# Reason, Rhetoric, and the Philosophical Life in Plato's *Phaedrus*

# Reason, Rhetoric, and the Philosophical Life in Plato's *Phaedrus*

Tiago Lier

LEXINGTON BOOKS
Lanham • Boulder • New York • London

Published by Lexington Books
An imprint of The Rowman & Littlefield Publishing Group, Inc.
4501 Forbes Boulevard, Suite 200, Lanham, Maryland 20706
www.rowman.com

6 Tinworth Street, London SE11 5AL

Copyright © 2019 by The Rowman & Littlefield Publishing Group, Inc.

*All rights reserved.* No part of this book may be reproduced in any form or by any electronic or mechanical means, including information storage and retrieval systems, without written permission from the publisher, except by a reviewer who may quote passages in a review.

British Library Cataloguing in Publication Information Available

**Library of Congress Cataloging-in-Publication Data**

Names: Lier, Tiago, author.
Title: Reason, rhetoric, and the philosophical life in Plato's Phaedrus/ Tiago Lier.
Description: Lanham : Lexington Books, 2019 | Includes bibliographical references and index.
Identifiers: LCCN 2019014594| ISBN 9781498562782 (cloth) | ISBN 9781498562799
    (electronic) | ISBN 9781498562805 (pbk)
Subjects: LCSH: Plato. Phaedrus.
Classification: LCC B380 .L54 2019 | DDC 184--dc23 LC record available at https://lccn.loc.gov/
    2019014594

# Contents

Introduction   vii

1   Phaedrus   1
2   The Urbane Speeches   21
3   The Palinode   43
4   The Art of Speaking   95
5   Writing the Eternal   155

Conclusion   191

Notes   195

Bibliography   231

Index   237

About the Author   251

# Introduction

The Platonic corpus as a whole can be regarded as a eulogy to Socrates and a defense of the philosophical life, but it is only in the *Phaedrus* that Plato takes the form of this defense as an object of inquiry. His inquiry is not limited to the various forms of discourse he might use in that defense, although they are represented here in a diversity unparalleled in the corpus, ranging from myth and poetry to rhetoric and dialectic to prayer and sacred ritual, each of which can be differentiated into still further forms. Plato's defense of philosophy in the *Phaedrus* is spoken through a dazzling array of "voices" that he brilliantly harmonizes, and it is in this harmonization that the persistent tension and question of the dialogue is most strongly felt.[1] Socrates tells Phaedrus that they must ask what it is "to speak and write well or not" (258d7–11, 259e1–2).[2] The reason that Socrates insists that this inquiry extends to all uses of speech (*logos*)[3] is plain: since all speech—even Socrates's parody of pastoral depiction—is at bottom persuasion, leading the soul of the listener, a speaker must be able to judge when to speak in one way or another.[4] Plato's *Phaedrus* is then principally an inquiry into the nature of *logos* and persuasion. Socrates's solution to the question of how one may speak well is that a rhetorician, a skillful speaker, must be able to discern the nature of his audience's soul and understand when to apply which kind of speech to produce what sort of effect. To become so knowledgeable, the speaker must become a philosopher.

This is the point of departure for the present study. The philosopher, Socrates tells Phaedrus, both generally and with respect to himself as a model, is someone who is ignorant and seeks wisdom out of a desire to know himself and the nature of things. Commentator's usually approach this paradoxical situation, that speaking well requires becoming someone for whom knowledge is not a possession but a question, as an epistemic problem, a consequence of Socrates's claims that true knowledge exceeds the capacity of mere mortals (e.g., 247d6–e2, 250a1–5, b1–5).[5] On this view, the art (*technē*)[6] of rhetoric is, at best, a "regulative ideal," an aspiration rather than a practical possibility, and philosophy is its best possible imitation, a means to acquire knowledge.[7] These concerns about the limits of the human capacity for knowledge are legitimate, but neglect the pragmatic nature of Socrates's solution, as Socrates explicitly calls on Phaedrus "to shape [lit. to make, *poētai*] his life towards love [*erōs*][8] and philosophical speeches" (257b).[9] But why does Socrates's answer to the question of what it means to speak well take this ethical form, an exhortation toward a way of life, rather than a body of knowledge? The explanation seems to lie in his characterization of philosophy as "searching" (*zētēsis*), animated by the fundamentally desirous or "erotic" nature of human experience: we are in a condition of imperfection, lacking the understanding with which we would be whole and stable (249d–e, 250c). The philosopher is someone dedicated to clarifying experience and understanding himself through reasoning.[10]

Socrates's depiction of the erotic nature of philosophy and reasoning raises the traditional scholarly question of the unity of *Phaedrus*: why does the dialogue speak in so many voices and address the themes of *erōs* and *logos* in such diverse forms? Why especially does the dialogue take this form when Socrates insists that a written work must be formed according to the principle of "logographic necessity," whereby the text must be arranged so that "every part fits to other parts and the whole" as if it were a living animal (264c)?[11] This contrast of themes, and discursive forms, is most sharply felt in the dialogue's division between three speeches on *erōs*, which culminate in Socrates's rhetorically and poetically brilliant "palinode" to Eros, and the subsequent discussion of rhetoric, which is comparatively prosaic and bereft of discussion of *erōs*. Plato seems to have divided the dialogue between *erōs* and *logos*, even while arguing for their necessary relation. According to Socrates, our desires both motivate and shape the use of speech, informing our selection and arrangement of words and the meanings we attribute to them (e.g., 234d, 235c, 237a–b, 238c, 241e, 254b–d, 255e, 267c–d, 270b, e, 271c–d). Speech can be used more or less effectively, and so rhetoric can be understood as an art. What, though, are the ends to which speech should be directed and shaped? Socrates's palinode shows that *erōs* may be better or worse. Discovering the nature of a desire, and its appropriateness in a particular situation, is the work of reason and therefore entails the use of speech. A circle is thus formed between *erōs* as it guides *logos*, and *logos* as it examines and clarifies *erōs*. How then can *erōs* guide us in speaking well? How can a life immersed in this circular relationship provide the kind of knowledge required? Answering the question of what it means to speak well requires understanding this reciprocal relationship, even tension, between *erōs* and *logos*.

The question that this book aims to answer can be summarized as this: Why is speaking well an ethical matter, best embodied in the life of philosophy, and why does this ethical exhortation arise from the relationship between *erōs* and *logos*? Philosophy's ethical nature, that it is a way of life irreducible to argumentative means (as essential as some may be to philosophy),[12] is commonly observed by scholars of the *Phaedrus*, particularly in contrast to the "way" of the rhetoricians (269d, 272b–c).[13] What the present study contends is that the ethical nature of philosophy is essentially related to the tension between *erōs* and *logos*, which Plato deliberately expresses through the unusual but stimulating form of the *Phaedrus*. As the soul is constantly changing, the mutual dependence but incommensurability of *erōs* and *logos* entails that the soul must continually work upon itself, shaping itself in relation to others through language, as it judges for itself the reality it experiences. This constitutive power of *logos* is exploited in rhetoric, but only when the speaker's self-constitution is recognized can speaking well be understood neither to derive from nor inhere in a great vision of reality,[14] but in an ethic that seeks to order the soul through constant reflection both upon itself and the larger whole in which it lives.

## THE PROBLEM OF REASON AND RHETORIC

For Plato's *Phaedrus* to still command such attention as it does at a time when rhetoric as a credible practice, let alone academic discipline, is at perhaps its lowest ebb in over two thousand years,[15] especially since it is an inaugurating text of the rhetorical tradition,[16] is intriguing and puzzling. This incongruity suggests, first, the continuing relevance of the *Phaedrus* despite the practical dissolution of the rhetorical tradition, and second, that there is perhaps a general awareness that the modern contempt for rhetoric may be misplaced. This contrast thus affords Plato's modern readers the opportunity to read the confrontation between rhetoric and philosophy found in the *Phaedrus* with a genuine interest, born from the belief that the dialogue speaks to an issue of pressing importance. Ironically, this interest approximates the interest Plato's contemporaries must have felt, despite the fact that the modern contempt for rhetoric is diametrically opposed to the prominent place that rhetoric held in Athenian political life.

Rhetoric is now popularly believed to be synonymous with the deceptive and unprincipled, if not immoral, manipulation of opinions. In this sense, Plato's condemnation of rhetoric in his *Gorgias*, that it is a form of gross and harmful flattery, seems to have found a modern restatement, if not direct descendent. There are of course significant differences between the modern and Platonic attacks on rhetoric. Plato's *Gorgias* sets Socrates against the currents of contemporary popular opinion in Athens, for Athens's democratic regime gave such extensive authority to the assent of large assemblies and councils that political and legal success, and sometimes even one's life, depended on the ability to persuade crowds of the merits of one's case or the flaws of an opponent's. The ubiquity and political importance of rhetoric accordingly afforded it and its adept practitioners great status, and its teachers significant wealth.

In such a context, there were strong incentives to abuse rhetoric as an instrument to secure political power. Socrates, in the *Gorgias*, makes a stronger argument against rhetoric, that not only does rhetoric harm an audience by misleading it, but it also actively corrupts the souls of both rhetorician and audience, inflaming their desires for mastery and pleasure.[17] Although some commentators are so struck by Plato's defense of rhetoric in the *Phaedrus* that they suppose him to have reversed his position on rhetoric from the *Gorgias*,[18] Plato in fact sustains the ethical criticism of rhetoric made in the *Gorgias* from the very outset of the *Phaedrus*, albeit in relatively muted terms (this is discussed in chapter 1).[19] In chapters 3 and 4 it will be argued that Plato actually deepens the criticism made in the *Gorgias* in light of a more sophisticated psychology. Rhetoric may not only inflame the desiring part of the soul, but also cultivate a misunderstanding of the nature of *logos* to the extent that it diminishes the soul's capacity for reason and therefore self-direction. But Plato's view of the relationship between reason and rhetoric cannot be said to be one of opposition, due to the simple fact that Socrates argues for the possibility of an art of rhetoric, perfectible to the extent that it is grounded in reasoning and philosophy.

The widespread view that reason and rhetoric are opposed is one that arose within the context of modern philosophy, and therefore a brief summary will help to more sharply distinguish the problem of reason and rhetoric as Plato develops it in the *Phaedrus*. The modern problem developed in the early Enlightenment conception of rhetoric as irrational discourse that must therefore be excised to the furthest extent possible from both political life and scientific practice.[20] Thomas Hobbes's attack on rhetoric is a particularly notable example, given its cogency, consistency across his political works, and influence.[21] He charged that rhetoric, through "similitudes, metaphors, examples," fosters sedition by inflaming the ambitions of the eloquent and, particularly when joined with flattery, preying on the ignorance of the many who must rely on the authority of others.[22] This attack on rhetoric centered on common opinion and the corruption of reasoning. For Hobbes, opinion is fraught with the improper use of names, fallible reckoning of causes, great popular disagreement, and reliance on the authority of men and writings. In contrast, "infallible" science begins from a radical doubt concerning the spoken intentions of men and indeed all discourse: "no discourse whatsoever can end in absolute knowledge of fact."[23] Certainty only arises from recognition of this fundamental uncertainty and that the link between the fact of sensory experience and the signs used in reasoning is unknowable; there is no understanding of the things themselves but only of signs—that is, the names imposed on the consequences of sensory experience. True reasoning therefore requires a stability in language that rhetoric puts at risk. While Hobbes regarded Plato "the best philosopher of the Greeks" because he associated Plato with the precision of geometric reasoning, none of the ancient philosophers were spared for introducing into reasoning endless disputation and disagreement: "their logic, which should be the method of reasoning, is nothing else but captions of words."[24] The ancients' belief that knowledge concerning natural causes, let alone the existence of a natural end for human life, could be obtained from opinion was absurd, for opinion is nothing more than discourse without definition, and if such discourse begins not from oneself but another, it is but belief or faith.[25]

While Hobbes's attack on rhetoric echoes a number of Plato's arguments in the *Gorgias*—for example, the flattery of the passions, the susceptibility of crowds and assemblies, and the use of long speeches as opposed to the use of questions in private.[26] His criticism of Plato for believing that knowledge and true reasoning could issue from opinion is a useful starting place to survey the problem of reason and rhetoric as it emerges in the *Phaedrus*. Socrates insists that the human mind can only find "nourishment in opinion [*doxa*]," and that opinion, our use of *logos*, and the mania of *erōs* are ineluctably linked (248b4). Opinion, with all its flux and unreliability, is a necessary starting point for the intellect. Plato's concern with rhetoric, in contrast to Hobbes, is not that rhetoric necessarily opposes and corrupts reasoning, but that rhetoric may deviate in an unhealthy way from reasoning despite sharing the same roots. Conversely, Plato wishes to understand how reasoning may grow from the same roots as the rhetoric he so strongly attacked in the *Gorgias*.[27] Understanding this broad difference between the *Phaedrus* and *Gorgias* begins with understanding the most obvious difference between them, namely, the extensive discussion of *erōs* in the *Phaedrus*.

Rhetoric is inseparable from the problem of how *logos* relates to reality. Rhetoric's attractiveness is due to its power to persuade regardless of the truth of the matter. Plato's introduction of this problem, in the first lines of the *Phaedrus*, comes in Phaedrus's advertisement of Lysias's pseudo-amatory speech in favor of the "non-lover" (227c). Socrates soon makes it clear that the problem of deception is related to the desires of speaker and audience—conscious or unconscious—as encapsulated in the *erōs* that Lysias criticizes and ostensibly purges from his rhetoric. Throughout the dialogue, from Socrates's playful inspiration, his ironic presentation of the nonlover, and his defense of *erōs* in the palinode, through to his analysis of how speech persuades by appeal to the desires of the audience, *logos* never relates to reality directly by simple correspondence of "mark" and object, but rather through the soul, which is characterized by its *erōs* for reality. Herein lies the clearest distinction between the modern problem of reason and rhetoric and Plato's characterization of the problem, since for him *logos*—the whole of language—is motivated by and grounded in desire and purposiveness.[28] Although the relationship between *erōs* and *logos* is difficult to delineate, it constitutes a productive tension that animates the entirety of the *Phaedrus*.[29]

In the first place, Socrates and Phaedrus approach *erōs* as an object of speech, a free-standing object separable from the activity of speaking. That *erōs* can be perceived and rendered in speech as an independent object is of course necessary to understanding it, as Lysias's and Socrates's speeches begin to do when they portray it as an irrational and inconstant desire. Later, in the discussion of rhetoric, *erōs* is again an object of speech, both in Socrates's analysis of the three speeches and then in his discussion of the psychology that is part of the art of rhetoric. But the dramatic action of the dialogue, particularly the prologue and interludes between the speeches, shows the reader that *erōs*, despite the claims of the nonlover, is present in our use of speech.[30] Socrates's ironic inspiration during his first speech anticipates his claim in the palinode that *erōs* brings about "the greatest good fortune" by inspiring philosophical conversation, which is best able to recover and cleave to reality. Reasoning (*logismos*) arises from this erotic tension with reality: desiring perfection, we become aware of our incompleteness and use *logos* to gather together our otherwise fragmentary experiences. *Erōs* is therefore implicated in the use of *logos*; *erōs* constitutes a background of desires that we express in our opinions and in the meanings we attribute to the words that articulate those opinions.[31] Plato therefore takes care to render in the dramatic action and banter between Socrates and Phaedrus the nonlinguistic expression of *erōs*, whether in gestures, physical reactions, or interactions with the setting, all of which affect their conversation. Given this action and Socrates's account of *erōs* in his palinode, the possibility of obtaining a disengaged view of *erōs* is, strictly speaking, impossible, and *erōs* cannot therefore be a free-standing object for *logos*.

Socrates and Phaedrus also take up *logos* as an object, quite literally when considering the nature of writing (chapter 5), and more fundamentally when they reflect on rhetoric and what constitutes speaking well. There is a danger here of an infinite regress, wherein *logos* reflects upon *logos* endlessly without ever touching upon reality—a danger related to Phaedrus's easy-going skepticism about symbols of civic importance, discussed in chapter 1, and Socrates's warning against the belief that rhetoric is capable of transforming everything. This antifoundational danger sheds light on why Plato weaves *erōs* into the *Phaedrus*, for *erōs* helps obviate the attendant ethical, political, and theoretical dangers of rhetoric, insofar as *erōs* establishes the necessary ground for inquiry into *logos* itself.[32] At some point, if *logos* is to have the power to convey meaning and persuade that we attribute to it, it cannot find the meaning of words in other words, but must go outside itself and be about something other than the relationship between words. *Logos* must draw upon our relationship to reality that Socrates presents as *erōs*. Chapter 2 shows how the two speeches of the nonlover, the urbane speeches, open up this problem as they attempt to articulate the power of *logos* to define and so constitute objects for reflection and communication.[33] Chapter 3 argues that Socrates's palinode aims to provide this grounding through its mythical psychology, while chapter 4 argues that Socrates's account of persuasion and the noble art of rhetoric are grounded in this dynamic (or truer to the Greek, kinetic) psychology.

This relationship between *logos* and *erōs* is complicated still further by the fact that *logos* can itself be an object for *erōs*. Socrates and Phaedrus are both "lovers of speech" (*philologoi*), albeit of very different kinds (228a–c, 230d–e, 236e). Phaedrus in particular has a peculiar passion for *logos* and rhetoric, for he finds in them the possibility of painless pleasure. His love for *logos* is only understandable on the basis of the palinode. *Logoi* are among the "semblances" and "reminders" by which we recollect reality, and so partly constitute the appearance of reality for us (which is a crucial aspect of rhetoric's power), although in so constituting we risk confounding these semblances with reality. Just as there are better and worse ways of loving others, there are better and worse ways of loving *logos*. Phaedrus's error nonetheless vividly shows how the power of persuasion extends from our passion for reality, and that this passion is in turn reflected in *logos*. Speech, exemplified in reasoning and philosophy, is both object and instrument for *erōs*.

At this point, the relationship between *erōs* and *logos* emerges as a reciprocal one, as *erōs* turns to *logos* to clarify its objects, and *logos* derives meaning through our erotic relation to reality. Seen in this light, can *logos* be understood solely as an instrument for our desires, as the rhetoricians, at least in Plato's portrayal of them, tend to believe (see the discussion of rhetorical technique in chapter 5)? The answer seems to be no. In the first place, we do not fully understand those desires that move our use of *logos*, and they themselves require articulation if that use of *logos* is to be in any way self-aware and knowledgeable. Socrates's palinode seeks to inspire just this kind of introspection into the nature of our own desires. In the second place, we do not privately determine the meaning of words that we use, but always do so in exchange with others. Our words are not our own, as much as the likes of Lysias may give the impression of being fully in control of them. Just as we use *logos* to shape our own and others' understanding of reality, so too can we be shaped by *logos* as we use words, arguments, and opinions in communication with others. A crucial argument in chapter 4 is that the instrumental view of rhetoric and persuasion is incomplete because persuasion is only explicable by this communal nature of language and the attendant psychology in the palinode. Being caught up in a language not entirely our own,

Socrates prescribes a "private" rhetoric that leads Phaedrus toward philosophy by virtue of searching for a foundation for public rhetoric in the private judgment of the meaning of his words (261a–b). Phaedrus's ignorance of such private rhetoric makes him both susceptible to rhetoric—and other external sources of inspiration—and closed to the full power of *logos*.

Recognition of this reciprocal, mutually constitutive, relationship between *erōs* and *logos* is especially important for understanding Socrates's enigmatic statements about his own ignorance and the need for self-knowledge. Socrates is able to recognize himself not in spite of this circular relationship but because of it, as he sees himself reflected in others (chapter 1). Chapter 3 argues that Socrates, in seeking to know himself, also comes to work upon, order, and develop himself—which development is not incidentally related to his argument that speaking well requires philosophy (the relationship between Socrates's ignorance and his way of arguing is examined in chapter 4 and then situated within Plato's way of writing in chapter 5).[34] The overarching purpose of chapter 3 is to show that Socrates's proof of the immortality of the soul through its self-motion, and his subsequent story of the soul's "deeds and experiences," not only redeems *erōs* as a form of mania, but shows—in myth—that our capacity to go outside our narrowly construed self-conception is necessary for self-development and self-perfection (245c4). In other words, the ethical nature of philosophy is implicit in rhetoric and the possibility of persuasion.

Although the close relationship between *erōs* and *logos* may suggest their identification,[35] or that one is somehow a kind of the other, neither is reducible to the other.[36] Clearly, *erōs* cannot be reduced to its linguistic expressions, as both Lysias and Socrates emphasize when criticizing its physical expressions. But perhaps *erōs* is an expression of *logos* understood more broadly as the rational nature of the cosmos? On this understanding, *erōs* in its highest form—the desire to grasp the nature of things—would be reasoning. Indeed, Socrates seems to suggest that nothing can be understood except through *logos* when he says that without dialectic he can neither "speak nor think" (266b3–5). Chapter 5 explores the possibility of this kind of universal *logos* in the context of writing, which holds out the promise of transmitting knowledge as if it were a mere object. But this kind of universal *logos* or cosmic rationalism, and its possible identification with *erōs*, can only be a matter of speculation, since it must be expressed linguistically and therefore through semblances of things rather than directly manifested.[37] The functioning of *logos* depends upon it being a semblance of what is signified rather than the signified itself; at some point there must be something outside of *logos*, and the identification of the desire for reality with its representation obscures the natures of both.

A central argument in chapter 5 is that, as much as Plato uses myth and other forms of discourse to show the conditions of *logos* and philosophy,[38] the nature of *logos* is best expressed in Socrates's searching approach, arising out of his self-ignorance and ignorance of a "divine" *logos*. In that case, perhaps there is a weaker link between *erōs* and *logos*, such that Plato uses *erōs* and *logos* as metaphors for each other (e.g., the godlike "semblance" a lover makes of his beloved is a metaphor for the "semblances" a rhetorician uses as argumentative steps [253b, 262a])?[39] But this view only postpones the issue, since it does not explain why *erōs* and *logos* are presented separately, and requires that the suitability of that metaphor be explained with reference to the natures of *erōs* and *logos*, which explanation of course involves the use of *logos*. The metaphorical relationship between *erōs* and *logos* thus returns the reader to their reciprocal relationship. This metaphor does at least show how the basic use of *logos*, to mark our experiences, bears on its relationship with *erōs*: how do we know that a speech, a phrase, or even a word "fits" our experience? We usually accept any given use of language, but sometimes we are perplexed, and where experience and *logos* do not "fit" together, we are forced to judge for ourselves our experience and formulate a better account. Drawing on other words, we are drawn outside of ourselves.

A key claim in chapter 4 is that Socrates examines the nature of persuasion within this problematic relationship between *erōs* and *logos*.[40] In persuasion, rhetoric and speech reshape and reorder the soul of the audience, redirecting it and changing its desires. But the rhetorician himself is already moved by *erōs* and must come to know both his audience and himself if he is to move others knowledgeably. The better his private understanding of words and speeches, both with respect to their relation with what they mark and to how others understand them, the better he will be able to lead his audience. In order to lead his audience, he must therefore become able to lead himself. In this way, Socrates's analysis of the art of rhetoric involves Phaedrus, and the reader, in reasoning and philosophy. Socrates aims to instill in Phaedrus the desire to understand how his words bear on and fit one another, and therefore calls Phaedrus to bring those words into relation with his own experience. In the end, Socrates does not resolve the problem of reason and rhetoric, rooted in the tension between *erōs* and *logos*. Chapter 5 argues that Plato reproduces that tension in the form of the dialogue as a whole, since he finds in that tension the animating force of a way of life that is dedicated to understanding the reality of one's own experience in order to live better in a world we do not fully understand.

## METHOD OF INQUIRY

In studying the *Phaedrus*, the choice between methods of inquiry, or whether a method should be adopted at all, is of unusual importance. This is because, even if the final purpose of the *Phaedrus* remains hidden, one of its themes is the nature of good and bad writing, and consequently how to identify, analyze, and read such writing. Different methods of interpretation will produce different accounts of the nature of Platonic writing and the literary form known as the Platonic dialogue, its ends, and its means. This account will affect all subsequent readings of the Platonic corpus. In short, the method by which any particular dialogue is read presupposes an understanding of the nature of dialogue in Plato's works. But if an understanding of the Platonic dialogue further depends on an understanding of the *Phaedrus*, a circle is formed. Methodical study seems to presuppose the knowledge it seeks. Is there a method for establishing a method? What are its grounds? This problem is not external to the *Phaedrus*, but intrinsic to its discussion of the art of speaking. Socrates himself differentiates two "ways" (*methodoi*) of rhetoric. The "short and smooth" way of Lysias and Thrasymachus is characterized as a knack for rhetoric, born from natural skill and practice (269d, 272b–c). The "long and difficult" way of the true art of rhetoric adds the criterion of knowledge—namely, knowledge of the subject matter being discussed as well as of the soul to which speech is addressed (271c–272d). The easy way can never ascend to the principles that ground or make possible the persuasion it uses, and without a precise understanding of how persuasion is achieved, it will never attain the perfection worthy of the title "art." But the way of the true art of rhetoric faces the same problem of method raised above: Socrates argues that dialectic can only be performed artfully if the speaker possesses knowledge of what is spoken about and of the soul he addresses, but then goes on to say that this knowledge can only be obtained dialectically (cf. 265c–266c, 270b–271c). Entry into this circle requires a nonmethodical element. One could appeal to practice, whereby the student artlessly stumbles forward, correcting his understanding of the subject matter as he goes, by trial and error. But how will the student know that he has erred if he does not already possess some kind of knowledge? Socrates claims that knowing is recollection of what one already knows, so that there is an intuitive element in coming to know that supplements any "method," including dialectic.

This intuition is vested in the very opinions that Socrates interrogates and makes use of over the course of his conversations, for an opinion expresses in speech one's own experience of reality. One sense of the Greek word for opinion, *doxa*, is that it is what "seems best," meaning that an opinion is formed for the sake of some end, and more generally, for the sake of living and acting.[41] Opinion is a link between speech and deed (a classical rhetorical contrast that Plato develops in his contrast between *erōs* and *logos*). Without the intuition of reality that is vested in opinion and action, any method would be but a sterile and unreal process justified only by its authority. Yet this intuitive grasp of how things are and whether one has erred remains an uncertain opinion and mere knack—the way of Lysias—until one can give the complete account that Socrates demands of the dialectician. As mentioned above, in contrast to the likes of Hobbes, Plato forms his dialogues around the necessity that reasoning begins with and incorporates opinion, both the particular opinions espoused by the particular interlocutor as well as the common opinions that allow for dialogue. The written dialogue imitates the way by which knowledge can be recovered through opinion.

Insofar as knowledge is obtained through opinion and conversation, the Platonic dialogue cannot be approached as the espousal of doctrine or the series of propositions in a proof, thinly veiled in the trappings of a drama. Rather, Plato's thought and intention are found in the arrangement or form of the drama itself and the interaction of his characters. Even when he writes in his own voice, he denies that words and writing can contain the most serious thoughts, let alone truth.[42] Nor is the unadorned opinion of Socrates, or whoever leads a given dialogue, ever given. Even when Socrates seems to express the highest truths, he always does so obliquely, by way of myth or simile, paradoxes, and puzzles, and these are frequently preceded by warnings: "But of course I am leaving out a great deal."[43] Still, Plato cannot simply rebuff the easy way of reading that proceeds on the assumption that what is most important in a particular dialogue is already known or self-evident, or that certain arguments and concepts are sufficiently known from their counterparts in other dialogues (the most notorious example being the *idea* or *eidos*, and Plato's so-called theory or doctrine of forms), or even from a second-hand exposition. To read in these ways is natural, for one can only read on the basis of one's own opinions and presuppositions concerning the meanings of words. But Plato does write his dialogues so as to confound this reliance on opinion.

In the first place, Socrates adapts his arguments to his particular interlocutor. He even tells Phaedrus that this adaptation is the basic principle of all forms of persuasion (271b, 271d–272b, 273e, 277b–c). His own arguments are always conducted *ad hominem*, not in the sense of attacking the character of the interlocutor (although he is not adverse to the rhetorical use of shame), but in that they address and are built around the actual opinions of the interlocutor. Moreover, persuasion is the leading of souls from one opinion to its opposite, a turning around and change of perspective attained, which Socrates accomplishes through the explicit refutation of opinion (261a–262a). Rarely does a Platonic dialogue end without an interlocutor's opinions having been supplanted or refuted, and never without them at least having been shown inadequate. The arguments that Socrates employs do not therefore plainly express his own opinions, but draw on his interlocutor's opinions or common opinions that may establish agreeable premises for a persuasive argument (262a–b). These formal considerations also compound the broader problem facing the interpretation of any Socratic dialogue, which is Socrates's famous irony or dissembling. This irony is pervasive and conceals his inner thoughts and meaning at any given moment, whether it is by feigning a pose, expressing false humility, saying the opposite of what he means, playing on the various meanings of words, contradicting himself, or formulating paradoxes.[44] In the *Phaedrus*, Socrates's irony is understood through the discussion of playfulness as the demeanor befitting someone who is cognizant of the limitations of words for communicating knowledge and expressing the most serious thoughts. This playfulness is then extended to writing, such that the serious author must demonstrate his knowledge, which is greater than his words alone, by refuting himself (278c–d). Should a reader of Plato consequently take hold of some part of a dialogue by itself, believing he had taken hold of some real knowledge, he could be easily contradicted and refuted by another passage expressing the opposite sentiment.

The method for reading a Platonic dialogue cannot therefore be insensitive to the nature of dialogue, nor its presuppositions, and so cannot come from outside the dialogue. A Platonic dialogue must be read with openness, to allow the meaning to unfold itself rather than to impose meaning upon it. Plato compels the reader to become an active participant and think through the arguments, their relation to each other, the character of the interlocutors, and the work as a whole; the reader must exercise himself in the art of dialectic-collection and division so as to engender an ethos of openness and to see the necessity and harmony that pervades the whole.[45] The search for the meaning of the Platonic dialogue, understood as Plato's opinion, gives over to the reader's own contemplation and learning of the subject matter—a pedagogic outcome that this present study argues is essential to Plato's arguments in the *Phaedrus* in defense of rhetoric and writing.

In light of these considerations, the interpretation of the *Phaedrus* that is given here does not proceed on any assumptions about the development of Plato's thought. This is not because of the insufficiency of historical evidence for establishing anything more than a provisional chronology of Plato's writings,[46] but because the presence or absence of certain dramatic features, personae, arguments, concepts, or elements of style in one dialogue, regardless whether it is earlier or later, cannot explain the features of another without disrupting its integrity as a logographically necessary and complete whole unto itself. To read in this way would also repudiate the principle that speeches must be adapted to souls.[47] Rather, this study aims to be an open-ended attempt to understand the coherence and argument of the text as a whole, as Plato intended it. At the same time, a dramatic reading of the sort proposed here cannot be taken for granted, particularly given its prevalence, and the interest of its proponents in the *Phaedrus*.[48] The assumptions made by this way of reading, including the belief that action and common opinion are philosophically significant, must be taken up and considered.

The criteria for artful rhetoric that Socrates provides in the *Phaedrus* may serve as provisional precepts for interpretation. Their ultimate sufficiency as rules of art can only be established over the course of the interpretation itself. First among these principles is logographic necessity, where every part of a text is necessary to all its other parts and the whole. Every character, every speech, every question, every contradiction, and even every omission or silence, is a part necessary to understanding the dialogue as a whole. Likewise, a part can only be understood in relation to the whole.[49] An interpretation must also consider the structure or form of the dialogue, as found in its setting, choice of dramatis personae, dramatic action, arrangement of arguments and topics, as well as its content, particularly the cogency and relevant implications of the arguments advanced, as well as the numerous mythological, literary, and contemporaneous references.[50] Tracing Socrates's references, allusions, and misquotations can be significant for understanding the mood and meaning of a passage. Similarly, Plato's use of language requires careful observation, as terms that only appear significant at later junctures will have been carefully prepared over the entire course of the dialogue, in such different contexts to imbue a richness of meaning in the word that requires interpretation in itself.[51] For these reasons, this book proceeds in the order of the dialogue's dramatic presentation, considering Socrates's and Plato's intentions in saying and doing what they do when they do, albeit with due consideration for the holistic, nonlinear, sense of unity also present in the principle of logographic necessity.[52] After a first reading, for example, one can hardly read the word *erōs* in the same way at the beginning of the *Phaedrus* without recalling the transformation of meaning it undergoes by the end—and in rereading the dialogue, Socrates does seem prescient in his usage of such important words. Since cleaving to the principle of logographic necessity tends an interpretation toward comprehensiveness at the risk of loquaciousness, some allowance should be made for the voice and purposes of the interpreter. Plato of course anticipates as much in his discussion of writing, and in fact encourages it in the spirit of growing the "seeds" he plants in others (276c–277a). Just what Socrates means by "logographic necessity"—and how strictly he himself applies this principle—is therefore scrutinized in chapter 4.

Second, since the art of persuasion entails the power to lead an audience from one opinion to its opposite, apparent contradictions must be identified and understood. This does not mean eliminating contradictions, but only understanding the reason for their occurrence, and thereby the aim of the argument as a whole. Socrates himself admits to leading Phaedrus toward a contradictory opinion about *erōs* that is not itself entirely true (265c–d); in addition to the question of the true nature of *erōs*, Socrates thus suggests that his purpose in so leading Phaedrus is also at question. Third, since speeches are adapted to their audience, the actions and speeches presented in the dialogue must be considered in relation to the character of Phaedrus, as expressed in his particular opinions and passions. These are revealed over the course of his conversation with Socrates and in other works, Platonic and otherwise. Given that the *Phaedrus* is a conversation between Socrates and Phaedrus alone, and therefore that all of Socrates's speeches are formed in relation to this single interlocutor, this principle implies that the unity of the dialogue depends on understanding the man Phaedrus. This, then, shall be the method of the following interpretation to the extent that a method can be justified.

*Chapter One*

# Phaedrus

Phaedrus of Myrrhinus is the ordering principle of the *dialogue*, for whose benefit he and Socrates discuss the various matters that they do in the way they do, shaping the form and content of the dialogue. But with the title *Phaidros*, Plato also signifies something more than just this one man. The related verb *phaidrunein* means "to cleanse," in the common sense of scouring with water to remove obscuring matter.[1] Both *Phaidros* and *phaidrunein* derive from *phaos*, "light," and the verb *phainein,* "to show," which emphasizes the sensory experience of illumination. Plato is particularly interested in speech as a kind of showing, although he expresses speech in many forms—conversation, song and hymn, pastoral description, incantation, prophecy, poetry, myth, rhetoric, dialectical examination, prayer—that can be divided again into further forms. From this polyphony arises the question of the proper relation between these various forms of speech and their use—under what conditions should they be used—and whether there is a particular form of speech to determine this proper relation. Yet Plato does not only imitate ways of speaking, but also dramatic action, including expressive actions of imitation, invocation, ritual, and gesture, all of which inflect his characters' words to convey additional layers of meaning. Plato's interest in how speech "shows" something must be understood in relation to this other kind of showing, including the sensory, experiential, and intellectual. In examining the nature of speech, he reflects on and shows how speech acquires and develops meaning through this interaction with our nondiscursive experience. Discourse is in a sense embodied, rooted in the particular—and personal—experiences of the individual,[2] in contrast with the shared or communal aspect of discourse. Plato expresses this important theme through the dialogue form itself, in which particular individuals converse, and in the rhetorical principle that Socrates later defends, that a speech must be adapted to its particular audience in order to persuade (271c–272a). Plato has at least, then, selected an appropriately named man to discuss these matters with Socrates. What remains to be seen, and this is one of the great questions of the dialogue, is the extent to which the embodiment of discourse in the particular individual—in Phaedrus—determines what is persuasive, or if persuasive discourse can somehow range beyond adaptation to the present beliefs of the particular audience.

This first chapter will consider the elaborate prologue of the *Phaedrus*, in which the reader is introduced to Phaedrus as a historical figure whose character—his interests, desires, and general disposition—is revealed as he and Socrates leave Athens to find a quiet reading spot. This literal situating of their conversation establishes a background or context of biography, character, literary and intellectual climate, action, and physical setting. Plato brilliantly weaves these elements together with the spoken words of Phaedrus and Socrates to broach the primary questions of the dialogue, including the natures of love (*erōs*) and speech (*logos*), their relationship, how they shape our character and relationship with the larger world, and what it means to speak well. Not least amongst these questions is how this background and the conversation are mutually constitutive: Socrates and Phaedrus reinterpret the meaning that the scene can have for them as a symbol of the greater reality that lies in-between their words. At the heart of this play between their words and their background is Phaedrus's love of speeches, for his conception of speech, as something detached from the desires of the speaker and literal, emerges alongside his selfish character. This mutual reinforcement of his conception of speech and his character, although productive of some virtue, obstructs his self-understanding and recognition of the greater power of speech. That Phaedrus finds affirmation of himself and his beliefs in Lysias's urbane speech reveals the ethical problem at stake in the subsequent inquiry into the nature of rhetoric.

## PHAEDRUS OF MYRRHINUS

Phaedrus, son of Pythocles of the Athenian *deme* or subdivision Myrrhinus, was likely born in 444 BC, and was approximately the same age as his friend, the famous speech-writer Lysias. Through Lysias, contemporary rhetorical art and its major figures exert a profound intellectual influence on Phaedrus, which is the primary concern in his conversation with Socrates. While the specific nature of that influence only emerges over the course of their conversation, this influence notably coincides with important biographical facts of Phaedrus's life as well as the intellectual activity centered in Athens that has been called "the sophistic movement."[3] Historical sources corroborate some of the portrait of Phaedrus that Plato paints: his good family name and means, though modest, provides him leisure and, along with his reputed beauty, entry into the circles of other well-to-do citizens (237b2).[4] He was also among those exiled for profaning the mysteries of Eleusis, the major civic cult of Athens, but little can be known about his specific motivations or general character without turning to the Platonic corpus.[5]

Plato portrays Phaedrus as a young man engrossed in Greek literature and intellectual life, where the innovations of the sophists and the burgeoning art (*technē*) of medicine seem to have produced in him a passion for speeches mixed with a notable moderation of the body. Since his youth, he, like many other Athenian boys, expressed fascination with the novel teachings of itinerant "wise men" or sophists, often at the expense of more conventional teachers—in Plato's *Symposium*, Phaedrus derides Prodicus's book, which Socrates will allude to later in the present conversation when instructing Phaedrus in a more noble rhetoric (267b, 272b–c).[6] Accompanying him in these pursuits was his friend, the physician Eryximachus, whose influence on him plays a significant role in the *Phaedrus*.[7] Socrates will later ask Phaedrus to draw on his relationship with Eryximachus to help understand how the specific techniques of an art relate to the art as a whole, and it is on the medical advice of Eryximachus's father, Acumenus, that Phaedrus ventures outdoors (227a–b, 268a–b). This care for the body is part of Phaedrus's moderation, which will prove to be central to the appeal of Lysias's speech, which criticizes *erōs* as a kind of excessiveness and madness.

At various moments in his conversation with Socrates, Phaedrus will refer to sophistic and medical teachings that he has picked up, often without recalling from whom or what book. All these moments—most importantly Lysias's paradoxical speech on love (227c, 234c–e, 235b, c), but also his distrust of myth (229c), his favoring of Lysias's conception of *erōs* over that found in ancient love poetry (235c), his expression of love for speeches because they are painless pleasures (258e), his opinion on the nature of rhetoric (260a), his interest in rhetorical techniques (266d), and his familiarity with how prescriptions are made in the art of medicine (268b–c)—will catch Socrates's attention and prompt important digressions. Socrates pursues these digressions in order to discover Phaedrus's beliefs and character, which seems selfish and peculiarly hedonistic,[8] but also to clarify how these contemporary intellectual developments have shaped his beliefs about rhetoric and the power of speech. Plato's dramatic characterization of Phaedrus effectively illustrates how the convergence of apparently disparate intellectual forces, particularly the recent development of rhetorical art and a technically sophisticated art of medicine, have reinforced, if not produced, Phaedrus's irreverence toward traditional piety and his conception of speech as a neutral instrument for the gratification of his desires.

Phaedrus is a man for whom signs, particularly those ancient ones most central to life as a Greek and especially as an Athenian, have become problematic. Shortly before Athens's ill-fated expedition to Sicily in 415 BC, Phaedrus was charged with profaning the Eleusinian mysteries. Maintained for nearly two thousand years, these ancient mysteries were a set of annual rites in which all Athenians participated, devoted to the harvest and dedicated to the grain and mother goddess Demeter.[9] The rites held in Eleusis were considered the "Greater" and were preceded by "Lesser" rites held in Agra, a district that Socrates mentions as being near the setting of the *Phaedrus* (229c1–3).[10] To profane these sacred initiation rites meant to take upon oneself the performance of what must necessarily be an imitation—serious or jesting—of the rites.[11] In Phaedrus's case, fifteen men, including himself, Eryximachus, Andocides, and the famous general-cum traitor and friend of Socrates, Alcibiades, profaned the rites in the home of Pulytion.[12] As this was a capital crime, Phaedrus and his alleged coconspirators fled Athens in 415 BC, forfeiting their property, and remained abroad until they were reenfranchised in 405 BC.[13] Phaedrus's exile for this impiety looms over the dialogue as a historical and biographical background, giving greater significance to Plato's allusions to the Eleusinian mysteries[14] and inviting consideration of the ethical and political dimensions of the philosophical problems discussed.[15]

Dramatically, the conversation depicted in the *Phaedrus* occurs shortly before Phaedrus's exile in 415 BC.[16] The summer setting means that his conversation with Socrates occurred immediately before he and his fellows were accused of impiety, in the midst of Athens's preparations for the Sicilian expedition (230c2). This expedition signaled the resumption of hostilities between Sparta and Athens, following the six-year Peace of Nicias. Phaedrus's easy life of idle leisure is, unbeknownst to him, about to be darkened by the winter of Persephone and the harsh realities of political life. The "happy summer day" of the *Phaedrus* is a brilliant but momentary efflorescence.[17]

## OUTSIDE THE CITY WALLS

The *Phaedrus* opens just inside the walls of Athens so that Plato may illustrate Socrates's temptation into an uncharacteristic departure outside the city. As he and Phaedrus engage in a discussion about what constitutes speaking well, both are drawn outside their ordinary ways so that they may turn inward and consider not only what has, but what should, guide their use of speech. For two lovers of speech, this is to consider their ways of life (228a–c, 230d–e, 236e). Socrates begins the dialogue by asking Phaedrus, "Where have you come from and where are you going?" (227a). This everyday greeting takes on greater meaning as Socrates comes to learn more about his friend and the powerful desires that move him, sometimes unconsciously, in his love of speeches and in his relationships where he shares this love.

Phaedrus has, since morning, been in the home of Epicrates, formerly the home of Morychus. It was "there" (*ekei*) that the famous speechwriter Lysias regaled him and his companions with speeches (227a3). Phaedrus once again found himself in the company of rhetoricians, and this time in a residence notable for the dubious character of its owners. Morychus was a wealthy man given to extravagance and gluttony, and consequently became the butt of Aristophanes's jokes.[18] Aristophanes also ridiculed Epicrates, although the comic poet did not live to witness that man's greatest transgressions of taking bribes and using his ambassadorships for profit, for which he was sentenced to death in 392.[19] The fact that Lysias himself wrote a speech accusing Epicrates of these offenses no doubt informed Plato's decision to place these men in friendly relation in the *Phaedrus*, perhaps as a reminder to Athens that there is no direct correlation between wealth, rhetorical skill, and good character.[20]

The time Phaedrus spent with these men, over "there," evokes a common poetic figure. Many other personae in Greek literature had also once traveled from "here" (*enthende*) to "there" (*ekei*), to that other place below the earth, the realm of Hades that lies across the boundary of death.[21] Plato frequently uses this euphemism to no less striking effect.[22] Phaedrus thus sat toiling in Hades alongside the other shades of men and has now arisen for the sake of a walk; were it not for the needs of the body, Phaedrus might have remained there indefinitely. The time spent "there" did not seem to be toilsome to Phaedrus, however, and was simply a passing of the time, literally "rubbed away" (*diatribē*) (227a4). This willingness to so spend his leisure is the object of Plato's implied criticism; Phaedrus's turn of mind and choice of companions have cast him into a kind of hell, which is compounded by the pleasure he experienced, for it shows that he has not recognized it as a hell. Plato's inversion of the spatial orientation of "here" and "there," casting Athenian people and places—and, in other dialogues, institutions—as the underworld, can only be called subversive, although this subversion might prove to be beneficial to Phaedrus and the reader alike, once Socrates reveals the effects of common opinion in Athens.

Socrates's interest in Phaedrus's time "there" focuses on the presence of Lysias, rather than Epicrates. He notes that Lysias "is in town," presumably visiting from Thurii. Lysias is not rooted to the city in the same way as Socrates, who rarely leaves (230d). Indeed, Lysias's father Cephalus had been invited to Athens by Pericles, on account of the family's wealth.[23] Despite, or because of, his limited legal rights as a *metoikos* (alien resident), particularly his exclusion from courts and the assembly, Lysias developed a strong interest in political matters by writing speeches, mostly forensic, and fostering relations with the democratic party.[24] Lysias's eloquence, then, was not a trifling hobby but a skill for the protection and advancement of his interests. Rhetorical skill could mean the difference between life and death in terms of legal suits or currying public favor, and it was especially useful for Lysias, given his precarious legal position. Indeed, Lysias became a professional speechwriter only after his family's substantial assets were seized and his brother Polemarchus executed by the Thirty Tyrants, an oligarchic regime installed in Athens by Sparta, in 404.[25] For Phaedrus, however, neither necessity nor want of means has fascinated him with Lysias's skill. The true nature of Phaedrus's desire to become, like Lysias, a master of the art of speaking is only revealed to the reader, and perhaps to Phaedrus himself, over the course of the dialogue.

Phaedrus attempts to persuade Socrates to join him in his walk with the promise of telling him about what occurred at Epicrates's. Phaedrus will be a messenger from over "there," if Socrates has the leisure (*scholē*) to follow. Socrates denies that he has any leisure, but playfully declares that learning what Lysias said is, quoting Pindar, "business that surpasses lack of leisure [*ascholia*]" (227b). Socrates's lack of leisure seems to refer to his customary practice of conversing, often in the market, with whomever he comes across, purportedly in the pursuit of wisdom.[26] The song quoted by Socrates, Pindar's *Herodotus of Thebes*, similarly begins with the poet interrupting his duty to the god with a civic duty: Pindar begs leave from Delos, for whom he was writing an ode to Apollo, so that he might sing the praises of his compatriot's victory in the chariot race. Socrates has also described his *ascholia* as a duty assigned by the god, and later tells Phaedrus that his leisure is limited because he is consumed with self-knowing, as prescribed by the inscription at Delphi (229e–230a).[27] Has Socrates set aside this quest for self-knowledge in order to find out about the *diatribē* of Lysias and Phaedrus? It is more likely his conversation with Phaedrus will somehow coincide with his *ascholia*, just as Pindar claims that his praise of Herodotus will also serve to honor Apollo.[28] Socrates's duty, to Athens as a whole if not simply to his friend, will in some way contribute to his professed business of knowing himself.

Socrates playfully asks Phaedrus, "What? Do you not believe that I alongside Pindar would put these things above lack of leisure [*ascholia*], to hear the pastime [*diatribē*] of both you and Lysias?" (227b). In this gentle mocking of Phaedrus—gentle because Socrates does indeed wish to hear what the two spoke of—Socrates suggests that only a great thing like the victory of Herodotus, which drew Pindar away from Apollo, could today distract him from his usual business. The similarity between Herodotus and Phaedrus, however, ends with their shared willingness to forgo wealth in pursuit of their respective desires—glory for Herodotus, rhetorical skill for Phaedrus (228a).[29] Phaedrus's amateurish pursuit is but a dim reflection of Herodotus's athletic prowess. Plato deliberately draws this contrast between Phaedrus walking "among the colonnades [*dromoi*]" and Herodotus urging his team around the race course (*dromos*) (227a–b). Phaedrus's desire to walk in the country, in order to refresh himself from the exertion of his time over "there," is an anemic moderation compared to the toils that Herodotus endured.[30] Plato here marks the increasing honor bestowed, in Athens, on eloquence and the power of persuasion rather than martial virtue; Phaedrus is one of the many who have been lured into a new realm of contestation of dubious merit.

Although he is no Herodotus, Phaedrus is not entirely submerged in his activities in Epicrates's home, and has not succumbed to the idleness and gluttony of the home's previous owner Morychus. His physical fatigue draws him out of "there," and it is Acumenus's medical advice that leads him to cross paths with Socrates on his way outside the city. Socrates goes even further, saying that, for the sake of hearing of the *diatribē* of Phaedrus and Lysias, he would walk to Megara and back—a total distance of nearly seventy miles—as the physician Herodicus prescribed (227d). The pleasant and comfortable stroll that they are embarking on pales next to the arduous regime of that devotee to physical health. Socrates once again gently mocks Phaedrus's comfortable moderation. But Socrates is not simply criticizing Phaedrus's lack of zeal—in fact, Socrates roundly criticizes Herodicus in the *Republic* for contributing to "the bad and shameful state of education in a city" that, being accustomed to luxury and licentiousness, is in constant need of treatment and drugs. By devoting himself to the care of the body, Herodicus lost sight of any other purpose for living.[31] For the sake of what does Phaedrus live that he must so moderate his life? It is certainly not to indulge in bouts of eating or drinking. Phaedrus is neither an infamous epicure, nor a champion charioteer, nor an ascetic physician, nor a renowned rhetorician or sophist. In contrast to these men, Phaedrus's careful moderation has meant that he has not achieved anything exceptional.

Socrates's bemused remarks set a playful tone for their short journey outside the city, in which each man pursues the other in the jesting mode of lovers. Phaedrus first attempts to have Socrates join him by promising to tell him of his *diatribē*. When Socrates teases him with his reference to Pindar's *ascholia*, Phaedrus tells him to take the lead instead, and Socrates is forced to ask again about the *diatribē*. Phaedrus happily gives a preview of the subject, since he believes it would be suitable for his older friend: he and Lysias passed their time with a speech that was "about love [*erōs*] in some way I do not know" (227c). Phaedrus is apparently confused because the beautiful beloved (*erōmenos*) is pursued not by a lover (*erastēs*) but by a nonlover (*mē erōn*, literally "one who does not love"). Lysias's thesis holds two apparently opposite things together, "for he says one must gratify the non-lover rather than the lover." As Christopher Rowe (1986) notes, rhetoricians frequently employed such paradoxes in their "display speeches" so as to demonstrate their power of persuasion, and Phaedrus is suitably impressed by Lysias's "refinement."[32] Sensing this, Socrates immediately moves to disrupt Phaedrus's enchantment by exposing the deception in the speech. He recognizes that Lysias's speech will inevitably favor the wealthier and younger man; if only Lysias had written speeches that equally benefited the poor and old, they "would be urbane and friendly to the public [*dēmos*]," and particularly beneficial to Socrates himself (227d). Lysias's rhetorical skill could help Socrates as a lover, but is at present only directed to his self-interest—which betrays its pretensions to be free from love.

Phaedrus responds to Socrates's love-struck pose by adopting the guise of an amateur, unable to worthily relate from memory the words of "the most clever of those now writing" (228a). Through this false humility, Phaedrus would stoke Socrates's desire by coyly withholding from him the object of pursuit. It is at this moment, however, that Phaedrus reveals that he would rather be able to imitate Lysias's speech than have a stack of money, and Socrates decides to expose Phaedrus's ruse rather than further pursue him. Socrates's subsequent diagnosis brilliantly brings together the themes of their journey in anticipation of the greater one that encompasses the majority of the dialogue. Socrates reverses the game of pursuit by invoking his personal knowledge of Phaedrus, and enters into what Rowe (1986) observes is a parody of the forensic style of rhetoric: Socrates hides Phaedrus in the demonstrative pronoun *ekeinos*, "that man," as if he were being prosecuted for his deception.[33] Foremost among Socrates's pieces of evidence is that because the speech was written (*graphesthai*, 227c5), Phaedrus could have Lysias repeat it, and Phaedrus could later review it, many times over, "looking upon what things he greatly desired" (228b). This power, peculiar to the written word, would allow Phaedrus to "know thoroughly" (*exepistasthai*) the contents of the speech, provided it was not too long, and expedite his imitation of it. Phaedrus then "journeyed outside the walls in order to care for it," practicing it until he chanced upon a man who was "ill with respect to the sound of speeches" and whom he "joined in [performing] the Corybantic rites." Here, the calculating desire (*epithumia*) of "that man" Phaedrus, carefully memorizing Lysias's speech piece by piece, gives way to the frenzied dance of the corybant who has an ear only for the tune of his goddess.[34] This forensic parody charges that Phaedrus, having found an appropriately susceptible man, would take advantage of him by feigning restraint. Indeed, it is characteristic of Phaedrus, and would be familiar to his friends, to adopt a humble and moderate pose.

Plato uses this playful banter to betray the desire and intent of Phaedrus, whose coyness immediately arouses the suspicions of the reader. Socrates's own suspicions are cued by his knowledge of Phaedrus, as he prefaced his accusations by claiming, "If I do not know [*agnoein*] Phaedrus, I have also forgotten myself. But really, neither of these two is [the case]" (227a). At first glance, this claim is straightforward in the assertion that there is some quality to Phaedrus with which Socrates is quite familiar and in fact betrays his pose. What is peculiar, however, is Socrates's formulation of the proposition that his knowledge of Phaedrus depends on his memory of himself. This knowing of Socrates (*gignōskein*) differs from the knowing that Phaedrus pursues (*epistasthai*) in his memorization of Lysias's speech.[35] In this particular case, Socrates's ability to remember himself and Phaedrus implies some sort of self-knowledge or self-possession through memory. Without constancy of the subject, Phaedrus could not be a consistent object of knowledge or recognition.[36] Socrates's recognition of Phaedrus and of himself are mutually dependent, for Socrates remembers Phaedrus when he recognizes him, which entails recognizing that he himself has seen Phaedrus before. Coming to know and learning, Socrates will later claim, are matters of recollection rather than acquisition. This personal knowledge seems to depend more obviously on prior experience.

The calm gaze with which Socrates sees himself, placing himself in the third person, betrays his pose of erotic frenzy. The true crime that Phaedrus commits is not against a frenzied man, but rather against the man unwilling to listen, whom Phaedrus would compel to listen "even by force" (228c). Socrates thus adopts for himself not one but two poses, the corybant maddened by speeches and the unwilling listener. He is at once desirous to the point of illness and dispassionate with respect to Phaedrus's speech. His introduction of this second pose allows him to further amplify Phaedrus's injustice and the extent of his friend's desire—he paints the defendant as a man who is the complete opposite of what he claimed to be. What he shows Phaedrus is two men animated by the desire for speeches, rather than just the corybant, and that it is Phaedrus's desire for a listener that first sets this mutual pursuit into motion. Socrates shows Phaedrus the type of man he truly desires, a man so possessed by Phaedrus's speech that he would follow wherever his beloved should go. This also shows that Phaedrus is ignorant of Socrates, since he mistook him, albeit playfully and with Socrates complicit, for the corybant he so desires. This entire opening conversation is directed by Socrates to show Phaedrus something of the nature of his desire, both for speeches and companions, and it shows Phaedrus to be the opposite of what he believes himself to be. Phaedrus is not simply a beloved, but a lover as well.

This mutual and playful erotic pursuit ends with the disclosure of Lysias's written speech. When Phaedrus attempts to simply give a summary of the parts he remembered, Socrates disarms him by telling Phaedrus that he is not interested in hearing this dull imitation, but only the original words of Lysias, who by means of his writing "is also present" (228e). Phaedrus, in order to give the appearance of possessing Lysias's rhetorical power, hides the source of his inspiration, but Socrates spies the scroll that his friend holds in his left hand under his cloak: "You hold the speech [*logos*] itself."[37] Although Socrates's knowledge of Phaedrus had made him suspicious from the beginning, he willfully joined him in playful pursuit in order to illustrate by deed Phaedrus's deception and underlying desire. Socrates not only succeeds in having Phaedrus read the speech, but he also confronts his friend's posturing. Having rid Phaedrus of this, he draws their physical journey to a close. They will be able to follow the *logos* only once they have identified an appropriate site for rest and then ceased the motion of their bodies. This site will, at Socrates's suggestion, be along the Ilissus and off the road they currently travel, which they had followed upon the medical advice of Acumenus. Although the physician's prescription was "fine," according to Socrates, it is not appropriate for the reading of the *logos* (227b).

Nonetheless, Acumenus's advice has prepared Phaedrus for the final stage of their journey, as he is barefoot just like Socrates: "It is fitting [*eis kairon*], so it seems, that I happen to be unshod; indeed you always are" (229a). Although Socrates's habit may mark him as unusual in the city, he is ready to travel outside of it; Socrates has no need for the artificial comforts that would now impede Phaedrus. On this occasion, therefore, Phaedrus's care for bodily health serves to bring him outside of the customs of the city and interrupt his fixation on the speech of Lysias. That their lack of footwear is "fitting" or "in season" (*eis kairon*) of course depends on the setting of the *Phaedrus*, quite literally grounding their conversation in the context of the external world. Beyond the painting of a "not unpleasant" pastoral scene, Plato is able to use the setting as a font of literary allusion and to communicate a drama that occurs outside the explicit words and arguments of his characters. Phaedrus in particular seems to need reminding of the action behind the *logos* (229a).

## THE MYTH OF BOREAS AND SOCRATIC SELF-KNOWLEDGE

The problem constituted by this background emerges when Socrates and Phaedrus, while approaching their reading spot, discuss how to determine what is true. A background of local myth (*muthologēma*) shapes their present understanding of that spot and their purpose in reading Lysias's speech. In Phaedrus's distrust of these myths, he ironically reveals that he nevertheless relies on the judgment of others, albeit in the form of modern rationalism that would determine what is true according to what is likely and therefore part of common experience. Socrates urges Phaedrus to consider more carefully his own self, for only with such self-knowledge will he be able to discriminate appropriately between those things in the background—stories, popular opinions, and even the physical world—that direct and shape his judgment. Socrates urges Phaedrus toward a distinction between *logos* and myth that differs starkly from the one Phaedrus would draw, for Socrates finds a use for myth that accords with his search for self-knowledge, rather than dismissing it based on a conception of discourse that relies on literal meanings derived from common sense experience.[38]

With the tall plane tree in the distance, Phaedrus asks Socrates whether it is not "here" that Boreas, god of the north wind, reputedly seized Oreithuia (229b).[39] While Phaedrus is doubtful whether this is true (*alēthēs*), his recollection of it during this walk with Socrates indicates that it certainly made an impression. The place appears to him a suitable one for maidens (*korai*) to play in, given its charm and transparent waters, and so he presses Socrates whether "it was therefore really here [that Boreas seized Oreithuia]?" (229b). The violence of erotic desire, as that which compels the soul outside of its comfort and innocence, and which was implied by Phaedrus's willingness to compel Socrates to listen to him, has now erupted. Perhaps Phaedrus, frustrated by his failure to "exercise" his memorized speech on Socrates, suggested this particular site for reading because it brought to mind Boreas's compulsion of the maiden (cf. 228c, 228e). As already seen, Phaedrus understands love dualistically, opposing the frenzied passion of the lover to the flight of the apparently frightened and moderate beloved; Phaedrus may have here unwittingly appropriated for himself the role of the maddened lover Boreas rather than the moderate beloved, the pure maiden. Given such a portentous coincidence between the scene and Phaedrus's recital of Lysias's speech—a verbal compulsion to take possession of the beloved—it is significant that Socrates rejects Phaedrus's setting for the myth and refuses to stop here.

Socrates's refutation sheds some light on the differences between the two men with respect to the customs of the city as well as their conception of truth and understanding. Socrates acknowledges that "it is said" that this is the site of Oreithuia's capture, but dismisses this rumor on account of other evidence (229b). The actual site, he tells Phaedrus, is "two or three *stadia* [350 to 500 meters] further down, toward the crossing-place into Agra; and there is somewhere some altar of Boreas on the spot" (229c). Herodotus recorded that a shrine to Boreas was dedicated following the second Persian invasion, after two storms struck and destroyed nearly half the Persian fleet.[40] Socrates remembers the memorial to this great Greek victory, upon which Athens's current power was founded, but Phaedrus, some twenty-five years his junior, has never bothered to learn about it and has "not noticed it" (229c). Within a generation, both the location and meaning of the memorial have been lost. For Socrates, what determines the true location of Boreas's rape of Oreithuia is not simply hearsay, but the presence of a civic memorial; the actual myth seems to be of little interest to Socrates.

Phaedrus, as a consequence of his ignorance of this additional significance in the myth, assumes that Socrates may in fact "suppose this mythical tale to be true" (229c). Socrates's response is masterful in how it manages, all at once, to slight the sophists, instruct Phaedrus, establish a necessary ground for philosophy, and otherwise deflect the question. He says that he would be not at all "out of place" (*atopos*) among the sophists (*sophoi*) were he to distrust such stories (229c). He could appear wise by claiming that, while Oreithuia played with Pharmaceia (from *pharmakon*, "drug"), a wind arose and threw her down upon some nearby rocks, and that she "came to her end" (*teleutēsasan*) as a result of being carried away from there. Or, alternately, for the account (*logos*) also claims this, she was carried away "from the Areopagus," the ancient court that tried capital cases and was by legend founded on the site of Ares's trial for the murder of Halirrothius, who had raped his daughter (229c–d).[41] Such rational explanations, however, would require a "clever" and "toilsome" man, because it would also be necessary for him to likewise "correct the form [*eidos*] of Centaurs, and again of the Chimera, and [there] would flow upon [him] also a throng of such sorts as Gorgons and Pegasai and some other inexplicable natures of marvelous speech both multitudinous and out of place [*atopiai*]" (229d–e).[42]

The problem is not necessarily that such a man distrusts these tales, but that he would do so "on account of the likelihood [*eikos*] of each," which Socrates calls a "rustic sort of wisdom" (229e). When Phaedrus asked Socrates about the truth of the matter, Socrates suspected that the conception of truth held by Phaedrus and some of the sophists—Protagoras's dictum that "man is the measure of all things" being a case in point—is that truth lies in the *eikos*, that is, in relation to one's own experience or what is commonly attested.[43] Socrates will himself later insist that we must begin with our own experience, albeit with the important qualification that we do not fully understand it, and his employment of *eikos* will differ considerably from these sophists' accounts based on sense experience.[44] For them, form (*eidos*) is understood entirely through its basic meaning of a visible "look." They dispute mythical tales because those tales do not accord with ordinary experience: no one has actually seen the wind rape and impregnate anything, and so Oreithuia's "strange" or "out of place" tale must be false. The truth of the *logos* depends on the corroboration of sensory experience.[45] The distinction between myth (*muthos*) and *logos* arises out of the fantastic appearance of the myths, and Phaedrus's, and the sophists', use of the two words implies a deep-seated mistrust of ancient stories, for both *muthos* and *logos* originally meant "words," "stories," and "speeches." In Homer, *muthos* meant authoritative speech, and did not imply a fantastic tale, although those too could be authoritative. *Logos* meant calculating speech, and consequently it and its verb *legein* often connoted deception.[46] The modern distinction, even opposition, between *muthos* and *logos* is therefore coextensive with a depreciation of traditional authority, and not simply disbelief of fantastic tales.[47] Without the authority of the ancients, a modern *logos* must rely on new standards, although Socrates's ridicule of the toilsome sophist indicates that merely substituting rationalized hearsay is no improvement.

Rather than boldly stating the truth or falsity of things, Socrates begins from the humble position of his own ignorance. He lacks the leisure of the clever "wise men" that spend their time disputing the likelihood of mythical stories, and the "cause" (*aitios*) of this, he says, is that "I am not somehow able, in accordance with the Delphic inscription, to come to know myself [*gignesthai*]" (229e). Asides from this business consuming Socrates's time, it is not obvious why the business of "looking to myself"[48] would preclude the rendering of mythical stories into a likely *logos*. A further complication is that Socrates expresses his need for self-examination in mythical terms, since he is puzzled whether he is "some beast more complex and Typhonic than Typhon, or some living thing both quieter and simpler" (230a). On the one hand, Socrates may be the horrifying, enormous, and multiformed monster that attempted to overthrow Olympus, or on the other hand, he may be something of calm simplicity.[49] The tension between these two poles formulates Socrates's existence as a problem, but he only describes the Typhonic pole of complexity mythically. Socrates uses myth, what is out of place from the everyday, to disrupt Phaedrus's complacency; Socrates is also "out of place" and unlikely (cf. 229c–d). Yet the simple and calm animal has no mythical analogue, either creature or god; Socrates's self-examination must contemplate something beyond the multitude of forms found in *muthologēma*.[50] To conduct this self-examination in the method of the sophists, by way of likely *logoi*, would only mire him in an infinite succession of physiological forms.[51] Were he simply a chaotic and ever-changing multitude, the Delphic inscription would be ridiculous. His self-described ignorance inheres in this tension or problem, and his awareness of its parameters implies that his ignorance is not absolute (230a). Phaedrus, however, as Socrates implies by describing the sophistic version of myth, does not look to himself and is even prevented from doing so by his desire to inquire about the "truth" of things in such a pedantic manner. Unlike Socrates, Phaedrus is unaware that he might be something complex, a problem; he has not taken the inscription at Delphi seriously.

This problem of knowing oneself, however, does not entail a retreat into oneself. Socrates refuses to offer opinions on the truth of things, saying that it would be ridiculous "to look upon the things belonging to others" while he does not yet know himself (229e–230a). But this has not prevented him from coming to know Phaedrus, knowledge of whom he said depended on his self-knowledge. Self-examination seems to require participation in conversation with friends and others; he shares in the *logos* that binds himself to other human beings and their common institutions and customs (*nomoi*). Until Socrates is able to resolve the tension that he perceives in himself, he will act in the customary way with regard to the myths—that is, he will be persuaded (*peithomenos*). The elusiveness of this response—*peithomenos* also means "trusting" and "obeying"—is significant for two reasons. First, Socrates again juxtaposes his adherence to custom and opinion with Phaedrus's irreverence. Phaedrus's interest in disputing myths is trivial, and perhaps even worrisome given his own apparent enjoyment of them (here and in the *Symposium*)—he finds pleasure in their falsity and separation from reality. Dispelling myths in the manner of the sophists is not pertinent to his self-examination, and so Socrates finds no purpose in thus subverting customs that he knows, given his reference to the shrine, are important for public life.[52] Socrates, like everyone else, draws on the opinions of his fellows, but unlike Phaedrus adjudicates their likelihood and plausibility rather than accepting them according to his inclinations. Second, Socrates's "being persuaded" may imply obedience, but it does not imply conviction or understanding about these matters. This distinction will prove to be of great importance in the later discussion of the art of rhetoric and critique of Lysias. At the moment, it is sufficient to note that whatever Socrates's real understanding of the myth of Boreas and Oreithuia, it is certainly not in terms of the common opinions that the sophists dwell in.

Socrates's parody of these sophists serves to not only instruct Phaedrus about the true and the likely, but also about his interest in the written *logos* of Lysias. Plato's shift from the pursuit of Lysias's speech to this discussion of myth is abrupt but not unrelated. Socrates's addition of "Pharmaceia" to the myth—a hitherto unknown figure in Greek literature[53]—deepens the medical theme of the prologue by expressing not the restorative powers of that art, represented by Acumenus, or its potentially arduous and even consuming nature, represented by Herodicus, but a deadly side effect. Oreithuia's play with Pharmaceia establishes a relation between medicine and death, which is as yet only implicit in the advice of the aforementioned physicians. Death occurs only in the rationalized *logos* of the sophists, not in the *muthologēma* in which Oreithuia is brought among the gods and gives birth to semidivine children. Her divine ascent in the myth is translated by Socrates into her "coming to an end," *teleutēsasa*. The immortality that is accomplished in myth is beyond the sophists' comprehension. There is nothing beyond the death of the body, and although the *pharmakon* may work as a "remedy" in order to preserve the body, it might also work as a "poison" and so aid in the body's dissolution.[54] The clever but "rustic" wisdom of the sophists renders Oreithuia's violent ascent beyond the body and mortality into what can be recognized by the senses. She reaches her end (*teleutē*), but it need not simply be physical death.

Plato also uses *teleutein* to describe Phaedrus when he took hold of Lysias's written speech: "Phaedrus at last [*teleutōn*] borrowed the book" (228b). There, the participle form indicated Phaedrus was in a state of completing, where the satiation of his desire means that it comes to an end and as such dies. In that case, desire was sated by the possession of speech in a fixed and physical manner that is only possible with writing. Socrates later refers to the *logos* as a *pharmakon*, both Lysias's speech and generally (230d6, 270b4–9, 274e6, 275a5). The overt implication is that the *logos*, as Pharmaceia or a *pharmakon*, is dangerous as well as restorative. *Logos* as a *pharmakon* might prepare one for an ascent into divinity.

In fact, Socrates says that he believes the sophistic versions of myth to be "graceful in some other way" (229d). He used one such version to communicate a warning to Phaedrus in a manner that Phaedrus finds attractive, but then supplemented that warning by undermining the sophistic rationalizations. The culmination of this is not a return to the original myth, but a recovery of something valuable in it, something that comports with our experience. This recovery depends on the revision of the myth by the likely *logoi*, and then incorporating its warning so as to join death to the mythical ascent while at the same time redeeming death as a completion. This development of the meaning of myth indicates to Phaedrus that he must pass beyond the sophistic conceptions of *logos* and *alētheia* to which he has been accustomed.

Phaedrus's walk with Socrates has led them from the sophisticated licentiousness and impiousness associated with Epicrates and through the rustic local myths that suggest that their conversation partakes of something greater than what is "likely." Plato has conveyed the rich resonance of their experience with his careful depiction of the natural scene and allusions to other myths, poetry, and sacred cults, especially the mysteries of Eleusis that Phaedrus will profane. The journey itself evokes the traditional walk to Agra that precedes initiation into the Lesser Mysteries, with the purpose of purification before participation in the Greater Mysteries. Phaedrus's ironic initiation conveys a complex meaning, at once bringing attention to Phaedrus's crime while mimicking the mysteries in writing, and thus, publicizing them. Phaedrus himself undergoes that ancient ritual in a new form and language, so that Socrates does not cast aside the mysteries, which have become an object of ridicule, but reinterprets them as he reinterpreted the myth of Boreas in order to rediscover the truths that served as patterns for the ways of the ancients. Socrates thus leads Phaedrus to discern, however dimly, that a common experience underlies these two widely different orders of symbols, linking Phaedrus's need to reconsider his conception of *logos* with the Eleusinian purification. The recovery of this original experience coincides with Socrates's turn toward self-knowledge, as only by understanding the locus of our experience in ourselves can we understand the experience itself, and the adequacy of its symbolization. This is the reason Socrates turns from mythologizing about himself in order to announce their arrival at the plane tree, "in-between [*metaxu*] the *logos*" (230a).

## THE SYMBOL OF THE PLANE TREE

The plane tree appears before Socrates and Phaedrus in the midst of the likely speeches of the sophists and Socrates's quest for knowledge. The tree proves to be a place that is wonderfully situated not only near the boundary of Agra but on the limits of ordinary experience. The reading site is the first of several experiences in the *Phaedrus* of the tension of the in-between, the tension of the *metaxy*.[55] Here, it is a place of inspiration situated between Athens and the unknown destination of their conversation. Surveying the grove, Socrates exuberantly swears, "by Hera, a fine stopping place" (230b). The oath proves appropriate, as it was Hera who was responsible for Hercules's madness (and therefore his subsequent initiation in the Lesser Mysteries), and Socrates proceeds to depict the place in a most unusual manner that amazes Phaedrus.[56] Having just parodied the likely *logoi* about myth, Socrates is now effusive about the details of the scene and their mythological associations. In the center stands the "tall" and "wide-spreading" plane tree (*platanos*), gently shading the soft grass and a "most graceful fount" flowing with cool water. Below the tree sits a shrine of maiden figurines dedicated to some nymphs and Achelous, the many-formed river god from whose horn Hercules was said to have fashioned the horn of plenty.[57] A fresh breeze carries a sweet smell while the summer hum of cicadas resounds. Socrates has depicted the scene as one stretched between the heights of the plane tree and the overflowing life springing from the earth and water underfoot. Even the mythical creatures that Socrates mentioned earlier—the Centaurs, Chimera, Gorgon, and Pegasus—seem to have likewise sprung from this joining of the water god and the mother figure of Hera,[58] whose name Socrates elsewhere says means "air."[59] These two poles of air and water, which together form a source of generation, are not the only elements of the *metaxy* that Plato has introduced here.

Several themes of Socrates and Phaedrus's journey converge here in the figure of the tree. The plane tree is a steadfast center to the element of flux and motion in the scene; because of its presence Socrates and Phaedrus are neither buffeted by the divine wind of Boreas, nor made hot by the summer day, nor directly underneath the bright light of the sun. It is this middling realm provided for by the plane tree that makes it a spot suitable for resting and reading. The fittingness of the physical scene presented by Plato indicates that it is neither a superficial gloss nor a simple dramatic device to bring the characters together. The tree shows that there is an end to the journey, one that will at least provide temporary rest before Socrates and Phaedrus must return to the city, as well as an end in the sense of final cause or condition that allows for the unfolding of the dialogue. As the plane tree looms over Socrates and Phaedrus, so does the setting loom over the whole dialogue, providing its playful and inspirational tone while at the same time holding together the currents of separation and otherworldliness. Giovanni Ferrari (1987) has convincingly shown that when the setting does fade into the background, it soon reasserts itself between the monologues and the conversation, always calling to mind that Socrates and Phaedrus are "in-between the speeches," in the *metaxy*, and that there remains a greater whole that grounds—and therefore transcends—any given discourse.[60] The dramatic setting in which Socrates and Phaedrus find themselves joins together and justifies otherwise detached speeches, thus relating what might appear to be detached words—innocent play or *diatribē*—to an underlying and sometimes obscure reality.[61]

The playful pun on Plato's name with the plane tree—the genitive *Platōnos* and *platanos*—grandly appropriates the same role for the author.[62] Plato's self-allusion indicates how Marsilio Ficino's interpretation of the scene as a symbol of the soul can be fruitfully interwoven with Ferrari's. In a dialogue about the use of speech, the soul is perhaps the most important background of all, particularly since Socrates will argue that persuasion depends upon understanding the soul and how it can be moved. Plato points to himself not simply as the author, but as the soul out of which this drama unfolds and moves the reader, and therefore that which the reader must come to understand if the text is to be understood. Insofar as the dialogue reflects something of reality, Plato has made his soul the mirror in which it can be read—the experience of reality as in-between is in some way a consequence of the soul's involvement in that reality.

Accordingly, Socrates's expression here of being in-between is not simply inspired by their arrival at a tree, but rather arises from the dramatic context and words that he employs—he has been deliberate in his use of speech to disclose a crucial aspect of reality that Phaedrus has overlooked. For Phaedrus, Socrates's description transforms the otherwise innocuous sight of a large plane tree and its shade, astonishing him because it is so contrary to his ordinary experience. Socrates has prepared this astonishment through their discussion about the truth of the myths and self-knowledge. His dismissal of the sophistic account of myth may have given Phaedrus the impression that he was entirely uninterested in myth, while his depiction of himself as perhaps something Typhonic revealed that there might remain some use for myth. At this very moment, when Socrates describes himself as somewhere in-between Typhon and simplicity, he discloses that there is quite literally something in-between the *logoi*. Phaedrus still dwells entirely in the *logos*, holding to the belief that the sophistic *eikos logos* will give a true account of myth. Phaedrus's engrossment with such *logoi* has rendered him oblivious to the *metaxy*, and so Socrates's overwrought description of the reading site effectively puts into speech for Phaedrus both the nature—and implicitly, the soul—that he does not perceive. Phaedrus is not therefore inspired by the scene, but he does wonder (*thaumazein*) at this strange man who interprets it:

> O wondrous man [*thaumasie*], you seem to be someone most strange [or: out of place, *atopotatos*]. For you speak artlessly, like a visiting stranger and not from this country; this comes from you being out of town, though you neither leave home going beyond its border [lit. into what is beyond the border, *eis tēn huperorian*], nor do you seem to me to go outside the wall at all. (230c–d)

Phaedrus begins to experience in their relationship the *metaxy* and the wonder that Socrates expresses, which he elsewhere describes as the beginning of philosophy.[63]

What might have been an otherwise tranquil and healing place for reading is transformed by the corybantic and "ill" Socrates, who confronts Phaedrus as a new source of excitement and inspiration. If the plane tree, said by some to be the Tree of Hippocrates the Asclepiad, really does have healing powers, its inspirational effects indicate a conception of health far beyond Phaedrus's limited concerns.[64] Phaedrus's life, primarily concerned as it is with the uninterrupted enjoyment of pleasures, now faces the wondrous spectacle of Socrates's "ill" and frenzied life, where the death of Oreithuia is no certain wickedness (258e). But if Phaedrus thinks Socrates is some rustic who communes with nature, the older man tempers his enthusiasm: "The country and the rocks do not wish to teach me anything, but the human beings in town do" (230d). The grove under the plane tree may excite his senses with its manifest beauty, but it does not in itself bestow knowledge or understanding. Socrates's purpose in journeying outside the city walls is, after all, to hear a *logos* that was written in the city. It is because Socrates is "a lover of learning" that he will follow Phaedrus "throughout Attica" (230d–e). Although speech may hide or distort nature and reality, without it nature remains an obscure and perplexing source of inspiration. Plato's self-reference further suggests that speech itself helps constitute our experience, as Socrates's language here articulates its ecstatic nature. Although Socrates seems to echo Hesiod's exhortation to country life in his *Works and Days*, the simplicities and virtues of nature and country life are recovered through art and the mediation of speech.[65] The meaning of our experience is not disclosed in a simple and direct manner as if in the full light of the sun.[66]

Socrates's and Phaedrus's short journey outside the walls of the city has been a preface to their journey into Lysias's *logos*, transforming what began for Phaedrus as a comfortable re-enactment of his habitual interest in speeches and inclination toward medical prescriptions. Socrates's pose of deep and frenzied interest in Lysias's *logos* incited Phaedrus to don his usual pose of a beloved who gratifies himself by enslaving his lover. This opposition between beloved and lover reflects Phaedrus's fascination with Lysias's speech, which seems to provide the spell by which a moderate beloved would gain all the favors a lover may bestow without being possessed by the compromising and disruptive madness of love. Phaedrus believes that he is the nonlover of the speech but does not recognize that his love of this *logos*—and *logos* generally—has brought him under Lysias's spell. He does not recognize how this *logos* has helped to articulate and direct his own passions, and if he is unwary, this *pharmakon* will bring about the very opposite of what he intended. In becoming a lover, Phaedrus fears he would become the sick and corybantic lover played by Socrates, and so come to the same end as Oreithuia—to be a lover would for him be the death of the moderate beloved whom he believes receives all benefit. Phaedrus's conception of love and the way he uses speech are thus intimately bound together in his way of life—his interest in rhetoric, his inclination toward the moderation prescribed by physicians, his skepticism toward myth, his irreverence toward Eleusis and the ancient ways of Athens, and not least of all, his comportment to his fellows.

Phaedrus seems to be susceptible to Lysias's *logos* because he is ignorant of any love that is outside the likely and simply observable. His own understanding about the relationship between a lover and beloved—the extraction of favors—is for him the simple truth of the matter. Phaedrus lacks awareness of his complicity in his own persuasion, that Lysias's words have meaning not as a direct reflection of reality, but as mediated by Phaedrus's desires and opinions. If he is to become able to discern what is true and false, whether in myths or speeches like Lysias's, Phaedrus therefore needs to turn inward and learn to scrutinize himself. Socrates recognizes this need in Phaedrus because Socrates knows that he himself lacks such self-knowledge: he is a problem to himself, lying somewhere in-between the Typhonic and the simple. Socrates represents this *metaxy* that he finds in himself in the plane tree so that Phaedrus may come to see that the world does not disclose itself directly but rather by inspiring us to reflect upon it. Socrates therefore makes himself an object of wonder so that he can lead Phaedrus into the problem of self-knowledge and the nature of *logos*, using the drug of the sophists and rhetoricians to remedy Phaedrus's accustomed ways.

*Chapter Two*

# The Urbane Speeches

Socrates described himself to Phaedrus as a frenzied and erotic lover of speeches, while the speech of Lysias presents itself as a remedy for lovers and a poison for *erōs* itself. The promise of this peculiar remedy is that once it has brought to light the shameful, worthless, and generally harmful nature of *erōs*, the listener will come to know the illness and so be able to deter its progress and engage in relationships with a sound mind (*sōphrosunē*). Socrates has placed himself in the very role of the lover that Lysias's speech is designed to combat. Given that this symmetry is Plato's contrivance, why has he chosen the work of Lysias in particular to be the object of Socrates's mad *erōs*? Lysias's reputation as a speech-writer only complicates the issue further, for why would Plato put in the mouth (or on the pen as it were) of such a man a speech that is of a private and frivolous nature, when he will, after his return to Athens in 404 BCE, write for the serious business of the law courts? What is the significance of this foray by a writer of public speeches into the genre of love literature? It is here that the problem of unity in the *Phaedrus* is first raised, for if the dialogue is intended to be simply an exploration of the theme of love, it would seem contrary to that purpose to have a political writer treat the subject. Likewise, if the dialogue's theme were simply rhetoric or *logos*, Lysias's unusual thesis—indeed, this so-called *Erotikos* is the only extant example of Lysias's nonpolitical work—would serve little purpose beyond being an example of poor writing, a purpose that could just as ably be served by work from an author's accustomed genre. These unsatisfactory consequences raise the question whether there is not a stronger connection between the substance of the speeches—*erōs* and its value relative to *sōphrosunē*—and the dramatic love-play between Socrates and Phaedrus, as well as their later discussion of rhetoric and *logos*.

Socrates will later call the first two speeches of the *Phaedrus* "urbane" (*asteios*, literally "of the town [*astu*]"), and accuse them of "urbane foolishness" on account of Lysias's thesis, namely that one ought to give favors to a nonlover rather than a lover (242c). But "urbane" also signifies the relation of this thesis, and *logos* generally, to the city and its opinions. The urbane speeches show how rhetoric presumes to rise above the private determination of meaning according to one's desires or *erōs* by invoking common opinions to support crucial arguments and terms. While this reliance on common opinions may lead the audience away from itself, it also permits an ambiguity of meaning that can be exploited for deception, encouraging the audience to find in the words what it desires, without reflection. Despite this shared reliance on common opinion, Lysias's speech and Socrates's rendition differ in a crucial respect: while Lysias exploits the seeming power of *logos* to free itself from *erōs* and relate solely to itself, Socrates's speech demonstrates the rhetorical force of logical necessity derived by grounding *logos* in reality. In opposing Lysias from within the thesis of nonlove, Socrates reveals the problematic nature of *logos*, that although *logos* has the power to lead one beyond the private determinations of *erōs* and bodily desire, which allows for linguistic deception, that deception is only effective insofar as the audience believes it to reflect reality. Conveying the irony of his speech not only with his words, but also expressively and mimetically, Socrates shows that it is precisely through *erōs*, experienced personally by concrete and embodied individuals, that we relate to reality and determine the meaning of our words.

## LYSIAS'S NONLOVER

The defense of a paradoxical thesis was the height of fashion in Greek oratory and a potent advertisement for the talents of a speechwriter.[1] Lysias's thesis is of this sort: he claims that the beloved should bestow favors not upon a lover, but rather upon a nonlover. But while paradox is common in exhibition rhetoric (*epideiktikos logos*), Lysias's speech defies easy categorization in a specific rhetorical genre, employing and playing on the content of private amatory rhetoric in his familiar forensic style, which aimed for persuasive efficacy with the diverse jury of the Athenian democracy.[2] Anticipating the potential diversity of his audience, Lysias preferred to create a concrete character suited to the tastes of the audience rather than to make use of "psychological generalizations."[3] His style as a whole aimed at the cultivation of an appearance of respectability and moderation.[4] Antitheses thus featured prominently in his speeches, often contrasting a person's words and deeds, or a culprit and his victim.[5] Evidence of Plato's parody is seen in the exaggeration of these features of Lysias's style,[6] although this style and mixture of rhetorical genres serve the serious purpose of expressing the power of rhetoric, and *logos* more generally, to stand freely, separated from the meaning that any one individual may impute to it. In Lysias's case, he exploits this incongruence between private and public or common opinions to produce a speech that will be as effective as possible with the broadest possible audience, regardless of its size or particular qualities and opinions.

Lysias begins with his thesis, formulated as an antithesis: "On the one hand you know about my business, and have heard that I think it to be advantageous for us that these things come to be; but on the other I think it fit [lit. is worthy, *axioun*] that what I ask not be refused on account of this, that I do not happen to be your lover" (230e6–231a1). The thesis implies that the nonlover's proposal is of the sort that occurs between lover and beloved. The later confirmation of this sexual innuendo gives credence to Socrates's claim that Lysias begins with the end (232e, 234b–c, 264a–b). How can the professed nonlover give his speech without admitting to being in love?[7] How can he account for his own interest in sexual favors? In order to avoid this problem, Lysias lays out his thesis as a recollection so that the nonlover's intentions need not be explicitly put into words.

The main couplets of the speech, although not given in any immediately discernible order, may briefly be summarized. Since the desire (*epithumia*) of lovers is an illness and mania, lovers harm themselves and then repent when they come to possess moderation or a sound mind (*sōphrosunē*) (231a, d–e). They are therefore fickle and disloyal (231b). There are but few lovers of a beloved, and so there is only a small chance of finding a lover worthy of friendship (231d). Lovers are more likely (*eikos*) to boast of their success in love, since they are honor-lovers (231e–232a). Moreover, since many lovers desire the body before they come to know their beloveds' interests (*oikeiai*), a beloved will suffer more in a quarrel with a lover because he has given up what is most valued (232b–e). Lovers make their beloveds worse, for they are so consumed by desire that they will praise words and actions even if they are not good (233a–b). As a consequence, lovers actively impede their beloveds, preventing them from associating with others lest they are tempted away by someone wealthier or more educated (232c). The nonlover, in contrast, acts willingly and according to his power, not by the necessity (*anangkē*) of desire, and so is able to look to his own interests (*oikeia*) (231a). He is the mirror opposite of the lover: he does not cause strife, chooses what is best over reputation, does not embarrass the boy, is not jealous and wants his partner to be loved by many, does not want physical relations until they are friends, and provides a long-term relationship.

Despite the eccentric organization of these points, the general strategy of Lysias's speech is clear: one's interests can only be achieved through soundmindedness rather than the mania of *erōs*, which is the compulsion that shortlived desire exerts over the mind (233b). The force of the argument relies on this characterization of *erōs* as necessarily being at odds with the determination of interest. This effectively sets commerce above love, and gives the whole speech the tone of a coolly calculated commercial transaction.

Lysias uses the word "interest" (*oikeios*, from *oikos*, "household") to bring all goods under the auspices of household management and commerce. The goods which Lysias includes are things of common approbation, such as the attainment and duration of friendship, pleasure, "the best," "some good," virtue, and especially what is "worthy" or "valuable" (*axios*). He leaves their specific meaning indeterminate (e.g., 232a–d).[8] More concrete are the appeals to stable household relations as well as quantities of association, property, and education (232c). The nonlover alone is said to effectively provide these particular benefits, while those that are left indeterminate are construed to be beneficial simply because the *sōphrosunē* of the nonlover allows him to provide whatever may please the listener (231b). This ambiguity concerning the meaning of interest, and other crucial terms, is not unintentional. For example, "association" (*sunousia*) also means sexual intercourse (from the literal "being-with"). This would be otherwise immaterial had Lysias not provided for the possibility of physical pleasure between so-called nonlovers, as "memorials of things to come" in their friendship (232e–233a). The word play and innuendo is in part due to the need to account for the nonlover's attraction to and enjoyment of the listener, since *epithumia* has been depreciated as a mad bodily lust; Lysias must substitute terms of advantage, interest, benefit, and favors or services to conceal the madness behind his moderation. The economic overtones of the speech accordingly restrict the meaning of *axios* to its material connotation of balancing items on a scale.

The ability to calculate one's self-interest takes on special importance in the loveless economics of the speech. The lover is particularly poor at this because of the inconstancy produced by his madness, which has the additional consequence that he is susceptible to breaking oaths (231a, 231c). Normal economic relations can be preserved only through the sound-mindedness of the nonlover; only agreements and oaths that are made willingly upon a clear assessment of interest will be inviolable. Lysias appeals to the commonsense proposition that economic self-interest entails some interest in stable relations within the community and adherence to its ways or customs. He left the meaning of interest indeterminate in part because the specific determination of what is worthy or good should be the business of willing agreement between free citizens. This results in a semblance of universality where the most common interests are sanctioned. Lysias's audience is the everyman of Athens, who embodies the variety of interests and desires found amongst the people at large, the *dēmos*. The speech of the nonlover is a species of conventionalism.

Lysias, however, cannot maintain that there is a perfectly harmonious community of interest, which becomes clear in the tension between the beloved's private desires and freedom, on the one hand, and the authority of custom on the other. Lysias accuses the lover of being an honor-lover who will likely boast of his erotic achievements. This attack on the love of honor is preceded by a condition: "if" the listener is afraid of "the custom" or law (*nomos*)[9] that the relations proposed here are disgraceful, then he should be wary of the boastful lover (231e). Although pederasty was a common practice in Athens, sexual exploitation or purchase was odious, as testified by legal suits concerning prostitution.[10] The nonlover, by reminding the listener of this public censure, shows some concern for reputation, and even induces a fear of censure for violating the custom. The nonlover does not argue that the provision of "services" is not shameful or something that should not be censured; the nonlover follows the custom. Instead, the nonlover implies that he will be discreet. He regards the custom as a solely public, rather than private, matter. Indeed, the nonlover holds that there can be conflict between reputation and what is "best"—that is, the desires of the beloved—and so he invokes the custom not to chastise but to indulge the listener's concern for reputation (232a). On the other hand, if the listener holds the opposite opinion and is not predisposed to respecting the custom, the nonlover's reminder of censure will induce in him a fear that will drive him away from the lover's overt breach of custom and toward the nonlover's modesty and discretion.[11]

The nonlover's self-interest therefore is not incompatible with the custom, so long as the latter serves as an instrument for the former.[12] Custom is of no intrinsic value. This same ethic is found or instilled in the beloved; the nonlover is not brash in suggesting they perform shameless acts, albeit in private, but does so because his audience is susceptible to it.[13] Phaedrus's susceptibility to this speech suggests that he is of the same character.[14] The nonlover's irreverence toward the custom reflects the irreverence of the *dēmos*, who secretly prefer "what is best" to what is customary, while the nonlover's appearance of discretion reflects the fear of shame that custom imparts. Although Lysias's speech attempts to be universal in its appeal, it must nonetheless are private if its discretion is to be successful. Custom and household are in tension so long as self-interest remains the ultimate determinant of worth.

The nonlover's own concern for reputation further complicates this situation. Soon after condemning the lover as boastful, the nonlover proceeds to express his hatred for those who might look down on the listener (232d). The no-lover contradicts his attack on the honor-lovers, and now argues that he wishes for the listener to be well-reputed among his fellows, an object of desire for many. It seems that reputation might serve the nonlover's interests after all. Lysias's speech has said one thing and then surreptitiously moved to say its opposite. In doing so, it is able to address two contrary desires: the desire to act as one wishes, scorning reputation, and the desire to preen oneself before others.

Lysias here demonstrates a perceptiveness concerning the multitudinous and contradictory bundle of desires found in his audience. His rhetorical techniques are well-chosen to reflect this audience, and reflect a commensurate conception of *logos*. Lysias's ambiguous use of key terms has already been mentioned. He also frequently uses conditional clauses and qualifiers to give the impression of universality, as he does not preclude any possibilities—for exmaple, that a lover might actually *not* boast of his success. His argument as a whole is based on what is most "likely" (*eikos*) (231c7, e1, e4, 233a2). Likelihood is not only sufficient for Lysias's purposes, but even advantageous, for it appeals to common experiences and opinions (273b1). Lysias is thus able to address the manifold and at times contradictory desires that might be found in his audience, chancing upon something of interest to any given listener, exploiting controversy about the nature of *erōs* (237a–b).[15] Lysias is not concerned with finding a unified set of principles for his rhetorical strategy, or defining any of his terms, or appealing to a unified set of opinions. Indeed, Socrates will later have Teisias argue that this is precisely the power and purpose of rhetoric.[16] Lysias's exploitation of ambiguity through likelihood implies a conception of *logos* so malleable and untethered to what it signifies that an audience can be led to contrary opinions about the same thing—a conception that Martin Heidegger has called "free-floating *logos*" to suggest the untethering of a sign from the reality it signifies.[17]

Lysias's characterization of the nonlover likewise mirrors his reliance on likelihood. The nonlover's moderation actively suppresses any single-minded pursuit that would come at the expense of other interests, for a particular interest has no predetermined worth—interests were examined only with respect to how they can be effectively satisfied without precluding others. This is a hedonistic calculus that preserves this variety of desires, and the possibility of their satisfaction, in order to address a multiform audience and the desires that may strike the beloved over time.[18] Being ruled by such a moderation, the nonlover shares the same variety of desires, tensions, and even contradictions, as found in the *dēmos*. Yet the beloved to whom the nonlover appeals with such rhetoric, whether intentionally or as a consequence of the technique of likelihood itself, is not a particular person with particular qualities and desires, but rather an abstract person who may be attracted to any object at one time or another.[19] Concrete, particular, and personal qualities evaporate to the extent that the speech succeeds.

Toward the end of the speech, however, this semblance of universality gives way so that not just any nonlover, but only a particular and concrete nonlover, the speaker himself, may be chosen by his audience.[20] A nonlover's desirability depends on his being as ambiguous and flexible as the beloved may wish, so to now claim that there is a necessary reason to choose him is to delimit and foreclose this attractive potentiality and universality.

Given the nonlover's pretension that he may satisfy any number of desires, and the commercial tone of the speech, it is not surprising that the criterion of selection will be wealth, at the exclusion of the majority of potential suitors. He says that the listener must not give "favors" to those who need them, which would entail being charitable and not giving to the best. This, he continues, would be absurd for two reasons. First, it would imply that it is not worthy (*axios*) to spend on friends but only on "those needing to be filled up" (233d). Since a man is of finite means, a perpetual charitable relationship would be impossible. Lysias does not allow for the possibility of an unending hedonistic exchange, and so the listener who gives "favors" must conceive of their relationship economically. The second reason for the absurdity of charity is that these recipients would be unable to return the favor, and their gratitude and prayers are worthless, that is, not fungible (233d–e). In his summation, the nonlover states that one should not give favors to those "only in love, but to those worthy [*axios*] of the business" (234a).

Despite the nonlover's clear superiority over the lover, there remains a problem: should the listener give favors to any wealthy nonlover? Lysias, by building the case for the nonlover upon the excoriation of *erōs* and the lover, particularly on the grounds that lovers are jealous and restrictive, has not provided criteria for choosing among the many wealthy nonlovers. Although he relied on likelihood in his previous arguments, this particular speaker has no desire to leave the final selection to chance, and therefore must provide a transition from the likely good found in common opinions to the precise good only he can provide.

Lysias gives two reasons why the listener should not give "favors" to all nonlovers: the favor will not be worthy (*axios*) of equal gratitude; and one cannot keep things secret (234c). The first reason reiterates that the criterion for ranking nonlovers is wealth. More interesting is the implication that an abundant supply of "favors" actually depreciates their value; like goods in the market, the value of the favor lies in its particularity. The nonlover thus gives his listener the friendly advice that he must maximize his market value by choosing only one partner. Despite the democratic veneer cultivated particularly by the promise of free association, the listener cannot but favor the man of wealth.[21] Consequently, the second reason provided by Lysias, the need to preserve the secrecy that was imposed by fear of the custom, prevents the listener from selling himself around town. The nonlover is not jealous, but only interested in protecting his investment; an associate desired by many but possessed exclusively by him would be of the greatest value.[22]

The nonlover believes his audience, the *dēmos*, is susceptible to the temptations of wealth.[23] The *dēmos*, perhaps not so secretly, desires wealth as a means to fulfilling its many other desires. The speech of the nonlover is not only a case of an oligarch feigning to be a democrat, but a case of democratic taste feigning universality. Indeed, Socrates immediately recognized this when Phaedrus told him the thesis, commenting that such a speech would be of use to the wealthy and young to the exclusion of the poor and old, and so would not be beneficial to the *dēmos* as a whole (227c–d).

Lysias has demonstrated keen insight into the relationship between speech and *erōs*, and how speech consequently carries ethical implications. His reliance on the variety of common opinions and desires produces a speech and form of moderation that equivocates about worth or value. No single interest or desire has inherent value, and indeed even moderation and its *logos* are regarded as instruments of maximization. Josef Pieper (1964) aptly describes Lysias's speech as "a rationalistic view of life as a 'technique'" to maximize pleasure and minimize "complications."[24] Without any natural and necessary ends, likelihood becomes the principal rhetorical tool. But likelihood is still a means to achieve the aims of love and desire, and it is only when the likely gives way that desire can be satisfied. For his part, the nonlover desires to eliminate likelihood and chance in order that he may be given favors before all others, placing Lysias's rhetorical techniques in tension with his earlier contrast between the nonlover's freedom and the lover's mad compulsion. Lysias hid the nonlover's underlying compulsion by using the language of commerce and the household to build a case based on the estimation of probable means rather than on the nature of ends; without a hierarchy of goods, prudence demands a moderation that balances competing desires. This is a democratic ethic that regards freedom as the highest of goods, but because of its toleration of disagreement with respect to many other desires, allows enormous scope for rhetoric.

Nonetheless, it seems absurd that Lysias would adopt a demotic form of rhetoric for a private speech, even if its immediate purpose was to display rhetorical skill to Epicrates and his guests. One reason for Lysias's mixture of genres and his appeal to the *dēmos* rather than a particular beloved is the fact that it is written down—it is composed to be portable and easily passed to others, useful to whoever might come across it and wish to pose as a nonlover (275d9–e3). This would hardly be lost on a rhetorician whose career was based entirely on writing speeches for use by others in public settings. At another level, the nonlover's aspiration to universality expresses the power of *logos* to convey diverse meanings with the same words or the same meaning with different words (263a–c). But Lysias's skill (or rather Plato's) in expressing the content of the speech through its rhetorical form also sharpens the original problem in the thesis of the nonlover: a private and personal approach cannot be made without betraying the speaker's interest, which the speech itself points out would be construed to be evidence of sexual desire, therefore rendering the nonlover's thesis, and his universal pretensions, absurd from the outset (232a–b).[25]

The speech of the nonlover, despite the playful absurdity of its delivery, displays Lysias's talents as a writer of forensic rhetoric and his understanding of his Athenian audience. His speech, as paradoxical and at times as absurd as it is, is not the work of a fool, and order can be found within it.[26] Similarly, the claim that it does not contain any worthwhile moral teaching because of the speaker's deceit is too simple.[27] A reader of Plato would, for instance, be hard pressed to find any serious argument made in favor of the constant "filling up" of one's bodily desires or that friendships should not last beyond the satisfaction of immediate or base pleasures.[28] Any hints at a tyrannical sort of *erōs* are delicately moderated or attacked in the *Phaedrus*.

Lysias's speech of the nonlover concludes with a solicitation: "and if you are missing something, believing it to have been left aside, ask" (234c5). While this invitation to dialogue reveals the speaker's confidence that the relationship will continue, it also admits the possibility that his speech was incomplete.[29] Nonetheless, Lysias expects to have gained the attention of someone who might wish to feign a lack of erotic attraction. Such a ruse should not be unfamiliar to those acquainted with the coy play between a beloved and a lover, the pursued and the pursuer. Indeed, Plato wrote the final sentence as a beautiful play on words: He puns on "ask," *erōta*, with *erōs*, and "you are missing" (*potheis*), literally means "you are longing for," producing the ellipsis that, "if, believing it to have been left aside, you are longing for something with respect to love."[30]

## A BACCHIC INTERLUDE

Plato uses the interlude between Lysias's speech and Socrates's rendition to illustrate the principle of the *metaxy*, the experience of reality that lies in-between the *logoi*. Socrates shows Phaedrus, not by argument but expressively and mimetically, that *logos* cannot be separated from *erōs*. The passions of both speaker and audience ground and guide the use of speech while speech may in turn shape those passions by clarifying and ordering them. Ignorance of this relationship renders Phaedrus at once credulous and susceptible to external forces, for he cannot see how speeches work on his desires to influence his judgment and so remains confidently self-absorbed, as if he were the free and self-possessed nonlover. Socrates will subtly show him, by mimetic reflection, the ugly character of his passion.

Phaedrus, greatly impressed by Lysias's speech, craves Socrates's approval: "Does it not seem to you beyond nature both with respect to the other things [i.e., its content] and in its words?" (234c). Socrates's response bears quoting in full:

> Daimonically so, comrade, so as to strike me out [of my wits] [*eklēttesthai*]. And I experienced this on account of you, Phaedrus, while I was looking upon [*apoblepōn*] you, because in the midst of [*metaxu*] reading you seemed to me to be made to shine by the speech; since you are a leader more than me

concerning such things, I followed to hear you, and so following I joined in Bacchic dance with your divine head. (234d)

This divine inspiration is a Bacchic joining-together, something wild and rustic, verging on a maddened departure from everyday life in the city.[31] The Bacchants' dance is, though, far from being an expression of sheer disorder.[32]

Phaedrus believes the Bacchic mood that inspires them is merely a jest by Socrates, without any serious implications (234d–e). For Phaedrus, a serious assessment of Lysias's speech would consider its use of words or its "rhetorical aspect," and whether there has ever been a speech that was so "great and numerous" in its treatment of the same subject (234e). His primary concern is for the form of the speech rather than its content. Socrates enjoins Phaedrus to give more attention to how he assesses speeches: "And is it necessary for the speech to be praised by me and you on these grounds, that the maker has said the necessary things?" (234e). There are things necessary to a particular speech or subject; its form cannot be separated from what is said. What form must speech about speech—that is, the analysis of speech—take? Lysias, Socrates says, repeated himself because the things he had to say were "insufficient," which is to say that the content of Lysias's speech entailed a particular form.[33] Phaedrus was amazed with Lysias's speech because he did not notice how its apparently disordered form was a necessary consequence of its appeal to contradictory desires. Socrates's own assessment is that Lysias was "displaying" (*epideiknusthai*) his ability to say the same thing in two different ways (235a). The speechmaker does not simply speak frankly, but manipulates words and their organization to make one thing appear as another, love as nonlove.

Phaedrus replies that Lysias in fact did say all that he should, and did not leave out anything that was "to be expressed worthily [*axios*]" (235b). Lysias's speech is, for him, a complete and perfect whole. But this is far from an impartial and dispassionate opinion, for Phaedrus has adopted Lysias's word *axios* and does not see how the speech manipulated the very terms by which he assesses it. Separating form and content, Phaedrus can see neither the contradiction between the nonlover's words and deeds nor how his own attraction to that speech reflects his own desires.

Socrates presents his disagreement as is he were the more sober man: their previous agreement is now characterized as a going-together, *sungchōrein*, literally meaning "to join in chorus or motion." Phaedrus's overenthusiastic belief that Lysias's speech was a complete explication of the subject of love does not seem true to Socrates, reminding him of "ancient men and women" who did in fact say something other than what Lysias has said (235b, cf. 275b–d). Socrates's vague invocation of these ancients—he alludes to Sappho and Anacreon, who celebrated the madness bestowed by *erōs* as a blessing and thus contrast starkly with Lysias—reminds Phaedrus that their concern is not so much who the speaker might be, but rather what love really is.[34] They cannot judge the merits of a speech about love while being ignorant of it. Socrates must moderate their passion so that they may the learn the truth about love. This moderation is, however, paradoxically expressed as a counterinspiration to Phaedrus's: his vague memory has filled him and inspired him to boast that he can speak differently and no worse than Lysias (235c). Socrates has been "filled up through the ears by the streams of others, like an empty vessel," just like the "daimonic" Phaedrus had been filled up and "made to shine" by Lysias's speech (234d, 235c–d).[35] Their respective inspirations differ, though, in that Socrates knows he is being filled because he knows that he is naturally empty—that is, lacking and ignorant of what truly inspires him. Phaedrus, however, only sees the speech, and does not even recognize that it has "filled" him and gratified his desires (258e). Without knowledge of his ignorance and emptiness, Phaedrus readily accepted Lysias's arguments and became convinced that they had expressed everything worthy on the subject. Socrates's knowledge of his own emptiness is moderating, inspiring as it were restraint of his desire to speak.

Phaedrus, being a lover of speeches, is intrigued by Socrates's promise of a new speech. Socrates playfully encourages Phaedrus, over four stages, in order to reveal the extent and character of his passion. In the first stage, Phaedrus promises that he will build a golden memorial of himself and Socrates at Delphi, "like the nine archons" swore to do if they violated Solon's laws, in exchange for Socrates saying better and "no fewer things" than Lysias (235d).[36] Phaedrus's offer to pay the penalty on Socrates's behalf reveals that, just as Lysias predicted of lovers, Phaedrus thinks nothing of transgressing customs or laws.[37]

The second stage in Phaedrus's attempt to compel Socrates to speak is precipitated by Socrates's refusal, on the grounds that he cannot say entirely different things on the subject matter than Lysias, for not even the most incompetent writer could completely miss the mark (*hamartanein*). In particular, Lysias's thesis depends upon the argument that good sense must be praised and lack of it admonished (236a). There is a necessary relationship between what is said and what actually exists (e.g., Lysias assumes that "madness" is clearly understood), without which a speech would hardly be sensible let alone persuasive. How this relationship is formed or what it consists in is not stated, although their present state of "inspiration" implicates the *erōs* of the speaker and the audience. At the moment, however, Socrates is compelling Phaedrus to maintain his focus on the substance and truth of Lysias's speech rather than just flitter to another attractively formed speech. Phaedrus's next bribe is to erect a statue of Socrates at Olympia, beside the hammered, rather than solid, gold statue of Zeus that was dedicated by the tyrannical Cypselids.[38] Socrates again dithers, claiming that he cannot "truly say something different [and] more many-colored to set beside [Lysias's] wisdom" (236b). Lysias's "wisdom" is akin to the empty showpiece of the Cypselidean statue,[39] and although impure in "many-colored" (*poikilos*) appearance it is nonetheless attractive to the *dēmos* and Phaedrus.

Phaedrus gives up on bribery and, in the third stage, resorts to force. He now admits that he too acts under compulsion, and mimics Socrates's earlier jibe, that if he had forgotten Phaedrus, he would have forgotten himself, so he knows that Phaedrus put on a "pose" of reluctance in order to tempt him (228a–c). Phaedrus has not understood Socrates's allusion to self-knowledge and the recognition of one's own ignorance: he mistakenly believes that Socrates really does want to speak for the sake of pleasing him. But by mistaking Socrates, he therefore "forgets himself"—he forgets that he loves speeches that seem beautiful. Phaedrus failed to reflect on why Lysias's use of *axios*, depreciation of *erōs*, and apparent moderation held such great appeal for him. Nevertheless, he does recognize a similarity in Socrates's pose of reluctance to his own pose of the coy beloved. This reversal of roles indicates to Phaedrus that he too is a lover, moved by *erōs* and *mania*, although the source of Socrates's own inspiration is of a very kind.

The fourth and final stage of compulsion is intriguing, as Phaedrus's ultimate threat is to stop giving speeches in Socrates's presence. Irreverent Phaedrus swears this, not to any Olympian god, but to the plane tree that they sit under. He has adopted the private symbolism Socrates established, and tellingly made the bond between tree and their conversation the only one he is unwilling to transgress, since it serves to satisfy his greatest desire. Socrates relents and proceeds with his speech because he recognizes that Phaedrus has gambled his dearest possession, the possibility of conversation (258e1–4). Socrates has forced Phaedrus to make their conversation something with personal stakes, for otherwise Phaedrus's enjoyment of speeches merely on the basis of their outward form would never touch upon reality.

Reviewing the action of the interlude, Socrates has goaded Phaedrus into revealing the extent and character of his passion. When he is met with resistance, Phaedrus becomes more radical and less political, and so reveals his own hierarchy of valuation. The law is the first to be sacrificed, while his beloved discourse is last; only in the end is he willing to make some self-sacrifice. Phaedrus acts in the same fashion as Lysias's mad lover: he thinks his labors—the statues—will be sufficient payment for his transgression; he has no fear of the custom or law; he is indiscriminate in his love of speeches and fickle; and he is willing to do what is prohibited and will cause enmity (cf. 231a–e). On the other hand, Phaedrus's flagrancy recalls at least two strategies of the nonlover: Phaedrus promises to dedicate statues in exchange for speeches, while the nonlover promised that sexual relations would be "memorials of things to come"; and both Phaedrus and the nonlover promised wealth and reputation (233a, d–e). Phaedrus's actions betray his self-conception as a beloved, but also indicate something redeemable in his *erōs*, something greater than Lysias's portrait would suggest.

In a final act of defiance, Socrates casts his cloak over his head "in shame" (237a).[40] This gesture encapsulates Socrates's efforts in this interlude to break the linguistic spell that grips Phaedrus, communicating to him a new emotion, beyond the frenzied lust they have so far invoked, that nuances their conversation. Although this gesture reveals the hidden *erōs* of the nonlover, Socrates's shame points beyond that *erōs*. By veiling himself, Socrates separates himself from and ceases to see his present source of inspiration—the "divine head" of Phaedrus—because he is ashamed before some unknown third term beyond the lover and his beloved. He mimics the purification of the Lesser Mysteries of Eleusis, admitting to and acknowledging the shamefulness, corruption, and darkness from which he will be reborn.[41]

## SOCRATES'S CONCEALED LOVER

Socrates's rendition of the nonlover's speech, while sharing Lysias's thesis and his essential argument that *erōs* is a form of *mania* and therefore harmful, differs from Lysias's speech in at least one crucial respect. Socrates opposes Lysias's presumption of free-floating *logos* and free judgment with a rhetoric that presumes unrelenting necessity in its arguments.[42] He conceives of speaking well as deliberation informed by stable knowledge, and *logos* as a means of arriving at that stable knowledge and reliably working out its implications. This innovation over Lysias's speech lays out a contrast case for both rhetorical efficacy and the nature of *logos* in relation to reality, with the ironic qualification that all this somehow implicates *erōs*. As with the other two speeches in the *Phaedrus*, content and form are contrived to reflect one another, for the very form of argumentation derives from the psychology it defends.[43] Nevertheless, the speech cannot overcome the problems attending the thesis of nonlove, not least the inexplicability of its motivation, which Socrates deepens to a psychological impossibility. Like Lysias's speech, it too unreflectively adopts common opinion at the expense of private judgment, failing to explain how, if at all, someone may judge that the opinions one adopts are right and true.

Socrates achieves the relative clarity of his speech in no small part through its organization. The speech as a whole has five parts: a proem dedicated to the Muses; a prologue that reveals the speaker to be a concealed lover; the speech of the concealed lover proper; Socrates's interjection that he is inspired and uttering dithyrambs; and Socrates's refusal to praise the nonlover. The speech of the concealed lover proper is divided into three parts: an argument outlining the principles of deliberation; a definition of *erōs*; and an account of the ways by which *erōs* harms a beloved boy. In thus framing the concealed lover's speech, Socrates accentuates its purported rationality, sharpening the opposition of *erōs* and moderation that the concealed lover proposes.

Socrates confounds Phaedrus's modernism and ostensible sober rationalism from the outset, beginning with a proem that summons the Muses, as if his speech were an ancient epic poem (it is a "myth" [237a9]). Rather than merely invoke the Muses, he inquires whether they are so called because of their "form [*eidos*] of song" or because of their genealogy ("descent from the musical race of Ligurians"), raising the specific problem of the meaning of *erōs* and the general problem of how one may determine the proper or fitting use of speech (237a7–9, c2–5).[44] Can a name be directly fitted to the "form" of what is named without the use of other, inherited, names? For that matter, can the form even be apprehended without those other names? Vice-versa, how was the original name fitted to what is named if not according to its form? The self-professed clarity of this speech, Socrates hints, is achieved by concealing such difficulties in "rhetorical aspect," that is, appropriately forming one's speech (235a1).[45]

In the prologue, Socrates narrates a dramatic context for the speech, that the speaker is himself one of many lovers of a "beautiful boy" who has devised a clever thesis to win the boy over (237a). Socrates thus reveals Lysias's nonlover for what he is, and that the aim of his speech was to win the admiration of the "beautiful boy" Phaedrus. The prologue also undermines the coming speech by revealing the nonlover to be a concealed lover. This raises a number of questions with regard to the truth of the speech: is the speaker in fact immoderate? What is the status of the moderation he praises? Is a nonlover impossible? How does the speaker understand himself and his hidden *erōs*? Is a completely rational form of speech possible?

The speech of the concealed lover proper begins by exposing principles of deliberation. Clarity of speech and thought are paramount: "Concerning all things, there is one beginning for those who intend to deliberate beautifully; one must know what it is that the deliberation concerns, or it is necessary [*anangkē*] to miss everything" (237b–c). Ignorant deliberation may be the norm, since "the many forget that they do not know the substance [*ousia*] of what each thing is," but the concealed lover's use of the strict *anangkē* means that beautiful deliberation is not possible without knowledge (237c). *Ousia* is thus elevated from Lysias's usage, where it described the wealth that a lover withholds from his beloved (232c6).[46] Unlike Lysias's nonlover, the concealed lover will not allow the arbitrary determination of terms; he demands complete clarity about whatever he speaks of, namely *erōs*, so that he will not confuse or contradict himself as a nonlover. One could not claim *erōs* is unequivocally harmful without a clear and self-consistent view of it, and such clear-sightedness in turn requires that *erōs* be purged from the deliberative process.

At the heart of deliberation lies the need for self-consistency and the principle of noncontradiction, although this does not sufficiently guard against the conventionalism of the speech. Simply assuming that one knows means that deliberation will only result in a failure to agree (*homolegein*) with oneself or others (237c). Noncontradiction will therefore show the substance (*ousia*) of the object insofar as consensus is attained. While the concealed lover thus exhorts his audience to disinter their prejudices and break the love for one's own opinions, he does not consider, or perhaps suppresses the question, whether there can be agreement made in ignorance. He allows that agreement and a self-consistent account will be a sufficient condition of knowledge, and is satisfied to replace private opinions with common opinion. Socrates will later say of the concealed lover's definition of *erōs*, "whether it was said well or badly, at least it was clear and agreed [*homolegein*] with itself" (265e). Contradiction is eliminated by verbal agreement, rather than by possessing a self-consistent body of knowledge.[47]

Following from the need for self-consistency, the final principle of good deliberation is to agree to a definition (*horos*) that can be looked to (*apoblepein*) during the inquiry (237c–d). *Horos* means "boundary" or "limit," and it is only by clearly separating the object from confounding factors that one can know it. As he will say at the conclusion of his definition of *erōs*, "all things are perhaps clearer when said rather than not said" (238b). The concealed lover wishes to bound off or limit *erōs* in order to free deliberation from the confounding and inconstant—that is, from *erōs*. His deliberative principles therefore match the content of the concealed lover's speech. Still, if the criterion for definition is agreement, the problem stands: what if everyone is consistent in their error? What are the criteria for agreement?

In the present case, the concealed lover defines *erōs* by invoking common opinion, which presumes to attain the most universal agreement and therefore complete knowledge. He says that "it is clear to all" that *erōs* is "some desire," that is, a species of *epithumia*. Meanwhile, "we know that even nonlovers desire (*epithumein*) beautiful things" (237d). These propositions divide *epithumia* and the attraction to beauty into two: *erōs*, a mad desire, in contrast to a good and right desire. From these two types of desire, the concealed lover deduces two "forms" or "ideas" (*idea*) inside human beings that "rule and lead" (237d). The first is "the ingrown" or natural desire for pleasure, and the second is "acquired opinion that aims at what is best." When opinion rules by speech, the form of soul is named moderation or sound-mindedness (*sōphrosunē*).[48] Nothing more is said concerning the nature of moderation, which is defined only by the negation of its opposite. When desire "drags us without speech" or "irrationally" (*alogōs*) to pleasures and thus rules us, it is named *hubris* or, loosely translated, "over-reaching arrogance" (238a). This *hubris*, since it is "many-limbed and many-formed [*polueides*]," takes the name of whatever form "grows by chance" (238a). As for *erōs* itself, the concealed lover claims it is "evident" what he should say, that *erōs* is directed toward beautiful things but also seeks pleasure in them through the body.

Socrates has contrived the content of this definition and attendant dualistic psychology to derive from and thus reflect the form of the speech, with the result that the speech as a whole is characterized by the rule of common opinion and conventionalism. The deliberative reliance on consensus is parallel to the sober reliance on "acquired opinion that aims at what is best," while the rule of *hubris* that is limitless in its forms is parallel to the disagreement and self-contradiction that inhibits deliberation.[49] Hence, the rule of desire leads us irrationally (literally, "without speech," *alogōs* [238a1, b7–8]). Clarity of speech, reason, is attained by asserting the rule of opinion and extirpating *erōs* as the source of discordance. Since the object of such reasoning is *ousia*, one incredible result of the concealed lover's principles is that even *ousia* is determined by common opinion.[50] Accordingly, the order and necessity of the speech, which the concealed lover frequently claims, is a logical necessity in the sense of being linguistic, rather than natural.

Since the principles of deliberation implied that only what is self-consistent can be good, and that a consistent rule of opinion is based on what is "clear to all," there is no need for the concealed lover to substantiate the nature of "the best." In order to discredit *erōs*, he only now needs to provide examples of how it causes a separation from what is commonly thought to be the best. The association of *erōs* with the body is especially helpful toward this end, given that the ills of the body are the most self-evident (263a–b).

Socrates's interruption of his speech at this point, having defined *erōs* and prior to applying this definition to illustrate the harmfulness of *erōs* in various ways, makes three points. First, as already noted, this purportedly purely rational speech is itself a product of *erōs*.[51] Second, Socrates describes this underlying *erōs* as divinely inspired, in striking contrast to the mundane language of the two speeches. This subtly prepares Phaedrus for the coming reference to "divine philosophy," suggesting a relationship between philosophy and this *erōs* that exists outside of, and inspires, their speeches (238c5–6). Third, Socrates's interjection falls at an obvious juncture in the speech, inbetween the definition and its application, and thus connects his inspiration to the moment that links the *ousia* of *erōs* itself to *erōs* as it exists in particular instances. The concealed lover presented his definition as if only now is he able to perceive properly *erōs* in its particular expressions, although this artful structure conceals the fact that his definition can only have come from observing *erōs* in those particular expressions. His rhetoric conceals this antecedent gathering and fitting together without which he and his audience could not even understand they were referring to the same thing with the word "*erōs*." *Erōs* is in some sense already known and felt.

When Socrates resumes the pose of the concealed lover, he returns to his definition of *erōs*. What is harmful is separation from the rule of opinion that aims at the best, and so his argument proving harmfulness is the same in each case: the definition of *erōs* implies the "necessity" that a lover, ruled by desire for sexual pleasure, must make the beloved as pleasing to him as possible; this "sick" man finds pleasing that which offers no resistance and conforms to his wishes, and because of this he hates what is stronger or equal; therefore, the lover will seek to make his beloved weaker than he is and delight "by necessity" in that particular weakness (238e, 239a; cf. 232c).[52] Socrates then applies this argument to a conventional division of domains in which a lover may cause harm.

The first example of how a lover may harm his boy is with respect to the mind. The lover prevents the boy from learning "divine philosophy" because the lover wishes for the boy to remain ignorant and "look to [*apoblepein*] everything that concerns the lover himself" (239b7). The boy looks to the lover just as Socrates earlier looked to Phaedrus as a source of inspiration, and just as deliberators must look to their definition (234d2, 237d1). This unavoidable creeping in of meaning associated with the verb *apoblepein* suggests that the act of definition, perhaps because of its seeming clarity, may keep one ignorant and enthralled.[53] Phaedrus later proves the point, when Socrates must work with his definition of rhetoric while attempting to persuade him that the opposite is true.

The boy's body, the second area of harm, similarly suffers. "Compelled to pursue pleasure before the good," the lover seeks what is physically inferior (239c). Perhaps reflecting the book-loving Phaedrus, the boy is softened, raised in "shadowed light," unversed in exertions and labor, and dressed in "borrowed colors and ornaments" (239d).[54] In short, the boy will be weakened such that "in war and other such great crises the enemy is heartened, and his friends and lovers seized by fear."[55] Excellence of body is determined by the needs of the city rather than pleasure. Indeed, *erōs* understood as the desire for bodily pleasure cultivates neglect for the toil and self-sacrifice required for the well-being of the city.

In the third example, the lover deprives the boy of familial relations and friends, who would censure their life of pleasure. He will also deprive the boy of his property in order to make him more manageable, effectively removing his beloved from the household. The concealed lover's censure, on the other hand, means that there is no retreat from public view, but rather the opposite: a consistent appeal to public appearance and honor, reinforced by private relations, in order to condemn the lover and his private *erōs*.

The fourth example concerns the realm of pleasure, which would seem to be the most rhetorically powerful argument against the lover, whose essential devotion to pleasure will prove unpleasant to the beloved. The lover is a flatterer able to provide brief pleasures that some "daimon" has mixed with bad things (240b). But there is no real pleasure that can be had from the lover. On this explicit appeal to the boy's desire for pleasure, the concealed lover's guise of moderation and "nonlove" seems to falter, for it raises the question whether the concealed lover implies that he himself will provide pleasure, and if so, whether that is consistent with his moderation. Both lovers and nonlovers, after all, "desire what is beautiful," and the definition of *hubris* shows that only the rule of the desire for pleasure is contemptible, not the desire for or experience of pleasure per se (234d).[56] In order for the definition of the soul not to contradict itself by saying that the rule of opinion and the rule of *hubris* are the same, it must be the case that, for the nonlover, opinion determines what is desirable and when, and not his inborn desire for pleasure.

The concealed lover's appeal to the rule of opinion in his distinction between moderation and *erōs* thus extends to each of his specific criticisms of the lover. In all four examples, the lover himself contents himself with a worsened beloved whose capacity for judgement is diminished. Such judgment can only consist of choosing what is prescribed by "right opinion" and resisting the immoderate desire for pleasure. Appropriately, then, the concealed lover concludes on the issue of oaths and how *erōs* ruptures one's bonds with the community and arouses the anger of justice. Since there is no present benefit in the lover, only the lover's promise of benefits in the future will attract the boy. The lover, though, will break his oath when his love ceases, as Lysias repeatedly argued (231a, 232b, e, 234a–b). This "former lover" now becomes sensible and moderate rather than "erotic and mad," and defaults "by necessity" (*anangkē*), fleeing from his creditor, the boy (241a–b). The lover desires nothing less than to be the receiver of free gifts, and in this sense he is identical to the beloved so honored by Phaedrus. He is insatiable: "for the purpose of filling up, as wolves are fond of lambs, so do lovers feel affection for a boy" (241d). The boy is likewise compelled (*anangkazein*) to pursue for restitution, and regrets choosing "the one who is by necessity [*anangkē*] mindless" rather than "the non-lover and the one who has possession of his mind [*nous*]" (241b–c).

With the attack on *erōs* complete, Socrates breaks off his speech and pleads with Phaedrus to let him stop. Phaedrus complains that Socrates has stopped halfway through the speech—he still needs to praise the nonlover and conclude that "it is necessary to grant favors to the [nonlover] rather than that man [the lover]" (241d). Phaedrus not only wants the speech to balance itself as a complete whole, but wishes to experience the rhetorical turn, the delight of the original position—that is, granting favors to a lover, being turned upside down (261e1–4, 265a1–4). Were he to continue, Socrates says he would be completely possessed by the nymphs that inhabit the grove they sit in, for he has already gone from uttering "dithyrambs" to "epic verse," and indeed the speech culminated in a rapid and forceful ascription of necessity to its arguments and ended with the similitude of lovers and wolves (241e).[57] He refuses to praise the nonlover because he would completely assume the pose of the nonlover and become an overt lover and flatterer of Phaedrus.

A brief construction of the portrait that Socrates refuses to give shows that, as with Lysias's speech, the speech of the concealed lover cannot be delivered without contradicting itself, both in deed and in speech. Ostensibly, the nonlover would be moderate and so lead the boy toward philosophy, caring for his body in order to fulfill his civic duty, respecting his ties to family and friends without jealousy, preserving his property, enjoying pleasures in moderation, and keeping his oaths. These benefits resemble those that the true lover that will provide in the palinode.[58] But all this would be done here in exchange for "favors"—that is, sexual gratification—and if the exchange is on the basis of bodily desire, there could not be any moderate rule (see "favors" at 237b6, 241a5, b7, d5).[59] According to the concealed lover, these two opposite states of mind and mindlessness cannot coincide. Despite his clear definition, the concealed lover's dualistic psychology is simply insufficient for the task of accounting for himself, that is, the task of self-knowledge. For him, the lover's abrupt change into a moderate man was quite literally a change into "someone else," for no one can at once be opposite to himself, moderate and hubristic, sensible and mindless (241a4).[60] Ferrari (1987) rightly notes that the appropriate response to having such desire, while holding this understanding of *erōs*, is "self-hate."[61] Reason, construed here as moderation according the rule of opinions that aims at the best, does not itself exert any force on the soul,[62] and is an insufficient guardian against *hubris*, only tempering erotic outbursts and indulgences. It is no guarantor of trust, oaths, and thereby justice as it is defined here. As Paul Friedländer (1958) writes, "This specific mode of life is led to reveal its true nature."[63] For such a person, the actual delivery of the speech would be purely deceptive and its praise for common opinion false, such that the professed justice of the nonlover would be nothing more than a ruse to solicit the favors of the beloved and his oaths no more secure than a lover's. Here too the concealed lover is inconsistent, for common opinion is the necessary instrument for his deception, as it is the authority upon which he attacks the lover.[64]

Socrates has used the clarity afforded by the concealed lover's deliberative principles and psychology to reveal the kind of *erōs* that Lysias opposed, and imputes that character to him and other rhetoricians who speak in monologue as if detached from what they describe. This ignoble rhetoric would, like the lover, oppress the beloved in every possible way, not least in "the education of his soul," for the ultimate purpose of the rhetorician's own gratification (241c5).[65] This sort of rhetoric would refuse deliberative argument, eschew clear definitions, mix its terms, and obscure any logically necessary deductions that would follow from his words. This rhetorician would be the flatterer who mixes momentary pleasure with the bad things he peddles—just as Socrates argues in the *Gorgias*.[66] A conception of the substance (*ousia*) of things that cannot be entirely circumscribed in words would be anathema to this rhetoric.[67] If the *erōs* of the concealed lover is of the kind he portrays, his recommendation of clear deliberation is contrived to more effectively oppress the beloved and conceal his own intentions. His principles of deliberation must therefore be reconsidered in light of their origination from *erōs*.

To define is itself an act of *hubris* that oversteps boundaries for the satisfaction of desire. In no way is it a selfless or disinterested act, nor is the definition divorced from the precipitating desire. A defined object is seen not as it simply is, but irrevocably mixed to satisfy one's preconceptions as formed by *erōs*. The good deliberation of the concealed lover, depending as it does on definition, cannot be completely realized: the object of deliberation will always elude complete clarity in the need for a decision.[68] There is no possibility of a purely rational and dispassionate discourse; the clear and moderate speech of the concealed lover, understood on its own terms, cannot justify itself. Extirpating *erōs* from *logos* and good sense, the concealed lover has only obviated self-understanding and with it the possibility of his own satisfaction, for he must instead dwell in opinion without the possibility of touching on what truly inspires his own personal thought and action. Socrates's speech shows Phaedrus that rhetoric cannot be merely a matter of form, capable of arranging words to any effect, but relies on the opinions and therefore desires of both speaker and audience.

## THE URBANE SPEECHES

The urbane speeches revealed Phaedrus's attachment to the opinions of the city, despite his selfish indifference to its institutions and customs. His hopes for rhetoric as a dispassionate instrument cannot be achieved, for the speaker addresses his *logos* to the desires of the audience, vested in their opinions about reality, for the sake of his own desires. Deception is possible because of disagreement or contradiction within the audience, whether between multiple people or within an individual. Lysias took advantage of these contradictory opinions, including the tension between the private desires of the individual and what is customary, to affect a kind of comprehensiveness (particularly in his use of likelihood) that Phaedrus found attractive. Socrates's concealed lover, however, sought to eliminate contradiction in order to provide a more consistent account of *erōs* and moderation that would be able to satisfy the aims of deliberation with a logical necessity not found in Lysias's speech.

Despite its deficiencies and ultimate self-contradiction, Socrates's speech marked an improvement over Lysias's speech in at least three ways. First, Socrates's concealed lover showed that persuasive speech needs a self-consistent understanding of the substance (*ousia*) of the subject matter, presented as a definition from which all subsequent argument can follow. If definition can indeed make manifest to everyone the actual substance in question, it would be in principle universally persuasive. Lysias's aspiration to universality, on the other hand, foundered on his reliance on likelihood and its attendant ambiguity in concrete cases, such as his own. Second, Socrates improved the clarity of arrangement and development of arguments. The concealed lover differentiated in himself two opposing forces so as to formulate a clear view of *erōs* that is unequivocally negative and reflects back to Phaedrus *erōs* as he understands it—Socrates even calls it Phaedrus's speech (243e9–244a2). Lysias, in contrast, obscured his argument against lovers and ultimately his distinction between lover and nonlover with his use of antitheses and likelihood. From this clarity of form follows Socrates's third improvement over Lysias's speech, that Socrates makes and maintains throughout a clear distinction between the goodness of moderation and the harmfulness of *erōs*. Instead of playing on the variety of contrary opinions found in the city, as Lysias did, the concealed lover makes a more obvious claim to universality by firmly subordinating all goods to the rule of opinion.

Socrates shows Phaedrus that a consistent defense of nonlove necessitates adherence to a completely self-consistent common opinion, a kind of moderate conventionalism. Socrates plays on Phaedrus's valetudinarianism in order to lead him away from his selfish love and envision the possibility of a "nonlove" that would benefit others and respect the customs of the city. Socrates shows how the seeming clarity that speech provides depends upon detachment from private bodily attachments—hence the first use of the word "soul" in the *Phaedrus* (241c5). Socrates will later confirm that the moral teaching and rhetoric of the concealed lover need not be cast aside, for it abused that part of *erōs* that it found "with justice" (266a).

This power of rhetoric, and *logos* generally, to detach the audience from its private opinions, comes with the risk, however, of impairing private judgment concerning what is in fact good and right. While *logos* may not be so plastic as Lysias presumes, neither does it possess the simple and overriding necessity that Socrates ascribes to his speech. The concealed lover's assertions of clarity and necessity blind him, and his audience, to the implication of *erōs* in the very act of speaking. He persuades only insofar as his definition of *erōs*, or his other arguments, satisfy his audience. Simply admitting that there is disagreement on the nature of *erōs*, and hence a need for definition or for that matter persuasion, implies that his audience diverges from "right opinion." They are therefore not purely rational and moderate, and are, like him, occasionally afflicted with *erōs*. How though, do they determine what is right and true? On his account, they must do so by the assertion of moderation: if *hubris* ruled, judgment would be impossible, since one would be choosing moderation out of excess; and yet if one's moderation ruled, its assertion would be redundant and persuasion unnecessary. These moments when the speaker turns the audience from *hubris* to right opinion are inexplicable for the nonlover and concealed by his assertions of clarity and necessity. There must therefore be some other form in the soul by which judgment is made between moderation or *hubris*, restraint or pleasure. As Socrates's ironic presentation suggests, this judgment somehow relates to the speaker's hidden *erōs*.

The ethical danger of rhetoric lies in this concealment of judgment and its effect on Phaedrus's own capacity for private judgment. Someone like Phaedrus is not passive in the face of such rhetoric due to some predisposition, but made passive, and to the extent that he takes pleasure in this rhetoric and the experience it produces, his own capacity for judgment has been stunted. As amply demonstrated in the dramatic action preceding and in-between these speeches, Phaedrus flitters from one experience—one speech—to another, without reflection or understanding of what in each is worthy of his attention, as spare as at that attention is. He cannot explain his own actions, and when summed, his life. Only an awareness of and openness to his *erōs*, awakened by the refutation of the nonlover's moderation, will allow Phaedrus to engage in self-inquiry and find what is truly desirable (252e6–253a4).

Socrates does not immediately begin his palinode, which praises *erōs*, but instead literally turns to return to Athens. In doing so, he mimics the lover who refuses to pay his debt and makes Athens a symbol of the sensibility and moderation found in common opinion. In order to seek recompense and satisfaction, Phaedrus is once again compelled to pursue Socrates like a lover and thereby turn his back on the city. The city and its opinions must be left behind so that they may look inward to obtain a view of what it is that they so greatly desire.

*Chapter Three*

# The Palinode

Socrates has turned his back on the urbane speeches and now leads Phaedrus into a grand defense of the mania of *erōs*. This third and final monologue of the *Phaedrus* assumes the form of the show-speech, the *epideiktikos logos*, which rhetoricians would deliver on momentous occasions or simply as a piece of entertainment.¹ As demanded by the situation, *epideixis* eschews the restrictive vocabulary and techniques considered more appropriate for forensic and deliberative rhetoric. Indeed, Socrates will again speak as if he is a mouthpiece for the Muses, making use of a mythical narrative structure, fantastic imagery, poetical phrasings and extravagant word use (e.g., "the superheavenly place"), and heavy-handed plays on words. The sharp contrast between this resplendent, even ecstatic, form and the prosaic and sober appearance of the previous speeches establishes what is unquestionably the dialogue's most memorable moment. So appropriate does the form seem to this defense of *erōs*, and ultimately the philosophical life, that some readers are inspired to believe that it plainly communicates Plato's opinions or even truths about the human soul and the use of *logos*. In so believing, however, they overlook the implication of the speech's subtle depiction of *logos* in constant interaction with *erōs*, which is that the speech exhorts Phaedrus and the reader to turn inward, rather than accept the palinode unreflectively, to reflect on how one's desires encourage the acceptance of a *logos* as true even as those desires evidence the want of a still greater reality.

Socrates's rhetorical presentation makes the speech difficult to interpret, for it is, as Myles Burnyeat (2012) says, "all vision with no argument" for the defense of *erōs*.² This is not to say it cannot be readily analyzed, for it is incredibly self-consistent in its use of imagery and terminology, and follows a clear structure from beginning to end. Furthermore, many familiar hypotheses that, in other dialogues, Socrates defends through argument can be found here, most notably the so-called "theory of forms" and the hypothesis that knowledge is recollection. Indeed, Plato seems to have here integrated in a holistic account some of the most fundamental principles of his thought. Familiarity with these hypotheses and principles, however, may mislead the reader from the particular content of the *Phaedrus*, and many commentators are inclined to believe with Friedländer (1958) that Socrates has "unfolded the myth out of doctrine."[3] Although these commentators follow what Daniel Werner calls a "dogmatic" understanding of Platonic myth, their approach should not be conflated with the sophistic demystification that Socrates earlier criticized (229c–e).[4] This "dogmatic" approach does not attempt to render the myth into what is "likely" or evident to the senses, but rather into arguments consistent with Plato's other works. But this approach ignores, if not refuses, the interpretive need to understand the myth on its own terms and in the context from which it arises.[5] At the least, analysis and interpretation of the palinode must begin with the fact that Socrates has created it for the sake of Phaedrus (257a). The principal question must therefore be: why does Socrates believe that Phaedrus needs a speech of this form—and this content—at this time? This dramatic question takes precedence over any speculation about Plato's general understanding of myth or his use of it in his dialogues.[6]

The argument of this chapter is that Socrates's palinode is a rhetorical defense of *erōs* that looks beyond the redemption of *erōs*, aiming to motivate and substantiate the coming discussion of rhetoric. Socrates redeems *erōs* by revealing that it inspires and guides the soul toward reality though the use of *logos*, especially philosophical conversation. He thus explicitly places *erōs* and *logos* in fundamental relation for the first time, but, significantly, he does not identify them. Precisely because *logos* cannot entirely satisfy *erōs*, and is communal, it can lead the soul outside of itself toward a new understanding. The lover's persuasion of the beloved, far from being a one-sided affair, is part of the joint search for reality that is philosophical conversation. The whole of Socrates's account of the soul, from its existence as the first principle of motion to its tripartition in the individual, contributes to the explanation of this perpetual motion of individuals leading and changing one another through *logos*. In thus communicating to Phaedrus the causes of persuasion, the monumental aspect of Socrates's palinode lies not in its reflection of eternal truth, but rather in its capacity to awaken and inspire us—Phaedrus and the reader—with the scope of our own participation in reality through *logos*.

## SOCRATES'S SHAME

A remarkable feature of Socrates's palinode is that it is inspired by his shame. Socrates now feels his *erōs* as an emotion that restrains him and places him in a subordinate relation to the truth about *erōs*. This paradoxically inspired restraint is an incipient recognition of truth, a vague and nondiscursive awareness that he has gone astray, which will inspire, guide, and support his discourse. This relationship between emotion or feeling and *logos* will also be an essential element of the speech itself, such that Socrates now prepares Phaedrus for the discussion of that relationship by showing him the precipitating emotion.

Socrates articulates his shame in four ways that anticipate the properties of *erōs* as he will present them in his palinode, but more importantly, this articulation demonstrates the concrete way by which nonlinguistic experience shapes his speech. First, he claims that his "customary sign," his "*daimonion*," has restrained him, which he interprets as the demand that he atone for his disparagement of Eros (242b–c). While Socrates's shame is internal, it entails some form of fidelity to the divine, which is here an external object, the god Eros. Second, Socrates claims that he is "a seer" (*mantis*), who has been shown the path of purification by the "spot itself," that is to say, by the grove under the tree or the *metaxy* (242c).[7] Unlike the great seers who deliver prophecies, Socrates is merely "sufficient for himself" and able to learn his offense (242c). His shame makes an intellectual contribution. Somehow, Socrates recognizes what is "sufficient for himself" although he does not yet know himself, and realizes he has erred. Socrates anticipates here the hypothesis that learning is recollection of knowledge already possessed, which he defended in the *Meno*, and will now present in his second speech as a myth. He also shows here that recollection involves emotion, feeling in a way that calls to mind something and may then inspire analysis. Third, Socrates's internal shame contrasts with external shame, shame before custom or the opinions of others. Socrates illustrates this problem with a quotation of the erotic poet Ibycus: "Lest by committing some offense against the gods I should receive in exchange honor from human beings" (242c–d).[8] What is dear to the gods and dear to the community of men not only differ but may fall into tragic opposition. Fourth, Socrates's mention of Ibycus foreshadows the transformative power of *erōs*. Phaedrus, being fond of literature, would recall that the poet sang of Eros as not only an uprooting storm and violent compulsion, as did Lysias and Socrates, but also as a lifegiving force.[9] Socrates's shame—restraining, prophetic, internal and divine, and potentially transformative—corrects their feelings toward *erōs*, placing him and Phaedrus in subordination to Eros and supporting their intellectual task of coming to understand *erōs*. In reconsidering *erōs*, Socrates reconsiders how they feel about *erōs*, and how they feel in their use of speech generally, for their passion is a crucial guide in understanding their experience.

Equally though, speech informs their feeling of passion. Socrates must not only feel shame in an appropriate way, but articulate both the nature of that experience and why it is appropriate. Socrates's shame arose in response to the specific contents of his first speech, and he can articulate its faults. That speech was "stupid" (*euēthe*), "impious," and thus "terrible" or "clever" (*deinos*) (242d). The two speeches of the nonlover expressed "stupidity [*euētheia*] [that] was altogether urbane" (242e5). Socrates's striking equation of stupidity and cleverness, intensifying his gentle mockery of Phaedrus's urbane friends and clever flatterers (228a, 229d, 240b, 242e), implies a higher form of intelligence, one consistent with what is divine. He charges the speeches with impiety by arguing that if the speeches said *erōs* was something bad, they must be impious, because Eros is the son of Aphrodite. Phaedrus demurs on Eros's lineage ("So it is said"), perhaps because he would rather, as in the *Symposium*, place Eros first among the gods because the beloved profits so handsomely from the lover. Or perhaps he simply does not believe that gods exist. Regardless, he does not object to Socrates's further claim that a god "or something divine" must be good (242e). Phaedrus could point out that the myths are replete with gods doing bad things, such as Boreas killing Oreithuia or Hades kidnapping Persephone, but again that would only matter to him if he actually believed those stories had truth to them.[10] Neither speech said *erōs* was divine, but only a form of desire or experience. For the nonlover, Socrates's interjection of piety and gods is beside the point of determining whether it is better or worse to give favors to a nonlover before a lover. Phaedrus's indifference to the gods, and of course his desire to hear yet another speech, has therefore allowed Socrates to introduce with little resistance what will prove to be a key proposition in his praise of *erōs*.

Socrates's attribution of goodness to *erōs* sheds further light on the shamefulness of the urbane speeches, their "stupidity," for they are not simply impious but actively harmful. They were, Socrates claims, "unhealthy," made for the sake of winning reputation among *anthrōpiskoi*, literally "diminutive human beings" or, more colloquially, "small humans" (243a).[11] Human nature is apparently diminished by the speeches' vilification of desire and extolling as virtue the moderation of a hedonistic calculus. Even the concealed lover's commitment to a healthy body was in some way unhealthy—true health is something greater than what the speeches claimed. The urbane speeches have thus caused illness by obscuring—for the audience and for the speaker—the divine and good nature of *erōs*, and therefore the recovery of this divinity must take the form of a purification.

Socrates tells Phaedrus that there is an ancient (*archaios*) purification concerning the telling of myths, which will constitute the form of his own palinode and thus bears some consideration. The poet Stesichorus recognized that the cause of his blindness was his slander that Helen went to Troy and was the cause of war. Unlike Homer, Stesichorus sought to restore his health, so Socrates will follow his manner of reconciliation with divine Helen: a "palinode," literally "a singing back" or "song of return." Stesichorus sang:

> This [*houtos*] speech is not true [or: genuine, *etumos*],
> Neither did you journey in well-decked ships,
> Nor go to the citadel of Troy. (243a–b)

Stesichorus's song is explicitly a recantation of the previous speech ("this," *houtos*, refers to an antecedent) for the purpose of establishing the truth.[12] His use of the adjective *etumos* to convey "true" is significant in its difference from *alēthēs*, which Socrates and Phaedrus frequently use (e.g., when discussing the truth of the myth of Boreas and Oreithuia [229c4–5]). *Etumos* conveys concordance with local experience, in the sense of "genuine," and so corresponds with local myth rather than sophisticated and cosmopolitan *logoi*.[13] Stesichorus must bring his speech into conformity with local myth and practices that regard Helen as a goddess of beauty or love.[14] In admitting his falsity, Stesichorus restates two key points, Helen's journey to and presence in Troy. The palinode thus gestures toward what is true by preserving the original story in antistrophe, recognizing the transgression and then returning.[15] This triadic structure of statement, negation, and recantation is the lyric invention of the epode from which Stesichorus took his name: the chorus, having sung stanzas contrary in both lyric and meter while moving from left to right, holds (*stēsis*) in the middle of the stage to deliver the final stanza.[16] Such will be the structure of Socrates's own purification.

In invoking the rhetorical trope of exonerating Helen,[17] Plato also presumes to explain the efficacy of the trope itself. Socrates uses the trope to show how beauty reveals itself in epodal form. Two Helens are produced, one a "phantom" (*eidōlon*), as Socrates says in the *Republic*, and the other the true Helen. This means that the former, fought over in Troy, was only a dim shade of the latter, who remains hidden.[18] This revealing of the truth about the beautiful and bewitching Helen is a structure that recurs throughout the dialogue, and is formally expressed as dialectic, wherein the true object of inquiry is found behind the variety of semblances that dialectic collects and divides (265d–266c).[19] Socrates's prescience—he will be "wiser" than both Homer and Stesichorus by delivering his palinode even before he suffers divine wrath—indicates that he was not ignorant of the shamefulness of his crime, and delivered his first speech for the very purpose of repudiating it. He must show what is false in order to make evident the truth.

Socrates's shame is the emotional thread that leads from the rule of common opinion in his first speech to knowledge of a higher form of love. This shame was felt as an internal inspiration to speak the truth about Eros, and now Socrates tells Phaedrus that it was aroused by the thought of being repudiated by "Someone of a noble [or: well-bred, *gennadas*] and gentle character [*ethos*]" (243c3). In contrast to the preceding accounts of *erōs*, this noble lover knows of a more orderly *erōs* that is without jealousy or hostility over petty things. It is in the first place the experiences of noble and rare men that are hidden by the urbane speeches' invocation of common opinion and "what is clear to all." The definition of *erōs* that pleased Phaedrus was a narrow generalization of experiences, which took the *erōs* of "sailors" who "have never seen the love of a free man" to be the whole of *erōs* (243c). This external source of inspiration, however, seems at odds with Socrates's insistence on internal divine inspiration. How is this opinion any better than the other? What is important here is their contrast, for common opinion may in fact be contradictory, and this contradiction forces the question upon the individual to judge which is true. Insofar as the experience of shame relies on the esteem and opinion of others, rather than divine insight, it alone does not distinguish between noble and base *erōs*. Socrates's shame is not justified until he can judge for himself that the noble lover is correct.

This recourse to internal, private, judgment, is the meaning of Socrates's fear of Eros. His shame aligns with the fear that he, like the poets, may be deprived of his sight. Enjoying whatever honor may accrue from attacking Eros means depriving himself of the ability to distinguish genuine and false. Lysias and Phaedrus, who did not fear the wrath of Eros and even presumed to be able to master him, have become shameless because of their ignorance of Eros's divinity.[20] For Socrates's part, his shame and fear inspire in him the "desire [*epithumein*] to wash out the bitter sound with a river of words" (243d). To put Eros in words, to define or "bound" him, is not therefore the sin itself, for *logos* is the way by which Socrates will reveal the goodness of Eros. Working through Socrates's shame and fear, Eros inspires a better account.

## MANIA

Socrates opens his palinode with a discussion of mania in order to recover the possibility that the mania of *erōs* could in fact be good and beneficial. Drawing again on common opinion, Socrates finds there resources to inform their judgment about mania, for each case of mania will exhibit a different quality of goodness that will be combined in *erōs*. Socrates casts these *maniai*, then, as distinct forms of a more essential divine mania that will emerge in his palinode.

The previous speech, Socrates says, belonged to Phaedrus of Myrrhinus, that is, Phaedrus of a place of fragrant luxury. The palinode, however, belongs to Stesichorus of Himera.[21] This new speech of *himeros*, the ancient

## The Palinode

name for "desire" that accompanies the Muses (and puns on *erōs*), will wash out Phaedrus's modern luxuries, and, so the word *epithumia*, which the urbane speeches associated with bodily pleasures, disappears.[22] Rather than completely refuting the concealed lover's attack on bodily pleasure, he implicitly agrees with the concealed lover's opinion about *epithumia* (cf. 238–239c). Socrates's purpose in the palinode is therefore properly understood as accounting for the full nature of *erōs*, which may both provide for the greatest good and find expression in *epithumia*.

Socrates's palinode begins with a repudiation of Lysias's thesis: "The speech is not true [or: genuine, *etumos*] which says that, rather than to a lover who is present, it is necessary [*dei*] to grant favors to a non-lover, because the one is mad, the other sound-minded [*sōphrosunē*]" (244a). Adopting Stesichorus's *etumos*, Socrates signals his desire to bring the urbane speeches into harmony with their own experience, here under the plane tree, which has attributed both good and ill to *erōs*. Socrates has cleverly qualified his thesis to allow for this complexity. His alteration of Lysias's thesis now allows for the boy to favor a nonlover when a lover is not present, which implies that a nonlover is not simply unworthy. Similarly, Socrates's negation of the claim to necessity allows that it may be possible and even better to favor a nonlover, which concedes that *erōs* may in some form be bad, although his aim here is to reveal its goodness.

Socrates uses examples of good mania to question their previous assumption that mania is "simply" (*haploos*) bad (244a). As in the case of the noble lover, he appeals to opinions that he and Phaedrus have neglected due to Phaedrus's sophisticated tastes, namely those that are old-fashioned and filled with superstition. Oracles, he says, have achieved "many noble [or: beautiful, *kalos*] things," in private or in public, when mad (244a–b). Since Socrates says that this opinion is "clear to all," just as the concealed lover did in order to avoid demonstrating the truth, some caution is appropriate here (244b5; cf. 237d4). These opinions would of course be dubious to Phaedrus; it is far from clear that these oracles say beneficial things when mad. How can one be certain that they are truly mad? Or that their pronouncements are true? Moreover, can one know the conditions of mania without eliminating its divinity and goodness? Is Pieper right to say that mania confounds any attempt to grasp it "scientifically"?[23] Socrates does make it clear that one property of good mania is that it provides knowledge,[24] although his formulation in each case suggests that the difficulty of the issue cannot be resolved by merely invoking opinions contrary to those of the nonlover.

Socrates's first example of beneficial mania is the mantic art, the art of prophecy, which communicates, first, that mania can result in knowledge and art, and second, that the simple act of naming raises the question of how the products of mania can be understood. Socrates uses the example of distinct oracles, the prophetess at Delphi, the priestess at Dodona, and the Sibyl,[25] all of whom possessed "the most beautiful art [*kallistē technē*] by which the future is distinguished" (244c). This is the first use of the word *technē* in the dialogue, and its conjunction with madness the first explicit formulation of a central puzzle of the *Phaedrus*: if art is a human endeavor, directed by thinking and capable of being taught (270d–e), how can its proper use depend on divine inspiration? Indeed, Socrates says that sobriety is detrimental to the art, such that it will accomplish "little or nothing" (244b).[26] Even sacred Delphi did not avoid criticism for its moments of weakness and keen sense for self-preservation, and only when it transcended these human concerns was its authority incontrovertible.[27] Perhaps thinking of the failures of these oracles, Socrates contrasts the ancients' confidence with the modern assertion of the power of human sanity and seeking (*zētēsis*) over divine mania (244c–d). Changes in the name of prophecy's divine inspiration (from "manic" to "mantic"), as well as the name of sober and uninspired inquiry into the future (from "oionostic" to "oiōnistic"), reflect this changing understanding, subtly misleading moderns with a "high-sounding" name. Socrates's recovery of the good mania entails recognizing the subtle power of words to shape our perception of the actual object, with the slightest of differences carrying with them diametrically opposed opinions about the object.[28] Even if the gods have inspired a prophecy, it falls to mortals to put it in words and interpret it. Phaedrus, for his part, must defend the superiority of his modern knowledge against ancient knowledge.

The second beneficial form of mania arises amid the greatest illnesses, which stem from ancient wrath or blood guilt. Socrates does not mention specific symptoms of this illness,[29] a specific god that has been offended, or any specific crime. This ancient blood guilt has few historical examples, and although Socrates says the illness afflicts "some families," his indefinite diagnosis suggests a general application: great illness might be bestowed upon anyone at any time, so long as we are without foreknowledge and remain ignorant of our ancient origins and the deeds of our forebears (244d).[30] Socrates's claim that this mania awakens one to the sacred purifying rites or mysteries (*teletai*) echoes the rites of Eleusis, which extended the need for regular purification to the entire city, rather than for certain families and crimes. This purification needs an interpretive mania that resorts to prayers and services directed to the gods (244e). That is to say, these illnesses exceed human understanding. In contrast to the urbane speeches and contemporary medicine, which considered mania and illness to be identical,[31] Socrates indicates here that mania may serve as a remedy and conversely that moderation may preclude healthiness. This purifying mania seems to arise from the experience of pain and perplexity, providing the insight that one must change course and interpret the experience out of a desire to cure oneself and become healthy again. The goodness of this mania derives from its dim recollection of the past as the cause of present troubles.

The third form of beneficial mania, poetic inspiration by the Muses, also looks to the past as a source of insight for the future. This mania arouses a "soft and chaste" soul to a Bacchic frenzy with songs and poetry, which then "orders" (*kosmein*) the "myriad deeds of the ancients" into a whole image for the education of future generations (245a). The softness of the poet's soul suggests receptiveness to inspiration by the Muses, in contrast to sober and therefore hard souls.[32] This soft soul recalls the concealed lover's warning that *erōs* inculcates a softness of body that puts the city at risk (239c9), but in this case, softness benefits the city. The improvement of the soul follows a different logic than the body. Socrates played with this softness in his first speech, when he shared in Phaedrus's Bacchic frenzy, summoned the Muses, and then composed dithyrambs and epic verses.[33]

Like the previous forms of mania, the poetic art must be touched with madness, for art alone is insufficient: "He who approaches the gates of the poetic arts without the mania of the Muses, having been persuaded that he will be a sufficient poet from art [*technē*], is uninitiated [or: incomplete, *atelē*] and both he himself and poetry, the poetry of the sound-minded [*sōphronountos*], are overshadowed by that of the mad" (245a). The technician without inspiration, the hard soul, has "been persuaded" that he can become a poet, which in this case is to say that he has been deceived either by himself and his desire to become a poet or by someone else. Unlike the manic art, where divine foresight and art were one and the same, poetry distinguishes mania from *technē*.[34] Although poetic mania doubtless exhibits art, the whole is greater than the sum of its techniques. The sober man of technique remains incomplete (*atelē*), so that the mania of the Muses exhibits the same restorative and purifying power of the mania of blood guilt (cf. *teletai* at 244e2). Sobriety leaves one in a state of ignorance as to how the past may inform future fulfillment.

Each of these three forms of mania are discernible in Socrates's expressions of erotic inspiration. He re-enacted the oracle at Dodona when he heard the voice "from the spot" under the plane tree, which prophetically revealed to him that he had sinned against Eros (242c1–2). This daimonic voice corroborated Socrates's experience of shame, as discussed above, mirroring the mania that reveals purifying rites for crimes—this is, those against Eros. Socrates's own poetic mania seems to have been inspired by Phaedrus's Bacchic frenzy, culminating in his first speech. That speech was itself, however, Socrates's crime—his poetic mania was in that case harmful and glorified the nonlover as the poets glorify the ancients. Only the corrective palinode will properly order "the myriad deeds of the ancients," albeit not deeds of human history, but of discarnate souls. The palinode will be the product of mania, and insofar as *erōs* is the provider of the "greatest goods," it too will share in the beneficence of poetry, purification, and prophecy.[35]

The cause of beneficence in these forms of mania remains to be seen. Each mania was asserted to be good on the condition of divine dispensation, to the extent that any human and sober prophecy, illness, or poetry was useless (244a7–8, c3, d4–5, 245a1–2). This proposition justifies mania insofar as Phaedrus accepts the earlier assertion that what is divine is in no way bad. But how can he recognize the divine (242a)? What is the divine? It is first approached by distinguishing it from what is human. Madness allows Socrates to go beyond the probabilities and ordinary expectations of human experience, such that the "fine" or "noble" deeds of mania are the result of disturbance, of "having been moved" (*kekinēmenos*) (245b). The realization of "the greatest good fortune" depends on being drawn out of an ordinary pattern of goods (245c, 265a). But so long as the nature of the divine and the greatest good remain hidden, Socrates's argument that madness is good—his argument so far relies on what is "clear to all"—remains insufficient. The palinode must extend beyond the assertion of contrary opinions and authorities. Only when Socrates can show the nature of the divine, and that *erōs* is the most divine mania, will he carry off the "prizes of victory" and his vindication of Eros be complete (245b–c).

## IMMORTAL SOUL

In demonstrating that *erōs* can achieve the greatest good, Socrates transitions abruptly from his defense of mania to considering the immortality of the soul: "It is necessary first to consider [or: think, *noēsai*] the nature of soul with respect to both gods and human beings by seeing its true experiences [*pathoi*] and deeds [*erga*]" (245c). Study of the soul arises naturally because Socrates's first speech regarded *erōs* as a form of our "inborn desire for pleasure" (237d–238a). He will later also show that such an inquiry is essential to instruction in the art of speaking. One must show the student "the being [*ousia*] of this [the soul's] nature" and how it acts and is acted upon (270d–e, 271b–c). Socrates's palinode, being concerned with the nature of soul in general and in individual souls, thus looks forward to their discussion of rhetoric and the requirements of art. But one must first use *logos* on individual souls in order to distinguish the nature of soul (270d, 271a–b). Socrates is beginning, then, with a principle that could only be the conclusion of the investigation, even though the investigation presupposed the principle.[36] Socrates's insight here is akin to the inspired pre-sentiment he expressed in his shame and diagnosed in the discussion of mania. Indeed, the relationship between soul and *logos* will emerge as a circular one, so Socrates says here that "the beginning [*archē*] of the proof is this," and then goes on to demonstrate how soul is itself an *archē*. The necessity of thinking about the soul seems to originate from and presuppose the soul. Rather than the result of logical errors, such perplexities in Socrates's proof will prove to be necessary for his account of persuasion and the power of *logos*, and expressive of the reciprocal relationship between *erōs* and *logos* that is at the heart of his ethical defense of philosophy.[37]

Socrates's proof of the immortality of the soul is a remarkably concise demonstration that the soul is immortal (literally "deathless," *athanatos*) (245c–246a). In eleven sentences, Socrates deduces that the soul moves others, but is itself moved only by itself, and so also moves forever so long as it does not abandon itself. As a self- and forever-moving thing, it must be the *archē* ("beginning" or "ruling principle") of all motion. Being an *archē*, it could not have come from another *archē*, and so does not come into being (i.e., it exists but is not generated [*agenēton*]). The *archē* of motion is imperishable (or: incorruptible, *adiapthoron*), for if it were destroyed, it could never again come into being since it was not generated—and if it was susceptible to coming into being or perishing, the entire cosmos would collapse and cease moving, since there would be nothing from which things could again be moved. Therefore, since what is self-moving is immortal, "it would not be shameful for someone to say this is the being [*ousia*] and *logos* of soul" (245e). Indeed, the soul's self-motion is seen from its effect on bodies, which do not move themselves unless they are ensouled (*empsuchon*).

This proof is problematic from the beginning. Its first words, "all soul is immortal" (*psuchē pasa athanatos*), are ambiguous because there are no indefinite articles in Greek, and here *psuchē pasa* lacks the definite article *hē*. The sense of the phrase is consequently either distributive, "each and every" soul, or collective, soul in general.[38] Is Socrates saying that the soul of each individual living thing is immortal? Or that soul, collectively, as life itself, is immortal? Each has significant implications for interpreting both the proof and the remainder of the palinode, and has understandably divided commentators.[39] Given that the linguistic ambiguity is itself irresolvable, it is prudent to suspend decision for the moment and allow that perhaps Plato intended this perplexity. By doing so, there can be some resolution of the other problems found in the proof.

This first sentence of the proof is also its conclusion. Socrates, like Lysias did when his nonlover presupposed the beloved's knowledge of his intentions, places what comes last in thought first.[40] Even the object in which the motion of soul is perceived—body—is not introduced until the end of the proof, almost as an afterthought. By suppressing this relationship to bodies, and so the distributive sense of soul—that is, the individual souls that are perceived as individuals on account of occupying separate bodies—Socrates is able to suggest without delay that soul is itself an *archē* that stands outside all motion as perceived by our senses. Yet even this equation of soul and *archē* is not explicit. The mediating propositions concerning what is forever-moving and what is the *archē* of motion are more general and not explicitly linked to soul. Only the conclusions drawn from these general propositions are attributed to soul: soul is self-moving, not generated, and immortal. The burden of the proof is carried entirely by deduction from the distinction between the self-mover and that which can only be moved by another. Socrates thus relies on the distinction of soul from body that he made in his first speech, used to prove the noble intentions of the concealed lover (241c).[41]

The manner of the soul's motion, both as an *archē* and as found in bodies, is perplexing. Motion presupposes a multiplicity, such as a change in position or in another property, and is therefore only a monad insofar as it encompasses a two-fold relation of like and unlike.[42] As such, a self-mover cannot be said to be solely active (its "deeds"), for it is acting on itself, and being thus acted upon, it is passive (it has "experiences" or *pathoi*, from *paskein*, "to suffer"); the self-mover presupposes its duality. It is therefore not incorrect to suppose that the experience of mania as "being disturbed," *kekinēmenos*, is the true nature of soul, but it is incomplete, for that passive reception of the divine can only capture one part of the nature of the soul. The being of soul, which "never abandons itself," lies in its restlessness, always moving itself and being moved by itself (245c9).[43] The closest physical analogue is centripetal motion, a perfect unending motion toward itself, the circularity of which necessitates its perception through parts.[44] The perception of the soul as being in motion immediately differentiates it from soul in collective sense or soul as a principle.

Yet the soul as *archē* gives the proof an undeniably collective sense. Reginald Hackforth (1952) argues that "the logic of the proof" depends on it.[45] All moving things—and so all things that "come to be"—"necessarily" (*anangkē*) come from a beginning, which itself cannot have a beginning or it would cease to be a beginning (245d1–2). The use of *anangkē* here is the clearest expression yet of the nature of necessity, for its assertion is accompanied by a demonstration of why something is necessary: noncontradiction and its correlate, unity. What is must be itself; a beginning cannot have a further beginning. All soul must rest in one soul. This collective soul could be interpreted as a cosmological principle or world soul, in which all individual souls participate and are completed to the extent to which they do so. Although there is no mention in the dialogue of such a soul permeating all individual souls, there must be such a thing as "soul" generally, under which all souls are understood as souls.[46] Indeed, both human and god alike were said to possess or be moved by souls, and the subsequent myth shows the Olympians moving through the heavens as each "performs what belongs to him" (247a5–6). "All soul" seems to arrange each soul as lesser *archai* of their respective "provinces of activity," as Ficino puts it.[47] Socrates thus aptly calls the self-mover the "font" (*pēgē*) of motion, recalling the font of cool (*psuchron*) water that flows under the plane tree (230b6, 245c10). This beautiful attempt to reconcile many souls under one, however, founders on the very passage that stimulated it, because the existence of many *archai* of motion contradicts the concept of *archē* itself—that is, that an *archē* as an *archē* must be one (245d1–2). The proof thus points again to the original problem of its distributive and collective senses.

The proof builds upon the demonstration that soul is an *archē* to show its eternity. Being a beginning, the *archē* of motion does not come into being, which means it always was, and insofar as it is imperishable, always will be. The correlate "always," however, is suppressed and not stated. In fact, the verb "to be" (*einai*) is only ever implicit, and Socrates exclusively uses the verb *gignesthai*, "to come to be" or "to be born," which can only mean a temporally finite, rather than eternal, being. An *archē* is in privative relation to "becoming," the world of genesis or change and motion. At the same time, the *archē* is itself in motion, which, as noted above, means it too is always in a relation. How, though, can this self-mover be in relation to anything besides itself?[48] Moreover, how can it be in relation to itself without the supposition of something—a property for instance—with respect to which it changes or moves? This proof of the nature of soul in and of itself depends, then, on a further cause, for the sake of which it moves. What makes possible its movement, or rather, for the sake of what does it move? What is the cause of its being, or, in the language of the *Republic*, where is "the good itself"?[49] No such cause is forthcoming in the proof; when soul inquires into itself, it already presupposes the cause of its motion.[50] The perpetual motion of the self-moving *archē* necessitates that it never attain and be in conformity with that for the sake of which it moves; were it to do so, it would cease to move, and so abandon itself as something forever- and self-moving. The good for which the *archē* of motion sets itself in eternal motion is present only as an absence, a lack.[51]

Socrates goes on to prove that an *archē* is imperishable by conjecturing the consequence of its nonbeing in the world, that is, on the temporal existence of bodies. Its eternity is proven by the absurdity that results should that *archē* cease to be, for another could not come into being (because an *archē* cannot be generated), nor could anything else—that is, nothing could come to move again. Without this original source of motion, "the whole heavens and all the earth would come to rest collapsing into one and never again have something from which things will come to be moved" (245d8–e2).[52] Everything that depends on another for its movement will be incapable of arresting this slowing. An immediate objection suggests itself: if there are other eternal causes akin to this *archē* of motion, their being would not depend on the *archē* of motion, and so the collapse of the physical cosmos would have no bearing on them—they would continue to be as they always have. Although something might continue to be, either this "one" of everything that was once generated or simply all the eternal beings,[53] the force of Socrates's argument is that such things can only be said to be insofar as generated things, and therewith motion, exist.[54] Our own continuous existence, that we are in motion and temporal, is given as evidence that the *archē* of motion still exists, and there is no knowledge of eternal beings except through their differentiation and multiplicity, which is the work of the *archē* of motion and generation. The perfect rest of the "one" into which all is collapsed, echoing the one of Parmenides's monism, does not admit of direct perception or knowledge.[55] The scope of Socrates's claim cannot be overstated, since, by implying the identity of the *archē* of motion and soul, he is claiming that the being of the cosmos, at least generated being, is coextensive with life and soul. The fact of our being and thinking is a premise of not only the proof that the *archē* is imperishable, but of the very existence of the cosmos.[56]

With this, Socrates concludes that the immortality of that which moves itself has been shown, and that "were someone to say that this is the being and speech [*ousian te kai logon*] of soul, it would not be shameful" (245e). Socrates thus equivocates in the end and does not say that the proof is true, only that it can be justified before noble souls. It is justifiable in light of the shame that Socrates incurred from his first speech. Although that speech distinguished the soul from the body, it made no claim for its immortality or incorruptibility. On the account of the first speech, the lover corrupted the beloved in both body and soul. An incorruptible soul, then, serves as a bulwark against persuasion that would take possession of the beloved and corrupt him entirely. Indeed, Socrates's expression of shame served to reveal the soul to be something capable of purification from servitude to bodily desires. The soul is not only independent of the body, but rules the body—Socrates's new account has freed the soul in order to show that the mania of *erōs* can meet the judgment of the noble lover.

Socrates's conclusion introduces the corruptible and perishable body that the proof depended on. The "necessity" that the soul is not generated and immortal requires that the motion of bodies originates from souls (246a1). Socrates has given an account of soul's nature that is as much as possible limited to itself, so that its deeds and experiences are only with respect to itself, distinct from its relation to the world.[57] Indeed, the eternity of the soul is inconceivable without such a distinction, since the proof depended on the soul being an unmoved self-mover. Were the soul necessarily or always an other-mover, its essential being could not be said to lie in self-motion.[58] The immortality of the soul lies in its eternity, not in the conventional sense of forever being attached to an everlasting body. But the true self-motion of the soul is imperceptible, seen only in speech. Only the motion of individual bodies, which are in themselves "soulless" and moved "from without," allows the perception of soul in "ensouled" (*empsuchon*) bodies that seem to move themselves. The nature and cause of this embodiment remains hidden.

The soul's attachment to individual bodies, its distributive sense, presents again the problem of determining whether soul can also be the *archē* of motion, in the true sense of beginning all motion. Inquiry into the nature of soul does not begin in its unity as an *archē*, but in its many instances, although the soul's desire to know itself in order to find its greatest good returns to that unity. The restlessness of soul is active and endless inquiry into itself, which inquiry will extend through and between individual souls. Socrates said that "this is the being and speech of soul" and indeed its being and speech (*ousia te kai logos*) are inseparable. Soul's *logos* exceeds the boundaries it sets for itself because the object is forever in motion, yet also finds unity in "all soul" that makes possible *logos* itself. By this mysterious excess, the question of the nature of soul has brought into question the distinction that Phaedrus uncritically accepted, between precise *logos* and ill-defined fantastical myth.[59] The indeterminate *psuchē pasa* is a justifiable representation of the nature of soul, and its particular articulation within the proof will provide both inspiration and essential grounds for Socrates's myth of *erōs* and the good it provides through philosophical conversation.[60]

## FORM AND GOD

Since the proof has sufficiently established the immortality of soul, Socrates tells Phaedrus they must now speak of the form or *idea* of soul. The *ouisa* and *logos* of soul as presented in the proofs is therefore an incomplete account of the nature of the soul, requiring a discussion of the form of soul in order to harness its immortality as the *archē* of motion to the deeds and experiences of both divine and human souls. "Form" does not here refer to what has been called Plato's "theory of forms" or "doctrine of ideas," although they are related in that form of soul allows for its perception of the highest objects of contemplation, and therefore determined by its relation to those objects.[61] *Idea* literally means "a thing seen" or "a look" and therefore refers in the first place to generated things, and yet is plastic enough to describe the manner by which soul is apportioned so as to be soul.[62] Socrates says that to tell "what sort" of thing the form of soul really is would be an "altogether divine and long narrative," while it is within human capacity to show what the form resembles (*eoika*) (246a). The study of soul through a likeness is more properly human in that seeing the form or look of the soul entails seeing it in the image of a familiar physical object.

Socrates proposes a likeness for the soul that is appropriately mobile: "the combined power of a winged and yoked team and a charioteer" (246a). An important feature of this image that commentators often pass over is its precise referent: it likens the soul not to the chariot itself but to its capacity for accomplishment and activity, as it is specifically the "combined power [*dunamis*]" that unifies this fantastical complex of parts, which together recall the chariots and mythical beasts mentioned earlier in the dialogue.[63]

Indeed, Socrates's image seems intended as a playful counter to Phaedrus's inclinations, first to his "softness" and aversion to discomfort by recalling the charioteer Herodotus of Thebes (227a9–11, 258e1–5), and second to the "clever" men cast doubt on the truth myth by arguing from likelihood (229c–230a). Socrates here establishes a new ground for likelihood or *eikos* (derived, like *eoika*, from *eikein*, "to be like or resemble") that is not grounded solely in empirical observation. In transcending the everyday as well as Phaedrus's expectations—not least Phaedrus's self-conception and conception of *logos*—the myth establishes a background for the later discussion of rhetoric, not least by apposing the unifying power of the chariot to the "power" of *logos* for "leading the soul," which suggests an essential role for *logos* in fulfilling the nature of soul (271c10). Socrates's story of how the soul leads and is led, however, is long and nuanced, and it begins with the soul's perfection in the image of the gods.

Socrates distinguishes between the soul of a god and the soul of a human according to the nature and stock of their charioteers and horses. The gods' are good and of good stock, while the human's are mixed, explicitly having only a pair of horses, one "noble [or: beautiful, *kalos*] and good" and the other "the opposite," that is, ugly and bad (246b). Having these opposites within the soul makes the team troublesome and difficult to control. As for the charioteer of the human soul, Socrates's description is curious, literally being "the ruler [*archōn*] for the charioteer of the team," which suggests a further distinction in the image between the charioteer as a whole and his mind. The question as to whether the charioteer, and perhaps even the horses, are themselves animated with souls such that one soul itself contains several souls, will result in an infinite regress—defying the unity sought by a likeness—if the independent or active motion of each part is ignored.[64] These motions are nevertheless governed, in the case of a god's soul, by the *archōn* of the chariot in a manner akin to the *archē* of motion, serving as the origin or font of the chariot's motion, and thus distributing the power of the *archē* across each part as the *archē* does for each individual soul. The chariot as a whole would consequently be a self-mover insofar as it moves in accordance with its *archōn*.

Socrates is now able to more clearly distinguish between immortal and mortal living things, as the proof only distinguished immortal soul from body on the basis of self-motion as opposed to passive motion. Socrates is careful to eliminate the possibility of a body moving forever—that is, be immortal—for otherwise it would be impossible to distinguish the soul as the cause of motion. Whether or not a soul is found in a body reflects a difference between souls. When soul is perfected or complete (*telea*) and winged, it travels without difficulty and "arranges [*dioikein*] the cosmos," but "the one having lost its wings" is instead carried—that is, passively moved by external forces—"until it lays hold of something solid, where having come down to dwell [*katoikizein*], it takes an earthly body" (246b–c). The body is the home of the imperfectly winged soul, "but it is not immortal from any argument that has been reasoned through" (246c). It is only because of our limited perception of the gods, "neither having seen nor sufficiently thought of a god," that they are imagined (*plattesthai*) to be immortal living things, with a soul and body combined forever (246c–d). In a stroke, Socrates refutes the Olympians found in the poetry of Homer and Hesiod. Their portrayal is an imaginative extrapolation of the life and experiences of human beings, in whom soul and body are mixed together. Knowledge of the soul's movement in its pure and divine form must therefore come from some other source than sense perception alone. The palinode reveals that knowledge through a diachronic descent from perfection rather than through an ascent from imperfect perception in embodied life. This is in a way misleading, as our own temporal experience is of the latter, but Socrates's myth shows how our imperfect and mortal state implies, and can only be understood in light of, this perfection.

The gods themselves are not the source of their power to range the heavens, but rather their wings are nourished by "the divine" that is in turn "beautiful, wise, good, and every such thing" (246d–e). Socrates thus depicts the souls of gods in an archetypal journey motivated by the desire to commune with this source. Zeus, "the great leader [*hegemōn*] in the heavens," journeys about "ordering and caring for all things" (246e). Behind him follows "an army of gods and daimons," arranged in eleven further companies (or "parts," *merē*). A thirteenth god, Hestia, remains in the home (*oikos*) of the Olympians. The twelve traveling gods "lead as commanders [*archōntes*] according to the station which each has been assigned" and "do what is [assigned] with respect to themselves" (247a–b). Zeus's station is to order the others, and in so doing he assumes most clearly the power of self-motion. A rank ordering of souls is established, each owing their station to Zeus. From this, the gods and their companies proceed along their respective pathways (*diexodoi*), each a ruler within his or her own station, but not the absolute first principle found in the proof. This army of "the happy race of gods" is an orderly and harmonious "chorus"—no doubt the chorus that Socrates alluded to in his earlier mania, and wishes Phaedrus to join (cf. 247a7, 228b5–c1). The followers of the gods, however, struggle to participate in this chorus while their leaders easily ascend to their "feast upon the arch of heaven" (247a–b).

The gods' feast is a pivotal moment in Socrates's myth, for it is the heart of the soul's relation to reality, guiding its motions at every level—cosmic, interpersonal, and within the individual soul. In establishing this fundamental relationship, this divine feast will assume a similarly pivotal position in Socrates's analysis of rhetoric and his ethical exhortation of Phaedrus, which Socrates anticipates by rhetorically contrasting this feast with the "feasting of speeches" furnished by Lysias "over there," that is, under the earth in Hades (227a3, b6–7; cf. 236c8). Here, the gods leave behind any ordinary notions of place and feast. When they reach the arch of heaven, "having journeyed outside, they stand upon the back" of the heavens and are led around by its revolution (*periphora*). They then feast by turning their "gaze upon [*theōrousi*] the things outside the heavens" (247b–c). Even the gods now find themselves in passive subjection to a still greater source of motion that is perfectly circular in its path.

Although this "superheavenly place" of the feast is the ultimate destination of the soul, it is no place at all. Even the poets, who have given so many fantastic and strange images, have not "hymned nor will ever hymn the superheavenly place according to its worth [*axios*]" (247c). The poetic mania, dedicated as it is to the glorification of deeds, is insufficient for depicting the place here, which exceeds all deeds and objects of sense, and can only be spoken. The truth (*alētheia*) is that the place is "occupied"[65] by "that which really is," or more literally, "the being which is in the manner of being" (247c6–7). The difficulty of this rendering lies not simply in translation but in the nature of speech itself; Plato's formulation, *hē ousia ontōs ousa*, uses three cognates of the verb *einai*, "to be," as substantive, participle, and adverb. The circularity in this formulation still hides from sight the nature of being itself. "That which really is" must exceed all designation or description since it is the cause of designation, with the result that its attributes can only be rendered as privations or negations: it is "colorless and shapeless and intangible" (247c6–7). This entirely transcendent object—if it can be called an object—is that to which "true knowledge relates" and "is seen by intellect alone, the pilot of the soul" (247c7–8). The full extent of this negation of all earthly attribution is difficult to understate, for the absence of body in the most general sense—all physicality—and seems to be death.

Transcending physical being, "the mind of a god is nourished by unmixed knowledge and intellect" (247d1). This knowledge is not mixed with "genesis" or with anything "that is different in the different things we now say are"—that is, those things which come into being or change, and to which our words typically refer (247d7–e1). Such knowledge nourishes every soul so that each "should care to receive what is fitting [*to prosēkon*] [for it]" (247d2–3). The fittingness of such knowledge is not given any specific content, for that would entail mixture, but is simply the principle that it is only with knowledge of what really is, rather than what seems to be, that soul is able to receive precisely what it needs. The soul "fares well" by seeing, amongst "the other beings that really are," three specific beings: "justice itself," "moderation itself," and "knowledge itself" (247d3–e3). Each is the being of one of the four cardinal virtues, with knowledge taking the place of wisdom. Courage or manliness, however, is missing entirely. Although arrayed for battle, the gods seem to have, in their knowledge and lack of bodies, no need of courage. The good itself is also notably absent, given that Socrates is arguing that "the greatest good fortune" is bestowed through ecstatic mania—that greatest good fortune cannot be reduced to this superheavenly vision. What Socrates accomplishes here is to manifest the soul's need for truth and goodness, and it is that need that will guide its motions, including the use of speech. The Olympians are not only aware, as one commentator puts it, of the "absent presence" of the good, but are ordered by and reconciled ("with affection") to this perfect knowledge of their subordination to true being.[66] This is knowledge that they, lacking such being, are themselves not eternal but metabolic.[67] Even the gods must see being "through time," perceiving that which is outside of genesis, unmoving and unchanging—always being itself—as if it had a past, present, and future (247d3–4). Socrates accordingly describes being using a definite article with a participle, *to on* or *hē ousa*, to indicate that this perpetual duration must be perceived in a world marked by change.[68] The participle form points back to the soul, which is in motion while perceiving being.[69] Distinct from being and in motion, the gods, when their feasting is complete, sink "back into the heavens [and] go homewards," which is not the superheavenly place but the hearth of the cosmos. The gods, having ascended from their home, now look back upon it and perceive it as such.[70] If the gods remained forever in the superheavenly place, they would be indistinguishable from the period that carries them and cease to resemble mortals.

The feast of the gods therefore turns back toward the human souls which were the basis for conjecture about the gods' souls. The gods' perfect ascent and perception of the truth is extrapolated from a human capacity that is so often hidden. The colorlessness and seeming emptiness of "that which really is" is obscured by "multicolored" feasts such as Lysias's, which filled Phaedrus with desires for wealth, reputation, and pleasure (228a3–4, 234d, 236b7). Rather than inducing a divine mania for the perception of true being, Lysias used his rhetoric to please his audience with the promise of things that he found to have so much purchase in the city.

## MORTALITY

The grand and orderly ascent and descent of the gods is followed by the chaotic and partial ascent of those in their train. Socrates, having shown the perfection implied in mortal striving, now depicts the mortal experience in a series of reduplications of this cycle of ascent and descent in search of that perfection. Rather than in a singular vision of true being, the greatest good for the human being is obtained in the betterment of this search through continuous dedication and practice. Having begun with the gods, Socrates's depiction of mortality shows our potential, despite our imperfection and continuous struggle.

Even though "the best" human souls resembled (*eikasmenē*) the god they followed, and "lifted up the head of the driver into the outer place, and was carried along with the revolution [*periphora*], the charioteer was interrupted by the horses and scarcely looked down on the beings [*ta onta*]" (248a). These superlative human souls establish the limit of the human soul, and although they break through to the superheavenly place, they still see far less than did the gods. The human soul does not see *hē ousia ontōs ousa* in its full expression, but only fleetingly glimpses some of the beings (249c4). This limited perception of reality is the true origin of *eikos*, likelihood, which is established not on the basis of our experiences and opinions, as the sophistic disputers of myth and Lysias believe, but from what are truly the highest things. Socrates seeks here to reorient the soul in its entirety from the beings experienced in contradictory multiplicity to the beings in their true simplicity.

The proximate cause of imperfection in humans' attempt to imitate the gods is the quality of the horses pulling their chariots. The best mortal soul struggles with both horses, for the bad horse has effectively disturbed the good one, so that the driver must force the horses to lift him outside the heavens (248a5). He must resort to violence and compulsion, not words or other enticements, for there is an irrational element in the soul, as the concealed lover saw.[71] Phaedrus was himself the unwitting model for the driver's struggles when he compelled Socrates to give another speech. Phaedrus took control in the belief that he knew what was best for himself and Socrates, and although this leadership had "terrible" consequences, it was, as discussed earlier, instructive (242d4).

The other souls, unable to ascend to even glimpse the superheavenly place, "are carried around together below the surface [*hupobruchiai*],[72] treading and laying upon one another, each endeavoring to be before the other" (248a–b). This yearning of the souls for a glimpse of true being intimates the origins of *erōs* in the lack of nourishment, which emerges as their inability and unwillingness to hold their stations like the gods—they live in a disorderly competition. Struggle between souls thus originates from within an individual soul, not from the nature of being or the cosmos, so that peace and harmony must likewise originate internally rather than as a mastery over what is external. Without a glimpse of being, "all depart unperfected [or: incomplete, *atelē*]" and come to "desire [*chrōntai*] nourishment in opinion [*doxa*]" (248b4). Socrates makes the radical claim that human beings by nature—and by necessity[73]—seek out the truth, even though we must feed on opinions. Without seeing true being "where it is"—that is, by mistaking what is false for true—these souls will not know what is good or fitting for themselves, and so they seek out true being with "great earnestness" or "seriousness" (*spoudē*) (248b6–7). After these souls are incarcerated, most will be satisfied with opinion even though its power lies in imitation of truth. Phaedrus's own seriousness was of this sort, as he was seduced into defending Lysias's speech as if it were whole and perfect in itself (234c6–e4). Such eagerness for what is false means turning from that by which the wings of the soul are "made light" (248c1–2).

Now the journey of the mortal soul has returned to the point where the journey of the gods ended. Rather than nourishing their horses and going home, the souls are cast down by Adrasteia, literally Inevitability or Necessity, into mortal lives and bodies. In this moment of incarnation occurs the "chance" from which springs the great variety of forms of mortal life that inflects the human capacity to glimpse true being. In this iteration of the cycle of ascent and descent, mortal life grows organically. Necessity's "ordinance" (*thesmos*), more clearly a command or stricture than *nomos* ("law" or "custom"), lays down that "whichever soul becoming a follower of a god should look upon something of the truth, is free from sorrow until another period [*periodos*], and should it be able [*dunesthai*] to do this forever, it would be forever unharmed" (248c). The soul which, through "some misfortune [*suntuchia*]," is unable to do so, becomes heavy and "is filled with forgetfulness [*lēthē*] and badness" (248c6–7). Despite the eagerness with which souls attempt to ascend to the superheavenly place, they are unable to choose their natures and powers. Our forgetfulness obscures our natural power, but even in this state, something of the divine nourishment remains in the mortal and embodied soul, found through what seems to be true, *doxa*, so that the soul has the potential to be aroused and ascend again. Prior perception of true being is essential element of human life (248c3–4).

Being "weighed down," the soul falls to the earth and is planted (248c–d). The body seems to grow around the "planted" and hardened soul to become the "seed" or "birth" (*gonēn*) of mortal life. Socrates claims that there are nineteen human lives into which a soul could be first born into, arranged into nine ranks according to which soul has "seen the most." There are therefore only nine types of "seed" out of which the lives grow (248d–e). These lives range from the highest and first seed, which may produce "a philosopher or lover of beauty or musical [lit. man of the Muses, *mousikos*] and erotic man," down to the lowest and ninth seed which can only produce a tyrant (248d3, e3).[74] So there is a concordance between a soul's nature and way of life or profession in this first birth, but discrepancies may arise in subsequent births. There might be found followers of each god in every one of these lives, and discrepancies may arise between a nature and the way of life it pursues.[75]

This possible disjunction between one's nature and way of life does not mean, however, that those ways of life are not ranked. The lives of the poet, seer, and sophist really are subordinate to the gymnastic trainer; regardless whether the true nature of whoever tries to live such a life is fitted to it, the life of the trainer is closer to true being. Socrates gives some indication of this by his different introductions for the top four ranks ("into a seed [or: birth]" [*eis gonēn*]) and lower five ranks ("will have a life"). This point of separation between the ranks is more conspicuous given that the fourth rank is the only one explicitly concerned with the body,[76] and despite the palinode clearly situating the body within the lower rung of reality, this seed still ranks above many other lives. Someone who cares for the body and its health saw more of the truth than those other popularly revered positions, which are no longer concerned with what really is and is beneficial.

These lower ranks of soul are in fact dim reflections, poor mirrors, of the higher ranks, which will lead to their conflation. The politician's reflection by the demagogue and sophist is a case in point; although the former is "political" in the full sense of being devoted to the good of the city, and the others curry favor with the *dēmos* for the sake of profit, the inevitable mixing of the two will result in the popular disdain for the "politician." The poet, the imitative man, similarly sits in the sixth rank as a crude counterpart of the musical man—they would only be distinguishable to one who can recognize what is truly "musical."[77] The three forms of mania discussed earlier are now of questionable worth, as the prophet (*mantikē*), expert in mystic rites (*telestikos*), and poet are relegated to the fifth and sixth ranks. Perhaps the higher relation to music is one without the Bacchic frenzy of poetry. Socrates likewise distinguishes between the more humble prophetic powers of the soul and the mantic glimpse into the future given by the gods to such popular figures as the Pythia. A clear vision of the nature and origin of one's soul, realized to the fullest extent by the philosopher, is a superior glimpse into the nature of the cosmos.[78]

If the rank ordering of souls, according to how much they glimpsed of true being also reflects their relative concern with what really is, the preeminence of the philosopher means he is the one most concerned with what is truly beneficial. His ranking above those expressly political lives in the second and third ranks, "a lawful king or one fit for ruling [*archikos*] and warlike" and "a political man," indicates that the highest concerns—wisdom, beauty, music, and *erōs*—are private. If the philosopher-king is still present to Plato's mind, it does not seem to be a natural destiny of the soul.[79] Socrates makes a fundamental division here between the *erōs* found in the philosophic seed and the political order made by the king who abides and rules by law. The kingly soul is not amongst the most far-seeing, and so his law could decisively misconstrue the order that the philosopher perceives to the fullest extent possible for a human being. Socrates's later pairing of Zeus with philosophy, and not with the kingly soul, suggests a disjunction between the divine order of the cosmos and the static laws—if not whole political order—established on earth. What is erotic is more indicative of the highest order than the law by which the king wishes to order the city (cf. 249d–e, 256e3–257a2).[80]

The disjunction between a soul's nature and its way of life once embodied is exemplified in the case of Phaedrus. He appears to be a compound, who is a lover of beauty, is friendly with physicians, enjoys the company of poets, sophists, and, as seen in chapter 2, is not disinclined toward the tyrant. The fact that the lover of beauty shares the highest rank suggests that if Socrates does not find potential in his friend's soul, he at least wishes to give him that impression. Phaedrus's love of beauty is thus established to be the highest inclination in his soul, redeeming his lower inclinations, such as sophistry and demagoguery. Socrates's whole purpose in the palinode is, after all, to show Phaedrus that this love of beauty is of far greater value than he believes.

Similarly, the disjunction between the soul's true nature and embodied way of life is necessary to give meaning to its choices and judgment, which Socrates renders as an eschatology. All of these lives may be lived more or less justly, with the consequence that each soul will receive a better or worse "portion" (*moira*) in its ten-thousand-year journey of return (248e5). This journey is comprised of thousand-year periods (*periodoi*), each of which corresponds to one life and the soul's subsequent fate. These smaller periods resemble the period of the superheavenly place, and although they do not involve seeing the beings themselves, they are animated by the desire to return there (247d5, 249a3). A soul's relative rank and vision of being does not therefore determine its fate. Only one who "philosophizes without guile or loves his boy with philosophy" will return to the superheavenly place more quickly, if it chooses the life of philosophy three times in succession (248e).

Since souls are judged for their actions in their embodied lives, the myth of cosmic Justice, *Dikē*, can be interpreted as the present consequences of those choices. Socrates says life on earth is euphemistically "completed" or perfected (*teletuein*), as the myth of Oreithuia implied, through participation in the cosmic cycle of soul. After a thousand-year cycle, some souls are sent to "a prison under the earth [and] pay a penalty" (249a6–7). Others, "having been lightened by *Dikē* [go to] some place in the heavens" and spend their time in a way "worthy" (*axios*) of the life they lived while in "the form of a human" (*eidos anthrōpou*) (249a7–b1). As being "lightened by *Dikē*" suggests, the true "worth" of a life is determined by acting in accordance with intellect and perception of being, which also "lighten" the soul (246d6–7, 256b3–4), rather than by the honors, wealth, and pleasure extolled by Lysias; justice is not in the first place the judgment of particular actions, but the relationship of these actions to the condition of the soul. Socrates's claim that the soul chooses from an allotment "which life it may wish" to be born into in its next life indicates that our future is to some extent a consequence of our present choices and way of life (249b). Soul is only apparently freed from Necessity, since we are compelled, in our ignorance, to choose what is good and suffer what we must. Being in this way somewhere in-between knowledge of what is good and complete ignorance, the soul can become truly active and ascend to a higher life or descend to a worse one.

This judgment of *Dikē* and choice of lives is crucial to the palinode because it reveals that human nature lies in the capacity for judgment through reasoning, for the soul must be capable of seeing what really is—and erring—if "choice" and "judgment" are not simply instinctual action and arbitrary consequence. What is lower than the human, a beast, cannot take the "shape" of a human being:

> For it is necessary for a human to know, according to form [*eidos*], what is said [*legomenon*], by going from the many perceived things [and] collecting [them] into one through reasoning [or: calculation, *logismos*]; and this is recollection [*anamnēsis*] of those things which our soul saw then, having journeyed with a god and looked beyond what we now say to be, and raised his head into what really is [*to on ontōs*]. (249b5–c4)

The human being is essentiality its capacity to perceive form through reasoning. Although there is some ambiguity in whether reasoning is entirely linguistic—that is, enacted in words—Socrates is clear that "what is said" is only understood by reasoning, which gathers perceptions into one form.[81] Socrates shows here three things: the structure of reasoning; the condition of understanding language or of communication; and that communication depends on prior perception of true being. This does not exclude the possibility of error, the cause of which Socrates discusses later in the context of beauty, for although perceptions of being must have form and unity, form is not necessarily the being itself. Socrates disrupts, for a moment, the metaphor of vision for intellection and thinking—for mortals, clarity with respect to what really is obtained through speaking, not seeing, even while Socrates does not presume, unlike the concealed lover, that speech has an unequivocal power of clarity, since "what is said" must itself be gathered together, and the same thing may be spoken of in one way and "now" in another way (e.g., that which really is versus what is "now" said to be [247e]). The nineteen lives that Socrates distinguished indicate varying degrees of perceptiveness and varying approaches to "what is said." Humans come to know through conversation with other human beings, and that speech, Socrates claims here, cannot be meaningful if it does not in some way lead us to what really is. Every human being must enjoy some vision or knowledge of being if conversation is to be possible, such that reasoning, *logismos*, is already implicit in the capacity for speaking.[82]

This emergence of *logismos* is at the heart of Socrates's analyses of *erōs* and rhetoric because it is the way by which human beings apprehend what the soul desires and thereby the way to move the soul. There is no such thing as mere speech or conversation, wholly absent of reasoning and thereby absent of what really is.[83] To the extent that someone like Lysias believes he can persuade without possessing some knowledge is to misunderstand the natures of *logos* and belief as they relate to reality and our necessary desire for what really is. To confuse oneself and others about this essential human capacity is to diminish human nature—to make "small humans" (243a1). Nevertheless, *logismos* is precipitated by forgetfulness of being, so that the human being does not know either what it needs or what the "human form" (*anthrōpou eidos*) really is. The human being must gather itself. Socrates does not give a definitive answer to the problem of what is human, but articulates that problem so as to reveal its extent and intractability.

In showing that human form is essentially *logismos*, Socrates now makes clear that the premise of his myth, that soul is an *archē* and therefore immortal, could only be a conclusion he reached after gathering many souls into one (e.g., 245d2). Yet the *archē* is also the beginning, the principle, that makes *logismos* possible by endeavoring to find what is fitting. The *archē* is both the beginning and the end of reasoning, so that soul, in moving itself, returns to itself. This allows some clarification of Socrates's assertion that *logismos* is recollection: the soul could only perceive and come to know what really is if it had at one time seen true being; otherwise, its "gathering" would be done at random and could hardly be said to be gathering or perception at all. Socrates says that "it is always through memory [that soul] is able to be near to those things, which being near to a god is divine" (249c5–6). Furthermore, the soul's self-motion reveals that the soul does not simply desire to see again what it once saw, but to see it for itself, for its own benefit. As the soul desires and tends toward its own good, so too does it reason.[84]

At this crucial moment connecting the divine and the human, Socrates's myth points away from itself. On the one hand, the myth weaves together the whole that *logismos* recollects only in part, and so gives coherence to reason and its fruits. On the other hand, the only way to return to true being is to begin from our manifold and fragmentary experiences. What does it mean for *logismos* to be recollection if it is not the reproduction of a vision of the whole? In what way does *logismos* reflect reality? For that matter, how secure is the knowledge that *logos* and *logismos* must relate to "what really is"? Socrates's myth of *logos* thus indicates why *logos* must search beyond itself and take this mythical form, and why myth must point to *logos* in the sense of reasoning if myth is to adequately reflect the truth. The palinode is mythology in the highest sense.[85]

These difficulties in understanding how human nature lies in speech and reason take shape in the life of the philosopher. Socrates says that "justly only the mind of the philosopher grows wings" (249c4–5). The philosopher alone is able to gather so as to "recollect" best, "using reminders rightly" to grasp the beings. That is, he reasons best. In seeing most clearly what every human soul has seen to some extent, the philosophical life does not transcend the human, but is the human life par excellence. The philosopher nonetheless seems to stand infinitely far from the human, for his recollection of true being, which is "colorless and shapeless and intangible," must confront and be set against the ignorance of the many that is manifested in "what we now say is." Humanity dwells in the manifold of perception but without understanding or recollection, for it uses names solely as reminders of these perceptions, rather than as reminders of what really is. What we say (*phamen*) is not what is said (*legomenon*). This contrast with the "now" in which we live, the "present," and the "modern," must not be construed to mean merely the dramatic date of the dialogue, the corrupt state of Athenian intellectual and ethical life circa 415 BC, but rather the perpetual present separation from being experienced by every human soul.[86] Only the philosopher, "standing outside [*ekistamenos*] human seriousness" will be "perfected" by glimpsing being again (249c–d). As seen earlier, the objects of value listed by Lysias, which Phaedrus took so seriously, all pale in comparison with the true goods of the soul. The philosopher, as the human life most essentially human, separates itself from the apparent home of human beings, the body and what seems to be true—that is, opinion. In this enthusiasm, literally "having the god inside" (*en-thousiaszein*), the philosopher "has forgotten the many" that dwell in and speak of only what seems to be true (249d). On this account, the many regard him as passively disturbed (*parakinon*), and no doubt regard themselves active in their sobriety, although they do not know the truth of their words—that the philosopher is moved to return to the superheavenly place. To Phaedrus, Socrates seemed to be "wondrous" and "most strange" or "out of place" (*atopos*), always ready to walk outside the city although he never does (229a3–4, 230c6–d2).

## RECOLLECTION AND EROS

Socrates now turns in more detail to how the soul may ascend toward true being in this life through reasoning, which he also called recollection. Now Socrates tells Phaedrus that "therefore the whole speech [*logos*] having come here concerns the fourth mania" (249d). He told the story of the soul's ancient life, its cyclical ascent and descent, and its capacity for reasoning, in order to account for this highest form of mania. Reasoning and perception of being cannot be separated from the motions of the soul and should in fact be understood within the context of that motion. Without the interplay of discourse and desire, the uniquely human relation to reality is lost.

Recollection is precipitated by the experience of *erōs*, the eagerness upon seeing beauty to fly again despite being unable. This person who nonetheless continues to look upward is "slandered" as being mad, and indeed he "neglects [lit. does not care for, *amelein*] the things below," the needs and desires of the body as well as the city in which the body dwells (249d). Care for the body, however, was shown to be the privilege if not function of soul—"all soul cares for every soulless thing" (246b6). Although Socrates praises the soul that longs to return like "a bird" to true being and true nourishment, it will later be seen that that longing is not without its dangers.

Despite this danger, the mania that is induced by looking upon (*blepein*) something beautiful and being reminded of true beauty is the "best" mania of all (249d). This is the same mania that seemed to fill Socrates while he looked upon (*apoblepein*) Phaedrus as he read Lysias's speech and threatened to enthrall the beloved (234d3, 239b7). Phaedrus's own inspiration and shining face, Socrates now shows, was a reminder or even a "semblance" (*homoiōma*) of true beauty (250a6). Their mania was in fact love (*erōs*) of beauty (249e3-4). The lover was in fact in love before even meeting his earthly beloved, for otherwise he would not be receptive to or capable of perceiving his beloved. *Erōs* is participation in true being through the beauty found on earth—it is the experience of being inbetween (*metaxu*) the pure superheavenly place and the mixed life of the body on earth[87]—and in its highest form this participation requires speech to gather and clearly distinguish what is truly desired. This clarifies Socrates's meaning in describing himself as being inbetween the "simple" and "manifold," and that he knows himself through knowledge of Phaedrus (228a5-6, 230a3-6). As a desirous being he gathers together, through conversation, his manifold perceptions in order to find what he desires in its simplest and purest form.

*Erōs* is a tension, expressed here in the image of growing "wings" yet remaining rooted to the earth; the ascent of the soul will not be relived on earth in the manner of the gods. Indeed, the coherence of the myth seems to break down now that it is concerned with human life as we find it. Although wings were said to only grow every ten- or three-thousand years to lift one back to true being, now wings grow while on earth, at least for those with "sufficient memory" (248e-a, 249c, 250a). The great cycle is experienced in the "now," such that the nourishment of truth is found not only in "that place" above the heavens, but can also be glimpsed here.

The souls that can recollect more are most susceptible to the power of being, for they are "struck out" (*ekplēttesthai*) when they see on earth a "semblance" of beauty itself, just as was Socrates when he saw Phaedrus (250a6, cf. 234d1). When a man is struck out in this way, he ceases to be himself; the "self" and its regular and reliable boundaries are thrown into question before this vision of the truth. The self as such is defined in contrast to truth because it is what is filled up, colorful, and possessing shape, rather than transparent toward being. The heaviness of the self is the forgetfulness of being that must be "struck out." This is a strange picture of recollection, given the common belief that we hold on to our memories as if they were artifacts so that they do not escape us. Socrates is not saying that "memory" is emptiness, but that our original, best, state is one of clarity, without forgetfulness.

The human capacity for recollection is limited both by the powers of the particular soul and its "dulled organs" as well as the nature of the reminders or semblances themselves: "There is no light in the semblances here [i.e., on earth] of justice and moderation and other such things of value to souls" (250b1–4). With being so obscured by its appearance in semblances and by our organs, "few who come to the images [*eikonas*] see the race of the thing that has been imaged" (250b).[88] A soul dulled to the experience of being struck out, amazed, perplexed, does not perceive a semblance as a semblance of what is true, but simply as it appears, and will consequently maintain itself in its usual manner, believing itself secure. Socrates's claim that he still seeks to know himself, that he is ignorant, suggests that he would be in a constant state of being struck out or perplexed (229e–230a).[89] But Socrates playfully enacted this experience of being struck out to reflect back to Phaedrus his inspiration by speeches. Moreover, Socrates also said that because he knew Phaedrus, he had not forgotten himself (228a). How can he be both ignorant of himself yet not have forgotten himself? The only solution seems to be that Socrates knows himself as someone who is ignorant of himself, which is the suggestion made in the *Apology*.[90] Could he really therefore be said to be ignorant? His account of recollection shows that no human being is entirely ignorant, for a vision of the beings is a necessary condition for recollection—that is, reasoning—and even now our experience of *erōs*. Recollection is that capacity by which we clarify to ourselves our participation in being, and so that capacity by which we satisfy *erōs*. But since Socrates characterizes life as motion of soul, a life of reasoning is not one of completing thought by formulating a static doctrine, rather it is a life moved to seek the true and complete knowledge it only ever possesses in a preliminary or intuitive fashion. The perfecting of the soul that Socrates refers to seems to be a state of motion, of continual striving on account of recognizing its ignorance, both of the external world and of its own particular nature and power.

The beloved beautiful boy is not only an audience for the lover, an object of desire and persuasion, but also a semblance whose effect on the lover originates from the source of this semblance. The lover is not static, but himself moved, aroused because the boy reminds him of what he saw "then," in the ancient life of the soul, when it "was possible to see beauty shining" as all the souls followed the gods (250b). Now, moved by *erōs*, the soul longs for that time when we "were whole ourselves and untouched by evils" (250c). Recollection, Socrates says, is therefore an initiation in "the most blessed mysteries," the highest stage of which, the *epopteia*, is to see "whole and simple [*hapla*] and unchanging and happy showings [*phasmata*]" (250c).

Happiness lies not in experience and use of the things here, but in their use as reminders of these whole and simple showings where good things are found unmixed. Without Socrates's mythical arrangement to show that happiness is a condition of our present experience, one might believe human life to be tragic, full of darkness and suffering without reprieve. Socrates does not argue for the natural priority of wholeness, rest, peace, goodness, and happiness, as he does in other dialogues, but he does imply that one does in fact prioritize these objects when he identifies recollection with reasoning. Socrates's primary purpose here is to show that although living in the revelation of truth is beyond mortal powers, such a life may nonetheless be approximated or approached by constantly purifying the soul of the body's compulsion to dwell in what are only reminders. The greatest good fortune that is given through *erōs* is therefore not the complete vision of the superheavenly place, but the desire to attain it.

Socrates thus initiates Phaedrus into mysteries that recall the Greater Mysteries of Eleusis, although the civic cult of Athens has been transfigured and subordinated to the ecstatic view of the whole of nature through philosophy.[91] The rituals of Eleusis, rather than being the model for this recollection of true being, are an imitation in deed of what must instead proceed through reasoning. As an image of philosophy, the old rites are not discarded, but preserved on new grounds. But it is not clear whether Phaedrus recognizes this, or whether he only see Socrates's allusions to Eleusis as the demystification of ancient superstition. Reenactment of the mysteries is the crime for which Phaedrus and his associates are exiled from Athens, and Socrates has here been his leader in exactly this, for it is over and against the ordinary appearance of things that *erōs* inspires recollection. Socrates, though, should not shoulder all the blame for the destruction of custom, given that Phaedrus had begun the dialogue already afflicted with impiety and urbane skepticism. For Socrates, the mysteries of Eleusis, though deficient in reasoning, grasped something of the nature of human life and experience as being seperated from wholeness and purity.[92]

## BEAUTY AND ENTHUSIASM

In the next iteration of the soul's ascent, Socrates turns to the source of longing "here" on earth, which he identifies as beauty (250c). The particular nature of beauty, as "the most manifest" and therefore "most loved" of the beings, "found glistening most visibly clear through the clearest of our senses," makes it both a vivid exemplar for recollection and essential to human perception (250d). This manifest existence distinguishes beauty from the other beings: wisdom (*phronēsis*) and "the other things that are loved," remain concealed, "for it would produce a terrible love if it allowed some sort of visible phantom (*eidōlon*) of itself to come into sight." Recall that Socrates does not call the beings themselves "forms," which term he has assiduously restricted to the objects of perception and the work of reasoning, with the effect that perception of beauty is inseparable from the recollection of being, but is not the perception of true being itself.[93] Beauty is a special link between sensory experience and truth because of its clear manifestation and visibility—it presents to the senses the wholeness and purity so beloved in the superheavenly place. It seems to offer a visible completeness that has so far only been presented in speech, first in the concealed lover's use of definition to make clear and delimit the object of desire, and then in Socrates's description of reasoning as gathering into one form (237c–d, 238b6–7, 249b7–c1).

Socrates's contrast between beauty and wisdom is essential to understanding its nature and the prominence he gives it in the palinode. Beauty does us the good service of supplanting a most terrible and dangerous love with love for itself. The danger of the love of wisdom lies in the human inability to take hold of wisdom in its entirety; direct perception of wisdom and true being would destroy a mere mortal, or in other words, we would not be mortal if wisdom were so given. The love of beauty must then be relatively innocuous, as it allows us to perceive the things that have so far been called images, phantoms, semblances, or reminders, rather than the truth, which is not visible. Beauty is the manifestation of being, and therefore instills love of its instantiations perhaps more than any other being. Those fighting in Troy were drawn not by Helen, Stesichorus sang, but by her phantom. Indeed, if manifestation of a being obscures what that being truly is, the love of what is beautiful will draw one away from the being of beauty itself. The further implication is that the being of beauty, the manner of its being, lies in its concealment of being. The sheer manifest and evident perception of being conceals the nature of being. Nonetheless, Socrates says beauty draws one toward the recollection of being (249d). This apparent inconsistency may be explained as follows. The inspiration that beauty induces for its manifestations, rather than itself, leaves the lover longing for the true source of his inspiration when those manifestations prove to be just that—manifestations that hide the truth. Because of the very falsity of these phantoms, the lover is drawn toward being itself. The attractive superficiality of the beautiful points away from itself.[94] This is what Heidegger means when he interprets this passage as "beauty in felicitous discordance with truth."[95] He explains that "the essence of the beautiful . . . is what makes possible the recovery and preservation of the view upon Being, which devolves from the most immediate fleeting appearances and which can easily vanish in oblivion."[96] A central concern of the *Phaedrus* may be said to be how the "showing forth" or "manifestation" (*ekphainein*) of beauty conceals, for the perception of beauty is fundamental to the experience of *erōs* and therefore essential to understanding the power of *logos* that depends upon that experience (271c10). As Pieper (1964) says, since beauty is manifest to the senses and draws the human being toward the question of its being, "Plato envisages the utmost perfection accorded to man only as an encounter with divine Beauty, not as an encounter with the idea of Goodness or of Being."[97]

For someone who has not been recently initiated into the mysteries of being, this discordance between the appearance and being of beauty means that when he sees a "god-formed face" or "something that imitates beauty well," he will "give over to pleasure" and, like an animal, go "on all four legs to set upon them and father offspring" (250e). Not unlike his concealed lover, Socrates describes this pursuit of pleasure as *hubris* that is without fear or shame and "contrary to nature" (cf. 238a, 250e–251a). Dwelling on the pleasures of the body and producing bodily offspring is a diminution of human nature—it belongs to those "small humans," akin to the nonlover, who do not see the divinity of *erōs* (243a1). The true deficiency of this form of *erōs* is only seen in light of the experience of the newly initiated man who feels "fear" and "shame" when taken by the desire for bodily pleasure.[98] This divergence in emotional response to the same object, indeed to the same desire, reflects the potentiality in human experience, to be ennobled or corrupted according to the constitution of the soul.

The new initiate is fearful on account of the "reverence" he has for the beautiful body, and also fears having "the reputation [*doxa*] of madness" (251a). His fear and shame therefore originate from internal and external sources. With respect to the latter, all humans are nourished, to some extent, by opinion (*doxa*) and their recollection of being through speech, so the opinion of the community as a whole must carry enormous weight. But that the many are forgetful emerges in the opinion, first expressed in Lysias's speech, that castigates the lover for "sacrificing to his beloved as if to a statue and a god" (251a; cf. 248b4–5). The confusion of such opinion is reflected in the fact that it does not discriminate between the base and true *erōs*, and would restrain both. Regardless whether such opinion is correct in a given situation, the power of reputation produces an incentive to conceal this reverent madness in order to ensnare a beloved who fears for his reputation—as Lysias clearly saw—and therefore obscure the divine, internal, fear that the lover feels when recalling true beauty.

Playing on this conventional disdain for mania, Socrates diagnoses the "expected change [*metabolē*]" that overcomes the lover in the manner of an Ionian physician, analyzing the motions of bodies as they are acted upon and act on others. This experience is now a disturbance of the regular motions of life that produces symptoms of illness, including sweating, fever, itching, and throbbing aches (251b–d).[99] The resemblance of Socrates's diagnosis to the Hippocratics' physiological account of mania ironically reverses their demystification of mania in *The Sacred Disease*, using a physiological account as an analogy for a disturbance of the soul. Rather than madness arising from a failure to breathe, madness arises from a failure to remain open to beauty; rather than needing to discharge phlegm, there is a need to discharge a stored perception; rather than a melting of phlegm, there is a melting of the base of the wings; and so on.[100] But Socrates's physiology of *erōs* is not merely analogical and, serving a purpose similar to his allusions to the Eleusinian mysteries, purports to show that the true cause of bodily motion, both local and metabolic,[101] lies in the motion of the soul incited by its separation from the beings themselves. Unlike the Hippocratics, Socrates's understanding of the body entails understanding its nonphysical causes.[102]

Receiving the "flowing off" of the beautiful, the lover's wings are nourished and their feathers "begin" (*archein*) to grow anew (251b). The motion incited through *erōs* is the expression of the soul's nature as *archē* of motion.[103] Fulfillment of the soul's winged nature, its ascent, requires openness to being, which is literally sharing and taking part in: the simplicity of true beauty is now understood as a whole of parts, presumably because true beauty cannot be limited to a particular space or time. When "looking upon" (*blepein*) the beautiful boy, "parts" (*merē*) of beauty "come and flow (*rhēn*) from there" (251c).[104]

While the lover gazes upon the beautiful boy, "he rests from the pain" of growing wings "and rejoices," but when the lover is separated from the beautiful source, desire (*himeros*) becomes painful (251c–d). The base of the wings dry and the "passages" (*diexodoi*) through which the quills grow now close and harden (251d).[105] The nourished "shoots" of the feathers, straining to be released from this imprisonment, "sting" the soul. Just as the soul recalls the being it once saw, Socrates wishes Phaedrus to recall the earlier life of the gods, who traveled by many *diexodoi* ("pathways") in their ascent outside the heavens (247a). The lover, literally full of *himeros*, has gods inside him that move him to return. As Seth Benardete (1991) says, "God is wing," and so it is through *erōs* that a human gains the wings of divinity.[106] This pseudo-physiology of *erōs* is therefore a microcosm and macrocosm—a pattern—of the ascent and descent of souls; the life of soul has unfolded over the course of the palinode in successive iterations, and each iteration compactly contains or rather implies the whole. That is to say, the form of the palinode as a whole is implied in each part. If the human soul could be plumbed to its fullest extent, that inquiry would reveal the structure or form of the cosmos, and conversely, inquiry into the nature of the cosmos demands inquiring into the nature of oneself as the subject that shares in its object: the experience of beauty is communion of the lover with not only the beloved boy, but with being as a whole. To close the pathways (*diexodoi*) of the soul is to close participation in reality, and therefore close the possibility of self-knowledge.

Socrates's rhetorical parallels between the lover's perception and then his separation from the beloved, opening and closing, growth and decay, pleasure and pain, reveals the rhythmic pulsation of the soul with respect to being itself.[107] In this cycle, Socrates has rendered in temporal form the moment of change, in which both passive and active motion are experienced simultaneously, for the painful experience of this separation is at the same time a reminder of the beloved. This concurrence of opposites makes the soul "despair at the strangeness [*atopia*] of the experience" and it "rages in its perplexity [*aporein*]" (251d; cf. 240a9–b5). The soul becomes restless, moving night and day. Rest is only found with the beloved, whose presence reopens the lover's soul. The lover again "channels *himeros*" into himself and releases the parts of beauty that had been previously "compacted" inside him, ending his "birth-pangs" (251e).[108] Its parts compacted inside him, beauty is never entirely absent from the lover, and indeed because of the presence of these parts every human being longs for the whole it had seen before.[109] That which is held compact in the soul is only a partial gathering together of beauty, much like Socrates earlier said of reasoning. Despite this formal similarity, it is unclear whether the gathering of beauty relies upon reasoning, since perception also occurs in the animal-like lover, or whether Socrates's rendering here is itself the consequence of trying to understand beauty through reasoning—it is difficult to clearly distinguish the structures of reality and perception. Regardless, the compact perception of beauty, partial and incomplete, was not inert but disturbed the soul and consequently set it in motion, searching for peace in the beloved. This compact perception of beauty is the offspring of the soul, as opposed to the bodily offspring that was repudiated. In keeping with the motif of Eleusis, Demeter's seed is ready for harvest: the soul, ceasing from its birth-pangs, "reaps the sweetest pleasure" (251e–252a). The cosmic planting of "seeds" into bodies now finds a parallel in the planting of seeds into the soul, which seeds now grow in the presence of beauty.

The soul does not "abandon willingly" the great pleasure experienced after birthing, or its offspring, and accordingly values its beloved above anything else (252a). Beauty and *erōs* for it produces an ecstatic change by which the old heavy self is transcended.[110] Because the beloved appears good to the lover, his source of peace and relief, the compulsion to return is also willingness. Just as "all soul" was said to never abandon itself, the soul of the lover now includes the beloved as a necessary part of the wholeness it experienced in the presence of true being, thus making the beloved its own. Love is at its core love for oneself as a complete whole, which depends upon sharing in the larger wholes of soul and cosmos. This self-love can of course be interpreted, as Phaedrus did, selfishly. In the case here, what the lover refuses to be separated from is pleasure—there is no mention of its object being good in itself.[111] The lover will not abandon "the object of longing," "but he will forget mothers and brothers and all companions, and not place anything on wealth destroyed through neglect, and [neither on] what is customary [or: lawful, *nomimoi*] and graceful, and is ready to be a slave of all that he scorned" (252a3–6). Such is the fate of the civil and modest man who once followed custom because of fear for his reputation. Surreptitiously moving from condemnation to approbation, Socrates returns to the same hubristic desire that resulted in animal lust, but now on a higher level. Now, like Lysias, Socrates encourages Phaedrus to set aside his fear of reputation and aim his *erōs* beyond the mere opinions of the many. The *erōs* that leads the lover to forsake the broader community is also the *erōs* that brings the lover into community with his beloved, whom he now "reveres as if a god" and "the sole healer of his greatest troubles" (252b). The capacity for *erōs*, as love of one's own, to both bring together the community as well as divide, is the reason for which Socrates condemned *erōs* in his first speech, and now he closely echoes those earlier formulations—for example, the lover not allowing the beloved to leave day or night, depriving the beloved of associates, and wanting to reap pleasures endlessly (239d–240a, 240c–d). Here, though, it is the lover who is enslaved by the beloved; Socrates shows how the lover is drawn outside the bonds and conventions of the community for the sake of the beautiful.

If the beautiful were the good, then Socrates's palinode would have found here "the greatest good fortune" that is bestowed through *erōs*. The lover's desire to hold beauty forever is satiated only in the eternity of true beauty, and so to be without hardship, "whole, simple, unchanging, and happy." This, though, would mean that the lover would have to transcend his body entirely, for mortal life is hardship, and true unchanging beauty is seen only in the superheavenly place (248c, 250d).[112] Humans remain inexperienced in pleasure that is not preceded by pain, and even the gods never join with the beings. But the mortal lover, in creating a monument to his beloved, wishes to make fixed and unchanging the pleasant manifestation of beauty in the boy, and so forgets the being of beauty itself.[113] Hence we struggle to depict *erōs*:

> We mortals call him soaring Eros,
> But immortals [call him] Winged Eros [*Pterōs*], because it is necessary he grow his wings. (252b7–8)

"We mortals" are inclined to divinize and worship that which brings us pleasure, beautifying Eros—much as Phaedrus wished for in the *Symposium* (cf. 242e1–3). The second verse, supposedly quoted from the followers of blind Homer, is "altogether hubristic" and "not in meter" (252b). The words of the gods escape mortal beautification and art, but are nonetheless true, for Eros is fated to always come to be and never simply be winged, unlike the heavenly Olympians. The two verses together, human and divine, express the perplexing *metaxy* of human experience.

## SEARCHING FOR GOD

Socrates's revelation that the lover makes a monument of the beloved in the desire to enjoy beauty and pleasure forever shows the ambiguous destiny of *erōs*, that it may in fact lead one astray in the recollection of being and reflect back to the lover a narrow conception of his desire and soul. *Erōs* is not simply good, an uplifting inspiration toward true being, but rather it is dangerously fraught with the same "heaviness" that cast souls to the earth, namely forgetfulness of being (248c7, 263d1–2). The reason that souls differ in their capacity to manage this burden emerges in light of their self-reflective relationship with the beloved.

The followers of Zeus, Socrates tells Phaedrus, are more able to bear "the burden of the winged one," presumably because Zeus was the ordering god and his followers likewise seek order in their experience of *erōs* (252c). Socrates contrasts these with the followers of Ares to bring into relief the benefit that may obtain from *erōs* when properly directed. Instead of searching for true beauty, the lover sought to relieve himself of the heaviness of *erōs* before the particular beloved. Lovers who follow Ares follow the god of war and strife, and cannot bear separation from their beloved, which they express in a "murderous" jealousy and sense of injustice (252c).[114] Ares's love is the very real consequence of the desire for unlimited benefit that arises despite the finitude of the particular beloved. The subtle theme of war that runs through the *Phaedrus* now breaks through at the moment of the lover's frustration,[115] and justice takes its bearings from the rigid boundaries that are established around one's own, as if a sacred precinct. The Ares-like lover is concerned with preserving the present state, and so would be most amenable to the formation of statues—he is susceptible to becoming hard and closed to another, perhaps even higher, beloved.[116] At the most fundamental level, when the beloved is understood as true being itself, this jealous anger and wrath is a hatred of reality itself for refusing to bend to one's desire, with the result that taking vengeance can only mean repudiating what is and therefore embracing death. The utter devotion of an Ares-like lover could have disastrous consequences, forgetting once-dear relations and risking the well-being of the city. Only the mutual love of an even higher justice could ameliorate this tension in loyalties.[117] This further explains Socrates's subordination of the "warlike" king to the "philosopher" and "erotic man" (248d).

The character of Ares-kin is one example of the imitation that Socrates says all humans perform of their gods, for example, of their original natures.

Each lives with their beloveds, and others, in the manner of their god, and chooses the beloved from the beautiful "according to his disposition" (252d6). Socrates repeats that the lover will "build and adorn [or: order, *katakosmein*] a statue as if that same one were a god, thus honoring and worshiping him" (252d7). Knowledge of god, self, and the beloved are concomitant, so that the lover discovers himself in his shaping of others—although such knowledge is only realized in the case of the "incorrupt" lover "living his first birth here" (252d1–3). That is to say, only in that long-forgotten ancient life of the soul would there be perfect concordance between the lover's idol and his own nature. In the present, Socrates implies, the lover who is ignorant of his true nature may misconstrue the god in whose image he fashions himself. Since the lover cannot rely on what he merely believes to be his nature, the "search" (*zētēsis*) that a lover conducts for his beloved is of great significance. The search is an inquiry, as Socrates himself inquires, into the nature of soul and the different kinds of soul in order to distinguish clearly both the soul of the beloved and one's own soul. Love of oneself and another demands the Delphic quest for self-knowledge (cf. 230a1).

The paradigmatic followers of Zeus look for a Zeus-like soul that is "both a philosopher and leader [*hēgemonikos*] with respect to its nature" (252e). Such a soul would be most in accordance with Zeus who orders (*diakosmein*) souls, rather than simply adorns (*katakosmein*) them; the philosopher leads on account of his better understanding of soul (cf. 247e5, 252d7). When a Zeus-like soul is found, its god-like nature is only a potentiality, and the lover "will do everything so that he will become such a sort" (252e). That Plato himself undertook such loving labor would not be surprising, particularly given that his phrase, "those of Zeus search for someone Zeus-like," is formulated as the pun *Dios dion*, or "Dion of Zeus"—an allusion to the Dion of Syracuse upon whose urging he attempted to persuade the tyrant Dionysius of Syracuse to follow a philosophical life.[118] The lover's soul is reflected in how he tries to shape the world around him.

Socrates depicts the communion of Zeus-kin as the culmination of their search for god. Learning from others and his own efforts, the lover, "by following the scent from within himself to the discovery of the nature of his god, finds [the god] through the compulsion [*anangkesthai*] to look intensely upon the god" (252e5–253b1). This inward examination departs sharply from the ways of ancient oracles and seers, who would seek omens and inspiration from the world around them.[119] Here, Socrates says god is found in how the lover creates his monument and whether it is a fitting reminder, for "he touches him [god] through memory" (253a2–3).[120] As Socrates earlier described, the lover compacted desire and parts of beauty within himself, and so contained a god that would bear him aloft. Being thus "enthused" by recollection, he shares in the god by adopting his practices and ways, and then attempts to realize and express his experience of god in the world outside himself. Through this search, the lover regards his beloved as the cause of his enthusiasm, but not as the god. The beloved therefore pleases the lover not as a mere reflection of his desires, but as a reflection of the god he once saw.

Although the discovery of Zeus is only one possibility, it seems that it is exclusively Zeus-kin, those who are philosophers by nature, who are able to make the beloved in the image of god: "If it is from Zeus that they draw, like Bacchants they pour the draught upon the soul of the beloved, making him as like [*homoios*] to their own god as they are able" (253a6–b1). The goodness that *erōs* may provide is seen in how the search opens the lover to the divine—the true beings—and then in how *erōs* overflows the limits of his soul, inspiring the harmonization of lover and beloved with god. This is the beginning of the lover's persuasion. But the lover's affection for the beloved comes after he has discovered god, and therefore after he has determined what is best and most worthy of worship. Only if he had seen and not forgotten the truth, would he be able to do his beloved an unmitigated good deed.[121] The overflowing Bacchic frenzy is only rehabilitated under the authority of Zeus and his philosophers. Socrates thus implies that his own earlier Bacchic frenzy was drawn from Zeus. At the same time, by restricting the beneficence of that frenzy to philosophers, Socrates covertly criticizes the poets, who were said to glorify and memorialize the ancients for the sake of educating the young.[122] Although well-intentioned, the poets are incapable of truly making their beloveds in the image of god unless they become philosophical, and should that happen, it is far from clear that their monuments could remain poetic in any ordinary sense if they are to generate an internal inspiration. The poets, despite depicting the gods so beautifully, are bested by Socrates, who denied the gods bodies and subordinated them to the true beings.

As for those who followed other gods, Socrates only mentions by name Hera and Apollo (253b). Even those who now follow Apollo, the priests and prophetess at Delphi, must search for their god in themselves, despite the ancients' scorn for the merely human "search" (244c6). Socrates's allusion to the inscription at the temple of Delphi, "Know thyself," gives it a novel interpretation: the inscription does not simply warn petitioners that they will not understand the words of the god unless they know themselves—that is, that they should enter the god's temple complete and already possessing self-knowledge—but that the temple is the site at which self-knowing begins. Self-knowledge is the mission of the god.[123]

But the beloved will by no certainty understand his *erōs* as this search for god and self-knowledge. Socrates says that the beloved must still be "persuaded and disciplined, led into the practices and form (*idea*) of the god" (253b5–8).[124] That the beloved must be seduced into the search, even though he was perceived to have a suitable nature, means that he was not only ignorant of himself and his potential, but ignorant of his need for self-knowledge, which must constitute the core of his life. This is the problem that Phaedrus presents. Only when the beloved is persuaded to a life of philosophical self-inquiry, and there occurs a mutual exchange of constantly reflecting oneself externally in the other, will the lover be able to find god. Only then will the "eagerness of those who truly love, acting in the manner I say," Socrates tells Phaedrus, become "beautiful" (or: noble, *kalos*) and bring them happiness (253c). That this is a way of life—of practices—and neither mere words nor a singular vision is a crucial ramification of the relationship between *erōs* and *logos*, for the best form of discourse between lovers is that by which they lead themselves and keep themselves aligned in their pursuit of what really is.

## CAPTURING THE BELOVED

In the final iteration of the soul's cycle, Socrates turns to the inner experience and structure of the individual soul, as it is only here that greatest good of *erōs* can be realized through philosophical conversation, which harmonizes personal judgment with reality. All of the preceding myth of the soul's motion—its immortality as the principle of motion, its original perception of being and capacity for recollection, its inspiration by beauty toward true being, and its searching for god through communion with the beloved—contributes to the story of how the lover's persuasion and "capture" of the beloved is possible and may accomplish that greatest good by reordering both souls toward their highest form (253c6). Equally, the soul's self-mastery provides the premise of an individuated and embodied self-mover that was lacking in the proof of the soul's immortality, thus rounding out the circularity of the soul in a story of cosmic perfection by means of the individual soul's struggle to judge for itself what is best.

Socrates's articulation of the soul in its three parts—charioteer, good horse, and bad horse—allows him to explain the variation within a soul as it responds to different aspects of reality, particularly the difference between the appearance of beauty and beauty itself. This internal variation likewise explains the variation between souls, which will be crucial to rhetoric (271a–262b), and the possibility of a soul changing itself—that is, to be persuaded toward a new way of life. At the beginning of the myth, Socrates focused on the unity of this "form," its "combined power" to raise the soul toward true being (246a3, a6–7, 251b6–7). Now Socrates shows how this unity is the product of an interior struggle between the parts of the soul that originates from the horses' opposing "two forms" (253c).

The good horse is the "nobler" or "more beautiful," although Socrates's use of the comparative indicates that the horse is not simply or altogether good, and conversely that the bad horse is not simply or altogether bad. The goodness and relative beauty of the first horse is expressed in its "straight [or: correct] in form" (*to eidos orthos*) and white color (253d). As for its character, the horse is "a lover of honor with both moderation and shame, a companion of true glory [or: reputation, *doxa*], needs no whip, [and] is driven by command and speech [*logos*] alone" (253d–e). Unlike the middle part of the soul in the *Republic*, he does not exhibit the anger and steadfastness characteristic of *thumos* or "spiritedness"—these qualities are found in the bad horse—and indeed there is no mention of *thumos* in the entire *Phaedrus*.[125] Although the good horse's own parts appear to function well with respect to the whole, and the whole horse in turn to the charioteer, he is distinguished from the charioteer by its love of honor and the opinion of others. While the fact that it is the good horse, rather than the bad, that is attracted to opinion nuances Socrates's presentation of opinion, which he earlier attacked for inhibiting *erōs* (242c6–d2), it is clear that "that which truly seems best" is not necessarily the best. The white horse does not possess such knowledge to distinguish right and wrong opinion, let alone what seems best from what really is best, and must take direction from the charioteer's words. The confusion to which the white horse is susceptible is seen in the sequel, when he is led with misgiving by the black horse, which had been anticipated by Socrates's opposition of opinions contrary to those found in the urbane speeches. The white horse and his reliance on opinion alone is subrational; the charioteer may give spoken commands to the horse, but he does not reason with it.[126] Instead of physical violence, the charioteer may appeal emotionally to the horse's desire for honor and use shame to direct him.

The bad horse is the opposite of the white horse in every way. His physical appearance is one of disorder ("crooked," "manifold" parts almost heaped together at random [*eikos*]" [253a]), and so seems to be the source of Socrates's wonder that he may be Typhonic and the human attraction to the likely (230a).[127] This disorder is replicated in his behavior, as he acts with the excess and *hubris* that, for Lysias and Socrates's concealed lover, characterized *erōs* as a whole. His random appearance reflects his manifold purposes and excessive attraction to the immediate objects of desire; it is the black horse that drags the soul "on all fours" toward the semblances of true beauty (250e–a). His *hubris* is compounded by poor eyesight and deafness to the charioteer's commands, by which he might otherwise distinguish image and truth—his desire is undiscriminating. The horse seems black as a reflection of his distance from true being.

This darkness of the horse, his contrast to true being, links *erōs* as a whole, even in its lower form, with the need to search for the truth. Although the excessive desire of the black horse entails the confusion of images and monuments with truth, it is this initial attraction that leads the lover toward his god and his nature. Socrates does not therefore simply denigrate the black horse as an obstacle to overcome, but portrays him as necessary to the recollection of true being. This powerful desire, however, must be guided and disciplined lest the soul dwell in the chaotic motions that Lysias depicted. Unresponsive to words, the charioteer can only extend the rule of reason to the black horse through brute force and punishment.

The internal struggle for mastery that Socrates described in his first speech is now integrated into an account of *erōs* that requires that the lover himself attain self-mastery. In fact, the two horses form a team of opposites that happen to share the very same properties as the two forms of soul found in that earlier speech (237d ff.). One side listens to speech and is moved by honor and opinion, the other is "without *logos*" and moved by an insatiable *hubris* (238a1). Socrates now relieves the tension of that dualism by harnessing the two parts to the intellect, which is freed from its subordination to desire and "interest" in Lysias's speech, and to opinion in Socrates's first speech: intellect is that which judges when the passions of soul should be pursued. The nature of the soul has therefore been unfolded over the course of the three speeches of the Phaedrus, and the form of each speech has changed accordingly. In this concordance between the parts of soul with the speeches, Plato shows how different speeches may produce different effects in a soul, persuading in one way or another by appealing to one part or another. At the same time, Plato shows in the drama of Phaedrus's persuasion how speech shapes and directs the soul itself, and therefore changes it and its perception of the world, even though the soul's complexity and capacity for change implies that that new perspective may itself be overturned.

In perceiving the beloved, "all of the soul is warmed by perception" and "filled with . . . longing," but different effects are produced in different parts (253e–254a). The white horse "is forced by shame" to restrain himself from leaping on the beloved, while the black horse, "leaping with force, is carried [forward]" (254a). In contrast to the perfect passivity of the soul before the beings, the black horse here becomes active while it is pulled by erotic inspiration (see 247d5, 248a8, 250c5, e2; cf. the active voice at 252c4). The force with which he does this is irresistible and experienced as necessity (*anangkē*) by the white horse and charioteer. The black horse, unable to perceive anything else, is led to the beloved for the sake of sexual pleasure, which is the easiest way for the embodied soul to alleviate its painful separation. The black horse proposes things that are, for the white horse and charioteer, "terrible and improper [lit. outside convention, *para-nomos*]," and they attempt to resist (254b). After much agitation by the black horse, they finally succumb, and "the two follow his lead" and "agree [*homolegein*] to obey his commands."

This drama reenacts the drama that Socrates and Phaedrus had performed earlier, which placed Phaedrus in the role of the black horse. Socrates followed Phaedrus's lead after Lysias's speech, but attempted to resist the younger man's desire for a new speech once he was propositioned with things outside convention—namely the statues dedicated by the Cyselids and law-breaking archons (235d4–237a6). Socrates led Phaedrus in an imitation of the essential motions of the soul that he now articulates. Indeed, Socrates has at different moments assumed form of each part found in the soul. At the beginning of the first interlude, he assumed the form of the white horse and charioteer being dragged along by the black horse, but when Phaedrus resisted his analysis of Lysias's speech, he took the form of the black horse and promised the pleasures of a new speech. By doing so, Socrates was able to show Phaedrus how his moderation was an instrument for attaining the pleasures of speech, and that the *hubris* of desire lay below the surface; he is not reducible to the white horse. Socrates incited and so revealed to Phaedrus the importance of his black horse, particularly in our use of speech, which Socrates now displays in its disciplining by the charioteer.

The most important power of the soul is to determine when to slacken and when to restrain the horses, for it is in this moment of judgment that the soul as a whole becomes active and determines to some extent its own motion—whether it will grow wings and rise again. This power is one of self-restraint, restraining one passion for the sake of another. When the charioteer looks into his beloved's eyes, their "flashing" like lightning takes his memory to "the nature of the beautiful" which he once saw outside the heavens (254b). Nature is not simply what grows or is found outside of human making, but the very perfection or pattern to which that growth tends. The nature of the soul that Socrates sought at the beginning of the palinode is discovered in its relation to the nature of the perfect beauty that inspires it (245c). To this point, only conventions or laws, opinions, and associations have restrained a lover's desire for beauty (e.g., 252a). Now, the lover himself restrains his natural desire for the sake of another, higher, natural desire. Socrates thus subtly indicates that what is conventional is not necessarily in diametric opposition to what is natural and so could be brought into harmony with it (252e1–5). Manic transcendence and the fulfillment of nature need not be at the expense of the city and its opinions. Indeed, the moment that the soul perceives true beauty is a moment of moderation: the charioteer "sees it [beauty] again standing with moderation [*sōphrosunē*] on a holy pedestal" (254b).

Phaedrus will no doubt feel vindicated by moderation's appearance here, but also puzzled that he can become truly moderate only through *erōs*. He was attracted to a form of moderation in the previous two speeches that represses desires for the sake of satisfying them in the future. Now it appears that Phaedrus's moderation, because it originates in the desire to maximize pleasure, would actively preclude the transcendental erotic pursuit of true being and therefore true moderation. Moderation is the manner in which the true beings are seen in themselves, for that beauty which is pure and unmixed with any other being is distinct in itself, which is to say it is in perfect accordance with itself and never abandons itself; unlike soul, it is not ecstatic but at rest. The lover could not therefore experience true beauty with *hubris*, for he would always miss it; only through restraint will *erōs* allow the distinction of an image from what is truly desired. This is the essential power of the charioteer, the intellect, which by restraining holds the soul to the divine way, as does Socrates's *daimonion*.[128] The lover here coincides with the ambition of the nonlover, since it is the restraint of one aspect of *erōs*—the desire for bodily pleasure—that allows the perception of reality, although that perception of and judgment about what really is is only possible insofar as the soul loves and is thus led to true being.[129] Phaedrus's restraint is an inferior moderation in that its end is not determined by perception of what really is and that it only defers such judgment in favor of others' opinions and the hope for pleasure, whether right or wrong. The hubristic desire of the black horse is only vindicated insofar as his desire for unending pleasure points one toward the perfect perception of reality.

Moderation possesses the entire soul in this vision of reality. The charioteer, in fear and reverence, "falls on his back" before beauty, and "is compelled" (*anangkazein*) to violently pull both horses back onto their haunches (254b–c). True beauty and moderation seem to push the lover back, placing him in the passive state that his soul experienced so long ago, when the cosmic period carried the chariot on the back of heaven (247c). The soul is nourished and becomes most god-like in its motion on account of this conjunction of moderation and *erōs*.[130] But this moment of harmony between the soul and its true object of desire is fleeting, as the horses are restless in their natural desires, and so the soul reenacts in the present its ancient struggle to see the superheavenly place and is quickly cast back down to earth. The fall of the soul and its vision of truth coincide: the moment of the soul's complete satisfaction and rest is at once the moment the soul begins its descent to earth, its motion, and its longing.

The conversation and attempts at persuasion between the struggling parts of soul evince the rationality that extends, albeit unevenly, throughout the soul. The black horse in particular perceives the beloved only as a physical object of sexual desire. He reviles both the white horse and charioteer "for deserting their post and agreement [*homologia*] in fearfulness and cowardice," resorting to military language in Ares-like anger aroused by his separation from the beloved (254c–d). The discursive response of the other parts is limited, and they will "pretend to forget" their promise to the black horse (254d). Persuasion is in this sense always deception, since there must be an appeal to the soul's predominant desires and opinions. In contrast to the gods' perfect maintenance of their stations, living in self-possessed harmony with truth (247a3), the human soul's recollection of reality through appearances means it must always break from itself and its mistaken opinions. Since the soul must commit itself to successive perceptions of beauty, some part of it is deceived on its way to the truth. The ascent of the souls was not direct, but by turns (247a5).

Despite his limited perception, the black horse plays a crucial role in the rational activity of the soul. In his eagerness, he "reminds" the white horse and charioteer of their commitment to pursue the beloved boy, for the others would simply forget the boy in their enjoyment of their vision of true beauty.[131] Since the theme of this passage is the disciplining of the black horse, it is tempting to see the horse's continued struggles as mere distraction or nuisance in this process. But the black horse's power "to remind" reverses Socrates's earlier usage of reminders: here, it is a reminder of earthly things, not the beings themselves. This seems to contradict Socrates's earlier account of recollection—would not the black horse's "reminding" constitute a forgetting of being? This very question, though, mistakes the nature of the lover's enthusiasm, as it is not only for sexual pleasure in physical beings, but rather for any beauty that induces "reverence" and "fear" (251a, 254b8). Indeed, the charioteer now reveres his recollection of beauty just as the lover revered the beloved boy in the earlier account of enthusiasm. The charioteer monumentalizes his moment of recollection and insight. The danger of memorializing beauty therefore extends beyond sensory perceptions, so that when Socrates says that the black horse reminds the soul, he is reminding Phaedrus that the soul only comes to know true being through its manifold and mixed manifestations, that is, through the body and opinions (249b6–c4).[132] The earthly desire expressed by the black horse is consequently crucial for the soul's "correct" use of reminders, since memory of true being must also account for being as it manifests in the here and now (249d). Furthermore, since recollection proceeds through reasoning (*logismos*), and thus the use of words or speeches (*logoi*), even *logos* is liable to induce forgetfulness (see chapter 5). This is the difference between "what is said" by being and "what we now say is" (247d, 249b). This corroborates Socrates's point in his first speech, that the ostensibly clear use of definition actually obscured the object in question, namely *erōs*. The charioteer breaks his verbal agreement with the black horse because their words—whether the words used to describe their own desires or the beloved boy—have taken on new meaning.

Upon the recollection of true beauty, and the reminder of its instantiation in the beloved, the soul reorders itself by disciplining the black horse so that the soul as a whole may harmonize with true being and the beloved. This is the struggle by which the soul becomes whole in itself, a self-mover insofar as the charioteer brings the soul under his direction in the desire to become capable of perceiving what really is. The charioteer brings the black horse to heel with unsparing violence (254e). Since the horse only understands pleasure and pain, "many" such experiences will be required to train the horse to feel fear whenever it approaches the beloved and "ceases from its *hubris*" (254e5–6). The experience of *erōs* is, for the entire soul, "toilsome" and marked by "sufferings" as it struggles with itself. The capture of the beloved is thus preceded by the lover's difficult struggle to become moderate. Only when the lover, and then the beloved in turn, becomes open to truth, dedicated to realizing that truth in their lives, will the beloved be "captured" and the two bound to one another. The structure of the lover's internal struggle thus closely relates to the structure of the pursuit between souls.

With his black horse tamed, the lover again follows the beloved in reverence and makes a monument of him, giving him services as if he were "equal to a god" (251a, 255a). For this, the beloved eventually allows the lover into his company (255a–b). The lover's mania transforms the beloved into a lover in his own right, since the lover's "speech and company" exceeds the "friendship" of all of the beloved's relations, and so "strikes out [*ekplēttein*] the beloved" (255b). Recapitulating the experience of enthusiasm, the lover's soul remains open and the "stream" (*pēgē*) of beauty pouring into him "overflows" and returns to its source—just as the font (*pēgē*) of motion moved itself (255c, cf. 245c10). The stream that the lover pours over the beloved is thus drawn from the beloved himself, which Socrates depicts as the draught Zeus poured over his beloved Ganymede.[133] This beloved becomes divine through the stream of beauty which his lover sends "back into the beautiful [itself]" just as "a sound or some wind echoes off a hard surface and is carried back whence it had been set in motion" (255c). This true lover does not impregnate the soul of the beloved or fashion him in his own image, but inspires the beloved to bring forth his own "compaction" of beauty (cf. 251e3–5, 255d1–3).[134] The inspired beloved "is in love [*eraein*]" (255d3). Were Socrates not focused on the best case, however, the lover's mirroring of the beloved would show how deception can occur by reflecting back what seems to be true.[135] But in the present best and happy case, the two share a mutual love for the beauty manifested in one another.

The former beloved does not yet perceive the beings, but is perplexed (*aporein*), and now undergoes the same experience as the lover who was separated from the source of his enthusiasm (251d8, 255d3).[136] The perplexity of the beloved is the conscious experience of ignorance: the beloved was not attracted to the lover, but is now turned toward him and cannot account for this (255d). The beloved thus possesses a sort of knowledge, that it is not precisely the lover himself that he loves or that it is not precisely himself that the lover loves: their love for one another depends on the recognition of their own incompleteness. Their experience could be rendered as the question, why do I love this person? From this perplexity arises philosophy, which is a search for the divine through its images. Only in becoming a lover can one approach self-knowledge and self-satisfaction. The beloved does not at first realize that his own beauty is reflected back, "as if in a mirror," and inspires him—that is, that he is in love with himself. His failure to recognize this means that he is ignorant of himself, and so he will come to know himself by coming to know the lover. Lover and beloved discover themselves in one another, so that their immediate differences prompt in them the discovery of the fundamental likeness that binds them together, in one self as it were.

The beloved, having become a lover, is now also afflicted by the pain and pleasure of separation and reunion. Each lover "longs and is longed for" (255d). But as a consequence of the beloved's perplexity, the love that he holds is "a return of *erōs* [*anterōta*], a phantom [*eidōlon*] of *erōs*; but he calls it and supposes it not to be *erōs* but friendship. He desires [*epithumein*] in a similar way to that man [the lover], but more feebly" (255d–e). Friendship is thus derived from the erotic experience and does not repudiate *epithumia*, the desire for pleasure in bodies—semblances of true beauty—but controls it. Friendship is the proper erotic relation between these two humans, and indeed the proper relation to earthly things. A phantom of true *erōs* is the proper desire for a phantom of beauty. This restoration of friendship thus restores the friendship felt for friends and family that was lost in the ecstasy of *erōs* (239d–240a, 252a, 255b). This turn to friendship does not mean that true love and the experience of true beauty cannot be found in the lovers' relationship—quite the contrary in fact, for their friendship is sustained by a love for what is true and real. Far from repudiating community, Socrates's defense of *erōs* entails community as that in which the truly good can be embodied. Without Socrates's defense of friendship, the other side of *erōs* would be left unchecked: its forgetful heaviness, as opposed to its recollecting lightness, tends lovers toward selfish greed, jealousy, and ultimately strife (cf. 248c7, 256b4). *Erōs* therefore forms community at the risk of forgetting being—that is, at the risk of forgetting what is necessary for loving well and benefiting that community. A true lover, a true friend, remains in the tension of the *metaxy*, in between the desire for true and perfect beauty and the desire for immediate beauty, not only because he would otherwise forget the heavenly for the sake of the earthly or vice-versa, but because otherwise he could not see his beloved friend as he really is, in the light of the true beings. Their relationship is the best possible because of their impassioned moderation.

Should these friends be able to resist their sexual desires, with "the better [parts] of the mind victorious" in each soul, they will be led "into a well-ordered [*tattein*] way of life and philosophy," and achieve that greatest good: "neither divine mania nor human moderation is able to furnish a greater good for human beings" (256b). This is not simply the mythical growth of wings and ascent—Socrates reiterates that that occurs only after death—but "leading a blessed and harmonious [*homonoētikos*] life here" (256a–b). To follow in the orderly train of the gods (Socrates's *tattein* recalls again the *taxeis* of the gods [247a1–4]) is a way of life in the here and now, the forming of a manifold soul into a harmonious whole. How, precisely, that way of life will be conducted—presumably through *logismos*, that is, recollection—is not explained. Instead, Socrates shows a life of successive mirroring, beloved and lover each glimpsing in the other the true beings, their god, which makes them virtuous and truly beneficial to one another.[137] What is especially important for the subsequent discussion of rhetoric is that the lovers will come to be of the same mind (*homonoia*), not merely agreeing words (*homologia*): mutual understanding does not inhere in words alone, but in the view to which those words lead.[138] A man like Phaedrus, accustomed to being the nonlover or beloved, must be awakened to the power of *erōs*—already implicit in his nonlove—in order to lead him outside himself and his presumption of knowledge.

The truly beneficial friendship is safely guarded only by a life dedicated to wisdom and philosophy, which Socrates has shown to be characterized by searching for truth and therefore embracing one's ignorance. Yet the ignorance of philosophical friends seems to be of a different kind than that of other friends, for the former are alive to, even animated by, the distinction between the semblances that constitute immediate experience and what really is, while other kinds of friends forget that distinction. Socrates speaks of friends slipping into the love of honor characteristic of the white horse, and consequently succumbing to their bodily desires: "They take their souls unguarded [to] the choice which is said by the many to be most blessed" (256c). This derision for the many is particularly powerful, not in that they desire sexual pleasure, but that they honor it secretly while deploring it publicly (253a). To rely on the opinions of others is to forgo the capacity to judge when one should or should not act on such desires. But Socrates does preserve the possibility of a more moderate relationship, like that of the "noble and gentle" lover he recalled prior to the palinode, lightened by an awareness, if not dedicated pursuit, of something greater than pleasure (243c). Since "the whole mind" is not committed to sexual pleasure, these lovers will indulge sparingly and remain friends, "but less so than the other two"—that is, the philosophical friends (256c–d).

Thus, it is "from the friendship of a lover," not the gratification of bodily desires, that "such divine things" are given (256e). In contrast, the nonlover has no claim to friendship, but is merely an "acquaintance" (*oikeiotēs*), specifically, someone whose benefit is limited to providing for the interests of the household (*oikos*). In the final flourish of the palinode, Socrates completes his refutation of both Lysias's thesis and Phaedrus's moderation: "The acquaintance of a non-lover, mixed with mortal moderation [and] distributing [*oikonomein*] what is mortal and thrifty, engenders in the beloved soul an illiberality praised by the majority as if it were virtue" (256e–257a). Lysias's proposal was not attacked primarily because of its deceptiveness, but rather because it was in service of an ignoble ethic and way of life. The moderation proposed in the urbane speeches denigrated *erōs* for the sake of a wider variety of pleasures, repressing any overwhelming passion for a single object so that it might calculate the best means for attaining all of them. As discussed in chapter 2, those speeches did not distinguish, beyond following the judgment of the city, between good or bad desires, since any goodness was simply derived from moderate enjoyment. The man of mortal moderation will flitter from one desire to the next.[139] In the language of the palinode, Phaedrus's moderation, rather than separating him from earthly semblances, instead held his gaze intently upon them in the hopes of unencumbered enjoyment of them all (cf. 258e). Without inquiring into what is desirable and when, Phaedrus abandons his highest power and allows himself to be carried solely by external inspiration—always in motion, but discordantly and unhappily so, since he never knows whether his pursuit is a worthy one.

## LOVE AND ART

Having concluded his palinode, Socrates prays to Eros for forgiveness on both his own behalf and Phaedrus's, imploring Eros to accept "the best and most beautiful palinode I am capable of, both with respect to the other things and the fact that I have been compelled [*anangkesthai*] to speak with some poetical words on account of Phaedrus" (257a). This transition from his palinode to the discussion of rhetoric raises important questions about the status of the palinode as a piece of rhetoric that is also an offering to Eros, particularly in relation to Socrates's understanding of his own actions as a devotee to Eros. Socrates fears that Eros might strip him of "the erotic art" (*hē erōtikē technē*), and preserving that skill seems to depend on not only recanting the earlier thesis about *erōs*, but also on attempting to persuade Lysias and Phaedrus to change their lives and become better lovers (257b). Lysias should "cease from such speeches" and go to philosophy, and Phaedrus should likewise "fashion his life simply towards love with philosophical speeches" (257b2–6). Phaedrus must demand speeches from Lysias that do not simply flatter his mortal moderation, but that seek out what is best for them. Instead of being a selfishly passive beloved, Phaedrus must now turn toward Lysias as "his lover" (257b4). Socrates may find some political use in converting a well-known rhetorician toward philosophy, but his immediate purpose is to turn Lysias through and for the sake of his beloved, which Socrates depicted in the palinode as the mutual reflection and growing alike of lovers. The project of persuading Phaedrus may falter if it appeals to Phaedrus alone, only to be rebutted later by Lysias—Socrates must also appeal to Lysias and therefore communicate multiple messages to multiple souls.

For his own part, Socrates wishes to retain his erotic art so that he may "still more than now be esteemed by the beautiful" (257a). In claiming this end for his erotic art, to be honored by the beautiful, Socrates connects his palinode and the subsequent discussion of rhetoric, wherein he will argue that philosophy is required to become truly skillful in persuasion. But how is his claim to possess an art compatible with the ignorance he professes and finds at the heart of philosophy? Perhaps *technē* does not imply knowledge in the fullest sense of being able to articulate underlying principles or forms, but is rather a practical know-how or knack. Socrates takes this up later and conclude that art requires knowledge (*epistēmē*) (268d–e, 269d).[140] Socrates is therefore paradoxically knowledgeable and ignorant. This paradox seems to be resolved in the special subject matter of his art, *erōs*, which he presented in the palinode as an awareness of one's incompleteness that is concomitant with knowledge of one's ignorance.[141] But does this knowledge merely consist of such awareness? Any conventional sense of art could hardly consist of such a bare prospectus. Prophecy's art, for example, seems to consist in finding such inspiration that allows one to perceive and pronounce the future. An art must also be teachable (271b7–c4). Perhaps the power of the erotic art is similarly to find inspiration and inspire others—that is, produce fellow lovers, particularly of the highest things.[142] The erotic art would then consist of knowing souls and how they may be moved, and then moving them accordingly.

Art and inspiration are not necessarily opposed, as Socrates showed in his earlier discussion of poetry perfected through inspiration: "Poetry of the sound-minded is overshadowed by that of the mad" (245a7–8). But poetry's synthesis of art and inspiration consists in "ordering [or: glorifying, *kosmein*] the myriad deeds of the ancients" (245a4–5). In contrast, *erōs* was shown to be, at the highest level, the philosophical search, through reasoning, for what really is—that is, a search rather than the presentation of beautiful and pleasing images. The tension between mania and *technē* therefore expresses the tension of the erotic experience, between search and enjoyment of beauty, which Socrates engendered by raising the question of the nature of beauty. Although perceiving this tension does not sufficiently explain Socrates's knowledge, it does reveal a choice in Socrates's practice: either show *erōs* and its ends, as if one knew it, and thus beautify and monumentalize it; or embrace and engender *erōs*, the continual search that cannot rest in images of what it seeks. If Socrates knows himself as an erotic man, such self-understanding by definition entails going outside himself to find the knowledge he seeks.

Socrates admits this problem in the practice of his art when he claims that he spoke "with poetical words" for the sake of Phaedrus, despite saying earlier that poetry will never "hymn" the highest things worthily (247c, 257a; cf. 265b–c). The palinode was itself formed to be the "most beautiful" image of *erōs*, and by making *erōs* manifest and attractive to Phaedrus, its true nature was concealed (257a). The palinode cannot be understood as a simply frank revelation on the part of Socrates[143]—and indeed he will later say that the palinode only presented one half of *erōs* (265b–c, 265e–266e). Instead, the formulations of the palinode must be understood in light of what is known about Phaedrus's character, although that must be carefully done, since persuasion cannot be reduced flattery in the sense of validating one's opinions: persuasion is a leading away from one's present opinions even while appealing to them, in a way appealing to two possibilities even if they are contained in a single person (261e6–7, 262b2–3, 277c1–3). In Phaedrus's case, Socrates had to address his love of speeches, fear of pain, valetudinarianism, and tepid hedonism.

Socrates adorned his palinode by depicting the greatest pleasure, the relief caused by the presence of the beautiful. Chance itself, particularly the chance of having a Zeus-like nature, was suspended in order to show the best possible life. Someone might construe the philosophical life as being directed toward a most pleasing vision of reality, but Socrates denied both the possibility of a human attaining such a vision and the possibility of finding rest in whatever vision was attained—the soul moves perpetually and the palinode was accordingly cyclical. All mortal life entails toil and pain, and a life of philosophy, refusing gratification in semblances of truth, is no exception. While Phaedrus's valetudinarianism seemed to be validated in the face of such a life of separation from complete satisfaction, moderation itself emerged at the culmination of an erotic, mad search, rather than in balancing the desires of the body. Each aspect of Phaedrus's character can be found reflected in the palinode, and Socrates deliberately formed the speech in relation to their preceding conversation and actions. Phaedrus can find himself in this speech (see 265c4),[144] but he should also be perplexed by its commingling with the very opposites of what he enjoys. Moreover, with a good memory—which Phaedrus does not possess (e.g., 227e6–228c8)—he would recall many moments in the speech where a crucial proposition was not or could not be elaborated. The most significant of these was the nature of *logismos* as the means by which the intellect is able to gather together its perceptions—that is, reminders—of true being. Although Socrates identified *logismos* with recollection, its nature was not detailed explicitly, only indirectly through the connection between recollection and *erōs*. But why is *logismos* even necessary for the soul's ascent, and why must it consist of a way of life rather than the production of a single *logos*? The palinode could be regarded as a beautification of what might seem to many to be the ugly and tedious work of precise argumentation, a beautiful vision of a *logos* or doctrine underneath the myth, but Socrates gives no direct argument in the *Phaedrus* to support this. The persuasiveness of the palinode lies entirely in its ability to reflect back to Phaedrus beautiful images that first recall and then transform his own experiences.

The use of the mythical form was, however, a curious means of persuasion, given Phaedrus's express distrust of it (229c4–5). Socrates's strategy is ironic and playful, as he did not expect it to be persuasive in itself. Phaedrus confirms this when he says that "I pray with you, Socrates, *if* indeed it is better for us that these things come to be" (257b–c, emphasis added). Recognizing Phaedrus's inclination to disbelieve myth on account of their inconsistency with sense experience, Socrates uses fantastic imagery to suspend any ready agreement on the basis of the presumed truth of such experience. By proposing images that are fantastic—for example, that the soul possesses wings—Socrates compels Phaedrus to look beyond received opinion concerning both the meaning of words such as "wings" and "soul" and how they relate to one another, and consider the ramifications of their novel extension. Phaedrus must see, as Socrates showed with his first speech, that definitions and *logoi* do not exhaust the truth of a thing; he must interpret and ask himself what it means for the soul to possess wings, and somehow attempt to fit his opinions about these words to the things themselves, even though those things too must be put into words. This mythical talk does not preserve conventional piety, but opens Phaedrus to his own ignorance: "I have been in wonder at your speech" (257c1–2). Socrates accomplished this, for example, through the organization of the palinode in a mythical time that proceeded from a perfect but obscure ancient past ("then") to the modern and perplexing present ("now"). In the first place, it put into temporal sequence what actually occurs simultaneously in the present in the experience of *erōs*. Something is desired on the basis of having gathered together past experiences of what seemed good, presuming a continuity, goodness itself, across those experiences. Secondly, the placement of perfection in the past inspires future action toward return. The future is thus understood as a realization of what originated in the past, so that the whole of time—past, present, and future—is understood to be unified in form. Accordingly, the third accomplishment of this mythical arrangement was to transform Phaedrus's comportment toward his present objects of desire. Desire that seeks perfect wholeness in those objects or in their future arrangement is understood as degeneration ("forgetfulness"). Phaedrus cannot expect such perfection, such as endless pleasure, now or in the future, but only in a way of life that understands limitations.

The myth in the palinode beautifully depicts the whole of nature in both its motion and eternity, in which *logismos* participates if it is to be the discernment of what really is, and yet thereby reveals what *logismos* only perceives in part (249b6–c4, 250b1–5). Inasmuch as myth is a form of *logos*, Socrates thus subjects this beautification to his warning against monumentalizing: his speech exceeds what *logismos* can show. At its heart, the myth of the palinode points away from itself and its beauty to *logismos*, that is, to the gathering together of reminders. This does not mean that Socrates places myth and *logos* in diametric opposition—he in fact uses both terms to describe his two speeches.[145] But Socrates's palinode does place its own beautifying synthesis of the whole in tension with the dialogue on rhetoric that is to follow, paradoxically supplying the conditions for that dialogue while asserting that such dialogue is the only real means of recollecting the truth. Myth offers Socrates a way of putting into words what must always be behind our words, shaping and guiding them as much as they shape our perception of what they signify. Even in this, the myth succeeds only as a paradoxical call to search, professing that its incommensurability with the beautiful is in harmony with the beautiful.

## Chapter Four

# The Art of Speaking

Socrates's beautiful palinode impressed Phaedrus, but did not persuade him. Phaedrus's qualified praise, "if indeed these things are better," will become a familiar refrain, for what seems to be beautiful pleases him but does not ultimately satisfy (257c). Socrates's defense of *erōs* therefore remains incomplete. Whatever truth the palinode contains has not been made sufficiently clear to Phaedrus that he will take it into his life and consider devoting himself to the highest *erōs* and so to "philosophical speeches." Phaedrus's doubt is a reminder that this dialogue is alive, dealing with issues that are not abstract and distant from life, but of concrete significance to its interlocutors. For Phaedrus, the immediate cause of his doubt is his lingering attachment to Lysias. Phaedrus fears that Lysias, in the contest with Socrates, will "appear to me wretched" and will have to write another speech (257c). That Lysias must write seems to be something shameful to Phaedrus, for he once heard a politician abuse his friend by calling him a "speechwriter," as if writing rather than actually delivering speeches or speaking extemporaneously was inherently contemptible. A rift between Phaedrus and Lysias was opened, and Socrates's speeches have threatened to widen it further. This personal concern of a man for the true beauty of his friend raises the question that animates the remainder of the dialogue: what is beautiful or noble writing? How may Lysias become truly beautiful? Dramatically, then, the question of the nature of the art of rhetoric is subordinate to the question of writing, even though the former will prove to be the primary philosophical problem. *Erōs* as embodied in the lives of the interlocutors is what animates their joint, dialogical, inquiry. Through this embodiment, the promise of the palinode, that it persuade Phaedrus and Lysias toward a philosophical life, may be fulfilled and the two halves of the *Phaedrus* unified, as Phaedrus seeks true beauty in and for its manifestation here on earth, in what is particular and concrete.

This chapter will argue that the whole discussion of the art of speaking, despite its relatively prosaic and disengaged appearance, is an exercise in Socrates's own rhetoric, grounded in his erotic art. In the course of showing that the true art of rhetoric entails knowledge of both the subject matter and the soul of the audience, established through dialectical study, Socrates not only presents arguments that are questionable, but interjects reminders that their own inquiry, and speech in general, presupposes a fundamentally open-ended, erotic, and personal relation to reality. The rhetorician must develop a "private" rhetoric in order to perfect its public form, developing knowledge of subject matter and soul out of his own understanding of the nature of things. Building on the psychological insights of the palinode, the dialectical analysis of the soul that lies at the heart of Socrates's proposed art of rhetoric compels the rhetorician to look inward, interrogate his own beliefs, as he contemplates the various arrangements of the soul and what is most fitting for it. What began as a study of the conditions for perfect and artful persuasion proves to be an immersion in the highest activities of the soul. Socrates does not use this noble rhetoric as a blueprint toward perfect knowledge, but rather as an exhortation toward a dialogical practice that that will reconstitute the rhetorician's soul in light of its excellence. While this noble rhetoric may show the conditions for its perfection, rhetoric is in practice subsumed under Socrates's erotic art, which reforms rhetoric on the model of the philosophical ethos or way of life.

## LYSIAS'S SHAME

Phaedrus worries that the politician's abuse of Lysias will cause him "to cease from writing out of love of honor" (253d6). Phaedrus thus suggests Lysias follows "the coarser way of life" (256c1), but Socrates recognizes that Lysias is not so susceptible to the politician's abuse. Phaedrus, not Lysias, is ruled by love of honor (cf. 231e–232a). Ignorant of the full nature of *erōs*, Phaedrus fails to understand himself and misses the mark with others. Similarly, he believes that politicians scorn writing because they too fear for their "future reputation [*doxa*] . . . lest they be called sophists" (257d). Socrates does not deny this fear for their reputation, but rejects the belief that they repudiate writing simply. Politicians are lovers whose principal instrument is writing, since "the greatest thinkers" among them work to persuade the assembly to approve and write down their laws (257e). They wish to see themselves reflected in and loved by the *dēmos* as a whole: "The writer says 'it seems best to the council' or 'to the people' or both, and 'such a man said,' speaking of and praising himself with great reverence" (258a). Thus the politician enacts in "the theatre" of the assembly the encomia of the poets (cf. 245a), with himself as the object, realizing his self-love and desire for immortality.

Identifying this desire for immortality, Socrates recalls for Phaedrus the immortality discussed in the palinode and so places the question of writing in the context of *erōs*. Unlike the eternal life of the soul, the immortality of fame is limited, for the legislator is like "a god" until he dies (being subject to the higher, unwritten, ordinances of nature [cf. 248c2, c8]), and lives only as a memory recalled when future generations "gaze upon his writings" (258c–d).[1] With his immortality therefore depending upon its durability on earth, the politician is saddened "when his writings are rubbed out." Such immortality is a dim reflection of the eternal being desired and perceived by the mind, and produces only custom and habit rather than knowledge.[2] By recalling the higher immortality and natural law of the palinode, Plato indicates a difference in forms of persuasion that will become important for the later discussion of writing and his own project. While the legislator persuades the assembly with oral rhetoric, appealing to principles not currently established in law, once his laws are written down, his words become determinate and even customary or habitual in the broader sense of *nomos*.[3] Although the law may fix the meaning of words like "justice," it does not itself teach (275a, d–e, 276d), but relies on compulsion enforced by institutions like the Areopagus (229c). The threat of shame or bodily pain applied to the horses in the palinode vividly illustrates the limited power of persuasion that the law exerts on the multitude. In enforcing the law by disciplining the body and lower parts of the soul, the legislator's immortality suggests the limits of oral persuasion, and that even objects that are only perceived intellectually must be embodied in order to endure in this life.

While Phaedrus concedes the hypocrisy of the politician who abuses Lysias for writing, his response is tepid: "It is not likely [*eikos*] [that the politician reproaches Lysias for being a writer] from what you say, for he would reproach him, so it seems [*eoikein*], for what he himself desires" (258c). Responses such as "it is likely" and "so it seems" are common for Phaedrus, but his hesitation does helpfully remind the reader to more closely examine Socrates's arguments, the subtleties of which often elude Phaedrus in the quick flow of conversation. For example, Socrates's demonstration that the politician is hypocritical does not explain why the politician abuses Lysias in the first place. Perhaps the issue is the obvious difference between the kinds of writing he and Lysias perform: they may both be speech-writers, but Lysias's forensic writing aims to secure a beneficial verdict for his client, perhaps evading the punishments commanded by the law or disputing its meaning.[4] Moreover, Lysias himself does not enter into the contest to lay down enduring laws, but contents himself with his timely pieces.[5] Socrates does not distinguish between these kinds of writing, but quite intentionally so, for that distinction can be made clearly only after the long discussion of the nature of rhetoric itself. Indeed, Socrates's present argument suffices because Phaedrus, not Socrates, failed to distinguish between kinds of writing. Phaedrus does not ask, and Socrates politely passes over, whether Lysias's form of writing deserves abuse, although Socrates alludes to the possibility when he utters the truism that "what is shameful is speaking and writing not nobly [or: beautifully, *kalōs*] but shamefully and badly" (242d, 258d). Socrates reserves direct censure of Lysias's manner of writing until he obtains Phaedrus's agreement to the principles that justify censure.

Socrates here saves the possibility of good writing while revealing its full scope. His reintroduction of political life into the conversation gathers together the full range of subjects, and stakes, of the art of rhetoric, far beyond its private uses emphasized in the preceding three speeches. Socrates asks Phaedrus, "What is the manner [*tropos*] of writing nobly and not? Do we need to examine [*exetazein*, from *zētein*, to search or inquire] whomever else has at some time written something or will write, either a political or a private writing, in meter like a poet or without meter like a prose writer [or: private man, amateur, *idiōtēs*]?" (258e). Socrates suggests that the question that Phaedrus and Lysias should concern themselves with is a universal one that will disclose goodness of writing in all its forms—an unchanging standard that legislation can only imitate.

## THE IMMORTAL SONG OF THE CICADAS

Socrates appears ready to move directly into the extended discussion of writing that comes at the end of the *Phaedrus*, but instead enters into a digression that will develop into a lengthy examination of the art of rhetoric. This digression arises from Phaedrus's peculiar delight at the prospect of examining Lysias's speech: "For the sake of what else would one live, but than for the sake of such pleasures?" (258e). Unlike Socrates, also a professed lover of speeches, Phaedrus pursues speeches not for the love of learning but for pleasure (e.g., he praised Lysias's speech for its form rather than its substance [228b1–c3, 230d3, 234c6–7, 236e4–5]). This presents to Socrates the problem whether their inquiry can be conducted for such an end, or is thereby compromised.[6] Phaedrus, for his part, believes that pleasure is not only good but also the highest good "for the sake of which one would live": one lives "not [for the sake of] those [pleasures] which it is necessary to feel pain before or not take pleasure in, which indeed all the pleasures concerning the body have a small part of, so that they have also justly been called slavish" (258e). The highest principle of Phaedrus's life is therefore a hedonistic calculus, albeit directed toward minimizing pain rather than experiencing the greatest pleasure; great pleasure mixed with pain does not interest him. This view diverges from, or misunderstands, the transcendence of the palinode, effectively cutting Phaedrus off from the greatest pleasures, which arise from the relief of pain (248c2–5, 251c1–252a1) (this view also corresponds to the concealed lover's implicit promise of pleasure free from the harmful madness of bodily *erōs* [239a–e, 241e6–7]). If the soul's return to the superheavenly place by way of philosophy entails successively experiencing the erotic pain of separation and then joyful vision, Phaedrus's understanding of both speech and *erōs* prohibits any such return (cf. 272b5–6, 274a6–7). Moreover, Phaedrus discounts the psychological pains of *erōs* depicted in the palinode, which produces a curiously bookish hedonism that holds the body in contempt.

Given Phaedrus's superficial interest in speech as a means for gratification rather than learning, Socrates must find a way to convey in attractive terms the serious purpose of speech.[7] In the *Symposium*, Socrates discovered that his questioning and refutation held no special charm for Phaedrus, who was bent on eliciting rhetorical displays about Eros.[8] Tellingly, Socrates does not now refute Phaedrus's aesthetic interest in speech through arguments, but has recourse again to myth. The palinode's warning that the manifestation of beauty may grip the soul with pleasure has proven to be particularly suitable for Phaedrus, but Socrates must make that teaching still more explicit and with special attention to Phaedrus's evident contempt for the body.

Observing the cicadas in the plane tree, Socrates tells Phaedrus that they must continue conversing in order to resist the cicadas' song. If the cicadas saw them, "like the many who in midday do not converse but doze, being charmed by them [the cicadas] on account of not using the mind, they would justly laugh, thinking some slaves had come to their retreat in order to take their midday nap around the spring, like sheep" (259a–b). Phaedrus's urbane sentiments are thus rebutted: conversing for the sake of pleasure is akin to sleeping, and leisure should not be lack of employment, but employment of the mind. Dialogue versus sleep is analogous to Socratic versus Phaedrean speech, and what is at risk is not only the possibility of really examining Lysias's speech, but the possibility that speech has greater significance than the pleasure it generates.[9] Phaedrus's superficial *erōs* would turn speech into an empty instrument for dwelling in falsehoods, like those found in Lysias's "nonlover."[10] In referring back to the divine plane tree, Socrates makes a symbol of the protective shade it casts—light mingled with darkness—that allows two possible orientations toward *logos*. The sun rose to its apex over the course of Socrates's palinode, but the "stifling heat" of that vision now threatens to destroy the conversation. They can either revel in the relief provided by the shade, and thereby lose sight of the question of what constitutes noble writing, or they can use that relief as an opportunity to understand what they experienced during the preceding speeches (258e–259a).

Should they follow the latter way and employ their minds in conversation, the cicadas will see the two of them "sailing by them [the cicadas] unenchanted as if they [the cicadas] were Sirens" and give them "the gift for human beings that they have to give from the gods" (259a). In Homer's original story, Odysseus followed the divine counsel of Circe with regard to his men and instructed them to stop their ears, but he himself wished to listen to the terrible song of the Sirens, which promised wisdom, and so instructed his men to fix him to the ship's mast. Through this device, he was temporarily driven mad by the song yet nonetheless escaped the Sirens' island, which they had filled with their victims' corpses.[11] Socrates's allusion has two implications. First, he does not distinguish between the ignorant sailors and the divinely counseled Odysseus, and so makes his advice to converse a principle for all human beings to obtain the Odyssean wisdom that both hears the song and guards against it. Second, he transposes the Sirens' deadly island onto the plane tree, which has inspired Socrates (230b–d, 241e, 242d–c, 263d). Their conversation proceeds under the shadow of death; to indulge in the cicadas' beautiful song is to die. The myth of the cicadas expresses the limitations that mortality places on the divine ascent depicted in the palinode.

The cicadas, Socrates tells Phaedrus, were once men, before the Muses were born. When the Muses and their song came to be, these men were "struck out by pleasure" and devoted themselves to singing with such ardor that they "neglected food and drink, and did not notice that they had died" (259b). From these men, being pitied by the Muses, "the race of cicadas grew." Taking the Muses' gift, the cicadas sing until their death, after which they go and report on those who had honored the Muses in each of their respective domains, whether it was Terpsichore in dance, Erato in "love matters," and so on. But "to Calliope, the eldest, and Ourania who follows her, they report those leading a life in philosophy and honoring their music, who indeed amongst the Muses is most of all concerned with the heavens and speeches [*logoi*] both divine and human" (259b–d).

The dual purpose of the myth—both a warning and a call to honor the Muses—seems to originate from the nature of the immortal song of the cicadas. Socrates seems to agree with Hesiod, that although the Muses bring "a forgetting of ills and a rest from sorrows," a life without pain and laborious struggle is impossible.[12] When song "appears," it "strikes out" men. This moment of being "struck out," which Socrates playfully enacted after hearing Lysias's speech (234d1), is the moment of ecstasy when the soul grasps what is pleasing because it seems to satisfy our most fundamental desires (cf. 251a–252a).[13] Having found a source of great pleasure, the soul refuses to part with it, but the fate of the ancient men shows that an everlasting grasp of the beautiful and pleasant is outside the power of mortals. Neglecting their bodies in eagerness for pleasure, these men spurn a truly human life, and are reborn in subhuman form. Socrates earlier said that no soul that had glimpsed the truth would "be planted in a beast" in its first life, and now it seems that even the highest rank of soul, a *philomousos*, might fall in just that way (248c–d). What the myth of the cicadas clarifies from the palinode is that the cicadas lose sight of being because they lose sight of their mortality.[14] The argument is not that death is an inherent evil and the ancient men were fools for allowing it to happen,[15] but that their obsessive indulgence in the pleasures of song led to the obliteration of "the human form" and thus the possibility of recollecting being (249a–c). Pain and death may in fact be good so far as serve as negative reminders of true being.

The cicadas' song is therefore a test, bestowing a divine gift on those who hear it and honor the Muses but do not delight in the deceptive song alone, as Hesiod famously sung: "We [Muses] know how to speak many false things that resemble the genuine [or: true, *etuma*], but we [also] know, when we may wish, how to sing true things."[16] Perhaps the substance of this ambiguous gift lies in the disclosure that *logos* is dualistic, both "human and divine," and so may gratify what is merely human or what is divine.[17] Earlier formulations of this distinction suggested a higher but inscrutable articulation of the true nature of things (246a, 252b). If philosophy cannot be said to be the divine *logos* simply, it is at least the form of music, as Socrates interpreted it throughout his life and suggests here in his honoring of Calliope,[18] that seeks to couple human *logos* with what is heavenly.

Conversely, Phaedrus's love of speech conflates the pleasant and the good, and the pleasant may very well be harmful, whether this is understood to be the singers' deaths or their ceasing to be human. Socrates's myth warns Phaedrus of how deceptive is this desire for pleasure, particularly when it shapes the *logos* necessary for understanding what is truly desirable. *Logos* is capable of such superficiality—reflecting pleasant visions—because it entails separation from the immediate experiences and necessities of embodied life. Use of *logos* therefore risks producing the opinion that pleasant separation from necessity is the highest good while also allowing for the discernment of a good greater than mere survival. Mortality entails a tension between the necessities and pleasures of life, and this tension cannot be reconciled simply in favor of pleasure, as the cicadas believe. Socrates's myth of the cicadas shows Phaedrus how *logos* may serve a human life that is greater than either mere survival or the enjoyment of a licentious freedom.

Ferrari's interpretation of this myth is especially important in light of this warning against the danger found in the power of *logos* to beautify by virtue of its detachment from necessity. He considers the re-emergence of the setting or "background" of the *Phaedrus* as a deliberate allusion to the enabling conditions for dialogue.[19] The dramatic function of the grove is coextensive with *erōs*, understood as the desire to unite with an object that is absent yet somehow already known. There is a "background" presupposed and implicit in human action, in which the causes of its own being can be found. The "human form" is uniquely capable of perceiving and inquiring into this background through *logos*, and so truly human *logos* is that which does not merely assume or take for granted that background. When Socrates invokes the background of their conversation, he makes concrete the palinode's depiction of philosophical *erōs* as recollection, drawing Phaedrus's attention away from the vision of pure beings by which *logos* so easily obscures those experiences in which the beings are actually perceived. *Logos* does not open the soul to the nature of being by depicting pure forms, but rather by carefully distinguishing the appearance of those forms within the ever-present background that informs our desires and opinions. Socrates's myth of the cicadas remedies Phaedrus's urbane intellectualism, which flees from the unpleasant, painful, and ugly or ignoble aspects of human life. Their subsequent discussion of rhetoric accordingly turns on how the use of *logos* becomes knowledgeable when it confronts reality.

## THE PROBLEM OF RHETORIC AND KNOWLEDGE

When Socrates returns to the question of what it means to write nobly, his digressive myth has broadened that question to encompass speaking and provided the insight that speech must not be merely gratifying, as Phaedrus believed, but a means to learn what is truly useful. Alerted to Phaedrus's aesthetic approach to speech, Socrates probes further to determine Phaedrus's understanding of speaking "well and nobly"—does it require that "the mind of the speaker knows the truth about what he is about to speak on" (259e; cf. 258d7, 259e1–2)? Socrates's question links goodness and knowledge, although it is not clear whether for him speaking well means merely speaking persuasively or speaking in a way that benefits the rhetorician or the audience. Phaedrus, however, makes clear that he believes that speaking well means speaking persuasively for the benefit of the rhetorician.

Phaedrus's rejection of the argument that speaking well requires knowledge is predictable, given his solely aesthetic interest in speeches. Truth is for him secondary:

> I have heard that it is not necessary for the one who intends to become a rhetorician to understand what the just things really are but what seems so [*ta doxanta*] to the majority who judge, nor the truly good nor beautiful things but what will seem so [*dokein*], for persuasion comes from these things and not from the truth. (259e–260a)

Phaedrus's familiar resort to hearsay, "I have heard," reflects his approach to speech, adopting positions without consideration. His choice of words also hints at a basic problem in this opinion: Phaedrus could not claim "I know" that knowledge is unnecessary without contradicting himself, nor could he simply say "It seems to me," which would only confess that the opinion is itself not true because opinions are not true, as he claims. Phaedrus is in the impossible position of defending as true the opinion that knowledge of truth is irrelevant. His words tacitly admit the incoherence that creeps in through his reliance on a vague authority (a background of opinions he draws from as suits his desire). While Socrates is not concerned with the source of this opinion, only whether it is true, Gorgias' presence is felt here, as this opinion recalls his claim to teach how to speak persuasively about justice without knowing what is truly just or making oneself just.[20] There is a certain common sense to this, insofar as one can speak without knowledge and still persuade an audience. But how is it that we can persuade others of what seems to be if we do not know whether it is true? The problem expressed in Phaedrus's opinion is not a small one, and will reemerge at crucial junctures in the conversation.

Telling Phaedrus that his opinion is "not to be cast aside," Socrates quotes Nestor from the *Iliad*, alluding to the tradition of noble public speaking that seeks to lead an audience to the correct opinion, rather than the duplicitous rhetoric that Phaedrus offers (260a5).[21] In quoting Nestor, Socrates uses the theme of war to bolster his argument from the utility of words, that is, from the knowledge an audience has acquired through the actual use and application of words. Insofar as a word is meaningful, an utter lack of knowledge is impossible: "If I were persuading you to defend against enemies by acquiring a horse, and neither of us knew what a horse was, but I happened to know so much about you, that Phaedrus believes a horse is that animal of ours that has the largest ears" (260b). Phaedrus admits that it would be incomprehensible or "ridiculous" for rhetorical art to grasp the opinion of its audience without having any grasp of what it is an opinion about. Socrates carefully qualifies this, arguing that it only becomes ridiculous once the rhetorician "puts together a speech praising the donkey, naming it a horse and saying the beast would be an entirely valuable acquisition for both home and on campaign, useful both to fight from and able to bear baggage and many other purposes" (260b–c). That is to say, the ridiculousness of this belief depends on the unexpressed premises that a donkey would be useless for fighting and that such uselessness would be evident to its owner. The ignorance of buyer and seller is only exposed by use and experience; so long as the object exists only in speech it can maintain the guise of truth. Socrates therefore does not suggest that false opinion or deception by an ignorant person is impossible, but only that such opinions can be refuted by experience. Consequently, we do not have real knowledge of what we say unless our words can be brought into relation with our own experience—into relation with deeds—and accomplish their purpose.[22] This argument from use anticipates Socrates's introduction of the "private" rhetoric by which the rhetorician learns the meaning of words for himself.

But the ease with which this argument confounds Phaedrus conceals otherwise obvious objections. Some objects are not sensory and so their related words cannot be used and tested in the same way as, for example, a donkey is tested in battle. Moreover, use is no simple thing—were someone to use the donkey for tasks other than battle, he might not learn that he did not buy a horse. Socrates's argument is adequate only in relation to Phaedrus's level of understanding, which, as seen in his distrust of myths, tends toward a conception of speech as signs for sensory or "likely" objects.

When applied to political rhetoric, Socrates's argument from use becomes especially vivid. If a rhetorician who is ignorant of what is good and bad, "having practiced the opinions of the majority," addresses a similarly ignorant city "and persuades them . . . about bad as if it were good" and to do bad rather than good, he will "reap" a bad fruit (260c–d). That is, an ignorant rhetorician will make mistakes and produce the opposite of what he intends; he cannot determine which opinion he should have inculcated. But the question is ultimately whether the city will perceive its deception. Is injustice as clearly useless as a donkey is for war? Socrates's argument is deceptively clear because he uses the object "bad," forming the obvious truism that bad things result from bad things, which Phaedrus would immediately question if he were to ask instead whether injustice so obviously reaps bad fruit. Indeed, Socrates later describes all these objects as "disputable" in their meaning, and the palinode showed each to be visible to the mind alone rather than an objection of sense perception, like a donkey (263a). Without knowledge of the proper use of these things and of what actually constitutes "bad fruit," the question still remains whether persuasion only requires what seems to be true rather than knowledge. As Christopher Moore (2013) has pointed out, Socrates's rhetoric is not limited to the use of myths and images, but also extends to dialogical argument.[23] Were their discussion to end here, the reader would be justified in believing that Socrates employs rhetoric merely to persuade and win the argument. But Socrates does not end the discussion, and in testing Phaedrus's understanding, he instructs him in the very objections that would qualify and nuance his present argument, not least the need for the rhetorician to learn for himself how he and others actually make use of their words.

## PSYCHAGOGIA

Seeing that Phaedrus is readily disarmed by the argument that rhetoric ignorant of the good will lead to obviously bad consequences, Socrates takes the initiative to reformulate the claim on behalf of the art of rhetoric so that it does not deny the need for knowledge and therefore its own possibility. At the same time, Socrates takes care to explain the power for deception associated with the art. While Socrates's analysis of persuasion will not support the perfect persuasiveness to which rhetoric aspires, he will establish something of vital importance for Phaedrus, namely that the speaker must draw on internal resources that imply a stable foundation for *logos* rests.

Socrates begins the case for rhetoric by personifying the art of speaking, who advises the would-be rhetorician to learn the truth before taking up the art. But she also boasts that "without me [i.e., the art], the one who knows the beings will not be able to persuade by art" (260d). Socrates here carefully leaves open the possibility of artless persuasion, which will prove essential to Socrates's account of persuasion and his larger argument subordinating rhetoric to philosophy. But the boast is necessary if the art of speaking is to be an art in its own right, with an object distinct from those of the other arts. Distinguishing rhetoric from the other arts greatly expands the scope of rhetoric, for if rhetoric is necessary for all artful persuasion, even the practitioners of the other arts will have use, if not need, for rhetoric—perhaps to teach or even practice their own art. If rhetoric is not necessary for those arts, their knowledge could only be acquired without persuasion, perhaps nondiscursively, or acquired through an artless persuasion. The art of rhetoric therefore claims for itself an even greater scope than did Gorgias, who argued that rhetoric can aid the other arts.[24]

Socrates carefully qualifies his agreement with this great claim: "if she is indeed an art" (260e). If the art of speaking "lies" and is no art at all, but proves instead to be an "artless knack," her claims would be refuted while acknowledging rhetoric's capacity for some kind of persuasion. Socrates's objection is that artfulness entails knowledge of truth: "Of speaking, says the Spartan, a genuine [or: true, *etumos*] art without having laid hold of the truth [*alētheia*] neither exists nor will ever come to be" (260e). Socrates uses the Spartan's objection to supply what will prove to be a crucial premise concerning the nature of art: knowledge of the truth is the principal criterion of not just the art of speaking, but of art as such. The Spartan's contrast of *etumos* and *alētheia* provides a second criterion: only an art founded upon what is true simply (*alētheia*) will be fitting for local custom or practice (one sense of *etumos*).[25] Inasmuch as a genuine art will express that truth in practice, a genuine art will be one that bears fruit.[26] If, for example, the objects of rhetoric are justice and goodness, the Spartan demands that rhetoric produce what is truly just and good.[27] What appears parochial is in fact a demand that practice embody the truth, similar to Socrates's earlier argument that knowledge is confirmed in its use. Furthermore, the Spartan's demand indicates that whatever an art produces must be judged independently of that art; simply practicing an ostensible art is not sufficient proof of its genuineness. If rhetoric is to be proven an art there must remain the possibility of knowledge external to the art, and therefore artless persuasion and artlessly obtained knowledge.[28] When Socrates aims "to persuade Phaedrus . . . that unless he should philosophize sufficiently, he will never be sufficient in speaking about anything," he does not identify philosophy with art, but rather distinguishes them—philosophy's artless persuasiveness and proficiency with *logos* arises out of questioning concerning the grounds of art (261a).

The art of rhetoric "as a whole," Socrates says, is a *psychagōgia*, a leading of the soul, through speeches, regardless of context, whether it be law courts, in public or private, or on great or small things (261a). Socrates later claims that "the power of *logos* [itself] is *psychagōgia*" (271c10). Socrates's relation of rhetoric to the essence of *logos*, when taken with the Spartan's claim that the art of speaking must possess the truth, implies the amazing conclusion toward which Socrates will lead Phaedrus: that artful rhetoric— that is, perfect persuasiveness—requires knowing everything that can be expressed in, and addressed with, *logos*. Socrates laid the groundwork for this ambitious path in his palinode, which identified the philosopher with Zeus, hegemon and leader of immortal souls toward comprehension of true being (246e4–6).[29] The erotic struggle within the individual soul to achieve that vision is reflected now in Socrates's argument that a private and personal reckoning with reality must be the foundation of artful public persuasion.

Socrates's expansive definition of rhetoric means that the rhetoric used in public settings is only one part of the whole art, distinguishable from a complementary "private" rhetoric. Phaedrus's surprise at learning of this private rhetoric reflects the common association of rhetoric exclusively with speaking in courts and assemblies. Private speech was associated with household matters or love matters, differing in kind from public rhetoric and other uses of speech, such as in the other arts.[30] In the *Gorgias*, Socrates coaxes Gorgias to extend similarly the art of speaking to all these other matters,[31] which sheds some light on Socrates's purpose here: the extension of rhetoric to private uses forces Gorgias, and now Phaedrus, to consider its effects on the individual rather than the crowd. If rhetoric really is a leading of the soul, should it not be able to produce its effects on both many souls and one soul? If on one soul, not only on the ignorant soul, but also on the soul that is knowledgeable about the subject, or even on the rhetorician's own soul?

Socrates's illustration of this distinction between public and private rhetoric evidences his association of private rhetoric with the acquisition of knowledge. Nestor and Odysseus, who addressed the Achaean troops, represent the public rhetoric.[32] Palamedes, the ill-fated hero famed for his learned inventions, including the alphabet and arithmetic, represents the private.[33] Palamedes's inclusion suggests that private rhetoric includes the persuasion of oneself toward the nature of things—that is, the personal achievement of understanding. Both forms of rhetoric, however, follow the same principle of persuasion. Whoever possesses the whole art of speech will therefore know this principle and be proficient in both public and private rhetoric. For now, Socrates gives precedence to the private rhetoric as the foundation for the public, for his immediate concern is to show how the rhetorician cannot speak artfully in public without knowledge of what he speaks. Socrates's procedure here is dialectical, for he has distinguished the private from the public rhetoric in order to reveal their continuity, their unity in principle, which would otherwise remain hidden by the public appearance of skill.

The basic principle of artful speaking is "speaking the opposite" or *antilogic* (261c–e). *Antilogic* conventionally refers to forensic disputation, in which two parties oppose each other concerning the justness of the defendant. But Socrates also finds *antilogic* in the writings of the "Eleatic Palamedes"—commonly understood to refer to Zeno—which make "the same things appear to be like and unlike, one and many, at rest and in motion" (261d).[34] Artful speaking therefore lies in the ability to elicit contradiction. This is done by making something resemble everything it can possibly resemble, and "to bring into light the making of semblances [*homoioun*] and the hiding of another" (261e).[35] An artful speaker leads his audience by soliciting agreement to "many small steps" of such semblances, eventually "crossing over" to the opposite opinion (262a). Thus the importance of private rhetoric: without true knowledge of these semblances—that is, how things actually resemble and differ from one another—the rhetorician will not be able "to deceive another but remain un-deceived himself" (a significant risk when a rhetorician persuades with "artless knack," producing effects without clearly understanding how [262a; cf. 260e5]). Deception comes about because the audience is unable to distinguish for themselves the true beings from their images or semblances, which are mixtures: "Those who hold opinions contrary to what is do so on account of some semblances streaming in" (262b). Accordingly, the contradictions exhibited by such mixture may be exploited—as Zeno so ably did.[36]

On Socrates's account, opposites play an essential role in persuasion. Where the argument "crosses over," the listener's soul, believing one thing, must come to believe other than it, which at its most basic is moving from "what is" to "what is not," so that the soul comes to respond to the same *logos* in an opposite and entirely new way. Without this reversal or turn, the audience's opinion would be unchanged, and seeming persuasion would simply be a reiteration of existing beliefs.[37] In the case of deception, the listener is unaware that the mediating semblances are false and that he holds opposing opinions—for the deceived listener, there would be no moment of perplexity (*aporia*) in which the soul perceives a contradiction and division within itself—for example, the concurrence of pleasure and pain when perceiving beauty, or when the beloved turns toward the lover in confusion because he now seems to love what he does not love (251d–e, 255d3; cf. 247a5). The rhetorician is capable, though, of "bringing to light" this state wherein opposites resemble one another. This "bringing to light" seems to be a basic aim of private rhetoric: to perceive that what seems true to the audience is in fact contradicted by other opinions it holds.[38]

If *antilogic* is indeed the singular art "with respect to all that is said," as Socrates claims, persuasion by private rhetoric must take the same form. Learning how one thing resembles or does not resemble another, differentiating what actually is from what is not, also entails crossing over from one thing to the opposite (261e). One would, for example, come to learn that a donkey is not a horse by perceiving a contradiction between them with respect to a given property. Such knowledge is not attained through demonstration,[39] but through refutation of what it is not, using semblances or mediating propositions to reject the given opinion. Through this private use of *antilogic* to clarify his own beliefs, the rhetorician will become able to distinguish how one thing is like and unlike another in various respects. Knowing in which ways these things are alike, he will be able to make semblances by which he can lead his audience. Whether someone can, in this negative way, understand completely the object in question is another matter.

The force of *antilogic*, and therefore the force of the private rhetoric by which a rhetorician learns the nature of things, lies in the principle of noncontradiction and its correlate, unity. The thing in question cannot be the opposite of itself with respect to what is essential to its being. Psychologically, perceiving a contradiction throws the soul itself into a contradiction—pulled in opposite directions—that it desires to resolve. Its path to such resolution is implied in the experience itself, in the form of *antilogic*. Since one thing is brought into contradiction by means of a semblance,[40] the semblance must be examined to determine where the falsity lies: in the semblance and resulting conclusion or in the original opinion. Private rhetoric will therefore be concerned with inquiry into this semblance, this third term, to determine the nature of things as that which withstands refutation.[41] Just as the parts of true beauty "streamed into" the lover through its earthly "semblance" (*homoiotētos*) in the beautiful boy, so too is the "streaming in" of the semblance (*homoiotētos*) here the streaming in of assumptions about the nature of things—that is, the ever-present "background," as Ferrari puts it, or the memory of being in its wholeness (cf. 251b5, 253b8, 262b2–3).[42] In Socrates's account of *antilogic*, this stream of semblances shows how we draw on this shared background to give coherence and unity—form—to our words and experiences, without which communication and persuasion would be impossible. But because this stream of semblances reminds us of the true nature of things, it is also the vehicle for our deception.

Given the role of *antilogic*—and therefore also the principle of noncontradiction—in persuasion, Socrates's allusion to Zeno as the "Eleatic Palamedes" takes on special significance. First, Zeno makes the like unlike and the many one (as he does in Plato's *Parmenides*),[43] and so Socrates, by associating him with Palamedes, the representative of the private rhetoric, suggests that Zeno is fully conscious of the assumptions and implications of contradictory speech, particularly the assumption of unity and the implication that only the true beings, not opinions, exhibit perfect unity. Others who claim similar skill in contradiction, most notably Gorgias (267a–b), are not so aware. Gorgias, in his *Encomium of Helen*, asserts that all persuasion proceeds by false argument because human beings lack complete knowledge and therefore rely on "slippery" opinions.[44] Zeno regards opinion in similar terms, for reliance on opinion only results in contradiction: he shows that what is many must also be one, and since many cannot be one, the many do not exist.[45] Both men assume that what really is must be by itself, one, and unchanging. For Gorgias, this justified his argument that there is no being, only appearance, with the further consequence that the art of speaking that rules opinion rules over all.[46] For Zeno, the contradiction of opinions is an "exercise" and negative support for Parmenides's thesis that only the one is.[47]

This leads to the second point of significance in Socrates's allusion: according to Socrates, Zeno wrote his antilogical treatise out of *erōs* for Parmenides.[48] Without this erotic relationship to Parmenides and the transcendent one, Zeno's public *antilogic* would be incoherent. Socrates's allusion here reflects the coextensive tendencies of speech and soul toward unity—tendencies that the palinode speculatively fused in the perception of being itself by means of a singular form (cf. 249b6–c4, d4–e4).[49]

Third, the connection of Zeno and Palamedes suggests a possible limitation in the private rhetoric. In popular stories, Odysseus betrayed Palamedes and persuaded the Achaeans to execute him.[50] If Diogenes Laertius is to be believed, Zeno was tortured and then killed for conspiring to overthrow the tyrant Nearchus.[51] Palamedes's fate can be interpreted as the tragic sacrifice of wisdom, or even its political naiveté or imperfection, and became a rhetorical topic. Gorgias, among others, saw fit to write a defense speech for Palamedes, unable or unwilling to effectively defend himself.[52] Socrates too, in his own trial, will draw on this topic, comparing himself to Palamedes as a victim of injustice who refuses to speak other than in "his customary way."[53] Plato's recollection of these men's fates suggests that the discovery that private rhetoric is the basis of artful public rhetoric is problematic. Is there a need for a public defense of this private rhetoric, that is to say, the possibility of truth? Can such a defense be effective in the form of private rhetoric, given that public rhetoric addresses "the many" rather than an individual? In what way does the private rhetoric manifest itself in public rhetoric? This relationship between the public and private rhetoric becomes a fruitful problem for Socrates and Phaedrus, carefully nuancing their conception of the whole art of rhetoric as they analyze their own speeches on *erōs*.

## LYSIAS AND SOCRATES EXAMINED

The need for unity implicit in Socrates's account of *psychagōgia* now becomes thematic in his examination of their speeches on *erōs*, as Socrates demands that artful speech manifest unity in its content and form. This is a turning point in the discussion of rhetoric, as Lysias's writing can no longer be considered the principal object of their inquiry, but only understandable in light of a more general object, *logos* itself (see 258d8). But Phaedrus needs to see the abstract principles and *antilogic* that Socrates introduced manifested in familiar objects—those principles must prove true and genuine in accordance with practice. This expectation means dispelling the conceit that the rhetorician-cum-nonlover can conceal himself—and his *erōs*—behind his words. Public rhetoric must withstand the scrutiny of private rhetoric if it is to be considered artful.

Socrates and Phaedrus will assess Lysias's rhetorical skill according to his ability to lead the soul of the audience from one thing to the opposite—for example, from giving favors to the lover to giving favors to the nonlover. They will seek evidence of his knowledge of *erōs* in his use of its semblances. Since this examination is a form of private rhetoric concerning Lysias's artfulness, Socrates's objections to Lysias's speech constitute basic criteria for private rhetoric, which he presumes to extend to artful speaking as a whole. When applying these criteria—marking disputable terms, definition, and logographic necessity—to Socrates's own speeches, however, their limitations for public rhetoric emerge. Socrates's profession of artlessness indicates that the rhetorician's knowledge cannot be discerned simply in his use of certain techniques, since their power depends upon the opinions and current state of the soul of the audience.

Lysias's examination begins with Phaedrus reading out the thesis of his speech, after which "they must say where Lysias misses the mark [*hamartanein*] and what he does artlessly" (262e). Socrates establishes the first criterion of artful rhetoric, that the rhetorician marks his subject matter, with the argument that deception is easier when it concerns disputable terms. While terms like "iron" and "silver" are uncontroversial, "just" and "good" are greatly disputed (263a). Among Socrates's examples, the former refer to material objects that are easily indicated, while the latter are immaterial ("things of value to souls" [250a]), found only through discourse and thought. Given this disagreement, the rhetorician "must first in some way distinguish and take some mark of each form [*eidos*], both in which it is necessary that the majority wander, and in which [they do] not" and "perceive sharply which of the species [*genos*] it happens to be that he is about to speak on" (263b–c). The rhetorician must be able to precisely divide (as well as collect, e.g., iron and silver as different forms of metal) the objects of his speech with respect to popular consensus, which can only be done by applying a mark or name to represent in speech the beings in question. Without such a mark, Socrates implies, the difference will elude the speaker and he will "miss the mark" (*hamartanein*), as Lysias apparently does.

This power of *logos* to mark is mentioned throughout the *Phaedrus*, and was given a psychological basis in the palinode when the soul creates monuments out of reminders—that is, perceptions—of beauty and comes to provisional agreement with itself (and the beloved) concerning the beings (249b–c, 250a–b, 250e–251a, 254b). The mark is itself a sensory object that seems to fix or bring to rest what is in motion. In the present case, it is a spoken sound, but the concept of "mark" will also be used to characterize the written word that attempts to fix knowledge in the soul (275a). This need for marking seems to originate from the beings' transcendence—that is, the variation in the soul's perceptions of a given being as it appears in different objects. Corresponding to this great difference between the beings themselves and their spoken (or written) monuments, is the potential for a great deal of plasticity in the meaning attributed to a given word—meaning will vary according to the interlocutors' opinions, only becoming true in light of shared knowledge of the being itself (the "same-minded" lovers of the palinode [256b1]).[54] This plasticity allows for the "play in words" of the knowledgeable rhetorician, but the rhetorician must nonetheless use a mark to keep distinct in his own mind—what Socrates later calls "writing on the soul" (276a)—the real difference between uncontroversial and disputable types as well as the difference between what actually is and what "the multitude" believes.[55]

Socrates thus reintroduces part of Phaedrus's definition of rhetoric, that rhetoric's power lies in its persuasion of the many rather than any individual. This popular opinion about rhetoric is not entirely false, and by reintroducing rhetoric's effect on the many, Socrates indicates that the distinction between public and private rhetoric, although both share in *antilogic*, is real. Still, Socrates insists that the rhetorician manifest his knowledge of what is uncontroversial and what is disputable in his public speeches. Socrates takes *erōs* as an example: Phaedrus points out that it must be among the disputable things since Socrates was able to say opposite things about it—he interprets Socrates's arguments to have been that "it [*erōs*] is harmful to the beloved and the lover, and also the greatest of goods" (263c). Phaedrus does not notice that if indeed the two speeches said completely opposite things (they did not, as Socrates only argued that *erōs* may enable the greatest good, not that it is itself that good [245b7–c1]), and that deception is to persuade the audience to believe that something is other than it really is, it follows that he had been deceived by Socrates's two speeches. Lysias, on the other hand, failed to mark what was agreeable and disputable, and was consequently unable to lead his audience. Socrates indicates that effective persuasion—

including deception—requires such a clear statement of the object that will bring it out of the ambiguities of disputation.

Socrates's second criterion for artful speaking directly follows: Lysias did not define (or: bound, *horizesthai*) *erōs*. Were Lysias to define *erōs*, he would "compel [*anangkazein*] us to take *erōs* as a particular one being ... toward which all the rest was arranged" (263d–e). Definition brings what is otherwise contentious into one so that the listener can be led to the desired conclusion by the necessity of noncontradiction. This does not mean, however, that the definition must be true—Socrates later admits that his own definition of *erōs* was not (265d)—but only that its clarity and unification of the thing under discussion are necessary for persuasion.[56] Socrates similarly argued in his first speech that without agreeing upon a definition, either with oneself or with others, deliberation would "miss [*hamartanein*] everything" (237b7–d3). Socrates then used his definition of *erōs* to bring about the rejection of the lover. Whether or not the audience agreed with the definition would be an important limitation of public rhetoric understood as the delivery of a monologue to a crowd, but Socrates will only obliquely address this limitation later. For the moment, he only emphasizes that Lysias failed to make *erōs* clear to his audience. Socrates consequently claims that his own speeches (or rather, those of "the nymphs of Achelous and Pan son of Hermes"), because they used definitions, were more artful (263d). But it remains unclear whether definition is necessary or useful as a technique in public rhetoric, although it is necessary in private rhetoric that tries to distinguish reality from semblance.

Socrates's criticism of Lysias on this point appears to be superficial—why would a speaker define a disputable object if he intends to mislead the audience by that very disputability? Socrates himself said it is easier to deceive when a term is disputable, so why give up that advantage?[57] As discussed in chapter 2, Lysias's appeal to probability exploits the uncertainty of his audience, and indeed, his probabilistic statements about *erōs* acknowledge the possibility that there may exist good lovers, even as he discredits this as unlikely (231e). But Socrates demands that public rhetoric follow the same stringent criteria that define private rhetoric; the form of persuasion, *antilogic*, must be found in both public and private rhetoric. This does not mean that Socrates conflates public and private rhetoric, but it does establish the priority of the private rhetoric, since the persuasion of the individual soul is the basic unit upon which is built the persuasion of many souls. Persuasion is most effective when the rhetorician is able to move knowledgably, without error, between semblances so as to escape detection by the audience (262a5–7, b5–8). That is, persuasion occurs when the audience believes the semblances to be true, and the strongest form of persuasion occurs when the semblances are in fact true and the audience knows this. Rhetoric must therefore strive to imitate, if only for the purpose of deception, the clarity of knowledge. Rhetoric that fails to imitate such clarity, as Socrates finds in Lysias's rhetoric, fails to give the audience a definite semblance in which it may see its seeming knowledge reflected. To the extent that Lysias fails to provide a definite conception of *erōs*, let alone true knowledge of *erōs*, Socrates's argument is sound—Lysias's speech cannot claim to be done with art unless it demonstrates that it possesses such knowledge, and since it relies on what is likely rather than what is true, there cannot be such a demonstration. Unfortunately for Lysias, he is not here to defend his speech and elaborate on what it says (cf. 275d–e). As such, Socrates does not fail to treat Lysias's speech on its own terms, as Ferrari (1987) argues, since he has shown that, on its own terms, it says nothing really true.[58]

Lysias's unwillingness to define *erōs* leads Socrates to his third criterion of artful speaking, which is that a speech must possess an internal order or coherence he calls "logographic necessity" (264b7). As with the preceding criteria, Socrates develops the concept of logographic necessity from the unity implicit in *antilogic*, but undermines it with his own actions and in so doing indicates how logographic necessity depends upon the rhetorician's purposes and the soul of the audience. Socrates's basic argument is that Lysias, without a clear understanding of *erōs*, cannot order his speech in relation to *erōs*, and so cannot bring his audience to the desired conclusion in a compelling manner. His speech lacks a solid core around which its form may cohere. Lysias "[does not begin] from the beginning [*archē*], but from the end [*teleutē*], attempting to swim the speech backwards on his back, and begins from the things the lover, having finished, might say to the boy" (264a). His ordering of the speech seems random:

> Do not the [parts] of [Lysias's] speech seem to have been thrown out in a flood? Or does it appear that the second thing he says must have been placed second from some necessity, or any other of the utterances? . . . Do you grasp some logographic necessity by which that man placed these things thus beside one another in this order? (264b3–8).

Socrates here demands a linear order to speech, in contrast to the order exhibited by the soul's circular motion, where its perfection or end (*telos*) is a return to its beginning (249c6–8). Lysias's disordered speech, by beginning from the end and presupposing a relationship between lover and beloved, seems to parody a soul's erotic inspiration due to its recollection of a prior union with true beauty. In assuming this erotic link to the beloved and then concealing it, Lysias fails to lead his audience. Socrates's demand for linear unity recognizes the temporality of human experience, in which the soul will not seek what it already knows or believes itself to know. The soul's journey in the palinode was not only circular and cyclical, but also proceeded linearly by speech through semblances, rejecting what seems to be for the sake of what really is.

But in Socrates's demand for logographic necessity, another kind of unity is discernable, a holistic one. This holistic unity appears when he challenges Phaedrus to discover Lysias's purpose in ordering the speech the way he did. Rather than admit Lysias's arbitrariness, as Socrates insinuates, Phaedrus instead claims that he is not "sufficient . . . to see through" Lysias's artistry (264b–c). Phaedrus's belief that Lysias did have a purpose is not unreasonable (see chapter 2), and Socrates himself said that no one could "miss the mark [*hamartanein*] entirely" (235e). But because Phaedrus does assume Lysias's purposefulness and skill, Socrates easily elicits agreement that speeches should be ordered like "living animals," with an organized "body" that does not lack any parts and has all these parts arranged "so as to fit one another and the whole" (264c). Socrates seems to subordinate the linear ordering of the speech, since that order will be determined by the nature of the speech as a unified whole. This holistic unity of speech differs from the unity of the true beings that Socrates described in his palinode, since being is "simple" and "one" (248b7–c1, 250c2–3), while a speech is a whole of parts and always multiform.[59] As Socrates suggests when ridiculing Lysias, a speech requires a singular purpose to join together the parts, which are in turn functionally related to the whole speech. But the holism entailed in a speech cannot be limited solely by the purpose of the speaker, as Socrates's preceding criteria for artful speaking indicate: *antilogic* uses semblances, which are at bottom words that mark shared meaning between rhetorician and audience; and the rhetorician must mark, define, and ultimately know his subject matter. A whole speech therefore depends upon, and relates to, successively larger wholes, drawing on the background of meaning that comprises language and the unity of being portrayed in the palinode. Similarly, the analogous living animal is a whole constituted within larger wholes, for it is a body moved by a soul (245e4–6), and in turn the soul's purposes and desires. Whatever unity a living animal or a speech seeks, that unity is greater than, and confers coherence and necessity to, the unity of the animal or speech as a whole unto itself.

In contrast, Lysias's speech is characterized as a dead and therefore unmoving and, as Ronna Burger says, "un-erotic" collection of things that cannot even be called parts since they have no necessary relation to one another.[60] But Socrates's final blow to Lysias's speech, a comparison with the epigraph on Midas's tomb, reveals an important difference between the linear and holistic senses of logographic necessity that limits the principle and undermines any conception of a speech as self-contained. The epigraph sings of its own undying testament to Midas:

> A bronze-clad maid, I lie still upon Midas' tomb [*sēma*],

> So long as water flows and trees grow tall,
> Remaining on this much-lamented grave,
> I will tell whoever goes by: Midas is buried within. (264d)

Socrates says "there is no difference whether a part of it is spoken first or last" (264e). Lacking linear order, the epigraph lacks logographic necessity, and as such is not a whole, but a kind of dead body. Being a dead husk seems to be the fate of a "mark" or "sign" (*sēma*).[61] But the possibility of rearranging these verses without altering the meaning of the epigraph implies that the epigraph communicates a unified whole, namely that this testament to Midas is unchanging ("I lie still") and eternal ("so long as. . ."). Socrates's comparison of Lysias's speech to the epigraph is therefore, on the one hand, a criticism, for the true nature of *erōs* cannot be discerned except through linear argumentation and refutation. A speech's life is constituted by its motion and temporality, in contrast to the fixity represented by the bronze-clad maiden. On the other hand, Socrates says that what constitutes the whole remains outside life and death, and therefore outside the speech's strict linear order.

This qualification of "logographic necessity," that its appeal to holistic unity depends upon wholes greater than the speech itself, appears in the expression of eternity in the second verse. Without the verse, "So long as water flows and trees grow tall," the epigraph could not communicate the immortality of itself and Midas; although the four verses may be rearranged, they are all necessary to the whole. But the interchangeable order of the verses is Socrates's contrivance; he has removed from the original source two verses that follow the second and extend that verse's theme of immortality.[62] This continuity between these three verses would prevent the original epigraph from being rearranged in the manner Socrates intended. He has therefore violated the original's logographic necessity, understood as linear order, to suit his own purpose—to demonstrate the importance of logographic necessity. Socrates's rhetorical purpose shapes the epigraph, constituting it whole and bringing life to its dead words. Similarly, when the reader reconstitutes the original epigraph in order to test Socrates's assertion that it can be rearranged in any way, the epigraph emphasizes that eternity is observed in the enduring cycles of nature. But examining the original source provides the insight that logographic necessity depends upon the writer's intentions, and those intentions in turn depend on his relation to or understanding of the nature of things. Socrates, by qualifying logographic necessity, shows that it is a phantom or imitation of the eternal necessity ("Adrasteia" [248b5–c5]) that binds writer and reader, speaker and audience, and soul and reality.

Socrates thus sets aside Lysias's speech as a negative example of rhetoric, being unable to lead the soul, neither marking nor defining the unified nature of *erōs* nor proceeding in any necessary order. It expresses what rhetoric is not, useful in "that someone might profit from [it] by looking at [it], if not by attempting to imitate [it]" (264e). Their present examination is therefore a simple instance of *antilogic*, leading Phaedrus from the opinion that Lysias is artful, even "the most clever of those now writing," to the opposite, that he is artless (228a). Socrates used the techniques of artful speaking as the mediating terms of his argument. The technical inadequacy of Lysias's speech is contrasted to Socrates's technical mastery. But the preceding analysis has shown that none of these techniques were necessary to produce persuasion, at least the temporary persuasion that wins immediate approbation (cf. 276b). Nor does Socrates ultimately defend his technically superior speeches simply because they use these techniques. Rather, he examines his own speeches to show the fundamental conditions—the structure of persuasion itself—that enable those techniques.

Socrates's analysis of his own speeches serves two purposes: the first is explicit, to identify *antilogic* in their structure and the rhetorical techniques employed; and the second is implicit, to qualify this conception of rhetorical art and cast doubt on the true artfulness of his speeches, since *logos* is a leading of soul that is animated by *erōs* and its attendant ignorance of the true nature of things. First, Socrates notes that his two speeches "were opposites," where "one said that favors must be granted to the lover, but the other to the non-lover" (265a). Phaedrus misunderstands this opposition, saying that Socrates had done so "very manfully," as if it were an eristic contest in which the excellence of a man is demonstrated by his power to deceive, irrespective of real understanding. Instead, the speeches, Socrates tells him, were done "madly, which was the very thing I was searching for [in the speeches]." Socrates expresses here the reflexivity of the speeches, that he sought out the very thing that moved him—that is, he sought to know himself—and therefore it was out of madness that he distinguished the two forms of madness, one "caused by human illness," and "the other coming about by a divine sudden change from our customary ways." His artful distinction was done out of the "sudden change" characteristic of *erōs*. Reflecting on his speeches, he looks at himself as if in a mirror, and undergoes the "sudden change" of divine *mania*; in contrast to his speechmaking, he has now become moderate and sober in order "to gather into one" their previous experiences (cf. 249c1). Socrates's reference to his own madness as the cause of his artfulness indicates that his use of opposites for persuasion arises from the structure of *erōs* itself, which at bottom is not the desire for the prizes of a manly contest but the desire to perceive what really is.

Socrates's recapitulation of his speeches is not entirely accurate, however, undermining their claim to artfulness on the criteria he has just outlined. His speeches were not opposites in every respect, since it was their agreement on the point that "*erōs* is a kind of *mania*" that permitted their rhetorical contrast on the question of whether *mania* is harmful (265a6–7; cf. 231d, 235e–236a, 241b–c). This agreement reveals how a rhetorician introduces a semblance, for in his desire to move from the rejection of *erōs* to its acceptance, Socrates used this agreement to make a plausible transition from Lysias's—and Phaedrus's—understanding of *erōs*.[63] He then discovered the goodness of *erōs* by a second "division," this time of the form of divine madness. Divine mania, Socrates says, was divided according to the god who inspires it: "the mantic from Apollo, the telestic from Dionysus, the poetic from the Muses, and the fourth from Aphrodite and Eros, which we said was the erotic and best madness" (265b). This apparent recapitulation is in fact a novel analysis that reveals Dionysus's association with the second madness. Dionysus was considered a foreign god, and so the exemplary other, a hidden and mysterious external force that now represents well "the divine sudden change from customary ways."[64] His inspiration of telestic madness thus explicitly links the turmoil of separation from divine grace to *erōs* as the experience of a presence of something outside immediate comprehension.[65]

Socrates's introduction of Dionysus is appropriate to the context, for he admits now that the true nature of *erōs* eluded them, despite the apparent clarity offered by his discussion of the *antilogic* of the two speeches and his isolation of *erōs* as a form of divine *mania*. He "expressed by likeness the erotic experience, perhaps on the one hand laying hold of something true, but on the other also being quickly carried another [way], having mixed a not altogether unpersuasive speech, we played a mythic hymn, both fitting and reverent" (265b–c). Such mixture is the nature of semblance, which shares in two things. Socrates's palinode was not misleading simply because it used myth and imagery, but because it cast a vision of *erōs* in speech and speech is itself a semblance. As discussed in chapter 3, Socrates had woven this conception of speech's limitation into the palinode by contrasting the particular beauties that were only likenesses or images of true beauty with true beauty itself, the complete nature of which transcended mortal experience and expression. Hence Socrates can now claim that this misleading speech, this "mythical hymn," was "both fitting and reverent." But at the time, Socrates attributed the poetic form of the speech to Phaedrus—that is, he adapted the speech to the desires and expectations of his audience (257a, 271e–272a). These two qualifications of the palinode link the inability of the *logos* to manifest the truth (otherwise it would be the truth simply) to leading the soul to a new perception of being.[66] Socrates formed the palinode in order to disabuse Phaedrus of his original opinion about *erōs*. The opposite opinion to which Socrates led him was therefore formed in relation to his first opinion, and was not the truth simply; because he needed to address Phaedrus's present opinions, his approach to the truth about *erōs* was indirect. Persuasion and rhetoric are possible because our immediate experience is with semblances, not truth. By way of the example of his own speech, Socrates shows Phaedrus how even artless speakers such as himself and Lysias can produce persuasion, albeit imperfectly.

Despite having just been taught that the speeches were untrue, Phaedrus reiterates the pleasure they brought him (265c). Somehow their opposition formed a beautiful and pleasing whole, and so for Phaedrus contradiction remains an impersonal and strictly formal concept, rather than an experience that compels him to seek the truth. The ethical problem that Phaedrus poses is clarified somewhat: he regards *logos* as something so divorced from what it signifies, and from his private understanding, that self-contradiction is insignificant. Feasted on superficially pleasing rhetoric, Phaedrus is obstinate to more fundamental persuasion.[67] Socrates's argument, that artful rhetoric requires knowledge, must become ethically significant for Phaedrus, who is devoted neither to truth nor to ordering his soul, but to hearing pleasing speeches. Socrates must now show that the rhetorical success of his speeches reflected some fundamental knowledge of *erōs*.

## DIALECTIC

In order to demonstrate the artfulness of his two speeches, Socrates has shown that they were opposites and therefore together exhibit persuasiveness and *antilogic*. Now he must show just how they "crossed over from censure to praise," presumably on account of his knowledge (262a2). The techniques of marking, definition, and logographic necessity were only a prelude, but "by some good fortune" they found two basic "forms of speaking" that together comprise dialectic (265c8–9). This is a crucial moment in the *Phaedrus*, as dialectic appears to be the means to obtain the arguments and knowledge required for artful rhetoric.[68] But dialectic's function in coming to know is ambiguous, first because its artful use seems to depend upon prior knowledge, and second because it is ubiquitous in language. Furthermore, in reviewing the dialectical nature of his arguments about *erōs*, and by alluding to his own *erōs*, Socrates suggests that dialectic, far from being a neutral method for revealing the true nature of things, is grounded in an erotic relation to reality and therefore only intimates the nature of things.

The first form of speaking is "collection" (*sunagōgē*): "to lead the many scattered things that are seen together into one form, in order that someone may, by defining [*horizein*], make each thing clear concerning what one should ever wish to teach" (265d3–5).[69] Collection is the principle underlying Socrates's earlier demands for marking, definition, and logographic necessity, all of which help gather together manifold perceptions into a unified whole. This "one" produced by definition does not, however, necessarily reveal the true nature of the object. Socrates's example of collection makes this clear: "[with respect to] the things said about *erōs*, what it is when defined, whether said well or badly, the speech at any rate was able on account of this to say what was clear and agreed with itself" (265d). As noted earlier, using the technique of definition is insufficient for speaking well, although it does provide the clear object needed for the second form of speaking that comprises dialectic; the monument that collection produces is, or should be considered, provisional with respect to the nature of the object.

The second form is "division" (*diairesis*): "to be able to cut up again according to form along the natural joints, and to attempt to not break any of the parts, acting in the manner of an inept butcher" (265e). This implies that objects of perception can always be seen under general terms that are subject to division. The image of the butcher juxtaposes Socrates's analogy of speech to a living animal; now, the living speech is rendered a dead collection of parts. Analysis breaks apart the whole, removing the soul that coheres a speech and makes it self-moving. Only another collection would reanimate the object by putting it into relation to the form that gives it its shape and unity. The life or self-animation that Socrates alludes to seems to lie in the recursive coordination of cutting up and gathering together, which are joined together by the desire to clarify the nature of the object in question.

Socrates's review of his own division of *erōs* exhibits the necessary coordination of division and collection, but also their limitation for coming to know. Together, his two speeches took "the senseless [*aphrōn*] part of the mind as one particular form" and cut it into the left- and right-handed (265e–266a). In the first speech, he continued dividing the left side of "madness" (rather than *mania*, Socrates here uses *paranoia*, which conveys something outside of, yet near or alongside, intellection)[70] until he "found among the parts an *erōs* . . . that it greatly abused with justice." The fact that this division was at the time called defining (237c1, 241b7)—that is, a technique of collection—indicates that collection and division are coordinate, since collection is of diverse objects and division is of collected ones—collection and division presuppose one another, each implicit in the use of the other.[71] Accordingly, in the palinode, the collection of various kinds of *maniai* were also the division of *mania*: "[amongst] the parts of madness, we discovered and put forward an *erōs* homonymous with that other one, but divine, and praised it as the cause of our greatest goods" (266a–b). This example of collection and division also shows that they did not produce a form of *erōs* in its wholeness—its truth is only approached by re-collecting these two imperfect forms of *erōs*. Since Socrates's leading of Phaedrus to the opposite only proved the negative, that Lysias's definition was not entirely true and incomplete, this entailed that the new account would also be incomplete. Only Socrates's present review of his two speeches, which reconciles them as one antilogical movement, provides a comprehensive view of *erōs*.

This comprehensive view of *erōs* is notable for its reflexivity, providing in an example of dialectic a compact psychological foundation for dialectic. Here, *erōs* is a division of the "senseless" (*aphrōn*), which in turn is a part of mind (*dianoia*). Compared to Socrates's previous recollections of *erōs*, the new insight here is that mind comprehends sense and senselessness. Mind itself therefore cannot be equated with a determinate sensibility or rationality, as the nonlover would have it, but is only found by opposing and then transcending the sensibility that presumes to know. This structure resembles the image of the winged chariot, in which the charioteer harnessed together the obedient horse and the unruly horse, and recalls the form of the soul's ascent, looking beyond manifold appearances in search of being itself. This common structure links the desire of the unruly horse and the soul's ascent in self-overcoming, which disrupts presumed sensibility or "mortal good sense" (256e). But this structure of self-overcoming raises the question whether the comprehensive "mind" itself becomes determinate and therefore in need of a new opposition. Can *erōs* really be domesticated as a part of mind? The palinode was inconclusive on this point, claiming both that mind alone perceives true reality (247c7–8) and that mind desires the beauty that gives it coherence (251b6–c1, 255c6–d3, 256a7–8).[72] Plato has suggested a difficult problem in the psychology underpinning dialectic.

Given this problematic psychological foundation for dialectic, Socrates's professed love for dialectic—and lack of skill in it—idealizes dialectic but also its function within his larger argument that artful rhetoric requires knowledge. Although collection and division do not alone produce knowledge of the beings, Socrates claims that he is "a lover" of them "in order that I am able both to speak and to think" (266b). Together, they are the ability "to look to one and many"—that is, the unity of being perceived through its many semblances—and Socrates will "follow behind him in his footsteps as if he were a god" whoever "naturally" possesses this ability. Socrates calls this expert "a dialectician," and the art itself dialectic. The dialectician appears to possess the knowledge to perform collection and division perfectly. But since Socrates can only follow the dialectician and hesitates in so naming him, the full nature of dialectic seems to elude him (266b8). The problem seems to be whether conversation ("dialectic" is from *dialegesthai*, "to converse") can adequately unify the two opposite forms of collection and division, neither of which is by itself sufficient to reveal the nature of its object. Dialectic may constitute perfect speaking and require perfect knowledge of its object, but it only indirectly expresses that knowledge by leading the soul to contradiction, and is not that knowledge itself.[73] As Mary Mackenzie (1982) puts it, "collection and division is a method of analysis . . . but in order to analyse we must know what we're doing."[74] So if dialectic is to be more than a means to articulate what is already known, it must proceed imperfectly, collecting and dividing anew when one has "missed the mark."[75] Its fallibility indeed provides indirect evidence of its presence in all speech and thought, as dialectic can be found even in Lysias's artless and ignorant speech, when he generalized to, and deduced from, the forms of lover and nonlover, or in Socrates's admittedly inadequate definition of *erōs* (234c–d, 237d–238a).[76]

Socrates's love of the art of dialectic nuances his account of it, for his *erōs* expresses his ignorance of dialectic even while *erōs* is, as he claims, a part of mind. On the one hand, dialectic is necessary for, even essential to, speaking and thinking because it is the way to differentiate semblance and being. Yet on the other hand, dialectic's capacity to show the beings themselves, and therefore whether it is sufficient for and constitutes the true art of speaking, must remain elusive, for the form of dialectic can only be grasped dialectically. If dialectic is necessary yet also insecure, how will Phaedrus know that Socrates's dialectical account of *erōs* was in accordance with the nature of *erōs* except by inquiring for himself?

Socrates's earlier equivocation whether the art of rhetoric really is "one art" neatly expresses this ambiguous relationship between dialectic and knowledge, inasmuch as inquiry into the nature of the art must be dialectical and therefore collect together the art with what resembles it, thus multiplying the possible forms of an art of speaking (261e1–2). Not only does the question of the nature of the art of speaking remain open ("if someone would be able to grasp their power [of collection and division] by art" [265d1]), it remains fundamentally open because it is essential to all inquiry and must at some point become its own object, animated by the need to reconcile itself into one.[77] Dialectic in this way expresses the self-moving soul, animated by *erōs*, that acts upon itself. As such, Socrates formulates his following of the dialectician—the embodiment of the "one art"—as an allusion to Odysseus, who longingly followed the goddesses Athena and Calypso, never taking the lead and eventually parting ways with them so that he could find what is good for a mortal.[78] Though *antilogic* and dialectic clarify our opinions, they can only reveal the nature of being indirectly, through the opposition of opinions—that is, the opposition of what is said to be and what is not. Since the true nature of being remains hidden in the "background," Socrates's *erōs* for that truth sets in motion his mind and dialectical search.[79] At the apparent apex of the art of rhetoric, Socrates's attempt to grasp dialectic compels him to continue his inquiry by dividing dialectic from its semblances, and so he must distinguish the true art of rhetoric from its conventional practice by searching for the forms of collection and division through their images.[80] When he asks Phaedrus, "Is this [dialectic] that art of speaking by which Thrasymachus and the others have come to be wise with respect to speaking?" their search begins anew.

## Chapter 4
## ON TECHNIQUE

At this point in his argument, Socrates has explained that the art of rhetoric is the ability to lead the soul of the audience from one thing to its opposite—*antilogic*—and that in order to do this reliably and without error the rhetorician must know of what he speaks. Socrates's analysis drew on an implicit desire for unity at work in *antilogic* and in the techniques that evidence the rhetorician's knowledge—marking disputable terms, definition, and logographic necessity—and this desire then became explicit in dialectic. But Socrates cast doubt on whether any of *antilogic*, marking, defining, logographic necessity, or dialectic could themselves capture in *logos* the unified, singular, being that is the real object of knowledge. Instead, he pointed back to his own ignorance and *erōs* as that which inspires *logos* in its collections and divisions of the images of being. Socrates thus refers back to *erōs* as that which *logos* must satisfy in representing being. In suggesting this role for psychology in the use of speech, Socrates anticipates Phaedrus's objection to the definition of the art of rhetoric as dialectic. Phaedrus's objection is that this definition of rhetoric as dialectic overlooks the rhetorical techniques found in manuals and so, without these techniques, bears no resemblance to rhetorical practice. It will be shown that this great variety of rhetorical techniques—varying in form and efficacy—can only be explained with the introduction of another object for rhetoric, besides knowledge of being, and that object is the profoundly complex and erotic soul. Dialectic must accommodate the variation in souls upon which it works. Accordingly, in showing Phaedrus that the artful use of speech is determined in relation to the soul, Socrates accommodates and adapts his dialectic to Phaedrus's soul and the opinions he holds.

Socrates begins the next phase of their discussion by asking whether the rhetoricians, including Lysias, have this art of dialectic. Phaedrus confirms that they do not, which implies that they do not have the art of speaking. Phaedrus is not ashamed to admit this because he is not persuaded that dialectic is the art of speaking: "The form of rhetoric somehow eludes us" (266c). What Socrates presented does not resemble rhetoric as he, Lysias, and no doubt most people conceive it. Phaedrus presumes to possess, not unreasonably, some knowledge of rhetoric because of his experience with its practice. If dialectic is indeed the true art of speaking, Socrates must reconcile dialectic with that practice, showing how acknowledged practitioners either manifest or fail to manifest the art. In order to do so, Socrates must clarify Phaedrus's rather obscure opinion about the nature of rhetoric before collecting it together with dialectic. Phaedrus's objection is that they have neglected the many techniques written down in manuals of rhetoric. He poses the problem whether or not these techniques can be considered the art of rhetoric simply, and if not, what does the art consist of beyond its techniques? Phaedrus thus takes up the other part of rhetoric suggested by the personified art of rhetoric: not the possession of truth, but the way by which even truth is made persuasive (cf. 260d4–9).

Socrates displays, albeit in a mocking tone, a broad reading of the subject. He mentions to Phaedrus twenty-seven rhetorical techniques, most of which he attributes to nine famous teachers of rhetoric. With this survey, Socrates accomplishes at least three notable things that clarify the place of technique in the art of rhetoric. First, he suggests that these techniques are derivative of the principles and techniques already discussed. Several techniques—for example, "preamble" and "recapitulation"—refer to the ordering of a speech, which contribute to the linear sense of logographic necessity and establish the sequence of "small steps" in *antilogic* (262a, 264b, 266d–e). Prodicus's "fitting length" recalls how the rhetorician must move through those steps knowledgably, saying neither too much nor too little (267b). Several techniques are structured as contraries that deliberately recall Zeno's skill in *antilogic*, most notably Gorgias's technique "to make small things appear large" and Thrasymachus's alternately angering and soothing his audience (261d–e, 267a–b, c–d). Socrates attributes to Polus and Protagoras "correctness of diction," which derives from the marking of terms and definition (267b–c). Other techniques recall the use of semblances to deceive, such as Evenus's "covert allusion" and "indirect praise or censure," or Polus's "speaking with images" (267a, c). All these techniques are ways of relating parts of a speech, which is the formal function of the semblance in *antilogic* and ultimately achieved by collection and division—that is, dialectic. Although these twenty-seven techniques have particular functions or objects—for example, Gorgias's technique deals with smallness—this only confirms that while there is an endless variety of techniques, they all stem from the same root of dialectic. Socrates himself makes use, just in the *Phaedrus* alone, of almost all of the techniques he mentions (the exceptions are those techniques of Teisias, Gorgias, and Thrasymachus, that are explicitly aimed at a crowd—an exception that will prove significant to both Socratic and Platonic rhetoric).[81] But the weight that the rhetoricians give to technique, reflected in Socrates's mocking praise ("many fine things" [267c6–7]), indicates their ignorance of the basic principles of their art.

Socrates's second accomplishment in his survey follows closely on the first. In the sheer variety of techniques, some of which are merely inversions, reduplications, and extensions of others, and particularly in the contradictory tendency of some techniques, Socrates indicates that any individual technique will be useful in limited circumstances, to be supplemented with other techniques. Socrates exposes this problem when he rebuts Teisias (said to be Lysias's teacher)[82] and Gorgias, who boast of skill in "conciseness and unlimited length of speech concerning everything," with Prodicus's joking discovery that speeches should be "neither long nor short" but "fitting" (*metri-*

*os*) (267a–b). This need for fittingness points back to the presupposition of unity in *antilogic* and the need for speeches to be whole unto themselves. Socrates will soon argue that the rhetorician must develop this knowledge of what is fitting for any given speech.[83]

Socrates' third accomplishment in his survey is to indicate where the proper use of rhetorical techniques might be found. Thrasymachus's techniques, particularly that of alternately arousing and soothing, place *antilogic* within the context of the full nature of the soul, drawing on the passions associated with the horses rather than the charioteer (253c7–e5, 254a2, a7–b1, c3–7, e7–8; but cf. 254b5–c1). The fact that Thrasymachus is the ninth rhetorician that Socrates mentions strengthens the insinuation that such speech corrupts the order of the soul, for Socrates had ranked the tyrant ninth among souls in terms of its vision of true being (248e3). When this insinuation is taken together with his observation of Thrasymachus's power with "the many," Socrates suggests that rhetoric may derive strength or efficacy in part from the ineptitude and psychological disorder of the audience. But in the palinode, Socrates showed that the soul's passionate arousal is incited by its awareness of its separation from true being, which is the very separation that incites reasoning—the passions of the horses are therefore only parts or aspects of the passion that moves the entire soul (251b6–7, 253e5–6). Although Thrasymachus may exploit weakness of the intellect or even suppress its activation, he can only do so because the passions he arouses are akin to the soul's fundamental *erōs*. Socrates's invocation of Thrasymachus therefore hints at the place of technique within the art of rhetoric, as they achieve their effects insofar as their use is attuned to the desirous nature of the soul.

With Phaedrus's understanding of rhetoric now clarified as the invention and application of techniques, Socrates proposes that they "look more closely at these things under the light, and [see] what power of the art they hold" (268a). His approach is dialectical, gathering together this understanding of the art of rhetoric as technique with other arts. In doing so, he detects "a gap in [the rhetoricians'] warp." Socrates examines arts that are familiar and dear to Phaedrus, medicine and poetry, before comparing them directly to rhetoric. In each case, he asks acknowledged masters of the art whether the application of techniques is the whole of the art.

Socrates begins with medicine as it is a model art, with seemingly self-evident ends, and also the most familiar to Phaedrus, given his friendship with the physicians Eryximachus and his father Acumenus. Socrates presents the would-be physician who believes the mere application of techniques to be sufficient for medical art:

> I know how to apply such things to the bodies, so as to both warm and cool them if I wish, and if it seems best to me, to make them vomit, and again if [it seems best to me], to make their bowels move, and many other such things;

and knowing these things, I am a worthy physician and [I am able] to make another to whom I pass on knowledge of these things. (268a–b)

Phaedrus scoffs at the pretensions of this amateur physician: Eryximachus and Acumenus would think him "mad" to believe that he was a physician simply because he "had heard something somewhere from a book or chanced upon some trifling drugs [*pharmakia*]" (268c). As Socrates anticipated in his argument about the donkey presented as a horse, knowledge of an instrument implies knowledge of its proper use, and now Phaedrus confidently asserts that a physician must "also know for whom and when it is necessary to do each of these things, and to what extent." Socrates has chosen this first example well, as Phaedrus himself has provided the basic solution to the question of the place of knowledge of technique in art.

Phaedrus assumes that the end of medicine is bodily health, which determines the usefulness of medical techniques. But the *Phaedrus* has already alluded to some ambiguity in that assumption. Socrates contrasted the prescription of "noble" Acumenus with that of Herodicus, who devised regimens out of an obsessive fear of death (227a4–b1, d3–4). Other Platonic dialogues more explicitly question the ultimate end of medicine. In the *Symposium*, Eryximachus makes clear that he does not aim at simple bodily health, but instead seeks to establish a "harmony" in the body so one may enjoy the pleasures of both "good" and "bad" loves even when they would be "out of season" (*akairos*).[84] Eryximachus's highest aim, which guides his application of the two loves, is the continual experience of pleasure without obstruction by the body—the same end that Phaedrus elevated to the purpose of life (258e).[85] The end of medicine thus leads to the question, bodily health for the sake of what? In the *Republic*, Socrates raised this issue with reference to the good of the city, which subordinated all the arts. Should a physician treat the body of a man whose soul is corrupted or is useless to the city?[86] Since the body is only a part of the greater whole of the "living animal," the treatment of the body cannot be reduced to its preservation. Medicine is the first of the three arts that Socrates discusses not only because of its familiarity to Phaedrus, but also because its object is in the end subordinate to the object of the other arts Socrates discusses, which is the soul.

The second art that Socrates uses to illustrate the proper use of technique is poetry, which is represented by the celebrated tragedians Sophocles and Euripides. In poetry's use of speech, there is a closer resemblance to rhetoric than medicine. Indeed, Socrates has an amateur poet present to the two masters expressly rhetorical techniques—"making long utterances on small things and very short ones on great things, piteous speeches whenever he wished, and the opposite, frightening and threatening ones"—as evidence of his capacity to make tragedies and to teach others the same (268c). But Socrates's example of the use of speeches in poetry does not simply repeat the argument he made in the case of medical techniques, because the object of poetry is more ambiguous than that of medicine. Phaedrus sees that the amateur poet's error is the same as Lysias's, that he does not know the proper "arrangement" of these techniques "so as to fit one another and the whole"—he quotes verbatim Socrates's principle of logographic necessity (268d; cf. 264c5). As seen in the discussion of logographic necessity, however, the "whole" is ambiguous. Is the whole the poem itself, analogous to the whole of a living animal? This cannot be the case. Socrates says that the purpose of poetry is not simply to produce "the highest and lowest notes on a string," but to harmonize those notes. Like the drugs used by medicine are not the object of medicine, musical notes themselves are not the object of musical art or poetry. The application of these techniques is determined by the proper condition of the art's object, the body in the case of medicine and now the soul in the case of poetry. As suggested by the principle of logographic necessity, a speech or poem cannot be properly arranged without knowledge of how its words can be used to properly affect the soul. If the harmony to which poetry aims is believed to exist solely within the poem itself, on its own terms as it were, the poet would lose sight of his principal object, the soul that experiences the pleasures of speech and music and judges the harmony to be good or bad, and so lose sight of the highest harmony (cf. 277b–c). Hence Socrates subtly inserts "the musical man"—a life that he ranked among the highest, alongside the philosopher (248d2–4)—as the one who makes harmony, rather than the tragedians (268d6–e6). In addition to placing art in relation to its effect on the soul, Socrates indicates the ethical consequences of so doing, for the musical man does not abuse the amateur for being ignorant, as Phaedrus did the amateur physician, but rather "being musical [says] gently" that he only "knew the things to be learned before harmony, but not harmonics" (268d–e). Knowing harmony, the musical man produces harmony in his student and, conducting himself harmoniously, is himself harmonious. Since his object is a state of soul, the musical man is able to produce that state within himself.

Returning to the art of rhetoric, Socrates identifies as exemplary rhetoricians Pericles and "the honey-voiced Adrastus," the legendary king of Argos (269a).[87] In turning to statesmen, Socrates not only repudiates contemporary teachers of rhetoric, but also returns to the most public use of speech and most public of arts, concerned with the preservation of the city as a whole and therefore with the objects of both previous arts, the preservation of the body and the harmonizing of citizens (cf. 239c–d). Like the musical man, the "wiser" statesman follows a gentler course in instruction (269b3). Pericles thus says:

> One must not be harsh but forgiving, if some people who do not know dialectic prove unable to define what rhetoric is, and from this experience of having

the things that must be learned before the art believe [themselves] to have discovered rhetoric, [and] that when they teach these things to others they [believe themselves to] have taught rhetoric completely [*teleōs*], and as for each of them [the students] speaking persuasively and arranging the whole, since it is no work at all, they must furnish [this] in their speeches from their own learning. (269b–c)

Socrates ironically puts these words in the mouth of Pericles, whose own knowledge of dialectic, and therefore rhetoric, is doubtful. Through dialectic, the rhetorician will be able to give an account of his art as it truly is and so perfect it, as Socrates and Phaedrus are themselves attempting to do, alternately collecting and dividing its principles and practices in relation to other arts in order to clearly distinguish "the rhetorical form" itself. Here, the nature of rhetoric is described as a synthesis of the advice offered by the physicians and poets, including the knowledge of both "for whom and when . . . and to what extent" to use rhetorical techniques and how they are to be arranged as parts of the whole of a speech. "The whole" that rhetoric arranges thus entails both senses of logographic necessity, linear and holistic, and can only be understood in relation to the audience's soul. The object of rhetoric has doubled, now including the soul alongside the subject matter. Without knowledge of both, there is neither an art of rhetoric nor the possibility of it being taught. This contradicts the claims of a rhetorician like Gorgias, who believed rhetoric to be a neutral art and that he could teach how to speak well in a law court without teaching what justice is[88]—that is, he believed that there is no necessary relationship between form and content, between "speaking persuasively and arranging the whole" and knowing the subject matter of the speech.

Phaedrus now claims to be persuaded that the art of rhetoric does not consist merely of the knowledge of techniques, and that a rhetorician must also possess dialectic and knowledge of the whole—knowledge of how a speech is formed in relation to its audience. Socrates has thus led him to a fuller conception of rhetoric as "a leading of the soul," which does not just use techniques to produce various states, but to produce those states in the right souls, at the right time, and to the right extent. As Socrates suggested at the beginning of their discussion, the art of rhetoric has a proper use, which he has now shown to be partly determined by its object, the soul. But since Phaedrus has just now learned of the existence of dialectic, and since the rhetoricians do not seem to teach it, he is right to ask Socrates, "How might someone be able to acquire for himself the art of the real rhetorician and persuasive man?" (269c9–d1). Socrates gives three basic criteria for becoming a perfect rhetorician: a suitable "nature"; "knowledge" (*epistēmē*); "and practice" (269d). Such a man would be "a complete competitor . . . but with regard to so much of it as is art, the way [*methodos*] appears to be, it seems to me, not [the way] by which Lysias and Thrasymachus travel [*poreuesthai*]."[89] The true way of rhetoric is thus disclosed through the refutation of the conventional way of rhetoric that uses techniques according to the whim of the rhetorician—that is, without knowledge (*epistēmē*) of the soul; the way that travels under the heavens, as it were, is perceived through dialectic, but therefore only dimly, by negation (Socrates said the heavenly way entails turns [247a4–7]). To call this hidden and heavenly way a "method" would therefore assume too much,[90] but the present clearing of the way is the first step in acquiring the art of the real rhetorician.

## THE NOBLE RHETORIC

Socrates has now placed the art of speaking at the pinnacle of the arts, but claims for it such a grand object that some incredulity must begin to creep in. Commentators have widely criticized Socrates's account of the true rhetoric, generally regarding it as either a "regulative ideal" or ironic, although the purpose of such irony is usually explained by some variation of the former, namely that Socrates proposes a deliberately inadequate account as propaedeutic toward philosophy.[91] The inadequacy of his account of rhetoric is generally inferred from its scope, since it becomes a study of the whole of nature.[92] But this is only a practical consideration, not one in principle. Indeed, the art as Socrates presents it is inadequate if it is understood as unreflexive and instrumental (i.e., subject solely to whims of the rhetorician), a neutral and disengaged dialectical analysis of the soul, since this view does not account for the interaction between the souls of rhetorician and audience in the course of analysis, and the self-development that must occur in the rhetorician to properly execute that analysis and perfect his art.[93] Rather, Socrates's account of the noble rhetoric is an ethical one, not primarily in the sense that the rhetorician must apply speeches that are beneficial and conducive to virtue, but in the sense that the rhetorician must reflect upon himself, pursuing self-knowledge, and in so doing constitute his own soul sufficiently to achieve the highest knowledge of soul that will allow him to invent and apply speeches "fittingly."

The question before Socrates is how someone might acquire the knowledge of soul that guides the use of rhetorical technique. Socrates once again begins his inquiry with a commonly held opinion. Apparent reversing what he said in the *Gorgias*, Socrates claims that the celebrated[94] Pericles "likely proved to be the most complete of all in rhetoric" because he joined rhetoric with the study of nature (269e).[95] In fact, "all such great arts need in addition babbling and lofty talk concerning nature, for in all things this high-mindedness and perfect workmanship seems to come from such a place" (269e4–270a3). The ends of these arts, as suggested by the examples of medicine and poetry, must be placed in relation to the natures of their objects, not simply pure in themselves, but to those natures as expressed in their possible activities and uses. According to Socrates, this comprehensive view of the nature of an art's object requires a study of nature as a whole. His mocking tone for this claim, adopting popular terms of disparagement for the study of nature,[96] points to the problem of whether such study of nature can become true knowledge, as mere "babbling and lofty talk" will be of no help to the true and noble rhetorician.[97]

Pericles, for his part, "was filled with this lofty talk" by associating with the natural philosopher Anaxagoras, who taught "the nature of mind and mindlessness [lit. intellect and lack of intellect, *nous te kai anoia*]" (270a).[98] If indeed the study of nature is essential to rhetoric, Pericles's skill as a rhetorician depends upon the quality of that teaching. Given Socrates's low opinion of Anaxagoras's teaching, described in other Platonic dialogues but generally insinuated here in the tone of "babbling" and "lofty talk," it seems that the belief that Pericles was the most complete rhetorician must be qualified. But Anaxagoras nonetheless serves as a useful example for Socrates, since Phaedrus likely knew of his widely disseminated beliefs,[99] and because those beliefs—particularly that nature is mechanistic and materialistic, and in this way rational—reinforce Phaedrus's inclination toward judging according to sense experience and the nonlover's related instrumental conception of *logos*.[100] Indeed, Socrates inaccurately paraphrases Anaxagoras, claiming he posited a duality between "mind and mindlessness,"[101] in an allusion to his own first speech, wherein he posited a similar dichotomy between purely moderate "mind" (*nous*) and "mindless" (*anoētos*) *erōs* (241a3–4, c1).

In that speech, a moderate man's interest in intercourse was purely aesthetic, which consequently made his persuasion of the beloved inexplicable. Either he contradicted his professed selfless moderation or admitted that he was moved by destructively "mindless" *erōs*. On this view, the speaker's interest cannot be in benefiting his audience, but only his own self-aggrandizement. Absent a higher principle that could encompass both moderation and *erōs*, and therefore comprehend a self-interest in benefiting another—the good or right-handed *erōs*—the question of "for whom, when, and to what extent" rhetorical techniques should be applied can only be answered to the extent that those techniques serve the speaker's desires, as Socrates insinuated about Lysias and Thrasymachus.

Accordingly, Socrates's association of Pericles with Anaxagoras's teaching suggests that his rhetoric ultimately failed in the same respect, and if Pericles's study of nature did make him "the most complete of all rhetoricians," it is only because the others were entirely ignorant that their art requires the study of nature.[102] Just as the dichotomy of moderation and *erōs* led to their reconciliation in Socrates's palinode, Socrates characterizes Anaxagoras's philosophy as a dichotomy between "mind and mindlessness" in order to suggest the need for their reconciliation under a higher principle that would in turn explain when and to what extent a speech would truly be reasonable or unreasonable.[103] This will prove to be the fruit of Socrates's proposed study of nature.

That the goodness of the soul is part of the study of its nature is seen in Socrates's analogy to medicine's study of the body. Socrates explains to Phaedrus that the study of nature should be part of the rhetorician's education because "the way [or: manner, *tropos*] of the medical art and rhetorical art is the same," arguing that since medicine produces health in a body and rhetoric persuasion in a soul, the study of their respective objects entails studying their particular natures and nature a whole (270b). "In both [of these arts] . . . it is necessary to distinguish [*diairein*] a nature," otherwise one will only proceed by "knack [*tribē*] or experience." This also explains why the earlier analogy of these arts concluded that art requires knowledge of "for whom, when, and to what extent" its techniques should be used, for without knowledge of the nature of a body, one will not know how to apply various "drugs and diets." A nature is not merely the collection of distinct parts, anatomy, but includes what is good for the body as a whole, namely "strength and health." Without knowledge of the body in its complete and perfect state, one cannot produce the end of medicine, and therefore cannot be said to possess the medical art. By analogy, one cannot possess the rhetorical art if one does not know how to "apply speeches and lawful practices" in order "to pass on whatever conviction and excellence [or: virtue, *aretē*] one wishes."

This function of rhetoric is novel in the history of Greek rhetoric and to this point has only been hinted at in the *Phaedrus*, when the palinode's true lovers were joined in philosophic discourse by a love that sought the knowledge that would order, "perfect," and "nourish" their souls (247c–d, 249c–d, 253a, 255a, 256a–b). Socrates is only now able to state this function of rhetoric after he refuted a number of obstructive opinions, particularly the opinions that rhetoric does not need knowledge and that it consists of a collection of techniques, applied in whatever manner the speaker wishes. Socrates now claims for rhetoric the power that he attributed to justice in the *Gorgias*, which suggested a higher or noble rhetoric.[104] In suggesting that rhetoric may cultivate virtue, two forms of rhetoric are now distinguishable: rhetoric of artless knack and caprice, ignorant of dialectic, as practiced by contemporary rhetoricians; and noble rhetoric that knowingly cleaves to the excellence of the soul. This explains Socrates's equivocation, that rhetoric may produce "whatever conviction and excellence *one wishes*," for although rhetoric is a useful instrument for achieving one's desires, the true art of rhetoric is coextensive with knowledge of the nature and therefore excellence of soul. Therefore, like the teacher of harmony who speaks gently because he is himself "musical," and like the Zeus-kin of the palinode who "will do everything so that [his beloved] will become such a sort," the rhetorician, knowing what is good for others and for himself, will as much as possible be good and desire to produce excellence in others (cf. 268e3, 252e1–5, 253a3–b1). The question of the *Gorgias*, whether or not the rhetorician must know and teach virtue, and whether he must be virtuous himself, is thus implicit in the *Phaedrus* and emerges at the climax of Socrates's argument that the art of rhetoric requires knowledge.[105]

With Phaedrus, Socrates has so far approached the noble rhetoric exclusively through the question of efficacy, where even if the rhetorician's aims are low, they can only be reliably achieved if he possesses knowledge of soul "sufficient for his purposes."[106] But Phaedrus is not convinced medicine and rhetoric do indeed share the same "way," responding to Socrates's analogy with his usual "it is likely" (270b10). While ignorant use of medical techniques will produce relatively obvious ill effects, the effects of a sham rhetoric will not be so evident and easily distinguishable from those of a noble rhetoric, for the principal objects of soul are matters of great dispute (263a–b). A soul's "conviction" can be easily divorced from excellence, granting great power and scope to the ignoble use of rhetoric.[107] Socrates obscures this by saying that the rhetorician "applies speeches and lawful practices," relying on the common identification of law with goodness, even though his earlier mentions of the law suggested that it inhibits divine *erōs* (as well as merely human *erōs*), and it is unclear how a speaker could apply practices without having already persuaded or otherwise compelled the audience (cf. 252a). Socrates thus uses his own rhetoric to compel Phaedrus to judge the art not according to its current practice, but according to its perfection.[108]

Rather than take up the validity of the analogy of health to virtue, Socrates presses on to a still more radical claim about the knowledge required of a rhetorician. He asks Phaedrus, "Do you suppose it is possible to comprehend [lit. to thoroughly understand, *katanoēsai*] the nature of soul in a way worth speaking of without [comprehending] the nature of the whole?" (270c). Following Socrates's lead, Phaedrus applies the medical analogy: "If indeed one is bound to trust Hippocrates of the Asclepiads, neither [is it possible to comprehend] [the] body without this method [*methodos*]." In comparing body and soul on this point, Phaedrus inadvertently suggests a difference between them. Which "whole" is relevant? The whole soul for the rhetoricians and the whole body for Hippocrates? Or must one know "the whole" simply, that is, the whole of nature? On the one hand, Phaedrus surely did not mean the whole of nature, although Socrates's discussions of medicine and poetry implied that the arts constitute their objects as wholes in relation to a still greater whole. Most physicians are unconcerned with the soul or even nonhuman bodies, and the following discussion of the Hippocratic-cum-rhetorical method appears taxonomic and analytical, proceeding from a whole body or soul to its parts.[109] Moreover, the body, as a physical object, is perceived as a whole unto itself, whose parts are understood in relation to each other and the whole, and it is with respect to that whole that health is judged. On the other hand, the dialectical nature of the present passage suggests that "the whole" must be understood as the whole of nature. Socrates himself suggests considering the question of method in light of dialectic when he says that each art "must distinguish [*diairein*] a nature"—that is, divide, which is a component of dialectic. Socrates used the other aspect of dialectic, collection, when he claims that medicine and rhetoric share a "way": he placed the two arts in dialectical relation and so in relation to a more general form of art.[110] Socrates's subsequent analysis of their shared method shows that a dialectical approach depends upon placing the objects in question in relation to a larger whole.

Socrates says that the method of comprehending the nature of the whole is what "Hippocrates and the true *logos* say" (270c). In order to become an "expert," a *technikos*, one must first "comprehend [or: to think through, *dianoeisthai*] the nature of anything whatsoever" by beginning with the basic dialectical problem, which is to determine whether the object is "simple" (*haploos*) or "complex" or "of many forms" (*polueidēs*) (270c–d). This means that a complex whole may possess a nature unto itself, although understanding it entails understanding its constituent forms. How one determines whether the object is simple or complex is implied in the next step. The second step to becoming an expert is to study the object's natural "power" in active and passive forms: "the power it possesses for acting on some particular thing"; and "the power [it possesses] to experience on account of some particular thing" (270d). In other words, one must study "the deeds and experiences" of the object in relation to whatever it interacts with (245c4). As seen in the discussions of *antilogic* and dialectic, the purpose of this method is to isolate the form on the principle of noncontradiction; if, when an object is put in relation with another thing, it undergoes a change in one respect but not another, it cannot be truly simple.[111] Furthermore, that which produces a given effect must also be subjected to division in order to determine whether a particular form in it or the whole of it caused such a change. If the object is complex, the third step is to count its constituent forms and then, just as with the simple object, to study each with respect to its active and passive powers. A constituent form and the whole it shares in are therefore tested by the same method. A complex object as a whole is itself not tested as to its "powers" for the same reason that that test was able to isolate the simple form—since any contradictory effects indicate complexity, the forms responsible for these effects must be differentiated.

On the face of it, this "way" is analytical and taxonomic, representing only one form of dialectic, division, which "comprehends" the whole as merely a sum of parts rather than a whole with its own powers. That is, the object is rendered dead and "butchered" (cf. 264c2–5, 265e1–3). But the test for complexity shows that the forms of the object are only revealed in relation to what is other than it, in a larger context implicit in every use of speech. Socrates's earlier account of dialectic, and the examples he found in his speeches, showed that this relation implies a larger whole. For example, *erōs* was first collected as a form of senselessness, and on the basis of that larger whole was then divided into its human and divine forms, just as the difference between a left and right hand is comprehended only in relation to the whole body.[112] Marking and defining are relational activities, collecting together while at once dividing that object from other similar objects. This also clarifies why the simplest forms, those of the pure and unmixed beings, elude comprehensive definition, since any definition regards them through their relation to other words and beings. With respect to this "true account" of the method for understanding a nature, then, the implicit larger whole must be the whole of nature itself, because a condition for comprehending any particular nature is the possibility of comprehending nature as a whole.[113] Insofar as studying the natures of soul and body are studies of nature, and not some other property, they must share in the same way.[114]

From this analysis of the Hippocratic method, Socrates arrives at a general conclusion for all the arts. A supposed art with "[a] method that proceeds without these things seems to be just like that of the blind," that is, a stumbling about without knowledge—the way of "knack" and "experience" (270d–e). In contrast, "should someone teach [or: impart, *didonai*] speeches by some art," he must be capable of "clearly demonstrating the being [*ousia*] of the nature of this thing," and "this thing" is that to which speeches are applied and in which persuasion is produced, "soul" (270e2–271a2). While commentators often interpret Socrates's unusual construction, "teach speeches by some art," to refer to the teaching of the art of rhetoric, which he takes up in a moment (271a4), this ignores the generality of his conclusion from the Hippocratic method.[115] Rather, Socrates's purpose seems to be to remind Phaedrus of the scope and comprehensiveness of the art of speaking, as anticipated in the description of rhetoric as the art of leading the soul in every use of speech (cf. 261a7–b2). After all, all teaching and learning is done, and all natures seen, through speech and the persuasion of the student's soul (cf. 277c3–6). As Charles Griswold (1986) has shown, this expansive conclusion implies that every art, at least in its use of speech, would need to understand the soul, and so a physician would not truly possess the art of medicine until he understood the nature of soul and also became an artful speaker.[116] The soul's implication in every art blurs the independence of the arts and crowns the art of speaking—and thereby, as Socrates is arguing, philosophy—as the art of arts.

When Socrates considers how the art of rhetoric can be taught, he indicates that the Hippocratic method, seemingly applied in rhetoric, is in fact derivative of the art of speaking, for that method presupposes the dialectical analysis of soul that is the object of rhetoric. This is seen in Socrates's first step in teaching rhetoric, contrasting soul and body: the artful rhetorician "must first write and make visible soul, whether it is one and homogenous by nature or multiform like the shape of [the] body" (271a). This same distinction is implicit in medicine, since the very study of body implies the presence of soul, and if all was body, it could not differentiate itself as an object.[117] Even the Hippocratic writings go outside of the body in order to understand its forms, formulating diagnoses by analyzing the body's interaction with nature and the external environment.[118] Since body is complex, its analysis summons the soul, which alone sees "the being of the nature" of a thing and understands it as a whole of parts. Where Socrates's presentation of the method of rhetoric differs from his presentation of the Hippocratic method is that rather than simply divide the whole object into its constituent forms, only presupposing the whole, rhetoric also proceeds from analysis to reconstitute wholes.

The second step in teaching the art of rhetoric is to show "what by nature [soul] does to what sort of thing or experiences from what" (271a). In the case of the single soul and single speech, this appears to be a simple task, but when a speech fails to persuade, or persuades some souls and not others, there must be a complexity in either speech or soul that will need to be differentiated in order to isolate the cause. In thus differentiating speeches and souls, the rhetorician "arranges" or "classifies" (*diatattesthai*) "both the species [*genē*] of speeches and soul, and the experiences of these" (271b). While Griswold (1986) has interpreted Socrates's terminological shift—from the general "form" (*eidos*), used in his account of the Hippocratic method (270d5–6), to "species" or "kind" (*genos*)—to mean that this method involves collecting types of soul but not dividing soul into parts, classification of species would be impossible without classifying parts.[119] Differences between species entail differences between their respective particulars, which in turn are only explicable by differences among their parts. In the rudimentary taxonomy of souls in the palinode, an Ares-kin and a Zeus-kin differ in a particular form in their souls (e.g., dominance of the charioteer). Likewise, the possibility of persuasion—leading a soul from one thing to its opposite—depends upon the possibility of changing the soul from one form to another—that is, reordering the parts of soul rather than merely presenting what appeals to its current form.[120] As argued in chapter 3, a particular soul that is capable of change implies a multitude of soul types, such that soul is both many and one. Socrates's use of "species" is therefore a reminder that when a given speech differentiates soul, whether distinguishing between parts in a particular soul or distinguishing between types of soul, it also collects soul, either collecting together similar parts in a particular soul or similar souls into a type. The rhetorician "must know how many forms soul has"—that is, how many parts—from which he classifies souls into "such and such sorts" (271d1–2).

The third step in teaching the art of rhetoric shows how such classification into larger wholes is necessary for the rhetorician to understand differences between the particular souls with which he is practically concerned. "Having classified the species of speeches and souls," the rhetorician "will go through all the causes of these experiences, adapting [*prosarmozein*] each to each and teaching which sorts [of soul] are [affected] by which sorts of speeches, on account of which cause one soul is persuaded and another unpersuaded" (271b). The causes of the "experiences" of soul are revealed through the complete classification of the differences seen among the various kinds of speeches and souls. In using the verb *prosarmozein* ("to adapt"), derived from *harmos* (a "fastening" or "joint"), Socrates indicates that the true harmony to which the use of speech aims is between speech and soul, rather than the poets' suggestion that harmony could lie simply in the relation of words to themselves (cf. 268c5–d5). At the heart of rhetoric, then, is the development of the rhetorician's ability to judge what is fitting for his audience, which here seems to mean simply what is persuasive, rather than mean what is conducive to any natural psychological good or virtue.

This third step in the teaching of rhetoric, the fitting of speeches to souls, also reveals a fundamental reflexivity in the study of *logos*. In the first place, the teacher not only shows his student how to adapt speeches, but he too adapts his teachings to the soul of his student, rather than simply marking the truths he wishes to impart. He must discover the nature of the student's soul in the same way as others', through the observation of the student's response to each part of his teaching. In the second place, this education entails a reflexive study of soul—that is, knowing oneself. The teacher can perfectly adapt his teaching to students only if he can perceive every type of soul (i.e., ordering of its parts) revealed by a particular speech, which is to say that the teacher must be knowledgeable about, his soul harmonized with, the natures of *logos* and soul. The teacher can only become skilful in adapting his teachings by learning about himself through the same method he learns about others: testing speeches for himself and reflecting on the causes of their effects on his own soul. The question of how a speech affects a soul and how a speech ought to be used therefore depends not only on the audience's soul, but on the rhetorician's as well. Socrates's earlier account of dialectic now appears especially incomplete in that he obscured there the implication of the dialectician's soul in determining a fitting collection and division, whether done for another or for oneself. But the reflexivity entailed in the study of *logos* raises difficult questions about the possibility of a true art of rhetoric. How will the inquirer know that a given "adaptation" rightly fits his words to his own soul?[121] What are the criteria for persuasion? Furthermore, how can he test the effect of words on his own soul without in some sense going outside his soul in order to make it a discrete object for himself? The soul struggles to see what is found through *logos* in a way that is disentangled from the *logos* it shares in with all other souls (linguistic interpretation of the struggle of the charioteer to rise above its peers in order to glimpse the nature of being [248a–b, 249c–e]).

There is consequently a risk of infinite regress in trying to locate a first or foundational fitting of speech and soul, which has led some scholars to argue that Socrates's proposed matrix of speeches and souls is defective and not the "true account" he claims it to be.[122] But this view overdetermines what Socrates presents here. His three steps in teaching the art of rhetoric are simply a broad outline of what is entailed by the perception of a change produced in one kind of object (soul) by another (speech) on the basis of non-contradiction. This process becomes complicated because each object is indeterminate—perhaps each is simple (an orderly soul; a single word), perhaps each is multiform (a triapartite soul; an entire speech)—and results in a differentiation of forms, species, or kinds, and causes, because something cannot become other than it is on account of itself. This method of teaching is not a set of rules that prescribes and determines the nature of a being, let alone the nature of being itself, but the working out of the principle that what is cannot be what it is not (cf. 245d1–3).[123] What remains to do is the immense task of progressively discovering and giving an account of the forms that comprehend the vast differentiae that exist among souls, speeches, and the objects of those speeches.

Although the task before the rhetorician is enormous, Socrates concludes that "in no other way will something be demonstrated or said with art, being actually spoken or written, either with respect to this subject or any other" (271b–c). Socrates seems to have completed his argument that Phaedrus must "philosophize sufficiently" if he is to become "sufficient in speaking about anything" (261a). Philosophy, on this view, would be the perfection of dialectic.[124] Dialectic, as the art of speaking by which nature is known, is the art in which all arts must share insofar as they know and teach the natures of their objects.[125] Philosophy is likewise the highest and most necessary practice because it studies the nature of the human being that "gathers together into one through *logismos*" (249b1–c6). The other arts must look to philosophy qua dialectic to secure themselves in the knowledge of soul that judges the rest of reality. This reliance of the other arts upon dialectic substantiates Socrates's claims that he is a lover and follower of dialectic "in order to speak and to think" and that the art of rhetoric is a leading of soul by words in both public and private (261a7–b2, 266b3–5). The boast of the art of rhetoric, then, that "without me, the one who knows the beings will not be able to persuade by art," has in a way been confirmed, albeit with the qualification that no one can persuade by art *without* knowing the beings, including the being of soul (260d8–9).

Socrates ironically attributes this comprehensive psychological knowledge to contemporary rhetoricians. He tells Phaedrus that they must "keep secret the nature of soul," for how else could they possess the art yet not have revealed it in their writings (271c)? Only a private and secret knowledge can reconcile their claims to possess this art with their silence on the soul. Or perhaps they do not in fact possess the art at all. Only when they can "speak and write this way [*tropos*]," making manifest and public the knowledge upon which their practice rests, "shall we believe they write with art." Socrates thus demands the unity of the public and private rhetoric, a perfectly complete manifestation of the nature of things to all as a proof of artfulness. This expansive knowledge is the corollary of the universality that Socrates attributed to the art of rhetoric, which concerns all forms of speaking (261a7–b2). At this point, when the rhetorician's object is true knowledge, there is no distinction between teaching and persuasion; any deception would occur only on account of the ignorance of the student.[126] At the pinnacle of the noble rhetoric, however, Socrates demurs as to how, exactly, someone will speak and write about the soul in such a comprehensive way. Insofar as the rhetoricians claim to possess their art, his hesitation is ironic, since he is ignorant of the great things the rhetorician must know: "The words [*rhēmata*] themselves will not be easy to speak" (271c6). In using *rhēmata* rather than *logoi*, Socrates recalls the *rheuma*, the flowing, of the parts (*merē*) of beauty into the soul of the lover. His analogy implies that beauty itself—and the other true beings—eludes him (255c1, c6; cf. 251c7). But he can say "how it is necessary to write if it is to be as artful as possible"—that is, the basic conditions for the manifestation of knowledge (271c6–8). Socrates's qualified ignorance will prove important in distinguishing philosophy and Socrates's use of rhetoric from the noble rhetoric he presents to Phaedrus.

Socrates recapitulates the nature of the noble rhetoric acquired through an education in the nature of soul and its relationship to *logos*, but this time adds the element of practice. As described in the study of nature, the rhetorician must first "know how many forms soul has," enumerate and classify them into "such and such sorts" and whence "they come to be" of one sort or another, and "having distinguished these, again there are so many forms of speeches, each such and such a kind" (271d). From this he will know "which sorts of people are easily persuaded to this sort of speech on account of this cause, and which are hard to persuade on account of these [causes]." But once these preliminaries are concluded, the rhetorician will "see these in practice both as they are and being put into practice, and be able to attend to them sharply by perception, or they will be nothing more to him than the speeches he earlier heard when I was with him" (271d–e). The rhetorician must "be able to show to himself that this man he perceives is of the same nature which the previous speeches were concerned with, now present in deed" (271e–272a). An education in words alone is therefore insufficient, despite the apparent self-consistency that accompanies it; the rhetorician's knowledge is perfected not by speeches about immaterial forms, but in the active use of such words to differentiate reality for oneself. He must be able, in his own mind and not simply by rehearsing speeches, to account for the particulars themselves, satisfying himself that what exists in his own speeches "fits" what exists in deed.

Socrates only mentions this turn to practice after the student has gone through his classifications, as if the classifications were ready-to-hand and could be accomplished without prior use of speech in interaction with others.[127] This order of presentation reflects Phaedrus's learning of the art from books or sophists. What Socrates has hidden, however, is the artless stumbling of the autodidact, who does not fit particular souls to pregiven verbal categories, but must discern those forms as he converses, "following the scent" as it were, by observing the effects of his words on his interlocutors and marking patterns among these souls. While this must have been the way that the first teacher established his classifications, this also applies to every implementation of Socrates's prescribed program and every attempt to learn how to speak artfully. Even in the case of a perfectly executed taxonomy a test would be necessary, and in the case of an imperfect taxonomy, refinement, either of which would entail comparing one's account of soul and the soul as it presents itself through conversation. This iterative process becomes perpetual in light of the fact that persuasion means changing a soul: The soul of an individual cannot be reduced to a single speech and will therefore only be understood in its complexity through further conversation.

From continual practice in the use of particular speeches and observing their effects on particular souls, in light of their general classifications, the student will attain the crowning achievement of the art of rhetoric. This is knowledge of how speeches should be used:

> By having already grasped all these things, then taking hold of the right moments [*kairoi*] when he must speak and refrain, and again for both speaking concisely and piteously and indignantly and for each form of speech he may learn, distinguishing both the right moment [*eukairian*] and wrong moment [*akairian*] for these, will he beautifully [or: nobly, *kalōs*] and completely [*teleōs*] have brought to perfection the art, but not before. (272a)

Socrates has anticipated this emergence of *kairos*, the "opportune moment" or "season," as the ultimate object of the arts on several occasions, whether in Prodicus's "measure" (*metrion*) between two extremes,[128] or in the "for whom, when, and to what extent" medical techniques are used, or in poetry's fitting of high and low into a harmonious whole. But for rhetoric, what are the criteria for determining the "right moment"? Is it simply the accrued knowledge of what kinds of speeches persuade what kinds of soul? For what ends is persuasion sought? Socrates does not say and thus preserves the practical ambiguity as to whether a rhetorician will seek to impart virtue or not in his audience. Imputing the palinode's poetic account of the soul, however, does supply an imperative that is moral and instrumental, by which the most effective speeches, the most lasting and persuasive, will be those that lead a soul toward self-perfection through philosophical conversation ("the greatest good fortune"). Speeches that lead the soul away from its natural good will always be susceptible to refutation. It seems that just as the physician cannot be said to possess the medical art without knowing what constitutes a healthy body, neither can the rhetorician possess the art of speaking without knowing what constitutes excellence of soul, since this knowledge reveals the ultimate purposes to which speeches should be applied. Rhetoric is therefore a matter of soul-craft, such that the proper ordering of speeches called for by the linear sense of logographic necessity cannot be determined without reference to proper ordering of the soul. The rhetorician who does not seek out such knowledge, whatever the true nature of the good of the soul may be, will therefore never possess the true art of rhetoric.

Accordingly, the question still remains whether the artful rhetorician, knowing what is fitting for soul, has perfected his own soul. Can he "fit" speeches to another without having so fitted his own? The question is not, in the first place, whether such knowledge will obligate him to lead others into a similar condition, but whether he can even know such a condition without being in that condition. The palinode suggested that the capacity to discern clearly another's nature—or discern anything for that matter—required a self-disciplining, a self-ordering. If nothing else, Socrates's exhortation of Phaedrus toward this noble art of rhetoric will compel Phaedrus to enter into conversation with others, which may shape and order his own soul as he tries to determine how best to persuade them. Appearing to provide a merely, or rather, basely instrumental account of persuasion—that is, how to effectively persuade without regard for the benefit of the audience—Socrates's noble art of rhetoric will instead transform the rhetorician who takes it upon himself to pursue rhetoric to its fullest extent, showing that instrumentality in its highest form will benefit both the rhetorician and his audience.

Again, the scope of knowledge required of the truly artful rhetorician is difficult to overstate, as knowledge of soul and *logos* will relate to every art with respect to how the *logoi* concerning their objects affect and persuade the soul. This is not simply knowledge of which speeches are effective with which souls, because attaining that knowledge requires knowing what is truly persuasive, which can only be knowledge of the beings themselves. As claimed in the palinode and implied in the discussion of dialectic, knowledge of the beings themselves is irreducible to any given speech, which the rhetorician-dialectician somehow grasps. The dialectician would be like the palinode's gods, effortlessly ascending to and descending from the beings themselves, and most akin to Zeus, who leads and arranges the gods according to their natures (246e). But the being that would crucially determine what is fitting for soul, the good itself, was absent in the palinode, perhaps because the palinode was a merely "human telling" of what soul resembles (246a4–6). Socrates's vision of the complete dialectician does indeed set for rhetoric a high and perhaps impossible standard.[129]

Socrates's application of this standard to those who now practice rhetoric exposes their artlessness and is, then, as much a rhetorical strategy as an inquiry into the true nature of *technē*. Whoever claims to speak with art should not be believed if they are "lacking in any of these things"—that is, lacking knowledge of species of soul, of particulars, and of the *kairos* (272a8–b2). Perhaps Lysias does sense and have a knack for what persuades the many, but whether such speeches are really fitting for their souls is another question, and Lysias's indifference to that question refutes any claim he has to knowledge. Socrates, in contrast, takes a skeptical position and does not mistake his own speeches as artful. He knows the conditions for art and seeks the required knowledge in the proper manner, but until he comes to such knowledge, he will not grasp the *kairos* and can only lay claim to the erotic art and its knowledge, which is that one is in need of and must search for what is truly fitting and good.

In keeping with this skepticism, Socrates solicits further conversation concerning rhetoric: "Perhaps the writer will say, O Phaedrus and Socrates, does it seem best [*dokein*] in this way, or must the art of speeches somehow be recounted in another way?" (272b). This is a playfully ambiguous interjection by Plato, for Socrates cannot mean "the writer" is Lysias, whose "method" has been refuted. This "writer" is one who suspects that Socrates had misstepped in his account of rhetoric and that the true form of the art has been fully articulated. Of course, "the writer" may be Plato, for it is the author who determines whether or not a line of argumentation has satisfactorily reached its conclusion and should therefore end. Here, Plato hints that this account should not be entirely persuasive.

Despite such encouragement from Socrates, however, Phaedrus is unable to scrutinize the argument. Instead, he hesitates to embrace the noble rhetoric because its careful dialectical practice is long and hard (272b5–6). Socrates does not shrink from this objection and responds that "we must turn all the speeches up and down" to see if there is an "easier and shorter [*brachutera*] path." Phaedrus must go back over the arguments and review them. Socrates himself has suggested a number of points of doubt. Are the techniques of definition and logographic necessity really necessary, and if so how do they differ from the other surveyed techniques? How is dialectical argument judged in terms of its relation to the beings themselves? Is the analogy between medicine and rhetoric fitting? Will the artful rhetorician impart virtue or not? What is the substance of knowledge of the *kairos*? What condition of soul is required of rhetorician in order to really understand the psychagogic power of his own words? Socrates's advice to Phaedrus is to take the opposite arguments—that is, suppose the arguments are not true—and then see what is left of rhetoric.[130] Perhaps the way does lie with Teisias and Gorgias, who boasted of contradictory forms of speech, although Prodicus seemed right to say that a "fitting" speech is preferable, for one must be able to choose which technique is better at a given time. Indeed, Socrates has formulated the problem of these two ways of rhetoric on Prodicus's *Heracles' Choice*, in which the hero must choose between the paths of Virtue and Vice. In light of Socrates's myth of the cicadas, Prodicus's rustic and unsophisticated admonishment of the desirous Vice is a fitting lesson for Phaedrus,[131] whose desire for painless pleasure by way of speeches has made him indolent, preferring an escape from the toil that accompanies mortal life. The way of the noble rhetoric seems to him long particularly because of his own habits and inclinations, which originate from the desire to have what is pleasing before us at all times. But if there is no easy way as he hopes, the heaviness of the necessary way must be embraced, bringing into harmony desire and toil for the sake of what is best.

## PROBABILITY

In dialectical fashion, Socrates puts his own account of rhetoric to the test by opposing to it Teisias's probabilistic rhetoric. For Socrates, this is not only a matter of discerning the truth about rhetoric, but also a matter of justice: "It is said, Phaedrus, to be just to also give the wolf's side" (272c). Socrates thus sets himself above the nonlover, who claimed that the lover is "a wolf" and did not allow him to give his side, and so casts Teisias as the nonlover and true wolf. Socrates hints that Teisias's rhetoric, much like the nonlover precluded real deliberation, forecloses the highest possibilities of speech. But in refuting Teisias, Socrates reveals the broadest aspirations of the art of rhetoric and with it the possibility of a universal *logos* commensurate with the nature that all human souls share.

Teisias's objection is that persuasion occurs, and can be readily produced by the rhetorician, without true knowledge:

> There is no need to exalt [the matter] or lead up [to general principles], going around the long way, for it is as we said at the beginning of the speech: the man who is practicing to be a sufficient rhetorician would not need to share in truth concerning just or good things, or even whether humans are such a sort by nature or nurture [*trophē*]. (272d)

Teisias here makes the final case for Phaedrus's opinion about rhetoric, articulating a pragmatic objection that follows on Socrates's own introduction of practice—experience with particular and individual souls—to qualify a purely discursive dialectical analysis of souls. Since Teisias's objection points to potential weaknesses in Socrates's argument, its precise formulation is important. What is particularly notable is that Teisias's summary of Socrates's argument introduces "nurture" as a differentia of human types, even though Socrates only spoke of souls' unchanging "natures" (270a1, b4–5, c1–2, c9–d7, e3–4, 271a6–8, a10, 272a1), just once mentioning custom (270a7–8).

In introducing the difference between nature and nurture, Teisias draws attention to how a soul is moved and therefore changed by speech—which, as has been argued, is a necessary condition for persuasion and learning—and that consequently a soul of one type may become (or reveal itself to be) another. As a case in point, a soul persuaded by Socrates's arguments would become more aware of the use of "it is likely" or "so it seems" in arguments. The possibility of a soul's type being a result of nurture—that is, previous persuasion—raises two related problems for the psychological study at the heart of Socrates' proposed noble rhetoric. Given that one must apply speeches to a soul in order to understand it, first, that soul's responses may not reflect its nature, at least in the sense of directly addressing the nature that underlies its nurture. Second, the application of a speech to a soul for the purpose of studying that soul may change it, so that a speech that elicited a certain response at one time may not do so again, and thereby further obscure that soul's nature. As Socrates intimated in the palinode, an account of the precise nature of a given soul, let alone all soul, is extremely difficult to obtain—the ever-moving soul conceals itself.[132] In light of these problems, Teisias's argument should be taken seriously as an argument against theoretical investigation.

Teisias pragmatically aims for success in particular instances of persuasion. He argues that the rhetorician need only concern himself with what is "persuasive" to the audience, which is "the likely" (*to eikos*) (272d–e). Even if truth is on the side of a litigant, "sometimes it is even necessary to say not what has been done, if it is unlikely, but the likely things, both when accusing and defending, and to pursue saying the likely in every way, often saying good-bye to the truth." This distinction between what is true and what is persuasive depends on the obscurity or fantastic appearance of the truth. As Socrates alluded to in the palinode, images of the truth may be more attractive and persuasive than the truth itself, which is to say that people are drawn to what should be the case as they themselves conceive it—their own opinions. Socrates accordingly argued, in the context of *psychagōgia*, that the rhetorician must begin with his interlocutor's opinions and draw resemblances between them and those he wishes to impart. One cannot become knowledgeable simply by receiving self-evidently true statements. Therefore, what makes Teisias's argument credible, and is the issue at hand, is how natural tendencies within the human soul itself contribute to our preference for "the likely" over the truth.

For Teisias, people prefer the likely to the truth because "the likely [*to eikos*] is nothing other than what seems to be so [*dokein*] to the majority" (273a–b). Phaedrus recalls saying something similar earlier, although Teisias more specifically determines *doxa* by identifying it with probability (*eikos*) (cf. 259e–260a). Socrates does not recapitulate his earlier refutation of Phaedrus's opinion, since he has, since then, shown that the rhetorician must both know the true being of what is being discussed as well as the nature of soul. Socrates's specific concern here is how a rhetorician who lacks knowledge of either true beings or soul may nonetheless succeed—that is, how a practical "knack" for persuasion is possible. Understanding how probabilistic argument succeeds will be instructive about the nature of "the majority" or "the many," and, indeed, the limitations of the noble rhetoric that Socrates presented.

Teisias's example of his probabilistic rhetoric is revealing of this relation between probability and the nature of the many. His example is of a legal disputation when a weak but courageous man assaults a strong coward and steals his cloak. Teisias counsels that neither should tell the truth; the coward should tell the court that he was assaulted by several men, while the weak thief should insist that they were alone and argue, "How could I, being such as I am, have assaulted someone such as him?" (273c). This example is deceptively simple, as there is a complex relationship between the two qualities, strength and courage, and the jury's ignorance. There are two implicit probabilities at work based on the relationship between strength and courage: a strong man is more likely to prevail over a weak one; and a courageous man is more likely to prevail over a coward. There is also a third implicit probability: a courageous man is unlikely to be unjust. These probabilities arise because of the jury's ignorance of the facts of the case, of the character of the men as opposed to their physical stature, and of the exact relationship between strength and courage. They conflate strength and courage, which, though distinct, resemble one another (in Socrates's urbane speech, a weak man "emboldens enemies and causes fear in friends," on the assumption that a strong body contributes to success in battle [239d4–6; cf. 270b7]). Assuming that physical strength determines a physical contest, and seeing only the litigants' relative strength, the jury concludes that the stronger man could not have been assaulted by the weaker. The many judge the case according to what is visible in deed. Sight, Socrates said, is the clearest and sharpest of senses, although it is by virtue of seeing forms, which are seemingly clear and whole, that we are deceived. Courage is not a physical virtue, but a virtue of soul, and therefore one of the "disputable" words (like "justice" or "good"), which Teisias exploits. He advises the coward to hide his cowardice because the jury will conflate courage and strength, and could even exploit a further conflation of courage and justice—it is unlikely that a courageous man would be unjust, while, conversely, it is likely that a coward would be. Tellingly, Teisias does not say that the coward is ashamed—the reason he does not admit his cowardice is because no one would believe him.

From these common opinions, a plausible course of events can be deduced. There is no advantage, therefore, in disputing these opinions. This "cleverly hidden art" is of course no great discovery, for it is nothing more than collecting opinions that would not meet significant resistance in a jury deliberation that amounts to little more than a vote.[133] But the breadth of this audience and the limitation of discussion among them itself limits the potential for Teisias's way of rhetoric to be a perfectible art, let alone an adequate account of persuasion, since this approach does not address the particular opinions of individuals.

Socrates's response to Teisias, which is his final refutation of Phaedrus's opinion, is a recapitulation of the method of education in noble rhetoric. This reconciles Teisias's argument with what had already been established: "We have for some time been saying that this probability [*to eikos*] happens to be generated amongst the many through a semblance of the truth, and just now we came [to the conclusion] that in every case the one who knows the truth knows best how to discover these semblances" (273d). Rather than a rote recapitulation, Socrates's response is in fact his third formulation of the art of rhetoric that compares—that is, collects together—the preceding discussion with Teisias's probability and then divides them again to better clarify the art. What is notable in this formulation is that probability's effect on the many is "generated" and therefore natural rather than artificial. Despite Teisias's claim that the rhetorician doesn't need to know what kind of audience he is dealing with, let alone whether they are so by nature or nurture, he takes advantage of what naturally arises in the soul. Consequently, he cannot simply produce whatever conviction he pleases, but only that which relates to what is credible to the many. Furthermore, in order to know how to use those opinions, Socrates argues that the rhetorician, even the probabilistic litigator, must understand their causes.

Socrates's use of the term "semblance" helps to clarify the power of probabilistic arguments, since "semblance" is now weighted with the meanings ascribed to it in the palinode and his discussion of *antilogic*. Probabilistic arguments are powerful because they, like all semblances, encompass or unify what is actually a problematic relationship between that which is simply true and its manifestation in particular cases. By setting aside the truth, the probabilistic argument encompasses a range of opinions attached to "strength," which might contradict one another, and yet nevertheless infers from them a consensus. In this way, the desire of each individual for the truth (cf. 248b), expressed in their opinion, is reconciled to their ignorance of the true nature of "strength" and the particularities of the case at hand; many possible opinions can thus be collected under and addressed by one probability. As in Lysias's speech, the contrary individual opinions that exist in a crowd are implicitly acknowledged and thus ameliorated, and the crowd is reconciled with itself.

"What the many believe" is the natural tendency to holism—for example, that a word has a single meaning connecting its many uses, which may in the end be too ready and hence unsatisfactory. This springs not from any particular malignancy, but from the same cause of "the human form," namely a natural and necessary desire to be reconciled with that which truly and completely is, to reach a complete and uninterrupted self-satisfaction (249b1). Opinion is accordingly an articulation of this desire and a necessary product of reasoning, an attempt to give form in speech to the many things we perceive, to say what is true. Identification of the form of the being with a particular instance of that form produces a love of that particular, and one's own opinion, and this effect of self-love comes to be multiplied *en masse* in a large audience. Contention within this mass of particular opinions can be abated by the gratifying semblance of an encompassing whole—hence Teisias's dismissal of the need to differentiate soul types.

Nevertheless, Teisias's universal pretensions raise the possibility of a universal *logos*, one that will persuade "the many" in the broadest sense, irrespective of differences between individual souls. In his previous formulations of the education of the rhetorician, Socrates only spoke of classifying and fitting together speeches and souls. Now, Socrates is finally able to formulate this education in terms of the universal knowledge portrayed in the palinode. Only when the rhetorician "counts the natures of those who will be listening [to him], and is able to divide the beings [*ta onta*] according to their forms and to embrace each, one by one, in one form," will he be an "artist [*technikos*] of speeches" (273e). The full scope of the rhetorician's education entails the intellectual return to the beings through their division and collection, with the proviso that one must do this "so far as possible for a human being" (273e–4). Only a divine *technikos* of speech, who grasps "the one form," will be able to precisely divide that form in speech into all its particular manifestations. A human but noble rhetoric is therefore distinguished from the perfect and true rhetoric that constitutes the standard for art and directs the imperfect human form. Socrates thus casts aside the contemporary rhetoric that forgoes knowledge as merely human, akin to the moderation that Lysias encouraged, for it does not even recognize the natural causes of its own power.

Socrates can now claim that the distinction between ways of rhetoric is also an ethical one, where the goodness of one's life is at stake. His refutation of contemporary rhetoric is, he claims, a restoration of the division between the human and divine, and therefore finding the proper place for the human use of speech: "For indeed, Teisias, it is necessary, say those wiser than us, for those who have intelligence [*nous*] not to care for gratifying fellow-slaves, except as a subordinate task, but [for gratifying] masters who are both good and from good stock" (273e8–274a2). He does not proscribe probability as a rhetorical technique, but only rejects the way of rhetoric that does not see beyond the opinion engendered by probability—that there is no need for truth and that what only seems true is sufficient for human purposes.[134] Long and laborious dialectical education is redeemed by coming to know what is fitting and good for soul, and, in becoming truly good, would rightly be called "something divine" (242e2–4; cf. 252e1–5, 253b3–c2, 256a7–b3). What is at risk with Teisian rhetoric is that the rhetorician ceases to orient himself by that alone which can provide for his own good and flourishing.

Although Socrates's formulation of the human lot is one of bondage, either to fellow slaves or gods, to embrace the latter is to harmonize with what is truly good and beneficial. This harmonization is the fruit of education in the art of speaking or dialectic, continually exercising oneself in comparing one's opinions with others' in pursuit of what is true. Socrates tells Phaedrus that "if the period [*periodos*] is long, do not wonder, for it is for the sake of great things that one must travel around, not [for the sake of such things] as you believe" (274a2–3). For Phaedrus, who longs to escape this world through an indolent pursuit of painless pleasures, this reconciliation with the limitations and bonds of mortality is most fitting. It is no mean achievement of Socrates's rhetoric, then, that Phaedrus responds that this vision of slavery is "altogether beautiful, if indeed someone were capable of it" (274a6–7). Unlike the beautiful palinode, this prosaic discussion of art and technique, harnessed to what is useful rather than beautiful, has brought beauty into the realm of possibility. Phaedrus's hesitation is not to be despised, for it is the awakening of the philosophical wonder that dimly perceives an unwavering perfection; only in light of perfection is the smooth and easy road perceived as it really is. Awareness of the insufficiency of the easy road and recognition of one's own ignorance are what keep open the possibility of the higher way. When Socrates consoles Phaedrus that "for he who attempts what is beautiful, it is beautiful to endure what should befall him," it is quite appropriate that he leaves unresolved the problem of whether such an attempt can ever succeed, for only if the truth is unattained in deed will thought go out in search of it (274a8–b1).[135]

With the resolution of Teisias's objection, Socrates and Phaedrus conclude their discussion of "art and artlessness of speeches" (274b). The problem that was dramatically subordinate to the examination of Lysias's art of writing and way of life emerged as the most pressing and primary problem: how speech itself is capable of, and in fact depends upon, leading the soul toward divine truth. Socrates's refutation of Teisias did not answer, however, the most crucial question for those who would gratify the gods rather than their fellow slaves: "Do you know in which way you may most gratify a god with respect to speeches, either performing them or talking about them?" (274b9–10). This is a peculiar question, since the whole of the preceding discussion aimed to show the nature of the true art of speaking and how one might acquire it through the study of soul and its manifold relations with speech. At the very moment when the noble rhetoric, founded on the perfection of dialectic, was to be crowned as the highest and noblest way to bring oneself into accordance with what is divine, the spell is disrupted and this beautiful monument of rhetoric brought into question.

Socrates does not know the way "to gratify a god with respect to speeches," but he suggests that he has heard something of it "from the forbearers, and they alone know the truth" (274c). If the wisdom of the ancients could be discovered without assistance, "if we were to discover this ourselves, would we care anything for the opinions [*doxasmata*] of mere humans?" Not having such knowledge, they must therefore care for the opinions of humans, for what "seems best" (one of the connotations of *doxa*). Humans must seek the truth through opinion and conversation with their fellows. Martha Nussbaum (1986) rightly points out that our "food of opinion [. . .], though less fine than the gods' food, is both the best we can get for our horses and a necessary item in our search for understanding and the good life."[136] As Socrates showed Phaedrus, precisely because opinions are images of and therefore share in truth and goodness, we can develop a knack for persuasion without theoretical comprehension. Teisias's tacit admission of ignorance of the true nature of things finds then a kinship with Socrates's own professed ignorance, albeit with far different consequences for both rhetoric and philosophy.

## SOCRATIC RHETORIC

Socrates's admission that he and Phaedrus remain ignorant of how one may please a god through speech—that is, ignorant of the best use of speech—draws the reader's attention to the important counterpoint to the art of rhetoric that Socrates himself poses. Throughout the *Phaedrus*, Socrates has portrayed himself as a rustic man who is ignorant, artless, and inspired. His grasp of the comprehensive noble rhetoric founded on dialectic came to him through "some chance" and the inspiration of "the gods of this place," rather than his own possession of the art of speaking and the knowledge that accompanies it (262c10–d3). How is his own rhetorical practice to be understood, then, if he does not possesses complete knowledge of the soul, let alone the whole? How has he come to grasp the principles upon which the noble rhetoric is established? Moreover, how can his presentation of soul in the palinode—its definition and myth of its "deeds and experiences"—be reconciled with this professed ignorance? Socrates's example of a rhetoric led not by knowledge of the whole, but by knowledge of his own ignorance, ultimately undermines the monument of noble rhetoric and points back to his erotic art and his search for truth.[137]

Socrates explained that he was able to perceive the principles of art because he was inspired and maddened either by the cicadas of the Muses or the nymphs of Pan. That is, he was filled with a divine madness, shown in the palinode to be *erōs*, that disclosed the nature of things. Socrates's artless perception seems to be possible because of the pre-incarnate knowledge that inspires and guides *erōs*; his glimpse of the eternal nature of things is not acquired, but recollected. Moreover, his apparently artful definitions of soul and *erōs* are nothing more than reminders. This artless grasp of the conditions for knowledge seems to be the solution to the problem that dialectic, as the manner by which knowledge is acquired, can be secured and known by nothing other than dialectic. There must be a form of knowledge prior to dialectic, whether as a technical method or in the common sense of conversation, by which its operations are guided and judged. This is one reason why the palinode spoke of *erōs* mythically, for *logos*, understood as a rational account, could not directly represent the cause of its own being. Similarly, Socrates offered there an incomplete definition of soul that would accord with *erōs*: soul is animated by a longing for the unity it lacks. Since Socrates knows that he lacks true knowledge of the beings, his definition represented well the nature of soul as shown by his own experience. That definition of soul can be said to be artful because it is based upon the true knowledge that he is ignorant. That Socrates claims for himself an art is therefore not incredible, for he does indeed know something, "the erotic things"—that is, expressions of his knowledge of ignorance that inspire the desire to know. As argued in chapter 3, this art consists of such knowledge and how to produce it in others—just like any other art—which, in practice, entails the refutation of what others assume to know—that is, their opinions. The highest erotic life, philosophy, proceeds as a search for the god within oneself because of this basic human ignorance. Such a way of life does not seek to impart this or that speech as if it were knowledge, but to use speech as a way to secure knowledge, for oneself, of the true beings.

Lack of this knowledge, whether on the part of Phaedrus or Socrates, is accordingly the cause of the sequence of arguments made in their dialogue on rhetoric. Even as the basic argument of each part was resolved, the premises that secured that resolution—the mediating semblances or little steps—became the object for examination in the sequel. In each case, Socrates's awareness that the nature of rhetoric had not been sufficiently demonstrated propelled their dialogue forward, where each resolution was contradicted and brought into question. This was the action of *erōs,* and not simply Socrates's *erōs*, but Phaedrus's as well, evident in every question or expression of confusion. For example, Phaedrus wondered that dialectic was the art of rhetoric, seemingly contrary to all practice. In the case of dialectic, the relationship between the form sought through collection and division was only resolved through the activities of *erōs* and recollection, which bound together collection and division as a coordinated pursuit of the form; dialectic as a whole only proceeds in the face of a collection that is inadequate to the desired form, to be resolved by division, and vice-versa. When Phaedrus subsequently opposed rhetorical practice to dialectic, his *erōs* for the true form of rhetoric was embodied in the action of the dialogue. *Erōs* set their souls and dialogue in motion as it opened them to a philosophical search.

In retrospect, the erotic and dialectical structure of the dialogue on rhetoric is clear. The dialogue grew from the question of Lysias's shame, and whether writing was a necessarily shameful activity. Socrates seemed to refute the belief that writing is necessarily shameful through the argument that politicians also wish to be writers so that they may attain the greatest good—immortality. From this premise, the desire for the greatest good, developed the entire dialectic concerning rhetoric: rhetoric without knowledge is ridiculous because use and practice would reveal such ignorance to be harmful; *antilogic* and dialectic are essential to *logos* and persuasion because they are the way speech relates to the forms of things and the soul, graced by knowledge of what is fitting (*kairos*). Socrates finally placed the culmination of this dialogue, his account of noble rhetoric, in dialectical relation with Teisias's pragmatic probabilistic rhetoric. The dialogue therefore came full circle, ascending from Phaedrus's acknowledgment that the practice of rhetoric without knowledge fails to grasp what is fitting, to the collecting together of rhetoric as the fitting of speeches to souls in light of their true good, and then descending back down to practice and how a kind of persuasion can be achieved through probability, which distinguished between true rhetoric and Teisian rhetoric and furnished the insight that the truth and ultimately the good of the soul is implicitly sought in the opinions of the audience.

The desire for the good implicit in opinion is therefore closely linked to the erotic and dialectical unfolding of dialogue. Although opinion as such receives little direct attention, usage of the words *doxa* and *dokein* are conspicuous. As a semblance of being, opinion shares in being, but only shares—it is a concatenation of perceptions concerning a being (e.g., the "compacting" of the parts of beauty [251e4]) (cf. 247d1–5, 248b5). Dialogue proceeds through these semblances, persuading the interlocutor not by demonstration from true premises, but by drawing on a series of opinions that, whether true or false, are agreeable. Indeed, any frank dispensation of the truth is unpersuasive and no dispensation at all, for what is actually true is other than the semblance; the palinode's distinction between semblance and being provided a countercharm to the pleasure of a seeming good, which induces forgetfulness. Revealing what is true is as constrained as deception by the nature of persuasion or *psychagōgia*, which is to say the interlocutor must be led through a series of semblances. Dialogue and dialectic must thus be conducted *ad hominem* if they are to be persuasive in a particular case and turn the soul from its opinions.[138] This is the ultimate cause of Teisias's failure to achieve any real persuasion, for he neither directs his speech to the opinions of a single interlocutor nor refutes them, but instead allows the complex of common opinion to remain undifferentiated and ultimately inconsistent. He relies on and exploits the audience's awareness that it is, as a group, ignorant.

Socrates's own practice contrasts sharply, for he conducts his conversations in an *ad hominem* manner at all times, and his conversation with Phaedrus is no exception.[139] As Socrates later says, a farmer, "using his farming art, sows [seeds] in what is fitting" (276b). Accordingly, Socrates did not refute Phaedrus's dear Lysias immediately, but over the course of two speeches, and did so in a form particularly suited to Phaedrus's tastes (235e–236a, 257a). Even then, Phaedrus was not persuaded by the admittedly beautiful palinode, and although its beauty did lead Phaedrus to question his faith in Lysias and exhorted him toward philosophy, it could not lead him to it. Socrates needed to pursue another means: leading Phaedrus to philosophy was also the objective of their subsequent discussion of rhetoric (cf. 257b, 261a). Since Socrates could not make Phaedrus into a true lover, Socrates therefore cannot claim to possess the erotic art on the basis of his speeches alone. His erotic art does not lie in rhetorical skill in the presentation of a monologue or imparting of opinions—that is, leading his interlocutors' souls to what is beautiful—but rather lies in his ability to lead his interlocutors in the re-examination of their opinions. The speeches most fit to hear are those which can actually turn souls toward a life dedicated to true excellence. While it is questionable to what extent Socrates is able to persuade his interlocutors to philosophy, he is remarkably adept at leading them to refute themselves and come to realize that what seemed true cannot be true. Perhaps this is the product of his erotic art, for the experience of *aporia* accompanies the experience of *erōs*, which is aroused to search not for what seems to be but what is. A complete vision or understanding of being is itself not necessary for Socrates's erotics, but what is necessary is to persuade one that such a complete understanding is what the soul most needs. Socrates would make lovers, not souls that are self-satisfied and complete, for such perfection is not the lot of human beings.[140]

Socrates therefore forgoes the title of dialectician, which was reserved for whoever "by nature is able to look to one and to many" (266b5–6).[141] This complete *technikos* of speaking was shown to have an exhaustive knowledge of the beings, types of soul, how speeches relate to soul, and most importantly, what is fitting for soul and therefore humanity in general. Since Socrates does not even know whether he himself is one or many, he follows the dialectician "as if he were a god" (266b). Collection and division are the way of "thought and speech," but Socrates has not and perhaps cannot grasp these forms of speaking in their perfection. For mere humans, *erōs* must lead us through the collections and divisions of dialectic.[142]

The complete dialectician now seems to be inexplicable. Why would he speak and search for the whole if he knows the whole? As Socrates said, "If we ourselves were to discover this [the truth], would we still care for the opinions of mere humans?" (274c). Unlike the Eleatic philosophers, whose ultimate dismissal of mere human opinion as "that which is not" leaves their own speaking unaccounted for,[143] Socrates himself disclaims any knowledge of a pure "divine speech" divorced from human opinion (259d6).[144] Socrates's *erōs*—coextensive with his ignorance—dispels the monument of "the art of speaking" that he has created in the form of the dialectician, but he does not dispel the monument because it is wrong or false, for the unity which *erōs* seeks points to dialectic as the purification and disciplining of *erōs* into a perfected motion along the "natural joints" of being. Rather, Socrates dispels the monument of the art of speaking because it is a perfection that cannot be adequately grasped, only extrapolated from the basic forms of speaking, collection, and division, of which he also disclaims adequate knowledge.[145] Indeed, the complete motion of the erotic soul is not simply the ascent that is overtly portrayed in the palinode, but also its descent from perfection in order to understand how the being of beauty extends through and is produced in the life of a mortal. Socrates's erotic art, then, entails seeking the *kairos* by which a human can live in friendship with the truth.

From Socrates's erotics and dialectic simply—that is, perfected dialectic—the noble rhetoric can be further distinguished. Like Socrates's erotics, the noble rhetoric is founded upon dialectic, but its attainment of artfulness is entirely dependent on the perfection of the dialectical understanding of soul. On the basis of this knowledge, the noble rhetoric lays claim to a rigor and development hitherto found only in medicine. It is accordingly subjected to the standards of art, and if it is indeed capable of hitting upon the true nature of soul, it will achieve unparalleled efficacy and reliability in persuasion (as Socrates said, even the lower aims of rhetoric—for example, deception—will be better attained as a result of attaining the higher—that is, knowledge of soul and the beings [274a4–5]).[146] The presupposition of this knowledge carries further implications. In other dialogues, Socrates argues that every art is devoted to the good of its object,[147] and his analysis of rhetoric in accordance with what is fitting for soul shows that it is no exception. Rhetoric can thus be placed alongside the political art that Plato develops at length in the *Statesman*, each ultimately aiming toward the cultivation of human excellence, which is, in its highest form, the pursuit of wisdom.[148] But while this clear purpose is plausible for the statesman, it has hardly proven so for the rhetorician, who has achieved success by exploiting widespread and fundamental disagreement concerning the nature of justice, the good, and the beautiful. Socrates's argument that rhetoric must be founded upon knowledge of human excellence is therefore a call for the radical reformation of its public and political practice, from the forms of deliberation and legislation earlier mocked as flattery of the *dēmos*, to an art that can defend itself in terms of its beneficence, not only before a crowd, but also before the most searching of private inquiries. Unlike Gorgias's rhetoric, the public use of the noble rhetoric must proclaim and defend its utility for understanding and attaining what is good and just for its listeners and students.[149] Socrates and Plato do not express this incredible reinterpretation of rhetoric, its nature and purpose, without misgivings. As discussed earlier, the determinate and static formulation of soul assumed in the discussion of education in the noble rhetoric is at odds both with the account of the soul given in the palinode and the erotic state presupposed by dialectic. The noble rhetoric must therefore proceed in a provisional manner, and so long as its art is not perfected, it will be susceptible to error and abuse, for the rhetorician will be ignorant of the complete good of the soul.[150] The imperfection of rhetoric thus returns to the problem raised and exploited by Teisias's probabilistic rhetoric, that the nature of the good and justice are inherently disputed because they are so dear to the individual soul, and so reopens the basic ethical questions with which philosophy is concerned. In light of our ignorance, rhetoric acquires its nobility on account of the search for true knowledge that is essentially human.

Socrates's demonstration of Teisias's artlessness provides a useful contrast for understanding Socrates's own artlessness. Both are artless speakers due to their ultimate ignorance of the soul, yet both nonetheless attain a certain rhetorical knack or prowess because of their understanding relative to their audiences. Here, the distinction between the public and private rhetoric re-emerges, for there is no question that Socrates's ability to lead a private conversation by way of the opinions of his interlocutors, who are wonderfully varied in nature, opinions, desires, and prejudices, is demonstrative of a far more profound and subtle understanding of soul than Teisias's superficial grasp of "what seems to be to the majority." What has been called Socrates's erotic art or his rhetoric of course means, at bottom, nothing less than engaging his interlocutor in philosophical conversation. Socrates exercises himself in the collection and division of souls and identification of souls that "are present before him," deepening his understanding of the soul while at the same time leading his interlocutors to a fuller consideration of their own opinions—that is, to self-understanding and the pursuit of knowledge. Socrates thus devotes himself to private rhetoric that is *antilogic* in its most basic form, the refutation of false opinion, which is not possible with Teisias's rhetoric.

Conversely, Socrates cannot use such rhetoric before a crowd, for the opinions of the crowd are only uniform at a superficial level, and will prove to be insufficiently uniform for eliciting complete agreement to each of the "small steps" taken over the course of a refutation, since the most precious things are the most disputable (263a–b, 273a6–b1).[151] Socrates cannot isolate the individual opinions he requires in order to affect the necessary refutation.[152] Moreover, humans do not desire *aporia* or find it attractive or pleasing, preferring a beautiful wholeness (251d–252a). These conditions allow a Teisias or Thrasymachus to seize hold of "what seems to be to the many" and rouse their passions, even though this would be but a momentary madness and beauty, created "as if for a feast day" (276b). Socrates's unwillingness to proceed in "the way of Lysias and Thrasymachus" entails forgoing the effectual power he himself admits can be found in demagogically addressing crowds, although he denies that such efficacy is truly efficacious since it ignores the most important thing, namely excellence of the soul (260c–d, 268a).[153]

When Socrates and Phaedrus's conversation returns to the court of law in the course of examining Teisias, the reader is reminded of the fate shared by Socrates and Palamedes, who were unwilling to debase themselves like men more beholden to the preservation of their bodies than the true justice of the soul. But the court of law also recalls the impressive way by which the politicians have provided for their immortalization in law. The politicians, the flatterers of the many who draw on the talents of the likes of Lysias, Gorgias, Teisias, and Thrasymachus, have, however imperfectly, grasped the nature of soul sufficiently enough to fasten themselves in the memories of their fellow citizens through a unified, static, and constant code of law. Socrates's unwillingness to edify, on account of his *erōs* for what is truly immortal and eternal, leaves unfulfilled the possibility of a *logos* that is passed on and becomes immortal by gratifying the lower parts of the soul aroused by bodily desires or honor. With this possibility of a universal *logos* in the background, Socrates and Phaedrus return to Lysias and the nature of writing. Socrates will not let his friend go until he makes it clear how Lysias will have to write in the future, if he is to make speeches that are truly beautiful and beneficial, capable of leading Phaedrus toward philosophy.

*Chapter Five*

# Writing the Eternal

Plato's discussion of the nature of writing arises out of two questions in Socrates's conversation with Phaedrus. First, what is noble and what is shameful in writing? This question was the impetus for the preceding dialogue on the art of rhetoric, and Socrates now returns to it. Second, how may one gratify the gods in speaking or writing? This question was raised at the conclusion of the dialogue on rhetoric, and the noble rhetoric remains incomplete while it is unanswered, for the gratification of the gods is the highest purpose of rhetoric and speech. These two questions are addressed simultaneously and overlap: noble writing depends on what is gratifying to god, and, inversely, what is gratifying to god will be revealed through the discussion of writing. The criticisms of writing that Socrates will advance must therefore also be considered in relation to speaking in the broader sense, encompassing both its oral and literary forms.

This chapter will argue that Teisias's attempt to fashion a universal *logos* in the form of probability was an appropriate transition to the question of writing, since Plato will use the peculiar attributes of writing to develop a new and universal understanding of the *logos* itself that will act as the standard for noble and ignoble writing and thus complete the art of rhetoric. In Socrates's Egyptian myth, Plato advances the defects of writing as the wellspring for a more robust interpretation of the written word, which ascends to an understanding of *logos* that comprehends its oral and written forms, and is commensurate with the transcendent nature of being. This *logos*, however, cannot be reduced to any particular words or speeches, and can only be embodied in an ethos (*ēthos*), a way of using words and speeches, that is committed to the examination and refutation of false opinions in pursuit of what really is. Plato's playful writing and dialogue form incorporates this Socratic *logos* and ethic, but by writing it down he implies that Socrates's strictly oral rhetoric does not express the full natures of *logos* and soul, and therefore limits the potential for rhetoric as an aid to philosophy and the fullest development of human life.

## AN EGYPTIAN MYTH

The truth about writing, Socrates says, is found in the ancient wisdom of Egypt, which tells of the advent of writing and its dissemination (274b–c). Socrates's intention in making the myth an Egyptian one is not clear, beyond the well-known age and piety of Egyptian civilization.[1] It may be related to the myths of Typhon, alluded to at the beginning of the *Phaedrus*, in which the Greek gods fled to Egypt before the monster's wrath.[2] If Socrates has this story in mind, his Egyptian myth would concern the flight from chaos or disorder, in which case the popular themes of Egypt's ancient wisdom and piety converge as the origin of divine order. As in the palinode, if truth is found in eternal being, it can be fittingly represented as an ancient time out of which the present has necessarily followed. But if modernity is considered a deviation from that eternal truth, there must have been an original moment of deviation. Socrates's Egyptian myth is concerned with how writing emerges from this original modernism.

In Naucratis of Egypt, Socrates tells Phaedrus, there was a "god" and "demon" named Theuth (274c). Theuth was a god of learning, invention, and art—an Egyptian Palamedes. Once, he went upriver to "the great city of the 'upper place' that the Greeks call Egyptian Thebes" in order to display his discoveries to the king, Ammōn, "whom the Greeks call Thamos" (the Greeks' innovative name, a compound of *theos* and *Ammōn*, indicates that they did not believe the Egyptian name was a sufficiently clear mark of divinity) (274d). Ammōn, for his part, was known as the sun god and king of the gods, and was explicitly called the Egyptian Zeus by Herodotus, as well as "the hidden."[3] The city of Naucratis was the Greek emporium on the Nile delta, and thus a site of acquisition and wealth-making, as well as of mixing local and foreign customs, whereby new knowledge and art would be disseminated.[4] Theuth thus ascended to Thebes as a god of modernism, improving and correcting the customary ways.[5] As will be seen shortly, Theuth did not see his inventions as mere trifles for addressing the desires of a day, but for the lasting benefit and progress of the people.[6]

Of the inventions that Theuth brought to Thamos for judgment, Socrates mentions five: "both number and calculation [*logismos*], geometry, astronomy, further both draughts and gambling [or: deceit, *kubeia*], and also letters" (274c). This particular array of arts would of course be of significant utility for the commerce in Naucratis. In the *Republic*, however, the first three arts are also part of philosophical education, valued for their capacity for drawing the soul toward the *idea* of the good in order to ensure the lasting order of the city. The arts' immediate pragmatic uses are propaedeutic toward this end.[7] There too, calculation is the first and fundamental art, for it is the perception of unity that all knowledge and art consists of, and leads to intellection and what is in thought alone.[8] Dialectic is conspicuously absent among Theuth's arts, even though it is the crown of the arts and the philosophic education in the *Republic*,[9] and the essence of the art of speaking here in the *Phaedrus*. Recalling Socrates's earlier argument that rhetoric without dialectic is incomplete, "Most artful Theuth," as Thamos called him, only possessed the preliminaries of dialectic, and so did not possess knowledge of soul and what is truly useful—Thamos must provide such insight.[10] Neither did Theuth seem to possess the poetic arts—for example, harmonics—which are concerned with beauty and entail mad inspiration beyond sober utility. From its Egyptian origins, then, it seems that writing is an ugly utilitarian art designed to serve the pressing problems and desires of bodily necessity and luxury.

On the other hand, in the list of Theuth's inventions, writing follows the discovery of a twofold instrument of play, "draughts and gambling" or "draughts and deceit," which certainly can be used for wealth-making, but only if the probabilities involved in draughts are understood or manipulated. Unlike the three preceding arts, which seek to override or escape chance for the sake of order and necessity, this fourth art embraces chance and what is unknown. Deception, it should be recalled, is integral to persuasion, and can only be reliably performed with knowledge. So the same god who invented aids for humanity also invented games and deceit—his intention as a whole may have been serious, yet he nevertheless saw value in play.[11] Writing, as the last of the arts, was therefore the culmination of what is serious and playful, necessary and probable, true and false. Theuth presented writing to Thamos as a stabilizing supplement to the uncertainty seen in draughts and deceit.

When Theuth displayed his arts to Thamos, he wanted them to be "passed on to the other Egyptians" (274d). He was a popularizer of knowledge, a democratizing god.[12] Thamos did not criticize this intention, but rather responded as a king concerned for the welfare of the people by examining each art presented by Theuth to determine what "seemed to be noble or not noble" (274d–e). Thamos apparently had much to say about each, providing an extemporaneous judgment that penetrated behind the appearance of utility they had for Theuth. In the case of writing, Thamos's criticism reveals how Theuth's intentions would in fact harm the souls of those using writing by keeping them enthralled to earthly objects of sense and the conventional meanings attributed to words.

This is first seen in Theuth's defense of writing, where he reveals his belief that knowledge can be simply manifested and transmitted in writing as if it were an object: "This learning, O King, will produce Egyptians who are wiser and possess better memory, for I have discovered a drug [*pharmakon*] for both memory and wisdom" (274e). Theuth seems to make the same argument as the technician, who claimed knowledge of medicine from having read books about drugs and diets. Phaedrus rejected this argument (266d5–6, 268e2–4). But Socrates has Theuth claim something still greater: that writing corrects the condition of forgetfulness that threatens oral modes of learning, and is therefore an art by which all other arts may be acquired. Theuth thus believed writing would develop the greatest of powers—the wisdom and memory that Socrates earlier said are the most needful things for soul (247d, 249c). In this light, the dissemination of the arts appears to be philanthropic, since writing, on Theuth's argument, would allow us to attain the most divine things and so gratify god.[13] But Socrates's palinode also showed that the soul was not immediately inspired by wisdom, which remains hidden, but by beauty, which is apparent, such that only when the desire for beauty and pleasure was purified into the pursuit and recollection of true beauty would knowledge and wisdom emerge (250d–e, 253e ff.). Similarly, Thamos's criticism of the superficial benefit and appeal of writing reveals his prudence.

In his judgment of writing, Thamos claimed that Theuth, "being the father of letters," was led astray "on account of good intentions" toward the art he "engendered" (274e–275a). For this reason, "one man is able to engender the things of art, but another has the lot to judge [*krinein*] both the harm and benefit provided to those who practice [them]" (274e). Theuth's erotic impulse, his desire to redress the fundamental human separation from the wisdom that perfects the soul, has given birth to a solution for forgetfulness in the form of art, but the possibilities of that art do not conform to his hopes. The enthusiastic lover similarly clung to his perception of beauty as that which released him from his "birth pangs" (251e–252a). If Theuth wishes to learn the truth about his art, he must be able to judge or divide himself (*krinein*, "to judge," also means "to divide") and oppose himself—that is, put himself in dialectical relation or find a suitable interlocutor. Indeed, Thamos told Theuth that what he believed about writing was "the opposite of what it is capable of"—thus helpfully forming an antilogical structure out of which the true nature of writing can unfold (275a).

Thamos's objection was that writing in fact produces "forgetfulness in souls" rather than memory, and in doing so only gives an appearance of wisdom (275a–b). Lacking practice or use of memory, those who "trust writing" are only "reminded by foreign marks from without." Theuth, it seems, hoped to correct for the plasticity of the marks of oral discourse, that is, their instability and susceptibility to disagreement, for otherwise the differences between beings are difficult to retain (263a–c). But he had apparently misjudged the nature of memory and therewith wisdom and knowledge, for those who rely on writing "are not reminded from inside themselves by themselves." The effect on memory from the overreliance on writing is a familiar phenomenon, seen in Phaedrus's rote memorization and of Lysias's speech, but Thamos's distinction between external and internal reminding is less clear.

Thamos's argument for internal reminding is an epistemological correlate of the ontological distinction developed in the palinode, between the transcendent beings themselves and their earthly manifestation to the senses. As such, the Egyptian myth continues to explore the problem of beauty and manifestation. Relying on external marks means regarding knowledge as the possession and schematization of these sensible manifestations—reducing knowledge to what can be readily named and agreed upon, rather than seeing the hidden inner cause of those manifestations and, accordingly, comparing the apparent meaning of external marks to one's internal and personal experience.[14] A soul that relies on writing is content with what is made manifest by these external marks. Similarly, this reliance on external marks construes memory in the conventional sense of a collection of determinate sensory objects or images within the mind, rather than in the sense suggested by the palinode—the intellectual perception of the one form in which manifold perceptions share. Theuth believed the monuments that are written words sufficiently capture what they recall, and indeed, on this view, the difference between monument and what is monumentalized would be negligible. Theuth's implicit conception of knowledge is a natural consequence of its origins in commercial exchange and the "human concerns" that condemn philosophy as useless (249d).[15] Rather than a drug for memory and wisdom, Thamos said that Theuth had only produced "a drug [*pharmakon*] for reminding" (275a). In saying this, however, Thamos conceded that forgetfulness is a problem, and his acknowledgment of writing's power to remind suggests that writing may yet be redeemed—so long as the user of writing perceives the dual nature of this *pharmakon*, as remedy and poison, a reminder and cause of forgetfulness.[16] Just like the technician who learned that his drugs were not remedies in every case, the user of writing must learn the measure for judging its use.[17]

Thamos makes a second criticism of writing, concerning its political effects. Having produced forgetfulness rather than memory and wisdom, writing "will furnish to those who are learning an appearance [*doxa*] of wisdom, not its truth" (275a). The memorization and mere recounting of words as if they simply expressed the truth is not, of course, a problem that is exclusive to writing, as both Phaedrus and Socrates recall "having heard" a common opinion or pithy expression, something that's merely in the air (235c2–4, 260a1, 274c1). Thamos must mean that this problem in oral discourse is exacerbated by the written word; reading and writing seem to inculcate a different approach to words and their meaning. Students are equipped with an appearance as if it were clothing, much like the sophist Hippias, whose ostentatious dress was a testament to his vanity and superficiality (compare Socrates's jibe at Phaedrus's own "borrowed ornaments" [239d]).[18] Without a "reminding from within," an inner core, the fixity and rigidity of writing will paradoxically produce students who float on the realm of pure showing and externality, such that they would be unable to differentiate, even in principle, opinion and knowledge. One would merely collect together objects of common agreement—which was what Phaedrus believed to be the whole of the art of rhetoric. Wisdom does not consist, for Thamos, in the memorization of external marks, but must lie, as is fitting for a hidden god, in the background behind or in between those marks, judging their appropriate use.

From the effect of writing on the individual soul follows a broader problem when those souls interact with the community. Thamos charged that students would become stubborn and vain, believing that they possess wisdom and do not therefore have anything to learn. They would be "seeming-wise" (*doxosophoi*) rather than truly wise (275a–b). Believing that knowledge and wisdom consists of memorizing external marks, the only proof of it would be similarly external—victory in verbal contests. Plato diagnoses the political consequences of this conceit more fully in other dialogues,[19] although reverberations of it have been seen in the *Phaedrus*, particularly in the urbane speeches and Teisias's forensics. In the urbane speeches, disagreement did not produce doubt and a search for knowledge, but led to reliance on common opinions, while Teisias believed justice to consist of nothing more than the verdict. On the principle that the character of the individual will affect political relations, Thamos seems to imply that greater congeniality will obtain where the individual soul does not rely on writing and is consequently open to learning because he does not presume to know—that is, he knows he is ignorant.

Socrates concludes his Egyptian myth without mentioning whether Theuth gave a rebuttal or Thamos reached a final verdict.[20] If Thamos's judgment of writing was entirely negative, though, Socrates would have merely returned to the same conclusion of the politician who slandered Lysias, that all writing is shameful (257c, 258d). Instead, Theuth and Thamos have staked out the advantages and disadvantages of writing (and, implicitly, oral discourse), as well as the possibility of a middle way. It cannot be assumed therefore that Theuth and Thamos expressed the final position of either Socrates or Plato on writing. The Egyptian myth does, though, broach the question of why Socrates did not write yet Plato did, which is one of the few ways that Plato draws attention to a difference between himself and his teacher. Consideration of this problem in the following pages will be restricted to its particular function in the *Phaedrus*.[21]

Phaedrus is incredulous about Socrates's Egyptian myth, repeating his concerns about myths and the authority of their source: "How easily you make speeches from Egypt or whatever place you wish" (275b; cf. 229c,

235c). Socrates swiftly rebukes him for his modernism and superficial urbanity, reminding him that

> [s]ome said the first prophetic speeches arose from an oak in the sacred [place] of Dodonian Zeus. Some men at that time, inasmuch as they were not wise just as you moderns [lit. "young ones," *neoi*] are, listened to the proclamations of oak and rock on account of their simplicity [*euētheia*], if only they should speak the truth; but perhaps it makes a difference to you who it is that speaks and where he is from. For you do not consider only whether [what he says] holds in this way or another. (275b–c)

Phaedrus's all too easy skepticism must be refined so that he does not consider facts of time or place, or one's opinions concerning the person speaking, as sufficient criteria for the truthfulness of what is said. Phaedrus simply shifts the burden of thinking and discovering the truth to trusted sources, which is to say, to external marks and consequently to his prejudices. Speech and thought aspires, Socrates implies, to a truth and universality beyond the vicissitudes of time or place. Even if the sources that Phaedrus trusts really are trustworthy, this does not mean that he has understood them. Just as Thamos prophesied, the moderns will suffer from the detrimental effects of their "trust of marks from without" and ignorance of the reminding from within. Socrates seems to have adapted Thamos's words to another form, as if the Egyptian god moved to a place Phaedrus finds more familiar and perhaps more trustworthy,[22] and communicated in a familiar idiom.[23] He also began his Egyptian myth trusting that "the forbearers alone know the truth" (274c). Socrates himself relies on what is familiar and trusted to Phaedrus to make his point that one should only trust true speech; he has not abandoned the *ad hominem* character of dialectic. But his praise of the simple folk at Dodona is ironic. How could these people know whether oak and rock had told them the truth if they did not already know it or could interpret it from the words they heard? Socrates himself said at the beginning of the *Phaedrus* that "the country and the rocks do not wish to teach me anything, but the human beings in town do" (230d). It is therefore difficult to reconcile Thamos's warning with Socrates's invocation of Dodona, for the latter trusts entirely the external marks by which a prophecy or oracle is delivered. Perhaps Phaedrus should likewise examine more carefully the apparent truths that have been uttered under the plane tree—Socrates earlier warned that the presumed clarity of the urbane speeches was "simple" (*euētheia*, 242d). Phaedrus should likewise interpret for himself and ask questions about Thamos's judgment of writing—not least of all how an internal mark can be made—when Socrates calls the god's words a "prophecy" (275c7–8).

## Chapter 5
## SOCRATES AND PLATO

Following the Egyptian myth, Socrates interprets Thamos's criticisms of writing and continues to develop them in contrast to oral discourse. The indirect dialogue between Plato and Socrates thus begins in earnest. Socrates begins by making clear his reservations about the "simple" ancients who listened to oak and rock:

> If someone leaves behind or receives an art in letters, supposing there will be something clear and firm from letters, he will be full of simplicity [*euētheia*] and really ignorant of the prophecy of Ammōn, supposing words that have been written are anything more than reminders for the one who knows about the things that have been written. (275c–d)

Ammōn's prophecy for all the arts that are written down—Socrates says "an art *in* letters," not just the art of writing—arises from his original assessment of writing. In dwelling on these mythical origins, Socrates is able to return to and uncover the questionable nature of writing from Phaedrus's modernist prejudices—an echo of his earlier warning that the student of rhetoric must not rely on a verbal taxonomy of souls, but apply those teachings and discover their truth for himself. Socrates develops writing's power to remind in light of its questionable nature, which he poses as a problem between two opposing ways. Only if writing can be seen in its duality, as remedy and poison for memory, are its highest powers for recollection possible, for this duality keeps alive the distinction between eternal being and earthly manifestation. If writing is seen as simply a remedy on the one hand, or a poison on the other, it will never be able to recall being as something beyond our opinions, that is, in its transcendent nature: if writing is only a remedy, one will believe that it says what is "clear and firm," although it only points to other phenomena, rather than what is actually truly clear and firm, namely eternal being; and if writing is only a poison that would replace being with itself, which is the impression Thamos may give, one will be closed off to its highest power.[24]

Socrates's analogy to painting helps to explain the problematic nature of writing, how it encompasses both reminding and forgetfulness. Socrates says that painting and writing share a power that is *deinon*, both "terrible" and "clever," to make what is silent and dead appear alive, animate, and capable of speech (275d).[25] This appears at first to be an inappropriate analogy, given that the latter is a strictly visual medium of imitation, while writing is a visual imitation of the aural medium of speech—that is, even further removed from the object of imitation. Early forms of writing, however, particularly the Egyptian hieroglyph, were predominantly pictorial and designative in the simple manner of painting. It is on the basis of this designative function that Socrates establishes writing's defects: endless repetition; the inability to adapt to the audience; and the need for assistance.

With regard to the first defect, Socrates says that the "offspring" of painting stand as if alive but remain silent before questioning and endlessly repeats itself. Socrates's use of "offspring" is not merely a rhetorical flourish to contribute to the image of seeming-life, but shows the involvement of a human being; art is not a dead technical or mechanical process, but caught up in the purposes and actions of a living organism—that is, the motions of soul or *erōs*. As Socrates will show, the products of art are akin to the body and require the constant care of soul for their life and motion. Similar to painting, "words" (*logoi*) seem to speak "as if thinking [*phronēsthai*]," but if asked a question, "they only point forever to the same thing" (275d). The offspring of each art refers to something other than itself, but because it fixes it in place and cannot speak of it in any other way, it betrays its appearance of life and motion. Socrates's contrast of words to thinking therefore indicates that thought is not reducible to fixed and unchanging words or images, but entails moving through the various relations and appearances of its object, such as in the way Thamos was able to say "many things" about each art he surveyed. The fixity of the beings themselves ("whole and simple [*hapla*] and unchanging" [250c2–3]) cannot be replicated in speech. It is important that Socrates does not yet restrict this warning to written words, as some commentators suppose,[26] since he speaks only of *logoi* (275d7), and indeed repetitious utterances are also a problem when they are oral. Phaedrus, for example, asked Lysias to repeat his speech over many times so that he might memorize it, as if he was learning something, and the three monologues delivered in the first half of the *Phaedrus* were subsequently examined. Without continuous discussion, those words are no more conducive to thinking than written ones.[27] Even the next two defects that Socrates discusses, explicitly attributed to writing, are as much defects in oral discourse.

The second defect is that, whenever written down, "every speech is rolled out everywhere to those who give ear, and so in the same manner to those it is not fitted for, and it does not know to whom it must speak and to whom it must not" (275e). The written word assumes every soul it addresses is the same and what is fitting for one is fitting for all, much like the mass rhetoric that Socrates criticized earlier; there is no grasp of the *kairos*, the opportune moment, which is the keystone of the true art of rhetoric. But this presumed unity of audience is not entirely misguided, since "all soul" and every human being was said to be nurtured by what is the same—the true knowledge of being, which is fixed and unchanging and thus universal (249b3–7). Writing may then presume to give to all the complete and final truth by virtue of it addressing something found in every soul. As was the case with Teisias's probabilistic forensics, what is lost is the ability to address differences in soul—which at the extreme means failing to address individual souls—by taking into account and responding to their particular opinions and desires. This forgoes the *ad hominem* of Socrates's dialectic.

The third defect of writing is that such a static, unresponsive, repetitive, and insensitive form of speech is always in need of assistance from its "father" when it is abused (275e). The written text is always a child, whose thought is furnished by a parent able to respond to the particulars of a question, supplement its fixed words with further words, and judge the nature of its audience. This is the danger of attempting to learn from books alone, rather than thinking for oneself—one becomes a rhapsode forever fastened and enslaved to his source as if by a chain (277e).[28] Socrates thus sets up writing as the negation of oral speech, dead rather than alive, fixed rather than in motion, oracular rather than rhetorical, and beholden rather than free. It cannot therefore produce in itself the logographic necessity that makes speeches like "living animals" (264c).[29]

Socrates criticizes writing as if what is said in writing is self-evident, but it is possible for the same text to be interpreted in different ways, rightly or wrongly, as were the written prophecies of the Pythia and the Sibyl. A reader must, after all, use moving oral discourse to find meaning in the written marks and in this way himself become a kind of father to the words, making them his own. But perhaps Socrates is making the stronger argument that criticizes a manner of receiving words, rather than simply criticizing writing itself. As noted, his criticisms of writing are also applicable to oral speech performed in a similarly fixed and unresponsive manner—which is precisely the manner preferred by Phaedrus. In light of this unthinking manner of speaking, it is not without irony that Phaedrus agrees to Socrates's criticism of writing with the comment, "you speak most correctly [*orthotata*]," rather than his usual, "it is likely." Phaedrus understands the warning about the rigid nature of the written word rigidly, as if it is itself *orthos*, "straight" or "right" or "correct" (275e6; see also 275c3, d3). Phaedrus acts like the white horse that obeys without question the words of the charioteer (253d–254c).

The rigidity of the written word nonetheless provides the antipode to orality that allows Socrates to see "another speech [*logos*], a legitimate brother of this one" and "the manner by which it comes to be, and how much better and more capable [or: powerful, *dunamis*] it is by nature than this one" (276a). This confirms that the problem is between two forms of *logos*, rather than oral and written *logos* simply.[30] The legitimate *logos* possesses properties of both the oral and written. Indeed, it is only on the basis of the properties of writing outlined above—its apparent defects—that Socrates can formulate an adequate image of the legitimate *logos*, which is "that which is written with knowledge in the soul of the one who learns, on the one hand able to protect itself, and on the other knowing [when] to speak and be silent with respect to those it must" (276a). Writing has become an analogy for true knowledge. Socrates, having introduced the properties of fixity and reminding, is able to show Phaedrus, the difference between, on the one hand, the motion or plasticity of words with respect to meaning, and the fixity and self-same nature of knowledge, on the other. In the palinode, Socrates described "true knowledge" as "not that to which generation is present, nor what is different in the different things we now say are, but the knowledge that exists in the presence of that which really is" (247d–e). The legitimate *logos* is the "reminding from within" that Thamos spoke of; "writing" is thus exonerated when it is in the soul rather than just "alien marks from without."

But it is difficult to conceptualize what writing on the soul really is, as the image is a seemingly impossible compound: a reminder or mark that always points to the same thing as well as being a fluid discourse which changes according to its audience. This "writing" therefore transcends the visual analogy to painting, which would give it the clear properties of a particular sensible object, and instead stands in the soul like the beings themselves, "colorless and shapeless and intangible" (247c)—writing ceases to be a physical object or possession at all. Phaedrus interprets this enigmatic condition of soul in the terms of logographic necessity: "You mean the living and ensouled *logos* of the one who knows, of which the written [*logos*] is an image and would justly be said to be some phantom [*eidōlon*]" (276a; cf. 264c). Precisely when one might expect a single, clear, definition of *logos*, suitably universal, Socrates's and Phaedrus's expressions of the legitimate *logos* confound one another—the soul which is written on possesses yet another soul, and the writing on the soul would be but a phantom of yet another speech. The legitimate *logos* resists any singular determination, either by sight or by speech. Plato can only bring forth the nature of the legitimate *logos* through this confounding image, from in between the speeches as it were. Phaedrus does well, then, to see that Socrates's use of "writing" transcends writing in any conventional sense. In seeing how the meaning of writing can encompass these opposing senses, he perceives the manner in which the living *logos* emerges from Socrates's dichotomy of oral and written. The "oral" aspect of the *logos* is portrayed as that which sets beings in motion, characteristic of Lysias's disordered word play. The "written" aspect fixes being, brings it to rest, characteristic of Socrates's first speech which presumed to possess such clarity of speech that could circumscribe the disorderly world. The *logos* as a whole, if it is whole, is the manifestation and perception of transcendent being, and the human being is that animal that, holding the *logos*, "has seen the truth" (249b).

Building on Phaedrus's distinction between the living *logos* and its phantom,[31] Socrates can now address the question of what constitutes good and shameful writing, and he distinguishes between two kinds of writing. He uses the analogy of farming to imbue the life of the *logos* into the previously dead husk of writing, showing what might be the respective "offspring" of the legitimate and illegitimate *logoi*. Speeches are now "seeds" that a "sensible [*nous*] farmer cares for and wishes to become fruitful," and therefore natural and generative rather than the artificial and sterile products of painting (276b). Equipped with the distinction between legitimate and illegitimate *logoi*, Socrates now shows how art is now clearly directed to cultivating the human being rather than producing artifacts, bringing the principle of logographic necessity under that of *psychagōgia*. Would this sensible farmer, Socrates asks,

> in seriousness plant these seeds in the summer, in a garden of Adonis, and rejoice when he beholds [*theōrein*] them as they become beautiful in eight days, or would he only do these things for the sake of play [*paidia*] and a feast day, if he would do them at all? But for those things which he was serious about, would he make use of the farming art, and scatter seeds in what is fitting, glad that what he sowed would grasp perfection in eight months? (276b)

The use of seeds for a beautiful feast day is the rhetoric and writing preferred by Phaedrus, who, like a cicada, would have only that speech that delights and gratifies him. Socrates seems to have in mind those speeches that aim to please the audience at all times, as if there were an eternal summer on this earth, without regard for a more fitting or natural purpose. Recalling that Eryximachus directed his medical art toward this end,[32] it would seem that this problem emerges from an underlying ethos that is insensitive to the cultivation of the soul, and goes beyond the particular form of speeches. Socrates does not preclude the sensible farmer from using his seeds for "feast days"—for example, for the celebration of the harvest and its patron gods. The soul longs, after all, for the feast where it might likewise "behold" the cause of its longing (247c–e). But this vision cannot be the only end of the soul, for even the gods only feasted at the apex of their ascent, after which they continued their cosmic cycle; for mortals, that feast is but a moment, and dwelling in ecstatic beauty only hides the true nature of things. Rather, the desire to behold the superheavenly beings in their utter and simple clarity can only be accomplished through the longer path of perception in the things "that come to be" and inform practice such that they are manifested throughout our lives.[33] They must be, as it were, planted in a "serious" way and cared for so that they might flourish to their full nature, what is "fitting," rather than forced into what is merely believed to be beautiful.[34]

Socrates now specifically brings the analogy to bear on writing. He first has Phaedrus agree that a man who has "pieces of knowledge" of "what is just and beautiful and good" must be "sensible" (or: intelligent, *nous*) with his seeds (276c). Apparently, one cannot have knowledge without being intelligent with respect to the object in question, which in this case is what is fitting for soul; knowledge entails knowledge of what is beautiful and good, as Socrates pointed out a number of times in the discussion of rhetoric. This man who possesses some knowledge of these things will not be serious about writing, because these words cannot help themselves "and are unable to teach sufficiently what is true" (276c8–9). This new criticism of writing is closely related to its inability to adapt to different souls, but does not preclude writing so long as it receives some assistance or is otherwise able to accommodate its inability to simply manifest the truth.

This knowledgeable writer will instead "sow and write the garden of letters for the sake of play [*paidia*]," and this play will truly be "altogether beautiful," as Phaedrus observes (276d–e). Whenever this man does write, he will be "storing reminders for himself, when he comes into forgetful old age, and for everyone who shares the same track, and he will be pleased when he beholds their [the seeds'] tender growth." Thamos's judgment of writing is now shown to have been not entirely negative, for the function of "reminding" that he identified has become an instrument for planting and growing "pieces of knowledge." The playfulness of writing, then, is directed toward the serious purpose of helping others recollect the nature of things that their souls possessed before being planted in a body, the success of which would be a testament to the writer's own grasp of the nature of these things and his own artfulness. The knowledgeable writer writes for the purpose of education (*paideia*), yet it is a nuanced account of education that incorporates all of the preceding concerns about reminders being mere "phantoms" and inducements of forgetfulness, the fixity and insensitivity of writing, and most important for the character of the student, the production of a "seeming wisdom." Once these defects have been recognized, Socrates is willing to allow that writing may be useful for education and real thinking.

Socrates is careful to distinguish the play of the serious farmer and writer from the conventional understanding of play as mere entertainment and pleasure-seeking. He contrasts the knowledgeable writer's play with those who spend their time drinking in symposia, recalling Epicrates's hosting of Lysias and Phaedrus (227b). Socrates himself, though, is a frequent attendee at symposia and known for his prodigious drinking ability.[35] How, then, are we to understand his present slighting of symposia and differentiate it from his own use of symposia? Is he really condemning himself, since there is no evidence that he ever amused himself by writing? This does not seem to be the case, since there is much evidence that he conducted himself in a playful manner at all times, either in symposia or elsewhere, filling his conversation with levity and irony, often telling jokes and amusing stories or examples, and only rarely falling into quiet reverence and contemplation.[36] Phaedrus describes the noble writer's play as "mythologizing about justice and the other things you mentioned," much like how Socrates mythologized about justice, beauty, and the good, earlier in the *Phaedrus* and in the *Symposium*. Indeed, the "altogether beautiful" writing seems to be modeled after Socrates's own oral practice and constant sobriety concerning the highest things while others descend into the frivolity he only plays at.[37] Even if the historical Socrates was no poetic mythologizer, and his great myths are but dramatic inspirations wrought by Plato, Socrates's famed irony is akin. If nothing else, Plato's mythologizing is a beautification or encomium of Socrates's ironic manner, a showing out or display of "the most divine and greatest images of virtue" inside him.[38] There is little reason to suppose that the writer who prefers to play in his writings, rather than indulge in symposia, could not imitate Socrates's manner in symposia or appreciate the opportunities that symposia present for planting seeds.[39] But for a valetudinarian like Phaedrus, Socrates's straightforward distinction between the play of the writer and the play of the drinker usefully directs his moderation toward a more serious use of speeches. Socrates does not attempt here, or anywhere else, to disturb Phaedrus's bodily moderation while praising the erotic mania of philosophy.

Socrates now turns Phaedrus's attention to the serious business that the knowledgeable writer attends to, which must be clarified in order to maintain the distinction between his play and mere frivolousness: "It is much finer [or: nobler, *kalliōn*] to become serious concerning these things" (276e). He thus guards against speeches about justice, beauty, or the good that are playful without seriousness, that is, exploit semblances of these things without intending to impart true beliefs or to learn what is true. Teisias's probabilistic forensics, which seeks only to secure a verdict rather than reveal the truth, would be one example of this lack of seriousness. Such superficiality seems to be particularly problematic for literary men of means, like Phaedrus, who do not face the life-threatening necessities of a litigant—at least until their frivolous play brings them into conflict with the law, as Phaedrus saw with his desecration of the Eleusinian mysteries. Socrates says that at the heart of this seriousness lies dialectic, which is the nature or perfection of rhetoric. The serious "farmer" of the "garden of letters"

> makes use of the dialectical art [*dialektikē technē*], taking hold of a fitting soul, plants and sows speeches with knowledge, which are sufficient to help themselves and the one who planted [them] and are not fruitless but have seeds, from which others may grow in other characters [*ēthoi*] that are sufficient to make this one forever immortal, and make the one who has it happy to the greatest extent possible for a human being. (276e–277a)

Socrates reminds Phaedrus that the use of dialectic entails adapting speeches to souls, which writing was said to be incapable of, even though their discussion of rhetoric concluded that someone who writes without adapting his speeches would never "speak with art" (272a–b). Writing, if it is to aspire to this highest form of speaking, must somehow find a way to not just say the same thing always, but to communicate different things to different readers, or use different means to communicate the same thing, or bring diverse readers into the same position so that they can all be addressed in the same way. This is the knowing way by which speeches must be planted and sowed, which, being adapted to the soul of the audience, will be beneficial (cf. 270b). These speeches will therefore not be complete or perfect themselves, but only in light of what they grow toward and cultivate—the writing on the soul. Writing and speaking follow the same principle, which is to remind and lead the soul toward knowledge.

Building on the metaphor of seeds, Socrates conveys the immortality of the *logos* through the organic imagery of planting, growth, and reproduction, as opposed to the immortality of the gods, who forever moved as pure disembodied souls throughout the cosmos. Recalling, from his palinode, Adrasteia's—Necessity's—planting of souls in bodies, Socrates draws an analogy where the knowledgeable writer's relationship with his students and readers is a microcosm of the divine necessity that sets the souls of mortals on their cosmic journey. That the *logos* is true, planted with knowledge, will be evidenced by the return of those souls to the superheavenly place—that is, by developing their own, personal, understanding of the nature of things. The educator teaches by leading his students to think and discern the nature of things for themselves, such that the immortality of the *logos* is derived from each soul's perception of the beings themselves—affirming that words do not reflect being, like a painting, but rather lead the soul toward perception of being. The *logos* that is reproduced and immortalized is therefore not a set of speeches, fixed words, laws, dogma, or doctrine. Rather, the "living *logos*" and "writing on the soul" is knowledge that is embodied in the student's own life, seeking out how to act in accordance with its highest objects. If Plato is himself capable of producing such writing, he will be capable of reproducing the living *logos* in his readers.[40]

Having distinguished between serious and merely playful writers, Socrates can now "distinguish those things, Phaedrus," that is, the "reproach of Lysias concerning his writing of speeches, and the speeches themselves, which were written with art and [which were written] without art" (277a–b). Socrates has elicited Phaedrus's agreement to the limitations of writing, its status as a plaything in comparison to the writing on the soul, and that the possession of the art of dialectic is integral for the writer both to grasp the nature of things as well as to reproduce this living *logos* in his students and readers. His reproach to Lysias can then take the form of another recapitulation of the art of rhetoric, this one more precise about its objects, both the nature of things and the way speeches are fitted to souls. The man who wishes "to take in hand the race of speeches with art" must first know the truth about what he speaks or writes, "defining everything [*pan*] by itself" (277b). Having defined these, he must know how to "cut according to [their] forms [*eidē*] until [he reaches] what cannot be cut." Then, he must see "the nature of soul" in the same way, and "discover the fitting [*to prosarmotton*] form [of speech] for each [soul] by nature," from which he can then "set and arrange the speech," giving "panharmonic and multicolored speeches to a multicolored soul," and simple speeches to a simple soul (277b–c).

Socrates does not repeat the conditions of artful rhetoric verbatim, but rather reformulates rather them with a few suggestive variations. First, he emphasizes the particularity of the knowledge demanded, where "everything" (*pan*) is defined, without mention of the synoptic view of "the whole" (*to holon*) implied by the Hippocratic method (270c). Indeed, it is not clear whether it would be possible to define, "bound" or "limit," the whole in the same manner that its parts must be limited in relation to one another insofar as they are distinct parts.[41]

Second, Socrates for the first time distinguishes the kinds of speeches and souls, having hitherto only indicated that it is necessary to do so (cf. 271b). Following the dialectical procedure modeled on the Hippocratics', Socrates arrives at two broad kinds of parallel speeches and souls, the "multicolored" (*poikilos*) and "simple" (*haploos*), the former having been used to describe Lysias's speech, and the latter one of the two poles of Socrates's soul (*haploos* and *polueides*, 230a). Socrates has therefore taken into himself, or perhaps found in himself, the whole range of possibilities for the human soul and speech-making. In seeking the nature of soul, he sees it both in its many forms and in the fundamental tension this produces, between soul as a whole and soul as it manifests in any particular individual—the problem of "all soul" in its collective and distributive senses (245b). Phaedrus's soul could be readily identified with the "multicolored," as evidenced by the complex myths that Socrates must produce to hold his attention.[42] But Phaedrus must also be simple, being capable of speaking and reasoning, grasping the "one" being or form that can be gathered together from its numerous instantiations (249b–c). This psychological unity explains why Socrates says that the multicolored soul should not receive only multicolored speeches, but rather "panharmonic" speeches, that is, speeches that bring what is multiform into a single harmonious whole.[43] As argued in chapter 4, the harmony and logographic necessity of a speech must be understood in relation to the soul. The reemergence of harmony in this discussion of writing, having originally been raised in the context of poetry, thus opens up a place for poetry in the nobler form of writing, as a way to bring souls that exist in a multitudinous and perhaps disorderly fashion into form—which would be most souls, if not all human ones, insofar as they are always in motion and struggle within themselves to establish the rule of the intellect.

Socrates's third revision is small but important. He now speaks of the culmination of this long study as being able to grasp "the race of speeches *with* art," rather than "having brought to perfection the art [of rhetoric]" or becoming a "*technikos* of speeches" (272a7, 273e3). By emphasizing the general object of this art, Socrates reminds Phaedrus that it encompasses not forensic, deliberative, or epideictic rhetoric, but every use of *logos*, as he first suggested when he defined rhetoric as a *psychagōgia* by means of words, whether in public or private (261a–b). Socrates accordingly describes the aim of this art as two-fold, "either to teach or to persuade," although the two seemed to converge in the noble rhetoric, where persuasion depended on learning and teaching was itself the highest form of persuasion—namely, persuasion that follows true knowledge of the beings themselves (277c). But Socrates never eliminates the difference between teaching and persuasion, since this identification so would deny the possibility of being persuaded of what is false and the possibility of error—without which there would be no deception, no learning, and no meaning to "art." Socrates thus gives the less august, "feast day" persuasion its due, for in the face of human frailty and ignorance, it will remain both necessary and the most prevalent use of speech. A beautiful or pithy exhortation holds an important place when complete certainty and truth are sought but cannot be secured for all time. Socrates's own frequent "mythologizing" about what is just, beautiful, or good, or "making speeches from any place," is a case in point, as indeed is his whole ironic manner.

Taking in hand the conditions of artfulness, Socrates now returns explicitly to the question of shameful and noble writing, which began the discussion of rhetoric: "And what about it being noble [*kalon*] or shameful with respect to both speaking and writing speeches, and at which time it might be said in justice to become a matter of reproach or not?" (277d, cf. 258d). Socrates expands the question of shameful writing to include both "speaking and writing" (277d, cf. 274b6–7). In fact, the general problem of shameful speech was suggested from the beginning of Socrates's first speech, when he covered his head in shame (237a, 243c–d). What is shameful in writing will also shed light on what is shameful in speech simply. Socrates says that "at which time," the circumstances will in part determine shamefulness in speaking and writing—that is, "the opportune moment" (*kairos*) mentioned in the discussion of rhetoric—although those right circumstances can only be perfectly grasped after having grasped the nature of things, including soul, in all their similarities and differences.

Socrates's final admonishment of Lysias shows that the principal mark of shameful writing is its inability to adapt itself to its audience and circumstances, or rather the writer's ignorance of his medium's limitations in this regard:

> So either Lysias or someone else who has at some time written or will write in private or in public having laid down laws [*nomoi*], producing political writings, and believing [*hēgoumenos*] there is some great steadfastness and clarity in it, such is a reproach to the writer, whether someone says so or not; for to be ignorant, whether awake or asleep, about what is just and unjust and bad and

good cannot in truth escape being most reprehensible, not even should the entire crowd praise it. (277d–e)

The principal criticism that such writing lacks certainty and clarity had been developed earlier, when Socrates said it cannot engage dialogue with its reader to clarify the meaning of its words. Socrates provided a psychological antecedent in the palinode, where the soul of the lover had to look beyond the monuments he would make of his beloved in order to find the true nature of what he loved (250b, 250e–251a, 252a, 254a–d; cf. 235d–e, 236b). True clarity was found only in the superheavenly place and the plain of truth, without which the use of rhetorical techniques would itself be unclear. In sum, the writer who ought to be reproached is one who has closed himself off to the true nature of things by believing that its clarity is possessed by the words themselves.[44]

Socrates's criticism of shameful writing therefore does not aim principally at what is said, but at the writer himself, at how he "believes" or "is led" (*hēgoumenos*). The shameful writer is ignorant of how it is that living discourse leads him to the meaning of the external marks that he writes down. Indeed, the very belief that there is certainty in writing is something to which his soul has been led through uncertain discourse. Plato it seems has his own irony and sense of play. Plato's use of the external mark "*hēgeisthai*" aptly illustrates how it is not the mark but the soul being led that bestows this apparent certainty. Here, Plato deliberately uses the verb *hēgeisthai* rather than other verbs of thinking, especially *nomizein*, which is related to law or custom (*nomoi*) in the sense of doing what is customary (e.g., 230a1–2, 244c2–5, 258c3–5). *Hēgeisthai* is not so limited. In the palinode, "being led" was elaborated in the mythical leadership of the gods, especially the great leader or *hegemon* Zeus, in whose train lesser souls follow (246e4). This divine leadership acts through the *erōs* that searches for god and longs to return to the eternal beings, the clarity of which is often mistakenly attributed to their instantiations on account of them being pleasing reminders (252e, cf. 250b–e). One believes something to be true not in any active sense, but because one is led to it, and one is not ultimately led to it by another human being, but by the already-present desire that someone must address in order to persuade.[45] On account of this meaning developed in the palinode, *hēgeisthai* signifies that the one who believes or thinks is already caught in the complex of desires—and of language—that move soul, which sometimes confuses it, yet also directs it toward the perfection of the pure and simple beings.[46] The man who believes there is clarity and certainty in the written word does not realize the complicity of his *erōs* in forming his opinion. That is to say, he does not recognize how that opinion was produced by and must be supported by what is for him uncertain and unclear. Insofar as this man does not see the activity of soul by which his words gain meaning, drawing on meanings already present to him in the very act of collecting and dividing things, he is a nonlover whose soul and *erōs* remain hidden behind what is manifest to him, the "marks from without."[47] Only when this secret *erōs* is itself revealed and made manifest to the nonlover will he be able to look beyond the words he has written or read to that which is truly clear and makes things clear. Lysias and the ignoble writer do not manifest the play that would evidence a higher understanding of speech in relation to the being itself. This appears to be why Socrates can so readily declare that this kind of writer is ignorant of justice and injustice, and goodness and badness.

On Plato's interpretation, Socrates's own decision not to write would seem to have been born out of these considerations: the written word is of limited utility in leading the soul, since it fixes in place words whose meanings require constant review and revision in light of the opinions brought to bear on them, given that different souls with different experiences and capacities will respond in different ways. Through such a medium, Socrates and his interlocutor could not engage in the dialogue and refutation of opinions that is necessary to light on real understanding and knowledge. The cultivation of the highest capacities of the soul appears to have been the abiding concern of Socrates's rhetoric, while writing would have forgone the thinking by which the soul grasps its real objects, and simply descended into the common *logos* of the crowd.

## PLATONIC RHETORIC

In dialectical fashion, Socrates's criticism of the writing characteristic of Lysias allows him to now unfold a noble form of writing.[48] As with the ignoble writing, the form of speech and nature of soul that produce the noble writing are closely correlated. Someone who believes that what is just, beautiful, or good exists or is clear only insofar as it is written down or spoken will never produce writings in the manner of Plato, which Socrates presently describes: "But the man who believes [*hēgoumenos*] there is much play in the written word" believes that "there has never yet been written a speech, either in meter or prose, worthy of great seriousness" (277e). This man does not believe that the written word is entirely opaque and in flux. Rather, writing is understood as "play," somehow childish but also educational since it is play in light of a great seriousness. Socrates does not exclude any kind of writing from this playfulness—not only are laws and political writings implicated, but also the great poetic works of Homer and Hesiod, a pious Pindar, and even the sacred written prophecies of the Pythia and Sibyl.[49] Perhaps this is why Socrates cites the Delphic inscription, "Know thyself," which turns one away from the hope for an easy path toward the cultivation of the true *logos*.

Socrates also brings the criticism of writing to bear on oral speech. His analysis of rhetoric is not complete until he takes into account the form of speech that the use of writing tends to produce. He says that there has not been a speech worthy of great seriousness "spoken as the rhapsodes have spoken, persuading without examination and teaching, but that the best of them have proven to be in reality reminders for those who know" (277e–278a). Writing produces rhapsodic-like speeches—monologues that only speak and repeat themselves without examining or teaching its reader. Retrospectively, oral rhetoric that likewise does not teach will fail to attain the highest end of the art of speaking, namely producing virtue (270b). Only teaching in this true sense of leading a soul toward what really is will produce the true virtue that is really "fitting" for a soul. The three speeches delivered in the first half of the *Phaedrus*, if understood to be earnest statements of the truth, would be guilty of this incapacity to really teach or lead their audience, despite or perhaps because of their inspirational quality.[50] Their rhapsodic manner could only dazzle with the momentary efflorescence of beauty—fruit from the gardens of Adonis. Without examination and teaching, the audience could not come to knowledge. These significant limitations are not restricted, of course, to the speeches of rhapsodes, but to any *logos* that is a mere pronouncement or product of rote memorization and not understood as merely a reminder. Such speech is an all too common part of rhetoric, which seizes on the opportunity to reduce the audience to a silent passivity, and so remains indifferent to the attainment of knowledge and development of character.[51] These limitations would also apply to exhortations to virtue, such as Prodicus's *Choice of Heracles*, which Socrates thought fit to repeat, although it acquired a reputation for being pedantic.[52] Socrates is himself no traditionalist who merely retells ancient stories of virtue, for his storytelling has a youthful or modern quality in that they redress the complacency and overconfidence of his interlocutors.

In light of this, will Socrates's own exhortations to philosophy and virtue succeed with Phaedrus? Socrates has refuted or qualified Phaedrus's opinions concerning the nature, ends, and means of rhetoric, but has Phaedrus himself engaged in this learning by careful examination of his own opinions? The student must also be active and not simply receive and then repeat what is told to him, but bring himself to examine and question those speeches. Otherwise, the student will never become independent of his teacher and be able to defend his own words. A number of Socrates's own students suffered this fate, losing sight of what they once saw with his aid and even turning away from philosophy without his guiding presence.[53] So even Socrates, who examined his students' opinions through refutation and dialectic, could not transcend play and show with all clarity the true objects of seriousness. His speech could only bring the soul to a clearing freed of false opinion, but the beings themselves could be perceived only if that soul had joined in the exercise seriously, as a matter of seeking something of value, and understood the grounds upon which their opinions had been refuted. Therefore only if the soul follows the *logos* as a guide, rather than seeing it as the answer itself, can it be led to the experiences portrayed in the palinode. Yet Phaedrus's vague understanding of *logos*, which Socrates has only uncovered over the course of their conversation, that speech itself is something clear and capable by itself of providing for the desires of the soul, was a great obstruction of this real leading of the soul, since it both hid the nature of those desires and refused the possibility that they could be explored through *logos*. Moreover, Socrates was compelled to first address him on his own terms, in monologues of professed clarity that were filled with rhetorical flourishes.

In contrast to the understanding of *logos* held by Phaedrus and the ignoble writer, the noble writer will be "one who believes [*hēgoumenos*] that what is visible and perfect and worthy of seriousness is only in those things that are taught and said for the sake of learning about what is just, beautiful, and good, and really written in the soul" (278a). These things to which one "is led" here is a return to the highest objects of the palinode, the beings themselves, looking beyond the words themselves. In the palinode, Socrates said that only by "standing outside [*ekistamenos*] human seriousness" will someone be "perfected" by again glimpsing being (249c–d). True writing in the soul is being devoted to and capable of learning, rather than the possession or acquisition of teaching. The noble writer does not seek to produce Daedalean statues that walk and speak upon command, but human beings who are able to converse in search of what is true; the writer wishes to produce souls that are themselves fertile and capable of passing on this "seed." These speeches, Socrates tells Phaedrus, "must be said as if they are legitimate sons," rather than just the "legitimate brothers" of the written word, which is to say that they are the writer's own offspring and products of a certain character (278a, cf. 276a).

Once this father of speeches has "discovered" the "one in himself"—that is, the writing in the soul or the living *logos*—he must see if "some offspring and brothers" of it will "grow in the souls of others according to its worth" (278a). This *logos* within himself is tested by its ability to take root in others, since only then will he see whether it has been planted with knowledge of what really is and the many ways that the beings themselves are manifested. This noble speech will therefore finally transcend the particularity of the audience, living in different souls at different times in different forms, while being akin as brothers and sons of the same pattern, in the same manner that every kind of human life shares in the same "form of the human" by virtue of its capacity for reasoning (*logismos*, 249b–c). The truly living and immortal *logos* will thus resemble the beings themselves, the manifestations of which are all necessarily different yet refer to and share in a single being that transcends each of them. On the basis of this, the father of speeches cannot be interpreted as someone to whom every soul that carries his "offspring" are beholden.[54] Such a result, as likely as it may be, would in fact be the very opposite of what is intended here, for the *logos* is fertile only so far as it is the fruit of the soul's search and a living memory of the beings themselves—it is fertile so far as it gives rise to real thinking that has no need of recourse to its father (cf. 275e).[55] The greatest father of speeches is he who is able to derive his lineage from the beings that transcend any of his own speeches or writings.[56]

The *logos* that is planted in us and is written in the soul is that *logos* which is able to differentiate being, and is no longer a monologue, a set speech, a monument, but living and moving according to the hidden form of things by which we are led between the one and many. The noble writer therefore does not implant this *logos* simply passing on "phantom" speeches, but through *psychagōgia* that involves, at its heart, *antilogic* that refutes opinions and dialectical purification of thought.

The noble writer intended here is undoubtedly none other than the man who playfully wrote this critique of writing. Plato, through his own irony, tells his readers that he is the divine answer to Socrates's prayer and attained what Socrates never could (he is one that "you and I should pray that we might become" [278b]). Plato's intention in having Socrates make this prayer, however, should not be reduced to self-flattery. Rather, the reader should ask what the problem is that Socrates advances here that would make him pray and hope for divine assistance?

The paradigmatic human being that Socrates and Phaedrus pray to become is, first and foremost, someone who believes that there is no serious and clear writing or speaking without examination and teaching. He is not strictly a writer or rhetorician. What Socrates outlines is an emos, a manner of living or character, rather than a particular profession or activity, which may be characterized in the terms used to describe the true lover: openness to being. This man does not seek or find perfection in *logos*, but only in what it enables him to perceive by shaping his soul so that he is always able to keep before himself the nature of speeches as reminders. Although such a man does not find justice, beauty, and good in speeches, neither does he lose sight of these things, for speeches must be used to teach and help him examine these things. His knowing will not consist in the memorization of texts or speeches, which he will only do so far as they assist in the serious work of learning and clearing the way so that the living *logos* may grow. This is an ethos of continual exercise in openness, which must be done in the manner Socrates has frequently repeated—dialectical exercise in the refutation of the opinions and speeches that are continually presented to him by himself and others. Finally, his manner of being and ability to see the *logos* as a reminder is only maintained in relation to others, since the legitimacy of his "son," his *logos*, is only discovered in conversation with others and proven by his persuasion of them, having understood their natures and the *logoi* for which they are suited. His ethos is consequently nothing less than discovering and producing justice, beauty, and good in himself and others, as the crowning achievement of rhetoric. His *logos*—or rather, the living *logos* in which he shares—is reproduced, not through a feast-day monument, but through instilling a like ethos ("other *logoi* in other characters [*ēthoi*]" [272a2]) of perpetual initiation and practice.[57]

All this is a prayer, for such a man would never succumb to those natural desires that would close him to the search and lead him to believe he had found truth and perfection in a speech or object he had grown fond of; this is a life of self-refutation that could never take its particular works seriously. If Plato did not intend to merely flatter himself, but to embody this serious purpose, his writings must somehow admit of this playful self-refutation and be capable of cultivating thinking in his readers (278b).[58] This playfulness will be the heart of Socrates's message concerning how one writes in a noble way: "Tell this to Lysias and anyone else who puts together speeches, as well as to Homer and anyone else again who composes poems that are bare or in song, and third to Solon and whoever in political speeches writes compositions he calls laws" (278c). This broad message is addressed to Lysias as well as any writer, past, present, or future, and thus goes far beyond the scope of Phaedrus and Socrates's personal relations. Socrates gives no indication whether he believes that this universal message, imparted only to Phaedrus, will find a similarly universal audience.

Socrates's final message is a puzzle that points back to his own limited knowledge, his erotics, as the heart of knowledgeable writing. This message is a concise set of three conclusions, with the first being that the writer must compose knowing that he holds the truth. Second, since he is able to come to its assistance and elaborate on what is written, he can "go into a refutation [*elenchos*] concerning what he wrote" (278c). Third, when the writer speaks, he is able to show that his writings "are wretched." The first conclusion in the message has been an abiding concern of the conversation since Phaedrus opined that rhetoric did not require knowledge (260a). This of course does not mean that a composition written by a knowledgeable man is simply true, as has been shown in the discussion of writing. In fact, the other two points of this message, and the proof of the writer's understanding of his medium, depend on him showing the opposite, much like Stesichorus insisted that "this story is not true" (243a8).

The second point, that the writer is able "to go into a refutation concerning what he wrote," is derived from the ability of someone who is knowledgeable to assist his written speech (see 278a). More than just being able to elaborate on its arguments, the writer is said to refute his writings and himself. This would indicate, indirectly, that he possessed something of greater worth than his writing. It also means that the writer must somehow be present and always accompany his composition; as Socrates said before they examined Lysias's speech, "Lysias is present," although Lysias's speech proved unable to defend itself adequately let alone refute itself (228e1). Unless a particular way of writing to ameliorate this authorial absence could be found, the need for the author to be present would defeat the purpose of writing altogether. Socrates hints that maintaining the author's presence has something to do with the ability to refute himself. Such writing would contain contradictions—the very contradictions or opposites indicative of *antilogic* and persuasion. The knowledgeable writer, knowing that any single speech could by itself not really manifest the truth to his reader, would leave reminders of his intent in the form of inconsistences, contradictions, and paradoxes that point beyond themselves.[59] Socrates earlier mentioned numerous techniques that could achieve this purpose, not least of all Evenus's covert techniques that were said to be "aids to memory" (267a2–5). Writing of this kind thus aims to produce *aporia* in the soul of the audience, which compels the soul to seek a resolution of those contradictions under a higher understanding of what is written (see 255d3).[60] Truth does not lie simply in the outward appearance or teaching of the text, but also hidden in its arrangement or form, which is also to say, its purpose. A writer therefore comes to the aid of his writings by writing speeches that will lead its readers not to a single dogma, a repetitious speech, but to a desire to understand and exercise that desire by making that speech their own. In order to assist his writing, the noble writer must cultivate a kindred ethos in the reader. The reader enters into a kind of dialogue with the text, thinking through its contradictions, and thereby develops his own reasoning and "writing on the soul." The author is thus revealed indirectly, as a consequence of the reader's own study and reconstruction of the purpose of the text. At the highest level, writer and reader will enter into community, attaining that *homonoia* or "being of the same mind" that Socrates earlier attributed to philosophic lovers (256b1). The author's "seed" becomes immortal because it is able to reproduce the tensions in the soul which arouse *logismos* and by which it perceives the beings themselves.

This soul's experience of beauty is paradigmatic, since beauty itself is paradigmatic for the tension experienced by the soul, for its superficial attractiveness conceals its true nature, and casts those who behold it back on themselves in search of that nature. The natural desire to take hold of, to make one's own, and never lose what pleases is a powerful, and indeed necessary, instrument for persuasion. That the being of the most manifest of beings is hidden yet inspires those who behold it is perhaps the greatest seed of all.

The third point in Socrates's message to Lysias follows closely from the first two. The author will be able "to prove" that his "writings are wretched" (278c). As noted, the refutation of his own writings demonstrates their inadequate and pale imitation of the truth. His audience is thus led to suppose that he does in fact hold something of greater value and worthy of seriousness, and so to inquire for themselves as to what is hidden behind the self-contradiction of the writing. One example of how an enlivening contradiction can be implanted in a text is found right here: how does a writer help something by demonstrating that it is wretched and refuting it? The readers who attempt to solve such riddles do not become sycophants that merely repeat the author's words, but seek to become capable in their own right.

Socrates crowns his message with the title of the writer who is able to embody this ethos. This writer cannot be called "a wise man," for wisdom belongs only to the gods (278d). Rather, a "more fitting" or "harmonious" title is philosopher or lover of wisdom, someone inspired by the knowledge that he lacks wisdom and must seek it. Only now does philosophy re-emerge to fulfill Socrates's aim, in the discussion of the art of rhetoric, "to persuade Phaedrus . . . that unless he should philosophize sufficiently, he will never be sufficient in speaking about anything" (261a). This late emergence of philosophy casts doubt on whether any of the particular moments of the preceding discussion of the art of rhetoric suitably reflect philosophy. Perhaps even the art of dialectic, although necessary for "thinking and speaking," does not adequately account for this way of life or ethos, given Socrates's claim that the real attainment and artful perfection of dialectic depends upon complete knowledge of the whole—knowledge that would mean one was not a philosopher but a god. If, then, it is questionable whether the philosopher is a dialectician in the strict sense, Socrates leaves the philosophic life, and hence the possibility of a noble writer, as a question. Is it possible for a human being to obtain the wisdom sought by the philosopher? Without the possibility of true wisdom, as found in the complete dialectician, there would not be either art or the knowledge it depends upon, but only eristic and artless stumbling to greater or lesser degrees of efficacy. Plato therefore brings the discussion of rhetoric to a close not with a solution to the problem of persuasion, but with one final problem concerning whether the art of speaking can ever be adequately grasped.[61]

Plato brings into sight the most serious of things—the living *logos* at the heart of the philosophical life, which seeks true being and the nature of the whole—at the same moment that he criticizes writing and therefore "shows to be wretched" everything that has come before in the *Phaedrus*. The emergence of philosophy saves the *Phaedrus* from the criticism of writing and the risk that it is trivial play that reduces all speech to meaningless contradiction and opacity. Plato has written a succession of refutations over the course of the *Phaedrus*, including refutations of Lysias's speech, the "merely human," Phaedrus's opinions, the ignoble rhetoric, and finally writing itself, which collectively serve to indicate the presence of a higher mind and understanding of the nature of things—a higher view and necessity that binds together all these refutations. The very form of Plato's writing is therefore an imitation of the philosophic life that, beginning with what is found in common opinion, engages in a truly enlivening and ennobling search for that which is only implied and dimly perceived in those opinions. In this sense, Plato has written a fitting monument or reminder of what is truly divine.

In the case of Plato's rhetoric, his writings both display and embody the Socratic life, the search for wisdom through conversation, and present that life as the paradigmatic human life. In this sense, the philosophic life is the "reminding from within," embodied in the "reminding from without" constituted by Plato's words. Plato's writing must imitate Socrates's rhetoric if it is to truly engage readers in the philosophic experience and persuade them of the necessity of philosophy. Plato's means to this end can be briefly summarized. Since Plato himself points out writing's defects—endless repetition, saying the same thing to every reader, and needing assistance—it is reasonable to assume that he thought he had found a way to counteract them or use writing's properties to rhetorical advantage. In the first place, Plato's dialogues endlessly repeat themselves so that future generations of students may carefully reread them in search of the single form that collects and binds together the subtle arguments, including paradoxes and contradictions, at work in Socratic play.[62] Phaedrus and Socrates demonstrated this use for writing by rereading Lysias's speech.[63] Socrates's guiding presence is to some extent replaced, as noted earlier, by the text itself and the need for the reader to account for its words and form.[64] Toward this end, logographic necessity is a useful heuristic principle.

Second, it is true that Plato's writings speak to everyone and do not adapt themselves to the particular reader, at least to the extent that the words do not change and can be read by anyone, but since those words must be interpreted, there is already a discrimination of audiences. A corollary of the rhetorical principle of discrimination is polysemy. Plato's use of the dialogue form, however, grounds his words in relation to the specific questions and answers of concrete and particular interlocutors. Conducted *ad hominem*, the dialogues are already limited with reference to the true nature of the whole and do not speak as if they were utterly clear; they can only embody that part of the whole which could be seen from the particular context of the setting, topic, and dramatis personae. Phaedrus's character, for example, has been shown to exert great influence on what Socrates says in the *Phaedrus*—which is not to say that a glimpse of true being is unattainable, but rather that this glimpse is only a glimpse and never consists of a plain monologue or disclosure. There is no universal speech like an oracular or rhapsodic pronouncement because persuasion must account for the differences between souls.[65]

Third, the apparent defenselessness of a piece of writing is counteracted by the dialogue form; the meaning of the work is not expressed simply, but through the peculiar features of a dialogue, just mentioned, in addition to the arguments of the interlocutors. A reader must account for both action and speech. There is a psychological, erotic background to *logos*, as indicated throughout the *Phaedrus*, that must also be interpreted in order to see the meaning of a *logos* not as it is manifested in words but in light of how it leads one—Phaedrus or the reader—to a certain view of reality. For example, Socrates's first speech, although clearly expressed, loses its meaning when taken out of its dramatic context and apart from its inspired proem and prologue. The defenselessness of a piece of writing is also counteracted by the presence of contradictions that naturally arise from Socrates's questioning and refutative form of dialogue.[66] The reader himself comes to the aid of the text in an effort to understand it.

The possibility of a noble writing, whatever its form,[67] does not explain specifically why Plato wrote. Even if writing's limitations can be overcome, what advantages over oral discourse inspire its use? Plato's decision to write can be interpreted as a political act to memorialize Socrates, but since that decision is based on the inadequacies of a strictly oral philosophical life, Plato's decision entails a supplement to or even correction of that life.[68] There is no explicit mention in the *Phaedrus* of the danger posed to the philosopher by publicly expressing his thoughts, so it cannot be said that the difference between Socrates and Plato lies solely in the desire to avoid persecution, as important a reason as that may be.[69] Nor can it be seriously maintained that Socrates was capable of writing at the level of Plato had he only wanted to, for his entire life was a testament to the fact that he did not see a manner of doing so that was worthy of philosophy.[70] Plato of course does not explain his intention directly, and so the extent to which his purpose in writing is revealed in the *Phaedrus* can only be ascertained by reconsidering the dialectic between oral and written word found in Socrates's dialogue with Phaedrus.

The dialogue between Socrates and Plato, the oral and the written, opened with Thamos's judgment on writing on the issue of memory. Socrates's identification of three defects of writing showed how writing fails to engage in the searching dialogue necessary for learning and teaching, which is the highest form of recollection. The potential advantage of writing became clearer when the "writing on the soul" was invoked as an analogy for true knowledge that transcends any particular speech. This moment sheds light on the difference between Socrates and Plato, since the writing on the soul, or rather the knowledge in the soul, transcends speech, either written or oral. Socrates's criticism of writing, and his refusal to write, is seriously qualified by this revelation of the transcendent nature of the "living *logos*," since it is a qualification not only of writing, but also oral discourse. More often than not, oral discourse fails to ascend to such heights. The inert and repetitious written word may be only a phantom of the living *logos*, but it nonetheless gives the appearance of possessing properties of true knowledge and being what oral discourse is incapable of, namely an unchanging universality.[71] Socrates's admission that writing too can be pedagogical, so far as it counteracts its limitations, is not balanced by the possibility of oral discourse that is unchanging and universal. To be sure, the knowledgeable writer must be capable of expressing himself and assisting his writing orally, but those spoken words are more limited by their own mortality, in the sense that they do not possess—and should not possess, insofar as they are adapted to a given audience—the fixity of what they are meant to signify, and also limited by the mortality of those who hear and speak them. The immortal living *logos* cannot be adequately represented in the spoken words of a single mortal; its universality is only manifested as a pattern that is capable of being replanted and cultivated in others across space and time. While Socrates was able to adapt his speech to the particular soul before him, he was unable or unwilling to address a crowd, let alone continue to speak after his death—and granting that he implanted his *logos* in his followers, it inevitably failed to live as does the truly living *logos* insofar as it was subject to the vicissitudes of human memory and intellectual capacity. Socrates would or could not persuade the *Dēmos* as a whole to cherish his *logos* and make monuments for the sake of remembering his *logos*.

Did Socrates's refusal to write originate from his indifference to that lower form of immortality, pursued by the hypocritical legislators who abuse Lysias, which consists of lasting glory and honor through the memory of others (258b–c)? Werner Jaeger suggests that Socrates did not write because his service was to fellow Athenians rather than some universal "humanity."[72] Perhaps Plato believed there to be something more universal in the Socratic experience that required an accordingly public and popular medium. Outside the city walls in the *Phaedrus*, the "spiritedness" or *thumos* characteristic of honor and political life is never explicitly mentioned, and only appears through the love of honor that keeps the soul beholden to the opinions of the city. Did Socrates's philosophic *erōs* so control the lower part of the soul that is concerned with the opinion of others, the *thumos* characteristic of the white horse, as to eliminate any desire for glory, as Leo Strauss suggests?[73] Was Socrates concerned that any monument made of him and his *logos* would only be a monument, and therefore an obstruction to following the *logos* toward knowledge of what is eternal? Any admission that he was in fact interested in such immortality would reduce Socrates to the sort of nonlover that politicians pretend to be, and a teacher despite his insistence that he was ignorant (257d–258d). As Strauss argues, Plato certainly would not have continued to write had he recognized that this form of immortality was in fact lower in every respect than the private striving of an erotic soul.[74] Socrates himself, at the end of his life, will express concern that "[my] *logos* may die."[75] Plato must have believed that there was something valuable that could be attained through that monumental glory—which does not imply that Plato desired glory as the highest end, only that he saw a use for it.[76] But if there was a use for the immortality that writing can bestow, one that did not compromise erotic openness, why did Socrates not pursue it? Socrates was not ignorant of the rhetorical opportunity afforded by reputation.[77] Socrates's refusal to write can therefore only reflect a failure on his part to see the higher power of writing, to keep alive the "living *logos*," and that Plato attained a deeper understanding of the whole range of erotic experience. Plato shows the ground of Socrates's speeches and experiences—especially the self-knowledge of his own ignorance that was essential to his life—in a way Socrates never could.

Plato's rehabilitation of writing means Socrates failed to understand how it is that the *logos* becomes immortal, which means he failed to understand both the nature of the *logos*, the living *logos*, and the human soul in which it dwells. To use the analogy of the two farmers, the one who plants for feast days and the other for real growth, Socrates only seems to be capable of the latter, and even then only to a limited extent because he is incapable of the former. His rhetoric would cease to be erotic in the sense of stimulating a mutual search if he gratified his interlocutors with the beautiful speeches of a feast day—he would be like a Gorgias or Thrasymachus and make cicadas of his audience. Plato on the other hand is freed from the strictly *ad hominem* constraint of Socratic rhetoric by virtue of writing, and may combine the talents of both farmers. Since he addresses many people at once, he can address both a range of souls as well as the range within the single soul (which range was seen to be implicit in the possibility of persuading—that is, changing—a soul), at one time amusing them with Lysias's speech before dispelling it, then at another giving a dazzling account of the whole in the palinode, which he then offsets with a rather plain discussion of the nature of rhetoric. Not entirely dissimilar to Teisias's probability, Platonic rhetoric addresses the multitude of soul types in a harmonious way that Socrates could not, as if Plato had perfected the art of dialectic so that he could collect and divide every kind of speech and soul. But his writing can become *ad hominem* insofar as a single reader cannot be reduced to a single soul type, but is capable of change.

Writing allows Plato to give the appearance that "all soul" finds its mirror in him (and flatter his readers that he mirrors them). He is "seeming-wise" (*doxosophos*), but knowingly and therefore playfully so. Plato's playfulness, especially evident in the *Phaedrus*, embodies beauty as that which is most manifest and superficial while concealing the truth. This must be the ultimate lesson in Anne Lebeck's essay: "in language and form the dialogue so perfectly *is* what it discusses, exemplifies what it advocates, awakens the reactions which it describes."[78] Socrates's irony and refutive approach can only imply a greater whole; he cannot gratify his audience's desire for unity and a complete vision of that whole, a desire he himself identified in the palinode. Dionysius Halicarnassus suggested that Plato took over the "grand and simple" style of Thrasymachus.[79] Al-Fārābī (1962) similarly claimed that Plato combined "the method of Socrates" and "the method of Thrasymachus."[80] This is to say that Plato is able to direct the passions of his audience (which he did most obviously in the palinode, in order to gratify the soul's longing for the whole), yet is also able to attend to the true art of planting seeds found in Socrates's elenchic rhetoric, so that his readers would be persuaded—or see for themselves—that something of greater value did in fact lie behind the surface of his poetry. Plato preserves Socrates's refutation of the idols of common opinion, and even accentuates it by setting opinion as such against the resplendent images of transcendent and eternal beings. Plato "rolls out" the Socratic experience "everywhere to those who give ear." If, then, Socrates lacked *thumos*, it cannot be that he did not recognize how to win honor and lovers by gratifying their desires and flattering them, for he was to some extent successful with honor-lovers such as Alcibiades and Charmides. Instead, a lack of *thumos* can only be understood in relation to the *Dēmos*—he won the honor of honor-loving men by refuting their own love of the *Dēmos*.[81] Insofar as Socrates refused to write, he failed to demonstrate that he had sufficiently laid hold of the *logos* and understood the soul to persuade the *Dēmos*, let alone every human being. He insisted that he was ignorant and that this is the wellspring of philosophy. The irony of Socrates' wisdom is that it could not be made manifest and clear to the extent that his interlocutors desired—his interlocutors often believed he only dissembled, concealing from them a teaching and "divine idols."[82] Only through the intervention of Plato could a "terrible longing" be generated for the wisdom that is the most desirable thing for every soul. Plato is able to keep open a view toward eternity in a way Socrates never could.

This view of Plato's supplement and correction of Socrates cannot be definitively proven. In the end, Plato has Socrates himself "mythologize" and deliver the monologues of the *Phaedrus* and the other dialogues, although one wonders whether the "nymphs of the place" that inspire him to speak with art are nothing more than Plato himself, and whether Plato really did place Socrates outside of himself in order to give an account of his rhetoric.[83] The beauty of the Platonic dialogue is largely transmitted through the mouth of Socrates, and the extent to which Socrates's conversations reached the splendid heights portrayed in Plato is an enduring problem, for the two cannot be decisively distinguished.[84] Neither do the limitations that Plato saw in Socrates's rhetoric indicate that he could have removed Socrates from his dialogues or his writing as a whole; his whole presentation of philosophy is derived from his interpretation of the Socratic experience and the soul of "the most just man of those then living."[85] Plato's refutation of Socrates's oral practice is proof that he can stand independent of Socrates, the father of his *logos*, yet also demonstrates that Socrates did grasp something of the immortal living *logos* because it reproduced itself in his student's independent thought.[86] Even as Socrates fades from dramatic prominence in what are called Plato's late dialogues, his presence is felt in the playful form of Plato's writing. There was always "the Socrates in him."[87]

## RETURN TO THE CITY

Socrates has given Phaedrus a message, an exhortation to philosophy, in preparation for their return to the city. Phaedrus will disseminate Socrates's teaching on writing to Lysias and perhaps, through the rhetorician, affect a new understanding of the *logos* in the city at large. But what sort of a messenger will Phaedrus be? Although he is an eager solicitor and, at times, dispenser of speeches, this eagerness is born from a superficial and hedonistic approach to speeches. What will he remember from this conversation? For the same reason that he is a lover of speeches and an eager messenger he is also unsuitable—his desire to be gratified by speeches has made him reliant on books and weakened his memory, and for the most part he has only followed Socrates's lead in the conversation (227e1–228a3, 228a5–b6, 228d1–5, 273a3–5, 277b4). No doubt his recollection of the conversation for Lysias will not be verbatim, and many of the particular arguments will be lost, but the outstanding images of the winged chariot of the soul, the cicadas' song, and the Egyptian myth will be sufficiently vivid to hold a place in his mind. Perhaps even Socrates's conclusions concerning the noble rhetoric will be recalled, given that he recapitulated them four times (271a–b, 271d–272b, 273d–274a, 277b–c). At the least, the general impressions produced in Phaedrus should remain—such as Socrates's rhetorical victory over Lysias, the rehabilitation of *erōs*, the need for knowledge in rhetoric, and the criticism of writing.

If nothing else, Phaedrus will be eager to recount his ecstatic experiences with Socrates, a rhapsode in his train. It is precisely his superficiality that recommends him. As is befitting his name and the theme of the entire dialogue, the man "Phaidros" is himself a "showing forth," and who could better serve as Socrates's interlocutor in a dialogue that warns against the dangers of monumentalizing? If Phaedrus's physical beauty and superficial love of speech could be harnessed to "something of greater value" to betray some wisdom beneath the "silver filigree," as one commentator has called it, Socrates would find a very useful friend indeed.[88] Socrates, for the purpose of "planting his seed" in others (which would not be idle vanity but great philanthropy),[89] could multiply the effect of his rhetoric by winning over the beautiful favorite of the speech-writers. A literary dilettante or "impresario," as Ferrari (1987) calls him, Phaedrus is the most adulatory audience, consumer, and disseminator of the work of speech-writers and rhetoricians.[90] Indeed, Phaedrus's multicolored soul is a helpful reflection of the panoply of soul types to be found in a broader audience, for which Socrates has produced speeches that are fittingly variegated yet harmonic. But if that is all Socrates has done, he would be guilty of producing "feast day" rhetoric and trifling pleasures. Instead, the harmony of Socrates's rhetoric is found in how he supplements the poetry and beautiful images, helping them take root in deeper soil, by discussing them with Phaedrus and showing how it is that they have worked on his soul. These two moments of myth and *logos* are sustained in a dialectical and fertile tension, the former providing an inspiring whole and the latter demanding a persuasive differentiation and analysis of its parts. Lysias and the speech-writers themselves would be compelled to compete with Socrates and adapt to the rhetorical countercharms that have been implanted in Phaedrus. Through Phaedrus, Socrates could reach Lysias, and if he could turn him to philosophy, like his brother, Socrates could reach the city as a whole by inspiring a noble rhetoric. Nevertheless, while Socrates's need for a messenger reflects the natural spreading of his seed, it also reflects the limitations of his strictly oral practice. Phaedrus, after all, will soon be exiled for defaming the Eleusinian mysteries. Will he recall the real reasons for Socrates's use of the Eleusinian symbols? Far more effective would be a written account that would remedy the limitations of Phaedrus's memory and "remind" whoever came across it.

But rather than point directly to himself as the noble writer whom Lysias should imitate, Plato points to Isocrates, another associate of Socrates who chose to write rather than strictly follow his teacher's oral practice. Phaedrus tells Socrates that they should not pass over his companion, "the noble [or: beautiful, *kalos*] Isocrates" (278e). Phaedrus seems to think of Isocrates because of his resemblance to Lysias as a speech-writer, another seeming antipode of Socrates in this regard.[91] Phaedrus does not believe the message for Isocrates will be the same, and therefore does not see where Isocrates fits in Socrates's account of writing. "What will we say he is?" Phaedrus asks. That is, is Isocrates a mere writer of political speeches, or is he a philosopher?[92] Apparently, Isocrates does not write in the manner of Lysias or for the same purpose, yet neither does he evidence the attributes and ethos of the knowledgeable writer—playfulness for the sake of teaching and the ability to refute what he has written. Are his writings philosophic?

Socrates's and Plato's assessment of Isocrates's work bears some scrutiny, since it helps, by contrast, to clarify Plato's understanding of his own writing and rhetoric.[93] So far, the only comparison cases have been Lysias, Teisias, and other rhetoricians whose principal purpose was simply persuasion. Isocrates, as an associate of Socrates who also exhorts his audience to "philosophy," seems closer to Plato.[94] But did Plato regard him as a peer, or find some limitations in this admittedly nobler rhetoric? Although the evidence is slim and therefore any historical answer to this question will be provisional, Isocrates's place in the context of the argument of the *Phaedrus* does suggest the possibility, and limitation, of a noble rhetoric that is not yet truly philosophical.

Drawing on his knowledge of Isocrates, Socrates prophesies about his prospects: "with respect to his nature he seems to me to be better by an order of magnitude than the speeches associated with Lysias, and to have a character [*ēthos*] mixed even more nobly [lit. in a more well-born way, *gennikōteroi*]" (279a). Isocrates therefore possesses one of the three elements of a successful rhetorician—a well-suited nature—and since he has already been writing at this point, he has the second—practice—as well (279a6, cf. 269d). Socrates implies that he possesses something of the third criterion, knowledge, by subtly changing Isocrates's epithet of "noble," from Phaedrus's *kalos*, to *gennikos* to impute to Isocrates a good natural capacity or descent. Socrates thus recalls his earlier use of the related *gennadas*, also "noble" or "well-bred," which described the "free man," the noble and gentle soul that was repulsed by Lysias's account of *erōs* (243c). Isocrates, similarly well-bred, would be aware of this higher *erōs*. This grasp of a higher *erōs* is borne out in the remainder of Socrates's prophecy, which says that when Isocrates grows older,

> with respect to the very speeches he now works on, he would differ [from Lysias and others] more than [do men differ from] boys in the arranging of speeches, and still more, if these things are not sufficient for him, some more divine impulse [*hormē*] might lead [him] to something greater, for there is some philosophy in the mind of the man. (279a–b)

This divine impulse that leads to philosophy is nothing other than *erōs*,[95] which desires to grasp the nature of things (cf. *hormēn* at 238b8, 251d2). This philosophy in him would draw him beyond competition for honors with rhetoricians like Lysias, who content themselves with the courtroom rather than the legislation and political reform that interested a young and ambitious Isocrates.[96] Surely Isocrates would not consider such longing to be a form of madness.

Nonetheless, Socrates's prophecy is uncertain, only stating that Isocrates "might" develop this philosophy. Nor is Socrates clear that this impulse will lead Isocrates to philosophy, only "to something greater." Plato may thus insinuate that Isocrates never did develop this philosophical potential, without invalidating Socrates's assessment of his character or suggesting that Isocrates's work was without merit. Indeed, Isocrates's writings never transcend political rhetoric, and he only ridicules the speculations concerning nature that Socrates said was necessary for the perfection of rhetoric,[97] and does not define the soul, as Socrates also demanded (270a, 270c–271c).[98] His own care for the grandeur of Athens and political devotion of its citizens is no doubt noble,[99] but perhaps obscures *erōs* as Socrates portrays it in his palinode, a great passion that must first lead the soul beyond the city in order to achieve a clear vision of what is in truth necessary for the individual soul.

Socrates only mentions, however, Isocrates's early work. Plato could be serious that there is a philosophical quality in Isocrates's work, perhaps more than is obvious. This does not imply that the two did not have real disagreements concerning the nature of political philosophy,[100] but there were interesting similarities in their political writings, not least concerning rhetoric. For example, a number of Isocrates's works possess the criteria for artful rhetoric, particularly the use of definition.[101] Also, Isocrates's *Encomium of Helen* emphasizes the development of the rhetorician's character and judgment concerning "the opportune moment" (*to kairos*), although he denies there is knowledge of the soul or that virtue can be taught, and denigrates precise knowledge (*epistēmē*) in favor of opinion (*doxa*).[102] It is also possible that Isocrates really was a noble writer as described by Socrates, capable of refuting what he wrote because he possessed "things of greater value": in *Against the Sophists*, Isocrates explicitly says that one must look beyond contradictions in speech, which the eristic sophists dwell on, to deeds as well;[103] he also seems to deliberately contradict himself by claiming to teach while deriding knowledge.[104] These considerations are sufficient evidence that Plato, whatever his final assessment of Isocrates, could find "some philosophy" in Isocrates. As such, Isocrates's presence at the end of the *Phaedrus* does serve a useful purpose for the work as a whole, for he is the possibility of a noble rhetoric that is not yet philosophical, even though it is to some extent inspired and reminded by it. He is akin to the lesser lovers of the palinode, who have not yet become philosophers because of their "love of honor," but "have an impulse [*hormēn*] to grow wings" in the future (256c–d). As seen in Socrates's first speech, it is the desire for glory and trust in the opinions of the many that prevents the flourishing of *erōs* and attainment of true knowledge.[105] Only if the noble writer is able to cultivate a higher desire that can rule his *thumos* will his rhetoric truly benefit the city.[106] This "impulse" will always place him in tension with the city and traditionalism as such.

Phaedrus is ready to return to the city, now that the nature of shameful and noble writing has been revealed, and a succinct message has been formulated for his beloved Lysias. "The heat has become milder," he tells Socrates (279b). The sun's descent from its zenith inspires the return to the city; its great heat resides in personal contemplation outside the *logos* of the city and its opinions (cf. 242a). Although the city may conceal the experiences and nature of the soul, this concealment has also been shown to be necessary lest the soul become dazzled and put to sleep by the sun. It is through this *logos*, animated as it is by common opinions and desires and the background of assumptions about the nature of things, that the individual soul must ascend to grasp the beings themselves. Phaedrus cannot have the pure, unadorned, and endless pleasures that he believes are found in speeches, but rather he must regard speech as a dim mirror in which he might spy something of the truth. Phaedrus and Socrates have therefore briefly ascended from the *logos* by examining the truth of their own opinions, but insofar as they must dwell in opinions that they shape with their fellow citizens, they can only strive to embody and put into practice that brief moment of clarity, and thereby develop an ethos worthy of that insight.

Since the gods of this sacred grove have filled them with the divine enthusiasm of philosophical *erōs*, it is fitting, Socrates says, that he and Phaedrus should pray to them before embarking on their "journey":

> O Pan and the other gods in this place, give to me that I may become beautiful with respect to those things within, and that I have so much of those external things as to be friendly with those things inside me. And might I think [*nomizein*] the wise man is rich, and that I should have a pile of gold as great as a moderate man is able to carry or bear. (279b–c)

Pan, the rustic god of the *logos* who is half man, half goat, has been their patron today.[107] His famously ugly countenance is charmingly mixed with wit and playfulness, in a fitting expression of the relation between the beauties available to the senses and the true beauty that is disclosed through *logos* to the mind alone. A similarly ugly Socrates wishes for only so much of that phantom beauty that will not weigh him down in those things he only believes to be true, and instead direct him to what is truly worthy of seriousness.[108] What is external—not just physical goods, but also the foreign marks, the words and speeches, we share with others—is not therefore scorned, for it is necessary for mortal life in the body and in community with others. Their friendship with what is within—perhaps a weaker bond than *erōs*, which wishes to possess and be in the presence of its beloved forever—appropriately arranges what is inside and outside, being and becoming, truth and appearance, and knowledge and opinion.

The *Phaedrus* comes to an end, then, by returning to where it began, with moderation, now understood with respect to both the soul and the body, and even the use of *logos*. The "pile of gold" that Socrates would carry away is a far cry from the "great amount of gold" that Phaedrus would give for Lysias's skill (228a). Moderation re-emerges after its apparent subordination to the madness of philosophical *erōs*, as it was only by hubristically penetrating what seemed to be fitting and measured that what is truly so could be discovered. This true moderation remains a prayer for Socrates, though, for until the hubristic searching of *erōs* can grasp what truly is, the nature of the truly moderate human being will remain hidden. Someone who believes he has attained something great by simply moderating his external things in relation to each other, rather than in relation to what is good for "the things inside him," that is, what is good for the soul, will only possess a phantom virtue.

Phaedrus joins in Socrates's prayer, "for the things of friends are held in common" (279c). While the two men first came together out of passion for Lysias's speech and Phaedrus's desire to show off the speech as his own, Socrates has led them into the truer community implicit in all speech. He was able to discern within Phaedrus's passion a common desire, to grasp what is always unchanging, and upon revealing this desire attempted to persuade Phaedrus and Lysias that only philosophy could satiate it. This real community of friendship is thus established as mutual participation in what really is, which alone can bring a human being into harmony with himself.

Socrates's final words recall the opening of the *Phaedrus*: "Dear Phaedrus, whither do you go and whence do you come?" Phaedrus was lost without realizing it, but through his serendipitous encounter with Socrates he has been reoriented, turned from his aimless *erōs* and stultifying moderation, which had produced in him the belief that the highest purpose of speech was to generate painless pleasures. Only when Socrates helped him bring to light that suppressed and hidden *erōs*, and they examined it in relation to what is truly needful, was Phaedrus able to see how he must lead himself. Only now is he ready to rejoin mortal life and seek the truly fitting *logos*, a living *logos* that does not stand in place of the truth, but aids him in gathering and dividing his constantly changing experiences in pursuit of the truth. Socrates's palinode and criticism of writing has pointed Phaedrus toward what is truly beautiful. Now that they have found the path, his journey may continue: "Let us go."

# Conclusion

Behind the splendor of Socrates's great palinode, Plato's *Phaedrus* has proven to be a rich, complex, and puzzling dialogue. The easy and smooth unfolding of the conversation between Socrates and Phaedrus, lightly touching upon such a variety of topics, is betrayed by and reveals a singularly focused meditation on how discourse is moved and shaped by—and in turn shapes—the desires of the individual soul. Over the course of the *Phaedrus*, Plato has brought to light, both by speech and by deed, the problem formed by the soul's desire to apprehend what is most fitting for it through its own opinions, which are a source of confusion and at best a reminder of what is truly desirable. No theory or doctrine of this phenomenon is possible, for Plato is concerned with how it is that the phenomena exist as phenomena—how their manifestation is constituted by the reciprocal relationship between *logos* and *erōs*. That is to say, because Plato wishes to bring to light the very conditions for speaking and writing well, he must have recourse to a way of writing that sees through itself and can lead the soul away from the words themselves to the reality they signify. For Plato, the highest form of writing embodies the problem just outlined—it shows how speech concerning the ends of human life originates from and also perfects desire and action.

In the opening pages of the *Phaedrus*, Plato illustrated the great power by which rhetoric grips the youth of Athens. Phaedrus in particular displays an ethic peculiarly well suited for exploring how *logos* acts upon the soul through the action of desire and pleasure, and for that reason allows a shallow kind of persuasion that obscures the full power of speech. In the urbane speeches of Lysias and Socrates, the ethic of this kind of rhetoric is introduced as the impossible position of a nonlover, which can appear plausible because of the wide range of incommensurable opinions to which an indeterminate audience may be led. Men like Lysias and Phaedrus desire, so they may exploit, a kind of passionless discourse based on what is evident to all. Socrates's cogent development of this position, and therewith its aspiration toward a pure rationality, reveals it to be an impossible conjunction of opposites. But the urbane speeches do express the power of *logos* to provide a kind of detached view of things that is essential to Socrates's mythical portrayal of the full nature of *erōs*, which is presupposed in every use of speech. Socrates feigns to transcend *logos* itself in order to illustrate how it is that *logos* is the manner by which the ever-moving soul perceives reality. Beauty emerges as the principal object of this myth because it is the principal object of *erōs*, and insofar as reason is moved by the desire for what is whole, complete, and fitting for the soul, it too is under the sway of beauty. When this desire is gratified by the perception of beauty, such pleasure is produced that it must be met with sufficient self-awareness to understand that this pleasure is the source of deception, for it leads one away from the truly simple and pure beauty that is perceptible by thought alone. The best lovers become moderate in their desires for one another and in relation to the external world as they pursue this most perfect beloved.

In hindsight, rather than simply being an exoneration of *erōs*, Socrates's palinode serves to show the true objects of speech and the psychological causes of persuasion. Over the course of Socrates's extensive discussion with Phaedrus on the nature of rhetoric, it emerges that rhetoric and persuasion are in fact only possible insofar as they touch on what really is and provide an image of knowledge and truth. Rhetoric must have at its heart some perception of reality if it is to become artful, just as *logos* must if it is to communicate anything, and this heart is nothing other than dialectic. *Logos* is essentially dialectical, and so dialectic resembles rhetoric; in their perfection, the two cannot be differentiated. But such perfection is only a goal of dialectic, which is an open-ended activity animated by the *erōs* of the interlocutors. Lacking the perfect knowledge of the true art of rhetoric, rhetoric that eschews the close reasoning of dialectic may retain great efficacy with variegated and inexpert audiences—which will include, at one time or another, the whole of humanity. This condition of ignorance therefore both animates Socrates's private rhetoric, which is the development of one's ability to discern the nature of things, and affords public rhetoric its power. For Plato, the tension between private and public rhetoric, internal and external marks, is also a way to inquire about his own medium of writing. From the inadequacies of writing in the manner of the rhetoricians, Plato points toward a kind of writing that combines the static and public nature of the written word with the fluid adaptation of oral discourse. Rather than writing as if a text were a fixed monument capable of endlessly dispensing the truth to all, a noble kind of writing playfully indicates its own insufficiencies in light of a truth that is perceptible only through the personal, private, efforts of the individual reader. Plato writes so as to first inspire in his readers an *erōs* for a coherent, unified, and timeless truth, and then, building from this desire, an ethic that, if not philosophical, is at least persuaded of and open to the needfulness of the truth and a life spent in pursuit of it.

The *Phaedrus* is not only an exoneration of rhetoric, but also the wellspring of Plato's written and therefore public project to situate philosophy at the heart of ethical and political life. Socrates shows Phaedrus how the manner by which one speaks both reflects our ethic, our way of life and comportment to others, and shapes how we conceive of and interact with reality. Socrates shows him that speech cannot be understood simply as the instrument and means to the indeterminate ends of a speaker, a reflection and arrangement of words that the speaker takes to be unproblematic. Rather, speech emerges as a medium in which we are immersed, and that precisely because it is not our own and allows a background of desires and opinions to stream into us, it may lead us outside ourselves and draw us into a shared search for what really is. Equally, in the face of this immersion, Phaedrus must himself become capable of leading himself, using speech privately to clarify his own understanding of the words that would otherwise dazzle and carry him away. He must become active in his use of *logos*, refining and thus realizing its dialectical nature in his own life. Through Socrates's intimate and apparently extrapolitical discussion with Phaedrus, Plato shows how the seeds of philosophy are sown within the individual soul as the way to discover and accomplish what is most fitting and desirable for our own lives, not in relation solely to abstract forms but in relation to those forms as they are found in concrete and particular experiences. As a politic exercise of rhetoric in its own right, the *Phaedrus* sows the seeds for this private rhetoric—to be either ardently pursued or at the least made amenable to it—through beautiful images of the goods of the soul that are by self-admission merely images and propaedeutic to philosophy as a way of life. Just as noble rhetoric grows from dialectic, so too does Plato's rhetoric grow as the resplendent exterior and simulacrum of the still greater beauty that lies in the soul's exercise of its highest powers. The place of the *Phaedrus* in Plato's larger political project can therefore be understood as a kind of prologue or initiation—or rather renewal, for the initiation never ends—by which speech, and therewith the possibility of philosophy, is rehabilitated as a way toward what really is.

For the reader of the *Phaedrus* situated within the modern malaise of rhetorical study, Plato's rehabilitation of the art of rhetoric stands out as a particularly strange defense of what has been, even what must be, indefensible. Plato advocates a rhetorical supplement to dialectic and reasoning—a recommendation that may be grudgingly acknowledged in the face of various fronts of resistance to scientific expertise and consensus. But this is the weakest aspect of Plato's rehabilitation of rhetoric. Stronger is his delineation, through Socrates, of a prospectus for a perfectly efficacious rhetoric; in modern terms, Plato proposes a science of rhetoric. Stronger still is that this perfect rhetoric is rooted in a dialectical analysis of soul and speech, animated by the soul's perpetual desire and struggle to harmonize itself with reality. Even granting that perfectly persuasive rhetoric may be impossible, this close identification of dialectic and rhetoric contradicts the clear modern distinction. If reasoning is rhetorical, one might wonder, have we already said "good-bye to the truth"? Is reason stripped of its secure foundations in reality? That may be, if speech is understood the way Phaedrus, Lysias, and Thrasymachus understood it, as a mere instrument.

For Plato, the power of rhetoric to captivate an audience by arousing its passions is not exclusive to rhetoric—it is a power shared by all speech, including dialectic and reasoning. The most controversial element of the *Phaedrus* was fittingly ornamented in the most resplendent rhetoric of the dialogue: the nourishment of the soul in the clear light of "the plain of truth." What is desirable and good is implicit in the use of speech. Not only is speech naturally related to and revealing of reality, but through speech we share in that reality for the sake of realizing what is good for ourselves. Only the power of speech to discern what truly is better or worse can justify the differentiation of rhetoric from dialectic, leading the soul in such a way that it may come to lead itself in pursuit of what is best. Rather than guard reason from the admittedly dangerous power of rhetoric, as people like Hobbes did, Plato shows their shared roots and runs the risk of defending rhetoric in his written work, for it is only in this way that philosophy and reason may really recommend themselves to the whole human soul. From this view, the enormity of the task of rehabilitating rhetoric is seen most plainly. The Platonic teaching upon which the classical tradition of rhetoric was founded is nothing less than the goodness of the way of the *logos*.

# Notes

## INTRODUCTION

1. Nicholson (1999) instructs readers "to be aware . . . of the polyphony [in order] to understand why [Plato] wrote that way" (1–2, 33; see also Kastely 2002).

2. All parenthetical citations refer to the *Phaedrus*, with other sources cited in the notes, following the abbreviations of Liddell, Scott, and Jones (1996), *A Greek-English Lexicon* (LSJ). All translations of the Greek are the author's. Translations of Plato's works are based on the Greek text of Burnet (1901), alongside the invaluable commentaries of de Vries (1969), Rowe (1986), and Yunis (2011). Translations of other Greek works are based on the texts of the Loeb Classical Library published by Harvard University Press. For clarity of meaning, Greek terms are occasionally transliterated rather than translated, with nouns and adjectives rendered in the nominative case and verbs in the present infinitive.

3. The original meaning of *logos* is simply "speech," related to the verb *legein*, "to speak." Only over the course of its use by philosophers to indicate the perception of the nature of things did it also acquire the meaning of "reason," although it never lost its basic connotation of speech or discourse. In order to preserve this continuity, the transliterated *logos* will be used frequently, especially where it is necessary to recognize both senses are relevant in the context.

4. Weaver (1953, 14); de Vries (1969, 23). Accordingly, any argument that Plato sought to defend the philosophical use of a particular form of discourse—whether rhetoric, dialectic, writing in general, myth, poetry, and so on—must be qualified as subordinate to the general question of what it means to speak well (see Ferrari 1987, 206, 213–14).

5. See especially White (1993, 202, 263–65); Werner (2007b; 2010); but cf. Griswold (1986, 43); Moore (2015, 34–35).

6. *Technē* is generally rendered as "art," although readers must bear in mind that *technē* does not necessarily imply the attributes associated with modern conceptions of art, such as creativity or expression of genius. Rather, *technē* is more closely associated with the crafts or bausanic arts, which are productive, require relatively precise knowledge, and are teachable.

7. Werner (2010, 22). A number of other problems are generated by Socrates's argument that speaking well entails turning to philosophy, particularly the relation between rhetoric, dialectic, and philosophy. Yunis (2009) rightly rebuts the attempt to collapse them into an indeterminate philosophical rhetoric (229–30, 236–37; see also Murray 1988, 279, 287n3–4). The relation between these discursive modes is discussed throughout chapter 4.

8. While "love" will be used to translate the Greek *erōs*, it is important to keep in mind that the English word has a broader extension, often including romantic notions that are anachronistic to the Greek as well as other senses that do not apply directly to *erōs*, such as friendship

(*philia*), brotherly love (*agapē*), and affection, usually parental (*storgē*). *Erōs* is best understood to mean love in the sense of sexual passion (LSJ s.v.).

9. Martin Heidegger (1997) neatly summarizes the issue: "The theme is speaking in the sense of self-expression and communication, speaking as the mode of existence in which one person expresses himself to an other and both together seek the matter at issue" (218–19).

10. Commentators have long recognized the importance of self-knowledge for the question of the nature of *logos* and therefore the *Phaedrus*. See, for example, Heidegger (1997, 219); Mueller (1957); Burger (1980, 5); Ferrari (1987, 6); Moore (2015, 136–84). Griswold (1986) notably elevates self-knowledge to the overarching theme of the *Phaedrus*, but see Ferrari's argument that this characterization of the *Phaedrus* is "at once too broad and too narrow" (Ferrari 1988, 409).

11. For Friedrich Schleiermacher, this thematic variety so verges on excess and superficiality that he declares the *Phaedrus* to be the product of Plato's youth and the first of his dialogues; others, for the same reason of thematic variety, see the *Phaedrus* as the product of weakened old age (Schleiermacher 1936, 59, 68; cf. de Vries 1969, 22). Still others go further and argue that the dialogue has no single theme or purpose at all (Jowett 1892, 9–10; Thompson 1973, xxi–xxii) (Heath [1989] similarly argues that the desire for thematic unity, rather than dramatic unity, is anachronistic for classical Greek literature). Some have even speculated that the *Phaedrus* is a pastiche of fragments and imitation by other authors (see the review and rebuttal in de Vries 1969, 3). Benardete (1991) calls its form "monstrous" (105). On the interpretive need to unify the dialogue, Schleiermacher (1936) memorably says that reading the *Phaedrus* without attempting to discover its unity is to render it "deformed in a wholly revolting manner" (48–49, cf. 14–17). Ancient commentators likewise saw the need to unify the dialogue (e.g., Hermeias of Alexandria surveys contemporary interpretations [1971, 8.15–9.6]), as do modern scholars (e.g., Benardete 1991, 103; Burger 1980, 3–4; de Vries 1969, 22–23; Griswold 1986, 10–12; Rowe 1986, 7; Rutherford 1995, 260–67; Yunis 2011, 1–2). See Werner (2007a) for a summary of the literature.

12. That the philosopher must use dialectic is one example immediately inferred from Socrates's argument that one must become philosophical to best accomplish the dialectical division of souls and speeches (261a, 277b–c, 278d). That the philosopher must use, or at least be capable of using, other forms of discourse is less obvious, but equally important to the *Phaedrus*. This issue is discussed in chapters 3 and 4.

13. For example, Weaver (1953, 5–6); Griswold (1986, 122, 208); Ferrari (1987, 62); Nicholson (1999, 9); Moore (2015, 181–82); and Irani (2017, 6–7, 21)—all emphasize philosophy's ethical nature in contrast to rhetoric or *technē* more generally. Nehamas (1990) pushes the question furthest in trying to discern the precise difference between philosophy and sophistry while observing their common argumentative techniques.

14. *Pace* Irani (2017, 4–6, 15, 20, 24), whose argument that Plato provides "a comprehensive understanding of the human soul" in the *Phaedrus* overstates the adequacy of that account with respect to the requirements of the true art of rhetoric that Socrates presents, the inadequacy of which is also suggested by the searching nature of Socrates's philosophical practice. Chapter 4 discusses the implications of Socrates's account of the soul, as well as his own practice of philosophy, in relation to the art of rhetoric.

15. In the introduction to his translation of the *Phaedrus*, Rowe (1986) claims that "[i]n our own society, rhetoric no longer exists as a subject for formal inquiry—except perhaps in relation to the criticism of literature—or for teaching (13). In the introduction to his own translation, Nichols (1998) makes similar remarks and goes further to attribute, in part, a decline in the quality of rhetoric to the decline in its formal study (2).

16. Schleiermacher (1936, 73); Jaeger (1944, 3.191); Kennedy (1980, 59–60); Cooper (2009, 66–67).

17. Plato (Pl.), *Gorgias* (*Grg.*), 462c–d, 502d–503d, 515d–516a–e.

18. For example, Jaeger (1944, 3.184–86); Hackforth (1952, 11); Nicholson (1999, 51–52).

19. Plato also alludes to, but does not explicitly develop, a "true rhetoric" in the *Gorgias* (504d–e, 508c, 517a), and similarly mentions beneficial uses of rhetoric in other dialogues, e.g., *Laws* (*Lg.*) 722d–723d; *Statesman* (*Plt.*) 303e–304e; *Republic* (*R.*) 498d.

20. Nichols (1998) argues that the Romantic movement's conception of art complemented and compounded the Enlightenment philosophers' attack on rhetoric, since it placed the highest value on the artist's creative acts of unique will and imagination, the expression of which would be obscured by rhetorical ornamentation (7–9).

21. Nichols (1998) similarly mentions the influence of John Locke on the Enlightenment attack on the practice and study of rhetoric (5–6). Taylor (2016) groups Hobbes with Locke and Étienne Bonnot de Condillac as originators of what has become the basic modern model of language, which he variously terms "designative," "encoding," "instrumental"—a model necessary for the flourishing of modern science that has been reciprocally fortified by that flourishing (3–5, 103–28, 131–32, 262).

22. Hobbes (1994), *Leviathan*, 20 *x*.12, *xi*.13–22, *xxv*.6–9.

23. Hobbes, "Introduction," 3, *vii*.1–3.

24. Hobbes, *xxi*.9, *xlvi*.11.

25. Hobbes, *vii*.4–5.

26. Cf. Hobbes, *x*.12, *xi*.13, *xxv*.6–8, 15, and Pl. *Grg.* 461d–462a, 462c ff., 471e–472d, 503c–d.

27. Pressing political concerns, not only in fifth- and fourth-century Athens, no doubt forced the question of the difference between philosophy and rhetoric. Socrates's execution in 399 BC hangs over the Platonic corpus, within which recur the themes of the political dangers of philosophy and the differentiation of philosophy from sophistry and rhetoric. Josiah Ober (1989) provides a useful summary of the context of popular mistrust of eloquence (170–74). In the early modern period, there was a similar ambition to distinguish philosophy from rhetoric, premised on the failure of the ancients in this regard. Consider again Hobbes (1994): Aristotelian eloquence is "vain philosophy" (*xlvi*). Or consider Petrus Ramus's (2010) criticism that the classical conjunction of wisdom and eloquence was "useless and stupid" because it gave moral authority to eloquence, which even an evil man could possess (84–92).

28. Even the most basic power of language, to mark something, which is the fixation of modern theory of language (see Taylor (2016, 103–28), is shaped by our own desires and intentions as we use the mark to distinguish an experience within a broader context. This is discussed in chapters 3 and 4, particularly in the context of dialectic.

29. Sallis (1996, 160–61, 173–75); see also Friedländer (1958, 3.241–42). Griswold (1986) similarly says that "a given text may turn out to be deeply aporetic in the sense that it defines a problem and shows that there are no available solutions to it" (12).

30. Some scholars have maintained that *erōs* is incidental to the dialogue's purpose, merely a topic for the speeches, the relative artfulness of which is the real purpose of the dialogue (see Jaeger's [1944] critical comments, 3.186–87, 190).

31. Ferrari (1987) uses the term "background" in relation to the setting of the dialogue to get at this issue (1–4, 21–36, esp. 25–26, 30). This term can be extended, as it is in chapter 4, to a speech's argumentative steps and the opinions to which those steps relate.

32. On the *Phaedrus*'s order of speeches and development of the nature of *logos* in parallel with a moral ascent, see also Friedländer (1958, 3.219); Pieper (1964, 92–93, 101–2); Rhodes (2003, 418–19); Weaver (1953, 6–11). Irani (2017, 1–7) rightly connects Plato's defense of rhetoric in the *Phaedrus* to his concern for misology ("hatred of discourse"), which arises from the belief that words do not touch upon the truth.

33. Zuckert (2009) emphasizes that "something about love requires indirect speech" (303–4), but does not explicitly draw the implication that, insofar as understanding love is essential to understanding speech, this oblique approach must also be taken with respect to speech itself.

34. Moore (2015) clarifies an essential aspect of the ethical nature of philosophy and the objective of the *Phaedrus* in his formulation of the quest for self-knowledge as one of "self-constitution," rather than simply the acquisition of knowledge of one's specific desires and attributes or of the general nature of soul (36–40, 140, 150–56, 174–81).

35. Capra (2014) comes close to this view ("true rhetoric is erotic and true *eros* is rhetorical"), but acknowledges the problem in this circularity (21).

36. Pieper (1964) speaks of an "everlasting problem" between divinely inspired "transformative upheavals," represented by Socrates's portrayal of *erōs* in his palinode, and the need for

moderate rational organization, represented by the two speeches defending the nonlover (23, 36, 51, 102).

37. Burger (1980, 2–4).

38. As argued in chapter 3. Similar arguments are made by Nicholson (1999, 73–74, 124); Griswold (1986, 150–51); Werner (2012, 98–100).

39. For example, Adams (1996, 7–16); Kelley (1973).

40. Weaver (1953) writes that "[r]hetoric moves the soul with a movement which cannot finally be justified logically" (23).

41. LSJ 444.

42. Pl. *Letters* (*Ep.*) 7.341b–e, 343a, 344c–d.

43. Pl. *R.* 509c.

44. Friedländer (1958) dismisses any conception of irony as "a mere swapping of a Yes for a No," and sees it rather as the temperament of the pedagogue who sets himself at the same level as his student, which originates from "the living experience of the unknown" and is expressed most succinctly in Socrates's avowed ignorance (1.137–44). Vlastos (1991) similarly notes that Socratic irony cannot be reduced to making false statements, but is also "complex" in that "what is said both is and isn't meant" (31).

45. Mackenzie (1982) shows how Plato deliberately uses paradox and *antilogic* (disputation of opposing opinions) in the *Phaedrus* for just this purpose of engaging the reader in dialectic and philosophy and thus making his writing "unequivocally alive" (69, 72). As will be discussed in chapter 5, Plato's stimulation of his readers in this way closely relates to Socrates's account of dialectic and the ethical nature of philosophy.

46. See, for example, Griswold (2002, 130–33), Howland (1991, 206–11), and Rowe (1986, 14).

47. Rutherford (1988, 222–23) rightly argues that understanding a given passage by drawing on similar passages in other dialogues can be helpful for understanding a given passage, but unless the "hazardous" nature of this approach is kept in mind, the point stands that the dramatic and philosophic unity of the single text is violated. See also Nichols (1998, 18–19).

48. A large amount of scholarship in this vein can be traced to the influence of Friedländer (see his account of the importance of dramatic action in Friedländer 1958, 1.158–61), and to some extent the influence of Schleiermacher's (1936) emphasis on esotericism (although esoteric readings do not imply dramatic readings). With respect to scholarship on the *Phaedrus*, the influence of Friedländer (1958) is explicit (e.g., Pieper [1964] 3, 102) or can be traced through Klein (1965) and Strauss (2001) to the works of Burger (1980, 77n24), Griswold (1986, 244n7), Benardete (1991), Sallis (1996, 17), and Nichols (1998, 19, 22). A notable exception is Rutherford, whose own dramatic reading stems from the field of literary criticism (see Rutherford 1988, 217, 219; 1995, 243).

49. Pl. *Parmenides* (*Prm.*), 137c–d; *Sophist* (*Sph.*), 244c–245a.

50. Capra (2014) is the best source on Plato's rich allusions to Greek poetry and his "appropriation" of poetic forms.

51. See, for example, Ferrari (1987, 101); McCumber (1982, 32); White (1993, 35, 40, 48–50, 52). In the context of reconciling Socrates's usage of *mania*, particularly in connection to *nous* and *sōphrosunē*, Scott (2011) rightly links such terminological development to Socrates's discussion of rhetoric as a way of "assimilating" seemingly disparate words and opinions (188–90). But this "assimilation" also speaks to the nature of language itself and, more directly to the point in the *Phaedrus*, the power of *logos* to "recollect" true being through the many semblances of being (249b–c).

52. Not to be confused with the "thematic" unity under discussion in Rowe (1989) and Heath (1989).

# 1. PHAEDRUS

1. For example, Hesiod, *Works and Days* (Hes. *Op.*), 752; Aeschylus, *Agamemnon* (A. *Ag.*), 1109.

2. The embodiment of discourse is not intended in the modern sense, wherein nondiscursive modes of expression are understood as modes of language in their own right (e.g., Taylor 2016, 16, 42–44, 149). There is nevertheless great scope in the *Phaedrus* for reflection on just that sense of the expression, although it will only be touched on here.

3. Barney (2006) provides a recent survey of the sophistic movement.

4. Lysias, *On the Property of Aristophanes* (Lys. 19), 15; Davies (1971, 200–1, 462–63).

5. Phaedrus's name was found in stone monuments, *stēlai*, recovered from the Eleusinion in Athens (Lewis, *Inscriptiones Graecae*, I$^3$, 1981, 422.229–30, 426.102) and mentioned in the defense speech of Andocides (*On the Mysteries* [And. 1] 15, 51). The incident is also an important episode in Thucydides' *History* (Th. 6.27–29).

6. Pl. *Protagoras* (*Prt.*) 315e–316a; *Symposium* (*Smp.*) 176b.

7. Eryximachus's influence on Phaedrus's moderation is also made clear in the *Symposium*. When Eryximachus suggests an evening of speeches rather than the usual excesses of symposia, Phaedrus strongly seconds the motion, as he obeys his friend concerning "medical speech" (176a–d; cf. 187d, 188d). They also leave the symposium together once it descends into drunkenness (223b–c). Eryximachus's ultimately hedonistic view of the purpose of medicine—to mitigate the natural ill effects of pleasure-seeking so that pleasures may be enjoyed even "out of season" (186c–187b, 188a–d)—closely relates to, if not directly informs, Phaedrus's view of the purpose of speech (see chapter 4.8).

8. Phaedrus's speech in *Symposium* reinterprets Achilles's fate in the terms of conventional Athenian pederasty, which he praises for the devotion a lover shows to his beloved (178d; see Dover 2016, 100–10, on the various benefits a lover was believed to provide to his beloved boy). He wishes to further honor the beloved'—that is, himself—telling his fellow banqueters: "For really the gods may honor most this excellence concerning love, although they more greatly wonder and delight and make well when the beloved is fond of the lover than when the lover [is fond of] the boy" (180a–b). Phaedrus's selfishness and instrumental view of love emerges in the *Phaedrus*, as discussed below.

9. Mylonas (1961) remains the principal work on the mysteries and the archaeological evidence recovered at Eleusis. Further interpretation is provided in Kerényi (1967). MacDowell (1962) provides a useful summary in his introduction to Andocides's *On the Mysteries*. Mylonas (1961) traces the origins of the Eleusinian mysteries through legends of a cult to Demeter c.1400 BC (24). On the importance of the mysteries to Greek life, see Kerényi (1967, 7–12), particularly: "*bios*, life, [Praetextatus] declared, would become 'unlivable' [*abiotos*] for the Greeks if the celebration were to cease" (12).

10. Apollodorus, *Library* (Apollod.) 2.5.11–12; Mylonas (1961, 240). In Euripides's *Heracles*, the hero claims to have succeeded "for I was fortunate enough to see the sacred rites of the initiated" (600–15). Plato refers to the Lesser Mysteries as preparation for the Greater in *Grg.* 467c.

11. William Furley (1996, 31, 33n10) points out that even if the profaning was lighthearted, "comedy is also a serious business," and gave insult to the cult of Eleusis.

12. And. 1.11–15.

13. And. 1.80.

14. Hades's rape and kidnap of Demeter's daughter Persephone, patroness of the Lesser Mysteries, is echoed in the story of Boreas and Oreithuia that Phaedrus mentions in the prologue (Homer, *Homeric Hymns* [Hom. *Hymn.*]) 2.1–32) and in the shrine of maiden figurines (*korai*) found at the reading spot (230b). The winged chariot of Triptolemos, the mythical founder of the mysteries, is echoed in the winged chariot of Socrates's palinode. Socrates's and Phaedrus's proximity to Agra suggests their own initiation into the Lesser Mysteries, which Socrates later mimics by covering his head before delivering his first speech (the Lovatelli urn similarly depicts one stage of Hercules's initiation into these mysteries, during which his face is veiled while he is cleansed with water [Kerényi, 1967, 55–56; cf. Aristophanes, *Clouds* (Ar. *Nu.*), 250–74]). Again in his palinode, Socrates depicts a procession of gods that ascend to true reality, recalling the procession of initiates that "culminates in the ceremony of mystic initiation" (Lebeck, 1972, 271). Socrates also uses the word *epopteia*, a sacred vision considered the highest mystery of Eleusis, to describe the lover's vision of true beauty (Mylonas, 1961, 274–78). These specific allusions suggest a structural similarity between the rites of the myster-

ies and the experience of *erōs*, which is discussed in chapter 3. For more extensive discussion of the allusions to the mysteries in the *Phaedrus*, see Farrell (1999) and Rinella (2010, 127–47).

15. Yunis (2011, 8n18) claims that "Plato ignored" the issue of Phaedrus's exile because of the time which had passed by the time Plato wrote the *Phaedrus*. But according to Thucydides, the Sicilian expedition was "by far the most costly and finest-looking force ever assembled by a single Hellenic city" (Th. 6.31), and its ultimate failure ensured it would never be dissociated from the ill omen attributed to the profaning of the mysteries and desecration of the Hermes. That an innocuous and naïve man like Phaedrus unwittingly played a role in these important events is not insignificant to a book bearing his name. Plato's choice of dramatic dating, setting, and dramatic personae for the *Symposium* suggests he had Phaedrus's crime in mind there as well. Further, as will be argued over the course of this book, the *Phaedrus* shows that Phaedrus's intellectual interests have produced the ethical conditions for such an act. Nussbaum (1986, 212–13), in contrast, does not deny Plato's concern with Phaedrus's crime, but suggests that the implications of Phaedrus's impiety are best understood in light of what she believes to be the historical impossibility of the dialogue, such that Plato set the *Phaedrus* in an alternate history of what could have been had Phaedrus heeded Socrates and turned to philosophy, in order to emphasize the fragility of these experiences of beauty that Phaedrus cherishes. But the dramatic dating of the dialogue is not historically impossible (see note 16), and the *pathos* of Phaedrus's fate is even more sharply with Plato's suggestion that Phaedrus and Socrates did converse prior to Phaedrus's exile.

16. Historical sources are provided in Dover (1968, 34–43), and Nails (2002, 314). A dramatic dating after 415 BC is unsatisfactory because it places Phaedrus in Athens at an uncertain time, since he could only have returned from exile after the amnesty of 405 BC (the first exile returned in 407 BC, but that was the exceptional case of Alcibiades, who was invited to return to serve as a general [Nails 2002, 190]), but he could not have returned later than 404 BC, when Polemarchus, still alive in this dialogue (257b4), was killed by the Thirty Tyrants. A dating earlier than 415 BC is also unsatisfactory, since the *Symposium* is clearly set in 416 BC, after Agathon's first victory for tragedy (Nails 2002, 314–15), and Phaedrus would not ask for encomia to Eros in that dialogue after hearing Socrates's great speech on Eros in the *Phaedrus*.

17. Nicholson (1999, 23), following Wilamowitz-Moellendorff (1917).

18. Ar. *Acharnians*, 887; *Peace*, 1008; *Wasps*, 506.

19. Ar. *Ecclesiazusae*, 71; Demosthenes, *On the Embassy* (D. 19), 277–78. For further sources see Nails (2002, 139–40).

20. Lys. *Against Epicrates* (Lys. 27), 1–9.

21. For example, A. *Suppliant Women* (*Supp.*), 228–30; Euripides (E.), *Hecuba*, 418, *Medea*, 1073–74; Sophocles (S.), *Antigone*, 76, *Oedipus Tyrannus* (*OT*), 776.

22. For example, Pl. *Apology* (*Ap.*) 40e–41c; *Phaedo* (*Phd.*) 64a, 68a–b; *Grg.* 525c, 527a; *R.* 330d. Plato employs this euphemism for Hades in a variety of contexts, often pejoratively, as he does in the *Gorgias*, referring to litigation and law courts as well as unthinking hedonism (471e–472a, 501b). Voegelin (2001) further notes that often Plato will subsequently invert this euphemism to indicate that the source of truth lies over "there," beyond the realm "here," which is now likened to hell (3.108, 114–16). The double meaning of death is discussed below.

23. Lys. *Against Eratosthenes* (Lys. 12), 4, 20; Davies (1971, 589). See also Pl. *R.* 330b.

24. Lys. 12.52–53, fr. 7 (*Against Hippotherses* in *Papyri Oxyrinchus*, 1606 fr. 2). On Athenian law regarding metics, see MacDowell (1978, 76–78, 82–84, 240–42).

25. Lysias gives his account in Lys. 12. Plato himself notes the potential gravity of the situation that necessitates rhetorical prowess (*Ap.* 38c; *Grg.* 511b–d; *Theaetetus* [*Tht.*] 173a).

26. Pl. *Ap.* 23b–c; Xenophon, *Memorabilia* (Xen. *Mem.*), 1.1.10.

27. *Pl.* 33c.

28. Pindar, *Isthmian Odes* (Pi. *I.*), 1.6–7.

29. Pi. *I.* 1.50, 67–69.

30. Pi. *I.* 1.41–42.

31. Pl. *R.* 405a–406e; cf. *Prt.* 316d–e. Socrates prefers the ancient Asclepius, who "said that he did not have leisure to be sick and it is not profitable to live this way, putting one's mind to diseases and neglecting the work that lies ahead."

32. Rowe (1986, 136).

33. Rowe (1986, 137).
34. To "join in the rites of the Corybant" renders the single verb *sunkorubantiein* (Pl. *Phdr.* 228b7; cf. Rowe 1986, 138, de Vries 1969, 41). The corybants worshipped the earth mother Cybelle, often celebrating her in a frenzied dance accompanied by rhythmic music. This cult was later associated with Dionysus, the god of wine and the revel, who was purported to have been initiated by Cybelle herself. On the exclusivity of the corybants' inspiration, see Linforth (1946b, 139–40); cf. Pl. *Ion* 536c.
35. Although each is frequently rendered "to know," *gignōskein* connotes "coming to know" and hence "to recognize," and is more often used in reference to human beings rather than other objects of study. Knowledge of oneself is never described by Plato as a matter of *epistēmē*, which usually refers to the knowledge possessed by craftsmen or through study. Plato's use of the two has puzzled scholars. Griswold (1986) argues that each verb signifies a distinct mode of knowing, the gnostic and the epistemic, corresponding to mythical and technical understanding. Gnostic knowing entails the pre-knowledge of the whole that Socrates depicts in the palinode as the condition for all coming to know as well as that which makes possible the technical, "quasi-mathematical" and "rule-governed" knowing of *epistēmē* (5–6, 200–1, 232). Although Griswold's distinction between these two modes is conceptually attractive, de Vries (1988) argues that the terminological distinction has no etymological basis (162). Nor does it seem to be supported by Plato's usage in the palinode, since the complete knowledge that Socrates seeks in the course of knowing himself is described as *epistēmē* (247d–e).
36. See Pl. *Tht.* 154a–b, 157a, 158e–159d.
37. This scene is undoubtedly meant to evoke the similar one in Plato's *Charmides (Chrm.)*, or vice-versa (155c–e). It is also tempting to see Socrates's words as referring not only to Lysias's particular speech, but to the *logos* as a whole—that is, the nature of *logos* itself; Lysias's paradoxical showpiece represents the nature of *logos*, with all that the faults of Lysias's speech would imply about the *logos* itself.
38. "Mythology" or *muthologia* appears to be a term invented by Plato, and occurs in the *Phaedrus* (243a4; see its cognates *muthologēma*, "mythical narrative," and *muthologein*, "to tell myths" or "to mythologize," at 229c5 and 276e3) and in four other dialogues (*Hp. Ma.* 298a4; *Lg.* 680d3, 752a1; *Plt.* 304d1; *R.* 382d1, 394b9). The word is a compound of *muthos* and *logios*, a derivative of *logos* that indicates a person concerned with speaking (but may play on *logion*, an oracular pronouncement—see LSJ S.V.). Plato's use of the word has a curiously paradoxical effect, given the contrary meanings attributed to *muthos* and *logos*, as discussed below.
39. Herodotus, *Histories* (Hdt.), 7.189; Apollod. 3.15.2. Apollod. 1.9.21 also tells of Oreithuia's winged sons.
40. Hdt. 7.188–90, 8.14.
41. D. *Against Aristocrates* (23), 65–66; Aristotle, *Rhetoric* (Arist. *Rh.*), 1398b25; Apollod. 3.14.2.
42. "[Things] of marvelous speech" renders *teratologōn*, as Rowe's (1986) "portentous" does not capture the two senses of religious omen (*terata*) and speech (*logos*), both of which are so important to the *Phaedrus* (LSJ 1776).
43. Cf. *Tht.* 152a ff. Protagoras can be related to the *sophoi* that are mocked here only by the shared assumption that an individual's sense experience is the standard for truth and knowledge. Protagoras is nowhere described as descending to the sophistic disputation of myths on the ground of their improbability, and indeed Plato portrays him as willing to employ his own myth (*Prt.* 320c–324d).
44. Pace Moore (2015, 174–80). Moore rightly argues that Socrates's quest for self-knowledge is "similar" to the sophists' "myth-rectification" on the grounds that everyone must seek to interpret their experience in a way plausible to themselves, but in so assimilating these kinds of myth-rectification, Moore suppresses their crucial differences. As necessary as myth-rectification may be, Socrates also makes the point that one tends to rectify to accommodate one's opinions, not change them, and that there are better and worse ways of rectifying myths—Phaedrus after all is himself a myth-rectifier, as seen here and in the *Symposium*, whom Socrates corrects (e.g., 229b4–c3).

45. Werner (2012) argues that there did exist an "intellectual movement" of "allegorical" myth interpretation, although the specific kind of allegorization varied considerably (28–30).

46. For example, Homer, *Iliad* (Hom. *Il.*), 3.188, *Odyssey* (*Od.*), 4.452, 9.335; Hes. *Th.* 27–28. See Beercroft (2006, 53–54), and Lincoln (1997).

47. Clay (2007) locates the ascendancy of *logos* and the discrediting of *muthos* in Herodotus and Thucydides (210–11; see also Naddaf's introduction in Brisson (1998, vii–x), and Voegelin (2001, 2.239–53). Herodotus gathered many stories, often disrupting the more fantastic ones, and used the word *muthos*, albeit only twice, in a depreciative manner (Hdt. 2.23, 2.45). In Thucydides, the modern distinction is evident (e.g., Th. 1.21–22). *Logos*, for the historians, does not seem to convey any particular authority (Morgan 2000, 19–20). The attribution of greater truth and authority to *logos* appears to have been a separate development that began quite early, by the time of Heraclitus (Heracl. fr. B1, B50 [DK]), and sometimes sharpened into an attack on *muthos* (e.g., Xenophanes fr. B1 [DK]), although philosophers continued to employ "myths" as late as the fifth century (e.g., Parmenides [Parmen.] fr. B1–2, B10–13 [DK]). In Plato's time, though, his invention of *mutholegesthai* (see note 38 above), "to tells myths" or "to mythologize," would have a paradoxical effect on his contemporaries' ears (see Protagoras' dichotomous use of *muthos* and *logos* in Pl. *Prt.* 320c, 324d). "To mythologize" could mean either: to make myths out of clear speech, that is, to obfuscate and obscure; or to make *logoi* out of myths and so clarify ancient stories; or to somehow accomplish both at once. This compound means that Plato to some extent restores the archaic meanings of *muthos* and *logos* and reconciles them, but he does not refute the modern distinction (he is often described as being complicit in, if not the principal authority for, this dichotomy [Brisson (1998, 90); Lincoln (1997, 363); Morgan (2000, 24, 27]). Despite the willingness of Plato's Socrates to employ myth, Socrates remains dedicated to the use of *logos* in the sense of calculation (e.g., 249c1).

48. *Skopō . . . emauton* should not be construed in terms of the customary distinction between public and private. Socrates's looking to himself does not imply a direct concern for *idia* or the business of the household, and has in fact come at the expense of such things (see *Ap.* 23b–c).

49. Hes. *Th.* 821–68; Pi. *Pythian Odes* (*P.*), 1.15–28. Later stories describe in greater detail Typhon's usurpation of Olympus: he succeeded in chasing the gods into Egypt, where they took animal forms, before he was destroyed by Zeus, who appeared "from the sky in a chariot drawn by winged horses" (Apollod. 1.6.3).

50. Moore (2015) argues that Plato alludes to Aristophanes's *Clouds*, wherein Typhon is "related to the function of manifesting the visible image of someone's self, thereby guiding that person to self-knowledge" (149).

51. In the *Phaedo*, Socrates says that such an inquiry would simply result in reductive physiological explanations, like those of Anaxagoras, rather than the disclosure of a true cause (97b–99a).

52. *Contra* Rowe (1986, 142).

53. Clay (2007, 213).

54. Pl. *Phd.* 63d8. See also LSJ 1917.

55. On the general nature and function of *metaxy* in Plato's work, see Friedländer (1958, 1.41–43).

56. Apollod. 2.4.12.

57. Hes. *Th.* 340; Soph. *Trachiniae* 9ff.

58. The Centaurs were born from a cloud impregnated by Ixion (Pi. *P.* 2.21–48; Apollod. *Epitome*, 1.20); the Chimera and numerous other beasts from the sea-dragon Echidna (Hes. *Th.* 297–322); the Gorgon from the sea-monster Keto (Hes. *Th.* 270–74); and the Pegasus sprang from the corpse of the Gorgon (Hes. *Th.* 280–81). Pindar sang of the great efforts made by Bellerophon to tame Pegasus with the bridle given him by Athena (Pi. *Olympian Odes*, 13.63).

59. In Plato's *Cratylus*, Socrates claims that the name Ἥρα is an anagram of ἀήρ (404c).

60. Ferrari (1987, 21–36).

61. Planinc (2001, 136–37, cf. 129–30). Planinc argues that the plane tree represents the *omphalos*, the sacred stone at Delphi that was considered the navel of the world that binds together the cosmos. Although nowhere in ancient Greece is the *omphalos* described as a tree,

there were numerous sacred trees (e.g., the oak at Dodona) that Planinc argues are manifestations of the *omphalos*.

62. The genitive *Platōnos* (from *Platōn*) means "of" or "from" Plato, used to describe origin, and so the force of the pun is to make the author the source or even father of both this particular grove and all that occurs underneath it. See Zaslavsky (1981).

63. Socrates claims in the *Theaetetus* that philosophy begins in wonder (155d).

64. Ferrari (1987, 32).

65. Jaeger (1944) argues that the very form of Hesiod's poem, which adopted the high style of Homer to exhort his brother to the life of the farmer, indicates that Hesiod was similarly aware that a return to the old and simple ways of country life was not straightforward and that a repudiation of the sophistications of urban life was not possible (1.73–75).

66. Pl. *R.* 515e–516b.

## 2. THE URBANE SPEECHES

1. See Aristotle's discussion of *epideixis* in *Rhetoric* (*Rh.*) 1.3, 1.9.

2. On the mixture of rhetorical genres found in this speech, compare: Dover (1968, 69–71); Rowe (1986, 136); Benardete (117); Kastely (142). The Athenian jury was composed of citizens drawn by lot for a particular case, but usually made up of the poor and old due in part to the fact that they were paid, by the public purse, a sum insufficient to lure the more well-off from their affairs (MacDowell 1978, 33–35).

3. Dionysius Halicarnassus (D. H.), *Lysias*, 11, 13, 19; Dover (1968, 76).

4. D. H., *Lysias*, 19.

5. See Dover (1968, 70). Theophrastus, a late commentator on oratory, criticized Lysias's use of antithesis (D. H. *Lysias*, 14).

6. Shorey argues that the "mechanical" transition *kai men dē* ("and indeed") is here overused in parody of Lysias's style (Shorey 131–32), to which Burger adds *hōste* ("so that") and *eti de* ("and yet") (Burger 1980, 23, 132n14); see also Nussbaum 1986, 209n). To determine the authenticity of the speech, Dover attempts a more systematic analysis that compares the frequency of vocabulary and constructions found in the so-called *Erotikos* to both Lysias's *Against Eratosthenes* (indisputably by Lysias) and Socrates's first speech in the *Phaedrus*. He finds a strong correlation between this so-called *Erotikos* and the genuine *Against Eratosthenes* in the use of *axios* and the related verb *axioun*, in addition to the transitions that Burger and Shorey mention. Dover concludes that although the *Erotikos* closely resembles Lysias's forensic style, this alone is insufficient to demonstrate its authenticity or parody (Dover 1968, 70–71).

7. See Burger (1980, 24–25); Griswold (1991, 46); Benardete (116); and Zuckert (2009, 309).

8. Yunis (2011, 99n231a4–6).

9. *Nomos* has a much broader meaning than simply "custom," for it also includes "law" and "ordinance," whether written or unwritten, as well as "melody" (LSJ 1180). This variety of meanings in the English can be gathered together under a holistic view of the recurrent practices by which the community orders itself, analogous to the bringing together of musical tones.

10. The *nomos* in question may refer to this general censure of sexual indulgence, particularly in public view, or even to a written law that forbade prostitution by men or women. See for example Aischines, *The Prosecution of Timarchos*, 19, 29–32, esp. 132–37, which draws a distinction between "noble" and hubristic pederasty (a similar distinction is drawn by Pausanias in Pl. *Smp.* 180c–e). Such a fine line between noble pederasty and prostitution indicates that Lysias's speech, *contra* Nehamas, does not "turn[] all accepted ideas about paederasty on their head" (Nehamas 1999, 333–34). For a discussion of the trial of Timarchos as well as custom and laws concerning homosexual acts, see Dover (2016, 19–38, 111–23).

11. Buccioni (2007, 21, 33).

12. Cf. Pl. *R.* 338e–39a, 358e–59a, 365b–d.

13. Society, Ferrari (1987) says, has a "tolerance" for these contradictions (89–90).

14. Rhodes's (2003) formulation is succinct: "Lysias represents the most persuasive logos of democracy and Phaedrus its libido" (418).
15. Socrates warns Callicles of vacillating in the assembly in order to gratify the ever-changing and fickle desires of the *dēmos* (Pl. *Grg.* 481c–482a).
16. Pseudo-Plutarch claims Teisias was Lysias's teacher in rhetoric ([Ps.–Plu.] *Lives of Ten Orators*, 835d).
17. Heidegger (1997, 235).
18. Socrates outlines this kind of moderation born out of a hedonistic calculus in Pl. *Phd.* 68e–69a.
19. McCumber (1982, 31). Lysias uses forms of address that give the sense of "a shadowy, almost immaterial, youth" (Giannopoulou [2010, 150]).
20. Burger (1980) notes the shift to the first person from the impersonal third person (24).
21. Rosen (1969, 435).
22. Callias son of Hipponicus similarly preened himself by allowing others to be entertained by the famous sophists he hosted (Pl. *Prt.* 311a, 314b–d).
23. Rhodes (2003) rightly links this aspect of Lysias's speech to Socrates's charge that democrats tend to find and promote to offices those individuals who promise to gratify them (418–19; Pl. *R.* 565b–d).
24. Pieper (1964, 37).
25. Compare the prologue of Demosthenes's *Erotikos*, a love speech for Epicrates, which discusses the function of an erotic essay as if the author were speaking to a second listener other than Epicrates (D. 61.1–2).
26. *Pace* Hackforth (1952), who writes that "this tedious piece of rhetoric deserves little comment" (31).
27. Hackforth (1952, 40); Nussbaum (1986, 208–9). Pieper (1964) argues that the rational technique advocated by Lysias is necessary for living (23).
28. Cf. Pl. *Grg.* 493d–95b.
29. *Pace* Griswold (1986, 45).
30. εἰ δέ τι σὺ ποθεῖς, ἡγούμενος παραλελεῖφθαι, ἐρώτα. The pun is discernible only by the reader of Lysias's speech, not the listener, since written texts did not mark pitch accents; Aristotle describes this as a species of linguistic argumentation (*Sophistical Refutations*, 1.4). The pun plays on ἐρώτα, the second person imperative of *erōtaein*, "to ask," with ἔρωτα, the accusative of the noun *erōs*. The rendering of the pun takes the latter, ἔρωτα, as an accusative of respect and leaves the condition without a concluding apodosis.
31. Following Ivan Linforth (1946b), both "join in Bacchic dance" (*sunebakcheusa*) and Socrates's earlier "joining in Corybantic things" (*sunchorubantiōnta*, 228b7) refer to instances of ritual madness or frenzy employed for the sake of therapeutic catharsis (140). In Plato's *Laws*, the Athenian Stranger speaks of Corybantism as akin to relieving a disturbed infant, "and thus artlessly they are able to charm the children, just as the remedy of the senseless Bacchants, using motion in this way together with dance and music" (*Lg.* 790c–91a). See Linforth (1946b, 129–34, 151, 155), for further discussion of this function of the Bacchic and Corybantic dances. On Dionysus as the god of wine, drunkenness, and generation or change, see, for example, Hes. *Op.* 609; Hdt. 2.123; E. *Bacchae* (*Ba.*) 535, 650, 770; Apollod. 2.29.
32. The dithyramb was a circular dance accompanied by the flute and antistrophic verse, which often depicted heroic deeds, and was always in celebration of the god Dionysus. See Pickard-Cambridge (1927, 10, 28, 38, 47–48). A more strict formalism accompanied later dithyramb, which was performed at public festivals (47; see also Pl. *Lg.* 700a–d).
33. De Vries 1969, 73n235a2–3.
34. See, for example, Sappho 2, 31, 47 (Campbell 1982), Anacreon 4, 84 (Campbell 1988).
35. Pl. *Ion* 533c–534b.
36. Arist. *Athenian Constitution* 7.1, 55.5. Note that the statue was to be erected in Athens, not Delphi.
37. The law that Phaedrus alludes to is unclear, and the only law-like thing yet mentioned was the inscription of the Delphic command (229e). This would suggest that Phaedrus violated the command to "know thyself" (Sallis 1996, 120–21). While Phaedrus is certainly guilty of failing to know his own ignorance, having him allude to the Delphic command would paradoxi-

cally suggest that he is aware that he is violating the command to know himself, which seems too clumsy an interjection by Plato. Rather, the "law" alluded to can only be what Lysias wrote—Socrates going beyond it is akin to a criminal breaking the law (cf. 254c5–d1).

38. See Morgan (1994, 384–85) on the manufacture of the statue. On the Cypselids' statue being an icon of Zeus, see Strabo, *Geography* 8.3.30. Epicrates's home, where Lysias read his speech, was also said to be near "the Olympian," that is, the temple of Zeus (227a). While Phaedrus gives voice to the institutional breakdown in the relationship between the human and the divine, he also made the first direct reference to Zeus, referring to him as the god of friendship (234e1). The desire to plead in Zeus's name, despite the corruption of the god's temple, suggests that the impulses that gave rise to the sacred institutions remain, and that these impulses may indeed provide the resources for the refounding if not renewal of those institutions (see Voegelin 2001, 2.200–204, 380). With respect to persuasion, Phaedrus's use of Zeus also illustrates how a broader context of usage may convey additional meanings, sometimes without the user's awareness, allowing the introduction of new or unforeseen connections (cf. 261e–262b, 263a–b).

39. Aristotle later wrote that tyrants are wont to build monuments, such as those of the Cypselids, in order to impoverish their subjects and deprive them of the leisure needed to conspire (Arist. *Politics [Pol.]*, 1313b19–26).

40. Like Lysias, Socrates puns on "to speak" and "to love," saying "I will speak [or: love, *erō*] while being concealed" (237a4). See note 30 on Lysias's pun.

41. On Socrates's imitation of the initiation into the Lesser Mysteries, see chapter 1, note 14.

42. Lysias uses derivatives of "necessary" (*anangkaion, anangkazein*) four times, all with reference to *erōs* (231a4, 232a6, 232b4, 233b4), while Socrates uses them fourteen times (237a9, c2, 238e3, 239a5, a7, b5, 240a4, b4, d1, e1, 241b4, b5, b7, and c2). In contrast, Socrates uses the word "likely" (*to eikos*) or a derivative only twice (237c4, 238e2), while Lysias uses it four times (231c7, e4, 232c2, and 233a2).

43. Irani (2017, 119–20) rightly disputes the common assumption in the scholarly literature that Socrates's improvements are only formal.

44. A special variation of this problem is that Phaedrus would judge the adequacy of a speech according to who delivers it, rather than a direct appraisal of its "form" (229c4–5, 235c1, 275b5–c2). Rowe (1986) suggests another variation, how a poet or prose speaker can account for his own craft and insight (153).

45. Socrates puns on the Ligurian descent of the Muses' name with *liguros* ("clear"), thus jokingly asking whether the Muses were named for descending from the "Clear Ones." Socrates will later refer to another race of "clear" (*liguros*) singers, the Sirens, who lured sailors to their death with their song (259a6-b2; cf. Hom. *Od.* 12.44). With respect to the present speech, the concealed lover asserts the clarity of his arguments at several points (*dēlos* at 237d4, 238b3, b5, 239d3, and 239d8, and *saphēs* at 238b7 and 239e2), and Socrates later again mentions its clarity (266d6).

46. McCumber (1982, 32–33).

47. Socrates emphasizes this verbal agreement by using *homolegein*, literally "same-saying," rather than *sungchōrein*, which suggests moving-together and therefore agreement in deed rather than merely in speech (237c3, c5, d1).

48. Cf. Pl. *Tht.* 210a8–b2.

49. The concealed lover even subjects thinking to that consensus, since one "must think" that there are two forms in a human being that struggle for command (237d6). A type of thinking that operates outside of this moderate rule of opinion is alluded to—the "accordance" (*homo-noein*) of both parts of the soul—but plays no further role in this speech (237d9). This will be taken up in Socrates's palinode, when he describes the agreement of true lovers as *homonoia*, literally "sameness of thought" (256b1).

50. Sinaiko (1965, 29); Rosen (1988, 100); Linck (2003, 271).

51. Socrates says he is speaking in "dithyrambs," the Bacchants' ritual song and dance, the antistrophic character of which parallels the duality of the two forms in the soul. See note 32.

52. Socrates here diametrically opposes Phaedrus's account of *erōs* in the *Symposium*, where *erōs* is agonistic without jealousy and thus makes the partners better. Socrates thus draws attention to Phaedrus's inconsistency and ignorance of *erōs* (Pl. *Smp.* 178e–179b).

53. These three instances are the only uses of *apoblepein* in the *Phaedrus*.
54. Dorter (1971) notes that this portrait "resembles perfectly the appearance of Dionysus" in Euripides's *Bacchae* (284–85; E. *Ba.* 455–60).
55. This parallels the city in speech of the *Republic*, which pits its well-trained guardians against the weak, pale, and luxurious oligarchs of foreign cities (Pl. 442a–c).
56. Hackforth (1952, 48).
57. Aristotle argues that because epic poetry links a series of episodes by narration, the imputation of necessity is most desirable, as it allows ample opportunity for the introduction of irrationalities and the concealment of absurdities. Homer, he says, taught us well how to tell falsehoods (*Poetics*, 52a, 60a–b).
58. The true lover, who founds his friendship with the beloved boy on the distinction of the boy from the true beloved—that is, the being of beauty itself (254b, 255d–e, 256e–57a)—is not identical to the ecstatic lover that abandons earthly relations (252a3–6). *Pace* Griswold (1986, 132).
59. With due consideration for the subtle qualification Hackforth (48) notes.
60. In the palinode, Socrates describes this experience as one of perplexity at the change, but ascribes it to the beloved rather than the lover (255d–e).
61. Ferrari (1987, 98); Brown and Coulter (1971, 420).
62. Irani (2017, 121–22).
63. Friedländer (1958, 3.225–6).
64. This is the dilemma that Callicles faces in the *Gorgias*: he despises common opinion and its attendant moderation yet is entirely dependent on it for his own gratification (Newell 2000, 34–35; see Pl. *Grg.* 510d–11a, 512d–13c).
65. Weaver (1953, 11).
66. Pl. *Grg.* 463a ff.
67. Weaver (1953, 11).
68. Ferrari (1987, 51–52).

# 3. THE PALINODE

1. Arist. *Rh.* 1358b–9a.
2. Burnyeat (2012, 238–39).
3. Friedländer (1958, 1.192). See also Pieper (1964, 97); Sinaiko (1965, 98–99); White (1993, 1–9).
4. Werner (2012) contrasts a "Dogmatic View" of myth interpretation with a "Debunking View," surveying versions of both (11–12, 48–49).
5. See the Introduction for a discussion of method in interpreting the *Phaedrus*. Werner (2012) draws attention especially to Socrates's claim that the proof of the immortality of the soul may be disbelieved by the "clever" but "will be trusted [*pistē*] by the wise" (245c1–4), since *pistē* does not imply certainty, but what seems reasonable or plausible, and is therefore an object of opinion ( 49).
6. *Pace* Werner (2012, 17–18). Put another way, speeches may produce different effects on different kinds of people (271b, d–e). Even though Socrates's use of myth for Phaedrus's benefit entails that Socrates has some understanding of what myth is and is capable of, in a general sense, his use of myth here first of all entails that Phaedrus has certain beliefs about what myth is and is capable of, which Socrates supposes will cause Phaedrus to respond to his myth in certain ways. Socrates probably understands more of myth, and what its effects will be on Phaedrus, than does Phaedrus himself, but even if Socrates's intention is propaedeutic, he must lead Phaedrus and so appeal in some way to his current opinions (261a, 261e–262a, 272a, 273d).
7. Clay (1979) argues that Pan is "another demonic presence in the background and setting of the *Phaedrus* . . . a source of both inspiration and danger," who emerges, as myths tell, at noon—just when Socrates notes his demonic inspiration (242a4–5) (348). Socrates elsewhere associates the erotic Pan with *logos* – see chapter 4, note 65, and chapter 5.

8. Ibycus (Ibyc.), fr. 278 (Campbell 1991).
9. Ibyc. fr. 282, 286, 287. Socrates's quotation of Ibycus may allude to Plato's *Parmenides* (*Prm.*) 137a, when Parmenides likens his dialectical inquiry to Ibycus's account of *erōs*, where an old racehorse remembers the labors of the chariot race and is seized by trembling fear (fr. 287; White 1993, 3–6). Socrates expresses fear of *erōs* at 242c, 254e, and 257a–b.
10. Socrates catches Euthyphro in the contradiction that piety is what is dear to the gods while at the same time asserting that they disagree with themselves (Pl. *Euthyphro* [*Euthphr.*], 6b–c, 7d–8b).
11. Rowe (1986) translates *anthrōpiskoi* as "poor specimens of humanity" (53 ad loc.).
12. Beercroft (2006, 49–52).
13. Beercroft (2006, 56–58). See Chapter 1 on the distinction between *muthos* and *logos*.
14. Hdt. 6.61; Isocrates, *Helen* (Isoc. 10) 63.
15. In his third letter, Plato exhorts Dionysius to "imitate [wise Stesichorus's] palinode, and change from the false to the true" (Pl. *Ep.* 3.319e).
16. *Suda* "Stesichorus." See also Philodamus, *Music*, 1.30.31.
17. E. *Helen*; Gorgias (Gorg.), *Encomium of Helen* (B10 [DK]); Isoc. 10. Isocrates mentions the long history of antipodal speeches in rhetorical and philosophical circles, and the use of Helen's case in particular (Isoc. 10.2–3, 14–15). Plato's articulation of the palinode or epodal structure here presumably allows speech to transcend the antipodal structure of eristic rhetoric. This issue is taken up in chapter 4.
18. Pl. *R.* 586c. This account of Stesichorus's palinode—that the Helen in Troy, over whom the war was fought, was in fact a phantom—is corroborated by the fragment of Stesichorus in *Papyrus Oxyrhynchus*, 2506 fr. 26 col. i. Herodotus's inquiry is similar, but makes no mention of fighting for a phantom (Hdt. 2.112–20).
19. Plato skillfully weaves into the *Phaedrus* other traditional elements of the Helen story; for example, Helen's prowess with drugs that suppress all pain and strife—a state for which Phaedrus longs (Hom. *Od.* 4.219ff, 4.264; cf. Pl. *Phdr.* 258e). On the "palinodic structure" of the *Phaedrus* as a whole, see Werner (2012, 243–47). Griswold (1986, 218) draws a clear connection between the palinode and dialectic, and therefore the dialectical structure of the *Phaedrus*.
20. Cf. Pl. *Lg.* 701a8–b2.
21. Nussbaum (1986) renders Himera "Desire Town or Passionville," but also finds the allusion to myrrh a reference to its pharmacological use as an aphrodisiac (211, 427n23; cf. Rinella 2010, 141n36 on Plato's general usage of *pharmakon*).
22. As Irani (2017) observes, across Plato's corpus, *epithumia* "does not always refer to an exclusively pleasure-seeking desire" (133). This makes it all the more notable that Plato concedes this exclusive usage here in the *Phaedrus*, making a deceptively clear distinction between *epithumia* and desire for the true beings. Strengthening the force of this distinction, Plato seems to allude to Hesiod's use of *himeros*, when he says that the Muses are accompanied by the Graces and Himeros (Hes. *Th.* 64).
23. Pieper (1964, 56).
24. White (1993, 72).
25. On these oracles' various modes of inspiration, see the works of H. W. Parke (1956, 1.17–25, 36–39; 1967, x, 3; 1988, 7–9).
26. Rowe sees this passage as "doubly ironic," citing the low rank Socrates gives to *mantikē* at 248d–e and the apparently obvious fact that "nor is it even a science (*technē*)" (172n243c1). The simple sense of irony implied by Rowe—that Socrates is lying—means that the passage depreciating the *oionōistic* art is "to be taken at face value" (172n243c5–6). But why then consider the mantic art ironic and not the *oionōistic*? Socrates is here developing the distinction between *mania* and *sōphrosunē* as it characterizes divine and human art. By not considering whether the mantic art might serve a serious purpose for Socrates, Rowe strips the present passage of meaning. As will be discussed, the apparent contradiction with 248d–e can be resolved without eliminating one of the propositions.
27. On the bribery of the priestess at Delphi, see Hdt. 6.66.

28. The *Cratylus* deals with the problem that the conventional nature of names poses for rational inquiry, as names are subject to a variety of relations depending on the opinions and intentions (and therefore desires) of the speaker (*Cra.* 411b).

29. While the palinode will show primarily psychological effects from one's separation from divine being, the example of Stesichorus indicates that a physical malady may also result, *pace* Pieper (1964, 59–60).

30. An obvious example of familial blood guilt is the curse of the House of Atreus, which is widely recounted in ancient myth and classically in Aeschylus's *Oresteia* (e.g., A. *Ag.* 1598–600). On Socrates's general application, in the *Phaedrus* of the mania arising from such blood guilt, see Pieper (1964, 60–61).

31. For example, Hippocrates, *On the Sacred Disease* (Hp. *Morb. sacr.*) 1.1–3, 20.1–6.

32. See Ficino (1981, 82).

33. Socrates's later image of the desirous soul as parched, however, warns against conflating true *erōs* with poetic inspiration (251d1–7). In the *Symposium*, Diotima declares Eros "hard and parched," contradicting the poet Agathon's inference that, because *erōs* greatly affects soft souls, Eros should be considered soft (cf. *Smp.* 195d–e, 203c–d). The poet's state of continual openness to beauty is more akin to Phaedrus's desire for continual painless pleasure, which Socrates warns against in the myth of cicadas (see Chapter 4).

34. In the *Ion*, Socrates similarly suggests there are two forms of art, one that lacks divine inspiration, the other being divine knowledge itself. There, seers and oracles are not spared the epithet "artless" (*Ion* 534b–e).

35. Burnyeat (2012, 242–43).

36. Cf. Pl. *Lg.* 894d–e; Pl. *R.* 511b–c; Arist. *Physics* (*Ph.*) 184a10–21.

37. Since the argument that Socrates's proof is rhetorical, even "fallacious," is plausible, the proof's significance lies in its purpose within the palinode and the *Phaedrus* as a whole. The proof is doubtless a testing ground for Phaedrus, and the reader, in terms of taking a more critical stance toward speech (Moore 2014, 200–1). But the specific contents of the proof—the ambiguity between collective and distributive senses, self-motion, incorruptibility, separation from the body while relying on its individuation—are also necessary for the integrity of Socrates's myth and his later account of persuasion.

38. The ambiguity of referring to the collective sense of soul as "soul in general" is the consequence of the very problem in *psuchē pasa*. Does the collective sense of soul refer to soul as a whole—that is, a whole of parts—or as a single and indivisible soul, in the sense of one soul? Is soul one or many?

39. On the ancient debate, see Hermeias, 102.10ff. Modern scholars are equally divided between the three possibilities. That *psuchē pasa* is distributive, see Griswold (1986, 84); Nicholson (1999, 156). That it is collective, see: Bett (2000, 919); de Vries (121 *ad loc.*); Ficino (1981, 6.i); Yunis (2011, 136–37 *ad loc*). That Plato intends both senses, see: Skemp (1967, 113–15); Hackforth (1952, 64–65); Burger (1980, 51); Ferrari (1987, 124); White (1993, 78–79); Moore (2014, 183–84).

40. This resemblance indicates that Socrates's criticism of Lysias on this point (264a4–8), like his other criticisms, is not as straightforward as it appears and necessitates a criticism beyond the level of technique (see chapter 4).

41. Sallis (1996, 136). Nicholson (1999) is correct to say that soul's self-motion is logically distinct from the motion of bodies, but it remains the case that such purely metaphysical, or "psychic," motions cannot be conjectured until soul's effect upon the body is clarified (162–63).

42. Pl. *Timaeus* (*Ti.*), 36b–d; Pl. *Lg.* 893c. See also Pl. *Prm.* 138b–139b, 145e–146a.

43. Pl. *Lg.* 894c.

44. Consider the example of a symmetrical top's centripetal motion, which can only be perceived by distinguishing a part of it that moves along with the whole (see Pl. *Lg.* 893c–d; Pl. *R.* 436c–e).

45. Hackforth (1952, 64). See also Bett (2000, 916).

46. On this issue, compare, for example, Ficino (1981, 6.i), who argues that the rational soul becomes one with the world soul and so "participates of alike immortality," and Griswold

(1986, 84), who argues that the only work of soul that is mentioned in the dialogue is the work of individual souls.

47. Ficino (1981, 6.i).

48. Moore (2014) approaches this problem as the difference between relative and absolute beginnings (187–88).

49. Pl. *R.* 504e ff. See Benardete (1991, 136); Burger (1980, 52). Ficino (1981) speaks of an "infinite" *archē* of *archai* as distinct from the "finite" *archē* discussed in the proof (6.viii).

50. This deduction of a further cause is not unique to the *archē* of motion, but in fact a necessary consequence of all thought and speech (*logos*), which at least presupposes "to be" (or simply "being," *to einai*) as a predicate. See *Prm.* 132a–133a and *Sophist* (*Sph.*) 243d ff. The close relationship between *logos* and the nature of soul is discussed below.

51. That which is at once at rest and in motion, unchanging, must exist outside of time (*Prm.* 156c).

52. Accepting Burnet's (1901)*gēn eis hen* rather than *genesis*, so as to: preserve the parallel structure *te ouranon . . . te gēn*; reject the insertion of the truism that eliminating the *archē* of generation would eliminate generation; and preserve the allusion to Eleatic monism described above (*pace* de Vries, 123–24 *ad loc.*; Hackforth 1952, 63n2; Rowe 1986, 176; Yunis 2011, 137 *ad loc.*).

53. As Moore (2014) argues, Socrates rhetorically conflates the "absolute" *archē*, the property of motion, and the "relative" *archai*, the self-motion of existent things, such as living animals, in order to use one to establish properties of the other (192–93). This is one aspect of the ambiguity between collective and distributive senses of soul.

54. "[T]he palinode has stopped arguing . . . [i]t has simply and brazenly begged the question" (Moore 2014, 193).

55. Parmen. fr. B8 [DK]; Pl. *Prm.* 132a–b, 141e–142a. Socrates's proof does not oppose Parmenides, for the apparent absurdity of all things being one points to the distinction between eternal being and the world of motion and multiplicity, transcendence and immanence, and the need to return to the "nonbeing" of opinion (*doxa*).

56. "Also, any rational soul's power is so great that any one soul in a way may be the universe" (Ficino 1981, 6.i).

57. Griswold (1986, 81).

58. Benardete (1991, 136).

59. Griswold (1986, 83).

60. Cf. Pl. *Tht.* 157a–c, 182d–183c.

61. Griswold (1986, 88–89).

62. When Parmenides asks Socrates whether there is form in things like "hair, mud, and dirt," he is emphasizing that form is found in every object of perception, and that Socrates's transcendent forms must consequently be reconciled with these apparently meager instances (Pl. *Prm.* 130c–131a).

63. The image of a winged chariot is pervasive in Greek literature, as indicated by the earlier allusions to Pindar's charioteers, the immortal horses given by Boreas and Zeus as compensation for kidnapping their beloveds (Nonnus, *Dionysiaca*, 37.155; Hom. *Il.* 5.265ff.), Pegasus and Chimaera, Typhon (slain by Zeus riding in a chariot led by winged horses), and the wild horses of Ibycus and Parmenides. Nor would Phaedrus forget Triptolemos, who was given by Demeter a winged chariot pulled by dragons so that he may spread the art of agriculture (Hom. *Hymn.* 2.145ff., 470 ff.; Apollod. 1.5.2). Drawing on this familiar image of a divinity journeying through the heavens, and related spatial metaphors, Plato did not intend his myth to merely reiterate or resonate with any particular one, but indeed to show how all of them originated from the "deeds and experiences" of soul as he describes them (245c4). Dwelling on Plato's use of traditional imagery without considering how he transforms and refounds them misses the purpose of the speech. Lebeck's (1972) article is exemplary in tracing Plato's development of such images through their suggestive extension to new contexts.

64. Werner (2012) argues for the agency of each part (62–65, esp. 64n39; see also Burnyeat 2012, 253–55). He argues this does not result in infinite regress because the parts are not whole persons in themselves and do not suffer from the inner conflict of the soul. But this is unpersuasive, as he also argues that the soul, by virtue of reasoning with itself, converses within itself,

and that the parts are able to speak to one another because they are to some extent reasonable or "sub-rational." If that is the case, the part is susceptible to change by persuasion, and such change is only possible if it is complex. Indeed, the allusive relationship between the "pathways" by which the gods travel and the "passages" out of which grow the shoots of the soul's wings implies reduplication and regression of the structure of the soul at micro- and macrocosmic levels (cf. *diexodoi* at 247a4, 251d4).

65. Literally, true being, "that which really is," *holds* (*echei*) the superheavenly place. What Socrates describes cannot of course "occupy" any particular place at all, and so the verb *echein* avoids predicating position, depth, or other physical properties.

66. Benardete (1991, 166).

67. Hesiod said that what did not taste nectar and ambrosia was mortal, "but if the gods lay hold of nectar and ambrosia to exist, how can gods who need nourishment be eternal?" (Arist. *Metaphysics* [*Metaph.*] 1000a8–20).

68. "Being," *to on*, is here treated as synonymous with *hē ousia ontōs ousa* (247c7) and merely differing in quantity from *ta onta* (247e3, 248a5, 249e5). Outside the palinode, *ta onta* does not necessarily refer to true beings, but also to "the things we now say are."

69. The gods' vision in the superheavenly place is accordingly expressed in participle form (*theōrousa*, 247c1, d4, and *idousa*, 247d3), although the use of the aorist participle *idousa* indicates that Plato was attempting to express, not with tense but with aspect, the perception of a perpetually enduring being.

70. Amongst the Olympians, Hestia alone does not feast, and it is her tending of the *oikos* that allows for the others' motion, their ascent and descent. She remains at the center and therefore seems related to the being around which the other revolve. In Plato's *Cratylus*, Socrates asserts that "what we call *ousia*, some say it is *essia*, and still others *ōsia* . . . and because we say that which shares in *ousia* 'is,' according to this she would also rightly be called Hestia, for we also seem to have called *ousia essia* in ancient times" (401b–e).

71. As Werner (2012) argues, the horses are not themselves irrational, for otherwise they could not be reasoned with or commanded at all, as Socrates depicts (62–68). They are more properly characterized as subrational, but not for that reason defective. The question of their rationality is further complicated by the fact that the motion of the soul as a whole depends upon the horses—their respective desires and attributes are essential to the soul's perception of, and motivation by, reality.

72. *Hupobruchios* literally means "under water." Socrates uses the language of water (*hudros*) to juxtapose the gods' easy ascent through the clear air with life in the world of motion and becoming, which the intellect must navigate as a "pilot," and wherein "the competition generates great sweat [*hidrōs*]" and the soul is embodied like an "oyster" (247c7, 248b1–2, 250c6). This fluidity of human life was also imaged in the setting, first in the crossing of the river Ilyssus and then in the stream under the plane tree.

73. *Chrēsthai* literally means "to be in need of," indicating the necessity underlying the desire for true being, without which the human soul could not have the form it does (248c8, 249b5–6). This can be contrasted with *erōs*, which also admits of the unnatural desires to which the horses may lead the soul (250e5–251a1).

74. De Vries (1969) argues that the conjunction ἢ in each seed (e.g., φιλοσόφου ἢ φιλοκάλου) is not disjunctive, so that the lives are identified as attributes of a single seed ("lover of wisdom *or in other words* lover of beauty") rather than exclusive lives ("lover of wisdom *or* lover of beauty") (143n248d3–5). But there is no need to preclude the possibility of distinct lives originating from the same seed. Socrates's palinode establishes the kinship between philosopher, beauty lover, and musical man, and although they are unified in the philosopher, they do not need to become philosophers. There are lovers of beauty and erotic men who are not philosophers, and indeed without the *logismos* characteristic of philosophy, these two lives appear very susceptible to mixing their pederasty with sex, contrary to the philosopher (256a–e). See Koritansky (1987, 39n14).

75. *Contra* Hackforth (1952, 83), it would be a grave misunderstanding to view this hierarchy as a clear scheme for the arrangement of human types in a city, since the nature of souls cannot be clearly determined.

76. The number four is associated with solids, the adding of depth to a shape (Pl. *R.* 528a–b; *Ti.* 31c–32c).

77. In the *Phaedo*, Socrates muses whether philosophy is "the greatest music" (Pl. *Phd.* 61a).

78. So Burnyeat (2012): "Plato has not suddenly gained a respect for prophets and poets. He thinks, as he always thought, that the marvelous and useful pronouncements they make are no credit to them, but to the god who speaks through them" (241).

79. There is no reason to assume, in a biographical or developmental manner, that Plato's omission here of the type "philosopher king" is a repudiation of it as a failed hypothesis following the disappointments of his venture in Syracuse (*pace* Voegelin 2001, 3.192).

80. "Although they are wise, those you educated as leaders of the city, they will not hit upon the good birth and barrenness of your people, but it will pass them by and they will bear children when they must not" (Pl. *R.* 546a–547a).

81. The "necessity" of this gathering into one is derived from the principles of noncontradiction and unity. These can be ascertained in the proof of the immortality of the soul (245d1–3). More plainly, the unity of form is coextensive with the perception of "what really is" because the beings must be seen as they are by themselves. For example, if one really perceives justice or knowledge simply, one must see "justice itself" or "knowledge unmixed" (247d1, d6). But, as becomes evident in Socrates's description of the mania induced by beauty, the necessity that perception is of form can also lead to a deceptive confusion of form and being.

82. Yunis (2011) argues here that Socrates has in mind "a discourse conducted on a higher, more abstract level" (146n *ad loc.*). Socrates no doubt includes in *logismos* such abstract discussion, but as argued above, his meaning is more fundamental, such that the "gathering" performed is necessary to all speaking (266b2–5).

83. To take one example, Griswold's interpretation that "Socrates is saying thought is recollective when it is motivated to understand the divine" goes wrong at the decisive point, for thought *qua* thought must be recollective and so is always "motivated to understand the divine"—whether the person thinking believes so or not (Griswold 1986, 113). This point is essential to understanding the nature of persuasion and the possibility of uncovering meanings in words or experience more generally (see chapter 4).

84. Weaver (1953, 6, 16–18, 22–23).

85. Friedländer's (1958) claim, that "Socrates . . . in the last phase [of the palinode], the erotic mania, *unfolded the myth out of doctrine*," can therefore be read in light of the qualification that this "doctrine" at its heart subordinates *logos* to divine being and truth, and so rediscovers the possibility that myth can be true (1.192).

86. Socrates's myth of soul has revealed the eternity we seek through *logos* by giving it a temporal form—that is, giving a beginning to what never came into being and will never perish (cf. 247d5–e1). See also Werner (2012, 81–85).

87. In Plato's *Parmenides*, Parmenides uses *metaxy* to characterize the "strange moment" when change occurs, when the thing is neither at rest nor in motion nor in time, and so reveals "the one" that stands outside of all properties—for example, outside of rest-motion, like-unlike, great-small, increase-decrease (*Prm.* 156d–157b). Awareness of and living in the *metaxy* would therefore be the most direct link to eternal being.

88. Socrates has transfigured the statue (*eikōn*) that Phaedrus promised to erect in his image at Delphi into a natural reminder of what is truly beloved (Pl. *Phdr.* 235d9).

89. For example, Pl. *R.* 475a5–6, *Smp.* 174d–e, 203c–d.

90. "That man among you, O human beings, is wisest, whoever just like Socrates knows that he is in truth of no worth with respect to wisdom" (Pl. *Ap.* 22e–23b).

91. There is limited historical evidence concerning the final Eleusinian rites, mentioning only the things "done," "seen," and "spoken" (Mylonas 1961, 270; Kerényi 1967, 92–93). Some sources suggest that the *epopteia*, the final stage of initiation, culminated in the revealing of a sacred flame (Mylonas 1961, 274–78; Parke 1956, 35).

92. See Pl. *Phd.* 69c–d.

93. Cook (1985) remarks that Plato uses the terms "being" and "form" "casually" in the *Phaedrus*, but it is certainly conspicuous and significant that Plato deliberately avoids the usage most familiar to readers of his other works (441).

94. In the *Symposium*, Socrates is perplexed when he cannot explain to Diotima what the lover of the beautiful possesses in possessing beauty, but he has no difficulty answering the same question concerning the good (*Smp.* 204d–205a). Pieper comments that beauty does not make us content or satisfied, "even on the most spiritual level" (85). While Burnyeat (2012) is surely right that "[e]arthly beauty is a good, not a poor, likeness of the ideal," this alone does not explain the differing responses to that beauty by the different ranks of lovers (256).

95. Heidegger (1991, 197).
96. Heidegger (1991, 197).
97. Pieper (1964, 83). Cf. Pl. *Smp.* 210e–212a.
98. Shame is one part or kind of fear, as it is linked to a fear for one's reputation (Pl. *Euthphr.* 12a–c).
99. Yunis (2011, 152n) *ad loc.*, and Capra (2014, 75–82), also note parallels with the symptoms of love mentioned in Sappho's *Helen*. Capra shows how Plato transfigures Sappho's depiction into a perception for true beauty, rather than forgetfulness of all else in the face of the beloved (82).
100. Hp. *Morb. sacr.* 6–8, 9.10–12, 13.7–10.
101. The two basic forms of motion (see Pl. *Lg.* 893c; *Prm.* 138b–139b, 145e–146a; *Ti.* 36b–d).
102. Consider the Hippocratic author's emphasis on the brain, which must remain open to the external world and freely circulating phlegm if intelligence is to be produced, as well as the emphasis on the need to study causation in order to discover cures (Hp. *Morb. sacr.* 10.46–54; 20.12–16). These affinities suggest that Socrates found such diagnoses to be not wholly without merit, but incomplete or reductive (see his rejection of Anaxagora's physiological explanations in Pl. *PhD.* 97b–99D). Socrates is rarely dismissive of the expertise of physicians, often using medicine as a model art analogous to philosophy—and the body is after all the object of care for the soul.
103. Benardete (1991, 134).
104. With an effect similar to his allusion to the Hippocratics, Socrates here alludes to Empedocles's hypotheses on respiration and perception ([Emp.] B84, B89, B100 [DK]). See also Pl. *Meno* (*Men.*), 76c–e.
105. The Greek is *ta tōn diexodōn stomata*, which resonated greatly with Ficino (1985), no doubt because of its prefiguring of the stomata of Christ, as well as the sharing of his blood in the sacrament of Eucharist (7.4 [159–61]).
106. Benardete (1991, 138, 141). Burnyeat (2012) similarly points to "the deity within," "inspiration from within a man's own mind," as the crucial source for recollection and hence reasoning (243–45).
107. Voegelin's (2001) interpretation of this process as a consequence of pulsation by both the subject and by "being" ("the Agathon") cannot be substantiated by the text and collapses together soul and "idea" (i.e., true being) (3.191). This relationship between the motion of soul and being is the very problem that Plato expressed in the proof of the immortality of soul, and more expansively over the course of the myth of the palinode. See chapter 3, note 112.
108. Emp. B71, B84 (DK).
109. In other words, the pre-existence of parts in the soul is a corollary of recollection, and accordingly the soul must have always possessed these parts to become human and capable of perceiving the beings.
110. Benardete (1991, 141).
111. Pl. *R.* 509a6–10.
112. Mystical union is an understandable but nonetheless erroneous extension of *erōs*. See Friedländer (1958, 1.80–84) for a relevant discussion on the differences between Plato and Plotinus on beauty, and Benardete (1991, 141, 146) on the irreconcilability of the desires to behold and to have. See chapter 3, note 107.
113. "The cause of all fault in each case is excessive love of oneself" (Pl. *Lg.* 731d–732b). Also see Emp. B2 (DK).
114. Ares's followers traditionally longed and prayed for peace and harmony (Hom. *Hymn.* 8.15–17).

115. Socrates's suggestion that the Areopagus, the Athenian court that tried homicide cases and especially those related to adultery, was the likely site of Oreithuia's death, alluded to this relationship between *erōs*, strife, and justice (229c–d). Also consider the resumption of hostilities between Athens and Sparta that looms over the dramatic setting, and Socrates's allusions to the gods' army and their war with Typhon, as well as his allusions to the Trojan War.

116. In the *Cratylus*, Socrates says Ares's name is derived from being "hard and unbending, what is called firm [*arraton*]" (*Cra.* 407d).

117. Cf. Pl. *Smp.* 178e–179b; *R.* 468b–469b.

118. Pl. *Ep.* 3.316c–317d, 7.327b–329b, 8.355a. On the pun, see Wilamowitz-moellendorff (1917, 1.537), followed by numerous others (e.g., Hackforth 1952, 99n2; Nussbaum 1986, 229; Voegelin 2001, 3.72). Yunis (2011) doubts the allusion, arguing that this advertisement of Plato's "private life would reek of melodrama and disrupt the elevated tone that is an essential aspect of [Socrates's] message" (156–57). This overlooks, however, the importance that Plato places on internal inspiration and pursuit of truth, both within the palinode and in his discussion of rhetoric—the recollection of truth is not a disengaged enterprise but engages one's own beliefs and is therefore essentially personal. Far from disrupting the tone, Plato's reflexivity conveys the seriousness of the message.

119. Burnyeat (2012, 240–43).

120. Yunis (2011, 157n *ad loc*).

121. Benardete (1991) describes this as "a forced fitting of the beloved into a previously fashioned image" (154).

122. *Pace* Capra (2014, 101).

123. Pl. *Ap.* 23b, 30d–e.

124. Gods and the beings themselves were clearly distinguished earlier in the palinode, and the present use of *idea* with reference to the gods is not inconsistent with this. Rather, it is an extension of the common usage of "form," which partakes in what are commonly called "the ideas." All that is perceptible, whether by sight or the intellect, must have form (249b–c; cf. chapter 3, note 81), but there is no indication here that such forms are identical to the true beings. An unusual and often neglected feature of the *Phaedrus* is that Plato's most direct representation of the true beings speaks of them as beings (*ta onta*) and not forms (*ta eidē*), while he carefully restricts the use of *eidos* and *idea* to less august objects. The reason for this seems to be that he needs to explain both true persuasion, in the sense of instruction and learning with respect to the true beings, as well as imperfect persuasion, which still gathers together various things in a single form, even if only to use the seeming kinship established by that form in order to deceive. As discussed in chapters 3 and 4, deception is possible because it uses a semblance of the true form of the objects under discussion.

125. See Pl. *R.* 375c, e, 410d, and esp. 440a5. There, Socrates also attributes to *thumos* the love of honor, which in the *Phaedrus* is possessed by the white horse (cf. Pl. *R.* 545a, *Phdr.* 253d–e). The absence of *thumos* in the *Phaedrus* is related to its general apolitical character, and particularly to Phaedrus's character, who lacks civic attachment (see the discussion in chapter 2 and the discussion of Isocrates in chapter 5). Werner (2012) overlooks this omission of *thumos* when he locates receptiveness to myth in the white horse and its love of honor (68–73). A stronger objection to the connection Werner draws between myth and the white horse is that the richness of myth appeals to all parts of the soul, particularly its engagement of the intellect in the gathering together and differentiation of forms both within the myth and then by extension to everyday language—just as Plato does by contextualizing the myth within the dialogue. Neither the white horse nor myth could otherwise be subrational and useful to the intellect (Werner 2012, 64).

126. The fact that the word *logos* and its cognate *logismos* only appear after the mortal soul had fallen from the superheavenly place suggests that *logos* is only of use when the mind cannot immediately perceive the truth. Pure thought is the power of the gods alone, to whom Socrates never attributes the capacity for speech (Hyland 2008, 76–77).

127. The argumentative appeal to likelihood (*to eikos*) of course involves more than the black horse, since likelihood is a judgment about the frequency of many perceptions and distinguishes between what is apparent and real. The rationality of such argumentation is a crucial implication in Socrates's later discussion (see chapter 4).

128. Following the suggestion of Friedländer (1958, 1.44, 53). Moore (2015) writes that "[the philosopher's] apparent *mania* might just as well be a higher form of rational coherence and self-mastery" (154–56).

129. Rosen shows that the nonlover's attributes anticipate those of the true lover, such that Socrates sublimates the former into the latter (1969, 426–28, 436; 1988, 91, 96–99). Others have advanced a similar reconciliation of nonlover and lover—that is, Weaver (1953, 18–19); Burger (1980, 27, 66); Griswold (1986, 67); Ferrari (1987, 102, 199–200); Benardete (1991, 126, 152); Linck (2003, 265); Sheffield (2011, 262).

130. Socrates's description, in the *Charmides*, of perfect moderation as the self-knowledge of "some great man" suggests the divine moderation here in the *Phaedrus* (Pl. Chrm., 169d–170a). Also see Klein (1965, 25).

131. This is the concern expressed by Vlastos (1981), that the beloved is not loved for his own sake, but only as a mere stepping-stone to the beings (26). Perhaps because he believes himself to be following Aristotle's account of friendship, Vlastos overlooks his alliance here with the black horse. In recognizing this, he would see how Socrates acknowledges that the black horse, by reminding the soul of its embodiment, helps prevent the soul from fixating on the beings in an impossible manner.

132. Compare Socrates's remark that he must run away from Parmenides as well as Heraclitus (Pl. *Tht.* 179d–181b), or Parmenides's refutation of both the hypothesis that "the many are" as well as that "the one is" (Pl. *Prm.* 136a–c), or the Eleatic Stranger's risking of "parricide" in refuting Parmenides's thesis that only the one is (Pl. *Sph.* 241d).

133. Zeus stole Ganymede and made him an immortal wine-bearer (Hom. *Il.* 5.265ff.; Hom. *Hymn.* 5.202–17). Ganymede's divinization through love is the happy counterpart to Oreithuia's.

134. Socrates says he is not the source of *logoi* in his interlocutor, but instead assists them in becoming "pregnant" and then "giving birth" to what is inside them (Pl. *Tht.* 148e–151d). This is in keeping with the account of the palinode that reasoning and learning are "recollection." Socrates's refutation of his interlocutors is not, then, simply an eristic victory, but a reflection back to the interlocutor the self-contradiction in their reasoning.

135. Bentley (2005, 243).

136. Consider how Plato puns on *aporein*, "to be at a loss," with *aporrein*, "to fall off" (i.e., wings): "Let us grasp the cause of the wing falling, why it falls from [*apporein*] soul" (246d3–5). This implies the two experiences are related by the soul's separation from being, which is to say that *erōs*, the desire to see true being or the desire to regain one's wings, is the perception of being in its absence. See also Pl. *Smp.* 192c–d.

137. This no doubt informed Aristotle's conception of agonistic friendship, perfected in the case of philosophic friendship (*Nicomachean Ethics* [*EN.*] 1156b6ff., 1169b30–1170a5, 1172a). Vlastos (1981) wishes to distinguish Aristotle from Plato on this point, claiming that love is purely selfless (6), but see 1156b6–7 (complete friendship is between good men, who "wish good for one another *insofar as* they are good"). Bentley (2005) similarly criticizes the urbane speeches for "treating [the boy] as a means rather than an end," in contrast to the purported selfless *erōs* of the palinode, but that obviates the self-benefit that accrues from *erōs* as Socrates describes it, and thus begs the question of palinode (238).

138. Socrates anticipated this distinction in his first speech (237c3, c5, d1, d9). See chapter 2, note 47.

139. Compare Socrates's account of the democratic man in the *Republic*: "He lives by the day gratifying the desire that falls upon him, at one time drinking and listening to the flute, at another drinking water and wasting away, and then again exercising, and again doing nothing and neglecting everything, and then spending his time [*diatribein*] as if in philosophy" (561a–d). The democratic soul does not possess true moderation (559b8–c1, 560c5–d6).

140. See also Pl. *Ap.* 22c11–d5.

141. Griswold (1986) writes that Socrates's knowledge seems to be "knowledge of being intermediate . . . "in between" wisdom and ignorance" (136; cf. Zuckert 2009, 321).

142. Zuckert (2009, 321).

143. *Contra* Pieper (1964, 39, 42–43, 97, 99).

144. Griswold (1986, 147–48); Werner (2012, 42).

145. Socrates's first speech as *mythos* at 237a9, 241e8, 243a4, and as *logos* at 241d3, 242e3, 243c2, 244a1, 264e7, 265c6, d7, e3, 266a3. His palinode as *mythos* at 253c7, 265c1, and as *logos* at 243d4, 244a3, 252b2, 265b8, c6, d7, e3, 264e7, 266a3.

## 4. THE ART OF SPEAKING

1. Zuckert (2009) seems to overlook the contrast between these two forms of immortality when she claims that the *Phaedrus* does not see "poetry or legislation" as "less pure forms of erōs" (320), from which she concludes that *erōs*, as conceived in the *Phaedrus*, is "not a desire to perpetuate one's own existence," although the palinode emphasized the lover's desire to hold on to his vision of beauty forever (252a).

2. There is a similar hierarchy of kinds of immortality in Plato's *Symposium*, when Diotima repudiates Aristophanes's celebration of political virtue as the striving after a form of immortality that is far surpassed by the immortality of being with the eternity of true beauty (Pl. *Smp.* 207c–d, 208c–209e, 211a–b, 212a; cf. 191e–192e).

3. Pl. *Lg.* 793a–d. On the broader meaning of *nomos*, see chapter 2, note 9.

4. For example, *Defense against the Charge of Taking Bribes* (Lys. 31).

5. None of Lysias's extant writings nor ancient commentary on his career evidence an interest in this higher art of writing. His defense of Athens's democratic constitution, *Against the Subversion of the Ancestral Constitution of Athens* (Lys. 34), comes closest to reflection on higher principles, but is not intended to endure like legislation.

6. Socrates's arguments in the *Philebus* and *Republic* provide external evidence that pleasure cannot be the highest good, for without wisdom one could not determine whether an experience is pleasurable or not (*Phlb.* 21a–b, 22a–b). In the *Republic*, Socrates is unequivocal that the highest good is not pleasure, yet later argues that the life of philosophy is a pleasure unmixed with the pains of the body (505c, 509a, 583a–587a).

7. The Athenian Stranger argues that a teacher must find a middle ground between the absence and presence of pain when educating a youth (Pl. *Lg.* 729b–e).

8. Pl. *Smp.* 194d, 199b.

9. *Pace* Klein (1965, 15), who argues that the purpose of the myth is to restore orality to its proper place. The immediate context, and Phaedrus's remark at 258e, indicates that the issue at hand is instead Phaedrus's manner of conversation and interest in speech, not orality per se.

10. Similarly, in the *Protagoras*, Socrates voices his contempt for symposia devoted to interpreting a poem in a variety of ways (347c–e). In the *Symposium*, Socrates rebukes his friends for giving encomia to Eros that are obviously and intentionally false, ascribing to the god everything believed to be good (198b–199b).

11. Hom. *Od.* 12.39ff. On the Sirens' promise of wisdom, see 12.188.

12. Hes. *Th.* 53–61; cf. Pl. *Phd.* 60b–c.

13. See also *Smp.* 211d7–e1.

14. *Contra* Capra (2014, 108–9), who neglects the rhetorical context of the myth—Phaedrus's hedonistic interest in speeches—and seems to accept the palinode's splendid image of transcendent beings, despite Socrates's repeated emphasis that the beings are only "glimpsed darkly" through opinion and reminders.

15. Burger (1980) rightly points out that Socrates's defense speech indicates that he did not believe death to be simply evil (74). In Plato's *Apology*, after his death sentence, Socrates notes that his *daimonion*, which holds him back from what is bad, never restrained him during his antagonistic defense speech, implying that it was good that he would come to die in the way he did (40a–c).

16. Hes. *Th.* 26–s8.

17. Ferrari (1987, 27) argues that the divine gift is that the cicadas will provide a good report to the Muses. But the value of this good report is not at all evident.

18. On philosophy as the higher music, see Pl. *Phd.* 60d9–61a5 (cf. Pl. *Euthydemus* [*Euthd.*] 295d–e). Socrates's distinction here, between the susceptibility of the *philomousos* and the

highest music of philosophy, indicates that the *mousikos* in the palinode is not simply attributive of the philosopher, but also an independent life. See chapter 3, note 74.

19. Ferrari (1987, 21ff).
20. Pl. *Grg.* 457b–c, 459c–460a; *Men.* 95c.
21. Hom. *Il.* 2.361. Two examples suffice to show the legacy of the noble rhetoric: the kings' address to the mustered army in the *Iliad* aims to win the soldiers over to decision of the council of kings (Hom. *Il.* 2.72–74); Aeschylus's Pelasgus persuades the citizens to heed the demands of justice despite its risks (A. *Supp.* 468–89, 516–23).
22. Socrates argues similarly in the *Republic*, albeit in the opposite direction, that a poet who imitates but does not use the thing he imitates cannot claim knowledge (601d–602a).
23. Moore (2013, 97).
24. Gorgias gives the example of his brother, a physician, who employs him, a rhetorician, to make patients receptive to medical prescriptions (Pl. *Grg.* 456a–457b).
25. See chapter 3, note 13.
26. Beercroft (2006, 57–58).
27. See the Spartans' demand that rhetoric produce virtue in Pl. *Hp. Ma.* 283c, 285d ff.; cf. *R.* 377b ff., 396e10, 548e.
28. For this reason Socrates asked whether the art of rhetoric "lies" when claiming that it is necessary for all persuasion: without such skepticism and the possibility of disproving the art, the art of speaking would presuppose itself.
29. Socrates reinterprets Hermes's traditional role of leading shades into the house of Hades as the power of *legein* and *logos* (Hom. *Od.* 24.1–15, 99–100; see also Pl. *Cra.* 408b–d). The word *psychagōgia* does not appear until the fifth century, in Aeschylus's *Persians*, where *psychagōgos* refers to someone who leads shades out of Hades in order to examine them, and in his lost play *Psychagōgoi* ("Necromancers") (A. *Pers.* 687; fr. 150–52 [Sommerstein 2009]). By analogy, Socrates's rhetorician is the *psychagōgos* who leads the soul out of (and back into) the mortal realm.
30. On the shamefulness of erotic speeches, see D. 61.1. Kennedy (1963) asserts that "love . . . was a common rhetorical theme," but only cites Demosthenes's *Erotikos* and Diogenes Laertius's late testimony that Aristotle composed four books on the subject (D. L. 5.1.24) (75).
31. Pl. *Grg.* 449d ff.
32. For example, Hom. *Il.* 2.207ff., 7.155ff.
33. On Palamedes's invention of the alphabet or "syllables," see E. fr. 578 [Collard and Cropp 2009]. On his invention of number, see A. fr. 252 [Sommerstein 2009], Pl. *R.* 522d. Gorgias gives a longer list of Palamedes's inventions that also includes military tactics, writing and written laws, weights and measures, messenger services, and even draughts (Gorg. B11a.30 [DK]). For further sources, see Woodford (1994).
34. The usual reason for this attribution, that Zeno invented dialectic (D. L. 8.57, 9.25), is insufficient, for this could as easily be attributed to Parmenides (Friedländer 1958, 3.215). But there is an additional reason for this attribution, discussed below, that Zeno, like Palamedes, was murdered.
35. Plato seems to be responsible for formalizing *antilogic* as verbal contradiction (LSJ 158 s.v.). On the essential function of contradiction in *antilogic*, see Kerferd (1981, 64); Murray (1988, 281); Nehamas (1990, 8).
36. Cf. 270d–e and Pl. *Prm.* 128e–130a, esp. 129d9–e2.
37. Moore (2013) argues that Socrates invalidly "assimilates" knowledge of the audience into knowledge of the subject matter (*ta onta*). Socrates suppresses the rhetorician's appeal to the audience's opinions and therefore circumvents Phaedrus's belief that rhetoricians only need to know the opinions of the audience. But Moore recognizes that knowledge of the audience's beliefs and knowledge of the object are "conceptually related," as Socrates argues in his discussion of Teisias's probabilistic forensics (see futher discussion below) (104).
38. Socrates's way leading of his interlocutors into *aporia* by exposing their self-contradiction, his so-called *elenchos*, shares the structure of *antilogic* (see Kerferd 1981, 65; Murray 1988, 281). Murray (1994) cautions that Socrates's use of *antilogic* should not be conflated with that of the sophists he criticizes (e.g., in the *Euthydemus*): Socrates demands an honest

response in agreed-upon terms, so that inconsistency or contradiction in the interlocutor's opinions may be discerned rather than hidden (130–31, 133–34).

39. Using Aristotle's definition of demonstration (deduction from true premises) for contrast (Arist. *Posterior Analytics* 71b).

40. Cf. Pl. *Ti.* 48e–50a, 52a–d.

41. Cf. Pl. *Smp.* 201c. Without perfect demonstration, reliance on argumentative victory as a criterion of truth blurs the distinction between philosophy and sophistry (Nehamas 1990, 7, 10, 13).

42. Heidegger (1997) similarly employs "background" (*hintergrund*) while interpreting the discussion in the *Sophist* of the presupposition of being (327).

43. Cf. Pl. *Phdr.* 261d6–8, *Prm.* 128e ff., esp. 129d9–e2.

44. Gorg. B11.11, 11.13; see also B11a.24, B11a.35 (DK).

45. *Prm.* 127e; Zeno A25–7, B1–2 (DK). In his poem, Parmenides similarly claims that "there is no true reliance in . . . the opinions of mortals" (Parmen. B1.30, 8.50–52 [DK]).

46. Gorg. B3.67–74 (DK); Pl. *Phlb.* 58a7–b3.

47. Pl. *Prm.* 128a9–b1.

48. Pl. *Prm.* 127b, 128a–e, 135c8–d7.

49. From his observation of the relation between the arguments of Zeno and Parmenides, Socrates postulates that the being of things lies in invisible, nonmaterial, and pure forms, which Parmenides confirms as the proper if imperfectly formulated foundation of "the power of conversation [*dialegesthai*]" (Pl. *Prm.* 135b–c). Kerferd (1981) writes that "Plato . . . was aware that his own view of phenomena was *anticipated* by those who concerned themselves with *logoi antilogikoi*" (67 [italics in original]).

50. The story of Palamedes's betrayal arises after Homer, and was a common theme in fifth-century literature. All three great tragedians wrote a *Palamedes* (A. fr. 96, 97, 252 [Sommerstein 2009]; S. fr. 478–79 [Lloyd-Jones 1996]; E. fr. 568, 581, 583 [Collard and Cropp 2009]). See also Gorg. B11a (DK); Pl. *Ap.* 41b; Xen. *Apology of Socrates* (*Ap.*), 26, *Mem.* 4.2.33; Isoc. *Busiris* (Isoc. 11), 24–30.

51. D. L. 9.26–27.

52. Gorg. B11a (DK).

53. Consider a fragment from Euripides's *Palamedes*: "A fine speech on shameful actions—such wisdom is not worthy of praise" (E. 583 [Collard and Cropp 2009]). In the *Theaetetus*, Socrates claims that the rhetorician who is devoted to giving an account of himself in private will come to scorn rhetoric—that is, "public rhetoric"—much as Zeno scorns his own writing (Pl. *Tht.* 177b; Pl. *Prm.* 128d–e). On Socrates's similar attitude toward public rhetoric, cf. Pl. *Ap.* 38d–e, 41b; Xen. *Ap.* 26; Cicero, *De Oratore* 1.54.231; D. L. 5.40–41. On account of this attitude, and Socrates's mastery of rhetorical techniques Nichols (1998) argues that Socrates was able, but chose not to use rhetoric in manner of his contemporaries (13).

54. In the *Cratylus*, Socrates shows that even the most important word for one who knows, "knowledge" (*epistēmē*), may admit of different meanings, whether following things in their motion (412a) or standing still before things (437a).

55. Alcibiades contrasts Socrates's consistent usage of words with the poets' and rhetoricians' indulgence in polysemy (Pl. *Smp.* 221e). Socrates's way of conversing therefore seems to be a form of private rhetoric that forces his interlocutors to maintain focus on the object at hand. See the discussion of Socrates's rhetoric below.

56. In the *Seventh Letter*, Plato (or the Platonist author) similarly stipulates that name and definition are the first two of five elements of coming to know, but because they are subject to change they are insufficient for knowledge (*Ep.* 7.342a7–b2, 343a9–b6).

57. Ferrari (1987, 46–52).

58. *Pace* Ferrari (1987, 56).

59. This complexity of speech exists at multiple levels. At the level of argument, the complexity of speech is seen in the discussion of *antilogic*, in which a pair of opposites are connected by semblances. At the most basic level, the sentence, this complexity is seen in the need for subject and predicate. Without these parts, speech ceases to be a whole and ceases to be speech. The discussion of being in the *Sophist* goes even further, suggesting that the simplest declarative sentence is itself antilogical and manifold, for *to on* ("what is" or "what exists")

cannot be understood without predication, which, being other than the subject, creates the opposite, "what is not" (244b–45c). The "semblance" in such speech is simply the verb "to be," *einai*. This is perhaps the most fundamental presupposition or "background" for any speech, and was accordingly identified in the palinode as one of the soul's fundamental objects. This need to predicate of the being in question explains why the soul only approaches being indirectly, through its "images" (250b1–5).

60. Burger (1980, 79).

61. Plato thus relates two plays on words: *sōma sēma*, "body is a tomb" (Pl. *Grg.* 493a) and body (*sōma*) as a "sign [*sēma*] of soul" (Pl. *Cra.* 400b–c). Plato takes up the association of body, death and tomb, and *logos* in the discussion of writing (see chapter 5).

62. *Contest between Homer and Hesiod* 324. Socrates omits the following verses: "and rivers fill, and the sea breaks on the shore, / and while the sun rises and shows its light and the moon as well." The dating of the *Contest* is uncertain, although recent papyri indicate it is part of Alcidamas's *Mouseion* (see the summary of the evidence in O'Sullivan 1992, 64) and therefore contemporaneous with Plato.

63. Scott (2011, 188–94) provides a careful analysis of Socrates's "assimilation"—that is, sequence of small steps—of *mania* to philosophical love, over the course of his two speeches.

64. For example, Hdt. 2.49; E. *Ba.* 25–35, 215–48.

65. White (1993) regards this "otherness" a "fixed certainty" as it is a condition of truth existing "as a dimension of reality apart from fields of discourse" (265, 275). This adds symbolic significance to Clay's observation of Socrates's repeated allusions to Pan, Dionysus's companion (Hom. *Hymn.* 7.36), whom Plato explicitly associates with *logos* in the *Cratylus* (408b–d), for the otherness of Pan represents the confrontation with otherness required to perceive the reality of things hidden in our use of language (see chapter 3, note 7).

66. See the discussion of the soul's immortality, in chapter 3, on the relation between the soul's motion and *logos*, which implies that *logos* too is in perpetual motion, constantly reformulating the soul's perception of being in pursuit of its truth.

67. Thus he risks becoming a kind of misologist, doubting one wants the capacity of speech to lead one to the truth because he believes all to be in flux, and consequently believes that the only use for speech is to make others to believe what they want them to believe (Pl. *Phd.* 89c–91c; Irani 2017, 1–3).

68. Yunis (2009, 229, 241).

69. Wedin (1987) makes the important observation that the objects of collection and division are not necessarily "forms proper"—that is, the forms of the true beings—but rather that forms are the means and criteria by which collection and division of things can be performed (208, 210–12, 217). Similarly, Socrates's usage of *idea* and *eidos* in this passage is not restricted to "forms proper," but rather form in general, whether that be the form of concrete and particular cases that exhibit *mania* or the form that encompasses species of *mania* (which is the case in Socrates's example of division). Hayase (2016) is therefore correct that the purpose of collection and division is not to discover the genus with reference to which the object in question is defined, but is wrong to say that "knowledge of what G-ness [i.e., the quality belonging to the genus] is seems irrelevant," since only knowing a genus will guarantee the correct collection and division of its species (118, 121–22).

70. LSJ s.v.

71. Sinaiko (1965, 34–35); Griswold (1986, 174–75); Wedin (1987, 212, 215–16).

72. The palinode's inconclusive support for Socrates's claim that *erōs* is a part of *dianoia* gives weight to Pieper's (1964) doubt that *mania*, and therefore *erōs*, can be wholly circumscribed in speech and reasoning (56). But this doubt cannot invalidate attempts to reconcile *erōs* and *dianoia* in reasoning (e.g., Santas 1982; Burnyeat 2012; Scott 2011), since *erōs* is the psychological experience that grounds *logos* and reasoning in an intelligible reality.

73. Parmenides aptly calls dialectic an "exercise" for the purpose of discovering the truth (Pl. *Prm.* 135c–d).

74. Mackenzie (1982, 70).

75. Mackenzie (1982) states "collection and division is not a method of acquiring knowledge at all, but rather a means of setting it out" (70). On dialectic's insufficiency with respect to

disclosure of true being, see similar discussions in Robinson (1953, 65); Griswold (1986, 174–76, 185, 198); Ferrari (1987, 151); White (1993, 217–18); Werner (2007b, 297–98).

76. See McCumber (1982, 19); Curran (1986, 68, 70); Ferrari (1987, 32, 69); Koritansky (1987, 45–46); Nehamas (1990, 9–10); Scott (2011, 195–96). *Pace* Yunis (2009, 240–41; 2011, 199) and Werner (2012, 178), who interpret Socrates' claim to mean that dialectic is a necessary instrument for speaking and thinking properly—that is, knowledgeably—but is not identical to either speaking or thinking. It is not clear how to explain that dialectic is essential to speaking and thinking while not identifying them or seeing them as applications—that is, species—of dialectic.

77. Gadamer (1989, 359–60). *Pace* Mackenzie's reading (1982, 70) that Socrates "describes [dialectic] as subordinate to a further skill" when he says they must grasp collection and division "by art" (*technēi*, 265d1). Mackenzie ignores the conditionality of the clause, which questions the possibility of artfully grasping dialectic.

78. Hom. *Od.* 2.406, 3.30, 5.193, 7.38; see also 5.192–226 on Odysseus's longing for home.

79. Faced with contradiction, "when the eye of the soul is sunk in the barbaric mire, dialectic gently draws it forth and leads it up" (Pl. *R.* 533c–d).

80. Pl. *R.* 511b7–c2.

81. A few examples are sufficient. Socrates's first speech included a "preamble" in which he summoned the Muses, an "exposition" in which he described the principles of deliberation and his definition of *erōs*, "testimonies" in which he appealed to "what is clear to all," and "proofs" in his examples of how the lover harms the boy (237a–d, 238d ff.). An important "covert allusion" from the palinode was Socrates's identification of *logismos* and "recollection," then relation of recollection to *erōs*, and then *erōs* to searching, which linked *logismos* and searching, although the link between *logismos* and *erōs* was never made explicit. Socrates also made the great seem small and made the small seem great when he collected and divided beauty and its "parts" (251c–e). Socrates does not make use of the "wailing speeches" in the *Phaedrus*, but does in a qualified way in the *Apology*, mentioning his poverty and the plight of his wife and young sons (31c, 34b–35b). On Socrates's use of rhetorical techniques in his *Apology*, see Seeskin (1987, 59).

82. Ps.–Plu. *Lives of Ten Orators*, 3.

83. Prodicus was one of Socrates's teachers (Pl. *Men.* 96d).

84. Pl. *Smp.* 186c–187b, 188a–d.

85. Pl. *Smp.* 187d–e, 188d. Compare Socrates's argument that medicine arises and develops out of the desires for luxury that produce a "feverish city" (Pl. *R.* 372d–373d).

86. Pl. *R.* 407c–e. Also see *Lg.* 728d–e on the political determination of bodily excellence.

87. Hom. *Il.* 2.572; Pi. *Nemean Odes* 9.30; Hdt. 5.67.

88. Pl. *Grg.* 456a–457c, 460c–d; cf. *Men.* 95c, *Phlb.* 58c.

89. Griswold (1986, 189) observes that Socrates and Phaedrus only take up "that which has to do with art," implying that the whole of rhetoric, paradoxically, encompasses more than art alone. This possibility, that there is a nontechnical element in rhetoric, will be discussed later in the context of Teisias's practical objection to Socrates's dialectical rhetoric.

90. Socrates's refutation of the definition of art as a collection of techniques qualifies any conception of "method" as a set of procedures, rules, or techniques of inquiry, for such a method must presuppose a determinate end that justifies the use of these techniques in their specified manner. That is to say, a determinate method presupposes a determinate object and that the method is necessary and sufficient for disclosing that object (Robinson [1953, 72–73] usefully contrasts Plato's and modern conceptions of method). But, as discussed earlier, dialectic is fundamentally problematic because it cannot finally determine the nature of its objects, the beings themselves, and therefore cannot demonstrate its sufficiency as a method.

91. See, for example, Werner (2007b, 297–98).

92. For example, Mansfeld (1980, 348–53); Werner (2010, 31–32, 36–37).

93. Yunis's view that Plato deals with rhetoric in instrumental terms is correct as a characterization of Socrates's rhetorical strategy, for his account of rhetoric shows Phaedrus the necessary conditions for his own instrumental view of rhetoric (Yunis 2005, 2009). But Yunis wishes to exclude a higher vision of instrumentality, what he calls "morality" (2009, 245–46),

when it is precisely the question of the proper ends of rhetoric that allows the discovery of its most efficacious means.

94. Thucydides testifies to Pericles's immense reputation for leadership and rhetorical skill (Th. 2.65.8), an opinion that Plato's characters echo (*Menexenus* [*Mx.*] 235e, *Prt.* 118b–c, *Smp.* 215e, *Thg.* 126a).

95. As he did earlier, the reason that Socrates chooses Pericles as the exemplary rhetorician, rather than a teacher of rhetoric, seems to be in part because Pericles is both a rhetorician and a statesman. This choice of Pericles thus alludes to a political art that must take up both the study of nature and rhetoric (cf. Pl. Plt. 303e–304e).

96. Socrates ironically mimicks Aristophanes's mocking of him as someone who studied "the things aloft and below the earth" (Ar. *Clouds* 227–34, Pl. *Ap.* 18b). Socrates's irony is that Aristophanes failed to understand his naturalism. On the popular use of "babbling" and "lofty talk" with respect to the study of nature, see Yunis (2011, 209–10n *ad loc*).

97. Contrary to the view of scholars who believe that Socrates's mention of Pericles here simply reiterates remarks in other dialogues (e.g., Guthrie 1975, 4.432; Rowe 1986, 204–5; Podlecki 1998, 28–29; Yunis 2011, 206, 209–10), Socrates does seem to find some value and insight, however limited, in Periclean rhetoric (Rhodes 2003, 531). Yunis (2005b, 207–10) supports the view that Pericles's example here is instructive, but his elevation of Pericles to an ideal of the true art of rhetoric does not consider the quality of Anaxagoras's teaching on nature.

98. An ancient tradition attested to Pericles' friendship with Anaxagoras, and his defense of Anaxagoras from charges of impiety (Plutarch [Plu.] *Pericles*, 32), although the earliest sources are only from the fourth century, not from the fifth in which both men lived (Yunis 2011, 209n *ad loc.*).

99. Pl. *Ap.* 26d.

100. On Phaedrus' inclination toward sense experience, see chapter 1. Another feature of Anaxagoras's book that may have appealed to Phaedrus was its style of dogmatic assertion (Schofield 1980, 22–33).

101. Following de Vries (1969), Rowe (1986), and Yunis (2011) in emending Burnet's (1901) redundant *dianoia* with *anoia*. Yunis (2011, 211n 270a1–2) rightly notes that *anoia* was not an element of Anaxagoras's thought.

102. *Pace* Yunis (2005b, 209–10), Socrates therefore does not make Pericles into an ideal.

103. Socrates's correction of Anaxagoras here implies the same criticism he elaborates in the *Phaedo*. He argues there that although Anaxagoras claimed that "mind arranges and is the cause of all things," he could not provide a principle showing "in what way it was best for a thing to be" and so "did not use his mind" (97c, 98b) (in the extant fragments, Anaxagoras's difficulty in distinguishing mind can be seen in his assertions that mind is at once separate from all other things yet also "present where everything else is" (B12, B14 [DK]). In the *Gorgias*, Socrates says that the result of Anaxagoras's beliefs was that "everything [is] jumbled together, without distinction" such that not the soul "but the body itself was the judge" of goodness (465c–d). Socrates draws out the political consequences of this cosmology in his criticism of Pericles, whose rhetoric could only pander to and inflame the passions of the many, making them wild and therefore worse (503c–d, 515e–516d, 517b ff.). *Pace* Hackforth (1952, 149), Pericles's "oratorical excellence" is necessarily related to whether or not he was "a bad statesman," for it is the expedient use of the former, in service of his policies, that produced the wildness for which Socrates convicts him as being the latter.

104. Pl. *Grg.* 463e ff., 504d–e, 508c, 517a; see also 480e–481b.

105. Pl. *Grg.* 456a–457c, 460c–461b. Irani (2017, 164, 170–71).

106. Yunis (2005a, 103–5) rightly claims that Socrates argues in terms of the efficacy of rhetorical practice, but this does not preclude a noble rhetoric that aims toward the production of virtue. In fact, Socrates's argument implies that the most effective rhetoric will be that which leads the soul to truth and knowledge, which would be the most secure persuasion, having led the soul to understand its "greatest good fortune." At this point, the distinction between teaching and persuasion disappears (see chapter 4, note 93).

107. In the *Republic*, Thrasymachus concedes that the strict meaning of art entails caring for the good of its object. Accordingly, a rhetorician who produces ill in his audience—intentional-

ly or not—would cease at that moment to practice the true art of rhetoric (345c–e; cf. *Grg.* 460b–461b).

108. Werner (2007b) argues that Socrates's "philosophical rhetoric" is, due to the epistemic limitations of discourse in general, a "regulative ideal" (297–98). Socrates's professed ignorance and his own actions, however, call into question this ideal and so reveal a relationship between philosophy and rhetoric that differs from what Werner suggests (see the discussion of Socrates's rhetoric in this chapter). "True rhetoric" rather than "philosophical rhetoric" is therefore the preferable term for this perfect rhetoric.

109. De Vries (1969, 234–5n.270c2, c3–5); Hackforth (1952, 150); Hermeias (1971, 245); Yunis (2011, 211n.270c1–2).

110. The interpretation that follows is indebted to Mansfeld (1980, 348–53).

111. In the *Republic*, Socrates argues that the whole of the soul cannot experience different things, and that it is instead different parts of the soul that are affected by a given thing. But rather than multiply the parts of soul *ad infinitum*, Socrates collects the desires under a single part of soul, the appetitive (436b–37a). Parmenides provides a succinct account of this test for simplicity: " whole cannot both do and experience the same thing at once, and so what is one would no longer be one but two," and "the one, becoming other than itself, can no longer be one" (Pl. *Prm.* 138b). See also Pl. *Sph.* 248c–49b.

112. Following the explanations in Mansfeld (1980, 350); White (1993, 237–38). On the general point that "the whole" must be the whole of nature, Ferrari (1987, 76), Heidegger (1997, 232–33), Jaeger (1944, 3.192), are in agreement.

113. Heidegger (1997, 232–33).

114. *Contra* White (1993, 238; see more recently Irani 2017, 171), it seems difficult to understand how soul can be completely known unless "each entity in the universe [is also] known," since soul necessarily experiences something when perceiving each entity, and the precise nature and cause of that experience cannot be elucidated without knowledge of the object perceived. As seen in the second step of the "Hippocratic" method, soul must then determine what in itself was affected by those experiences. Only in coming to know the whole of nature will the soul discover itself as reflected in those experiences.

115. For example, Rowe (1986, 206n *ad loc.*), and Yunis (2011, 213n *ad loc*). Hackforth (1952) is a notable exception, translating 270e2–3 as "to address people scientifically," explaining "that all important sciences . . . must apply to their several provinces the same theoretical treatment—the essence of which is the discovery of the One behind the Many, or the One-in-Many—as physics and cosmology apply to the universe. *All* science is, or ought to be, περὶ φύσεως ἱστορία [inquiry concerning nature]" (150 *ad loc.*).

116. Griswold (1986, 191–92). This is a conclusion that even Gorgias shied away from; see chapter 4, note 31.

117. See the Eleatic Stranger's refutation of materialism in the *Sophist* (246a–249d, esp. 249b–d).

118. See, for example, how changes in the direction of the wind affect the body (Hp. *Morb. sacr.* 13.10-15). Also see Hp. *Airs, Waters, Places*, 1.

119. Griswold (1986, 193–94).

120. Socrates's method of differentiating souls by applying speeches suggests a far more complex taxonomy of species and parts of soul compared to the palinode, and rightly so if a rhetorician must account for differences between particular human beings rather than groups (271e3–272a3). The tripartite soul should therefore be considered a provisional higher-order classification of parts, preparatory for the exhaustive division entailed in the noble rhetoric and philosophy, which may in turn require revision of the original classifications (see chapter 3, note 64).

121. Benardete (1991, 179–81); Sallis (1996, 173).

122. Burger (1980, 85–86), Griswold (1986, 193–94). The opposite risk is to believe that Socrates's psychology, either here or in the palinode, amounts to "a good account of the soul" except in Irani (2017, 24). For reasons discussed below, Socrates's psychology is only a bare prospectus.

123. *Pace* Griswold (1986, 193–94).

124. Yunis (2009) is critical of this common view, which effectively identifies philosophy, dialectic, and rhetoric under the name of "philosophical rhetoric," since it threatens to render meaningless the difference between the terms. He distinguishes (244–45) between philosophy and dialectic on the grounds that philosophy is concerned with "philosophical values" while dialectic is a neutral instrument or method of producing arguments. But this distinction cannot explain the difference between Socrates's use of dialectic and the sophists' or rhetoricians' use of dialectic, as Socrates has already shown that philosophers, sophists, and rhetoricians alike dispute these so-called "philosophical values" (e.g., 263a–b, 267a, 272d–e). Nehamas (1990) has shown the difficulty in trying to distinguish between philosophical and sophistic uses of discursive techniques.

125. On dialectic as the "synthetic" art of arts, cf. Pl. *R.* 531c–d, 532b–c, 533c–d.

126. Cf. Pl. *Ti.* 51e. Gorgias's ready acceptance of the distinction between learning and persuasion leads to his refutation by Socrates on the grounds that rhetoric, if it is only concerned with persuasion rather than learning, has nothing to teach (Pl. *Grg.* 454e, 456a, 458e ff.). Later in the *Phaedrus*, Socrates explicitly states that the art of speaking (and writing) applies to both teaching and persuasion (277c3–6).

127. Sallis (1996, 173).

128. Pl. Plt. 284e, 310d–e; *Lg.* 916e.

129. Koritansky (1987, 47); Burger (1980, 6); Werner (2010, 36–37).

130. Cf. Pl. *Prm.* 136a.

131. The principal source for Prodicus's speech is Socrates's quotation of it in Xen. *Mem.* 2.1.18–34. The story seems to derive from Hes. *Op.* 286–93.

132. Socrates anticipated the problem posed by nurture in the palinode, clearly distinguishing the "first birth" of a soul—in which nature and behavior correspond (252d1–5)—from the unknown number of subsequent "births" that the soul itself has a part in choosing (248c8–d2, 249a5–b5). Interpreted as a myth for persuasion, this suggests that ultimate causes for a particular soul's disposition toward certain speeches are obscure.

133. MacDowell (1978, 119, 251–53).

134. Moore (2015) similarly objects to the proscription of probabilistic argumentation as such. But by focusing only on the necessity that all speech must address opinions and therefore what is "plausible" (his translation of *to eikos*), Moore neglects the use to which Teisias has put *to eikos*, which diverts the audience's attention from the necessity and precision that attend truth (179–80).

135. Pl. *R.* 506b–d.

136. Nussbaum (1986, 214).

137. *Contra* Irani (2017, 150n8): "We need not take too seriously Socrates' disavowal of any expertise in speechmaking . . . this is [quoting Yunis 2011, 190] an 'ironic stance.'" Socrates's ignorance in this respect is crucial to understanding the difference between philosophy and rhetoric, since this ignorance is the well-spring for philosophy while at the same time limits the possibility of ever perfecting an art of persuasion. Socrates's "ironic stance" reflects the depth of the problem of rhetoric, and persuasion more generally, in the face of fundamental human ignorance.

138. Aristotle makes similar observations with regard to dialectic in *Topics* 1.1–2, 10–12, 14. *Contra* Klein (1965, 27), who distinguishes dialectic and *psychagōgia* in such a way as to deny *ad hominem* from the former. In what way, then, could dialectic really proceed? While a perfect dialectical analysis could collect and divide its objects by their "natural joints," this would assume an audience suitably prepared for such a dispensation. As discussed in this chapter, the noble rhetoric shows how the use of language, including dialectic, cannot be dissociated from the soul of either interlocutor. Dialectic must proceed provisionally, through fallible collections and divisions based on the opinions of the interlocutors.

139. In the *Gorgias*, Socrates objects to Polus's habit of arguing to a general audience, claiming that it is necessary for learning that individuals come to agreement (Pl. *Grg.* 475e–476a).

140. Gadamer (1989, 356–57, 359).

141. In a striking contrast, Socrates tells Euthydemus that he "knows how to converse [*dialegesthai*] far better than I" (Pl. *Euthd.* 295d–e). Surely he could not mean that the flippant play

of Euthydemus is of the same rank as the dialectician who knows the nature of the whole? His compliment is ironic, but not entirely false unless dialectic is supposed to be free of play and devoted solely to true statements. But it cannot be these things because it deals with common opinions and the opinions of its interlocutors. Nor does the intention of the dialectician provide a sufficient criterion to determine whether its practice is philosophical (Nehamas 1990, 6, 10–11). Euthydemus's mixed success—his interlocutors are left dumbfounded but unpersuaded—powerfully demonstrates the ignorance of the interlocutor as well as the limits of such play in the face of opinions formed by experience.

142. Weaver (1953, 21).

143. For example, Parmen. B1.30, B2, B8.50–2 (DK); Melissus, B7–8 (DK).

144. Cf. Pl. *Sph.* 216a–c; *Phdr.* 258e ff.

145. Analogically, Socrates said that we mistakenly ascribe bodies to gods because we have "neither seen nor sufficiently contemplated a god," which is to say we are compelled to represent the perfection we seek by way of imperfect mixtures, images, and so are prone to error (Pl. *Phdr.* 246c–d).

146. Yunis (2005a, 102).

147. For example, Pl. *R.* 341c–d.

148. In the *Statesman*, the knowledge of "for whom, when, and to what extent" one should use rhetorical techniques is attributed to the statesman rather than the rhetorician, thus subordinating rhetoric to the political art (303e–304e; see also *Lg.* 937d–938c). The attribution of this knowledge to a rhetorician in the *Phaedrus* suggests that the discussion in the *Statesman* does not distinguish between the public and private rhetoric, which calls attention to the fact that the statesman must have persuaded himself as to when to use persuasive techniques.

149. See Pl. *Grg.* 456a–457c, 460c–d, 517a ff.; cf. *Men.* 95c, *Phlb.* 58c. Socrates has misgivings about whether the good can ever be understood in its entirety (Pl. *R.* 506b–509c, 546a–547a).

150. Yunis (2005a) is for the most part correct to say that "there is nothing to prevent the rhetor from using his superior rhetorical skills, acquired by and buttressed with dialectical knowledge, for purely personal, corrupt, or destructive ends" (2005a). But one must add the crucial caveat that this misses the highest end of rhetoric, excellence of the soul, which perfects the art and one's persuasive ability. Plato's account of an art of rhetoric, founded in dialectic, which is inherently imperfect and deals in opinion, anticipates Aristotle's description of rhetoric as the "antistrophe" or counterpart to dialectic, which for him is also susceptible to abuse (Arist. *Rh.* 1356a; on the relation between rhetoric and dialectic, see *EN* 1.4.1095a31–b13, *Rh.* 1.1.1351a1–11, 1355a6–29, *Top.* 1.1–2, 11, 14).

151. Aristotle mentions the ineffectiveness of syllogism and lengthy reasoning before a group (*Rh.* 1.2.1357a8–22).

152. In his trial, Socrates singles out his principal accuser, Meletus, for dialectical examination, which only seems to confirm the prejudice among the jury that he is "a clever speaker," boorish, and, as he describes himself, "a gadfly," and does little to persuade them of his innocence (Pl. *Ap.* 17a–b, 26e–27a, 30e–31a).

153. See Pl. *Prt.* 335b–c.

# 5. WRITING THE ETERNAL

1. Plato's Critias recounts that the Egyptians considered the Greeks "always children" (*Ti.* 22b–23d). See also Hdt. 2.142.

2. Apollod. 1.6.3.

3. Hdt. 2.42. On Ammōn as "the hidden," see Plu. *Moralia*, 354c–d.

4. Hdt. 2.178–79.

5. Socrates mentions that Theuth's sacred bird was the ibis, a long-beaked water bird whose form the god assumed in hieroglyphs and paintings (274c). Theuth's sacred ibis represents his ascent from the formless change and becoming toward the substance of true being, parallel to his journey from the water and the port city of Naucratis toward "the upper region"

of Egyptian Thebes, where resides the king of the gods (274d3). Socrates arranges these Egyptian symbols in accordance with his earlier myths, particularly the soul's winged ascent from mixture and human commerce to the "superheavenly place," where it is purified by divine and true knowledge (249d).

6. The historicity of Plato's Egyptian myth and its symbols is an important problem, but one that unfortunately depends on unavailable information concerning the depth of Plato's knowledge of Egypt, whether firsthand or by hearsay and writings (Strabo claims that Plato traveled to Egypt after Socrates's execution in 399 BC [17.29]). Plato's references to Egypt in other dialogues are too general to draw any conclusions (e.g., *Lg.* 656d–657b, *Phd.* 80c–d, *Phlb.* 19b, *Ti.* 22b ff.), and are further complicated by problems of Platonic chronology. It is a reasonable assumption that he read Herodotus's account, and the relation between the two gods in the myth indicates some knowledge of the features of coffin texts from the New Kingdom (1560–1070 BC), such as spells describing Theuth's examination of the soul at the behest of Ammōn-Rē. Ammōn did not have such a significant and royal place in the Egyptian pantheon before this period, although he is attributed hiddenness in all periods (Budge 1955, 194). Theuth, by contrast, was one of the most ancient gods, at times even being assigned the role of creator god in relation to the power of the word and writing (Budge 1955, 183). Nevertheless, Plato's Egyptian myth is intended as a myth, not history, and these symbols are used primarily in relation to the other symbols of the *Phaedrus* and Socrates's arguments, through which their meaning is ultimately derived.

7. Number and calculation are used for counting troops, geometry for arraying them and surveying, astronomy for piloting ships and charting the seasons (Pl. *R.* 522c–d, 525a–b, 526c–e, 527d–e). In the *Laws*, the same three arts are the basis of the education of "the free man" (817e–818b–e).

8. Number and calculation are two aspects of the same art (see Pl. *R.* 524c–e). This is indicated in the *Phaedrus* by the conjunction *te kai*, meaning "both number and calculation," that is, both together.

9. Pl. *R.* 531c–d, 532b–c, 533b–d. Nor does Theuth mention the geometry of solids—that is, "the dimension of cubes and what participates in depth"—which Socrates says has not yet been devised because it is useless, but is nevertheless necessary to understand the nature of things, not least of all the movements of the heavenly bodies (Pl. *R.* 527b, 528b).

10. Theuth's misunderstanding of his own invention is also seen in the *Philbeus*, where Socrates shows that dialectic must be present in the invention of letters, mentioning Theuth's grasp of forms of speech in both their multiplicity and unity (Pl. *Phlb.* 18a–d).

11. On the Egyptian incorporation of play into education, see Pl. *Lg.* 819b–820d.

12. Derrida (1981, 143–44).

13. In later sources, Theuth is the author of the *Book of the Dead* (literally, "Chapters of Coming Forth into Day"), coffin texts which included an assortment of spells for use by the souls of the dead as a guide to the afterlife, and which also likely served as a moral guide for the living (Budge 1955, 343). The structure of that book, as a collection of techniques for living, comports with the technical and merely instrumental understanding of art characteristic of the rhetoricians. Plato once wrote that "[i]f it appeared possible for [these things] to be written or spoken sufficiently for the many, what nobler thing could I have done in my life than this, to write what would be of great benefit for humanity and bring the nature [of these things] into light for all?" (Pl. *Ep.* 7.341d–e).

14. Moore (2012) clarifies that the "location" of the mark—its externality or internality—is not at issue, since internalizing marks in error is wrong. Rather, the issue is whether a mark is foreign, someone else's, and not thought through in light of one's own experience and made one's own (295–96). Socrates's Egyptian myth therefore picks up on his earlier distinction between public and private rhetoric, which helped him demonstrate that a rhetorician needs to learn for himself how his, and his audience's, marks relate to the true nature of things.

15. This resembles but is not identical to Alcidamas's argument that writing is easy, common, and therefore ignoble (Alcidamas, *On the Sophists* [Alcid. *Soph.*], 3–8).

16. The duality of writing as a reminder may coincide with the two forms of writing that Herodotus says existed in Egypt, the hieratic ("sacred" or priestly) and the common (Hdt. 2.36).

For reasons that are made clear later, Plato would likely consider it impossible that writing could ever perform the higher reminding exclusively.

17. See Moore (2012, 292–93, 299). Derrida's (1981) well-known essay, "Plato's Pharmacy," makes much of the dual meaning of *pharmakon*, as conveyed by the English word "drug," but does not acknowledge that Thamos's play on this duality implies that there must be a measure by which the conditions for its use may be judged. Instead, Derrida regards each side of the *pharmakon* as merely the assertion of one difference against another (114–15). Throughout his essay, Derrida refuses to engage in conversation with Plato concerning the power of writing to remind—that is, to lead the soul toward an understanding of the nature of things beyond what is believed to be the meaning contained in words—and notably omits any discussion of the art of rhetoric, which showed the need to possess some knowledge of the nature of things in order to communicate, let alone persuade artfully (see, for example 121–24).

18. Pl. *Hp. Mi.* 368b–c; *Prt.* 315c.

19. A memorable example is the pretension of the politicians, poets, and artisans, who all believe themselves to know more than they do and have become proud (Pl. *Ap.* 21b–22e). In the *Theaetetus*, the opinion that perception is knowledge—that is, relative to each and every living thing—is said to produce a solipsistic ethos that is destructive of custom, law, and any belief in natural and true justice beyond instrumentality (171d ff.). A similar view produces the opinion that justice is merely what is agreed upon (Pl. *R.* 358e–359b). In the *Gorgias*, the eristic manner of argument that prides itself for its ability to persuade the crowd is criticized for submitting itself to the judgment of the mob (448d–e, 471e–472d).

20. Another possible verdict concerning writing, attested to in the *Laws*, is the use of strict legislation to prohibit innovation, as was done in the mimetic arts (656d–e).

21. A full consideration of why Plato wrote and Socrates did not would need to incorporate similar discussions in several other works, such as the *Laws*, *Phaedo*, *Republic*, and Plato's letters.

22. Herodotus reports a story that a priestess of Ammōn who fled Egypt established the oracle at Dodona (2.54–58). Ammōn is mentioned alongside Delphi and Dodona in Plato's *Laws* (738c).

23. Socrates borrows the proverbial phrase "oak and rock" from Homer (Hom. *Od.* 19.163). Penelope demanded to know the origins of her disguised husband, since he "was not [born] from oak nor from rock." Socrates, though, seems to use the proverb to the opposite purpose of freeing speech and thought from particular circumstances. He again uses it in this way in the *Apology*, demanding that the merits of the case not be judged by the personal circumstances of the defendant, but by its truth (34d).

24. An adverse consequence of forgetting the duality of the word is "misology," which Socrates diagnoses as the belief that there is nothing sure in argument or *logos*, such that there is no rest in anything. Rather than look to himself for the source of error, the misologist blames *logos* itself (Pl. *Phd.* 89c–d, 90b–d). A useful modern example is found in Derrida's (1981) criticisms of "logocentrism" and belief that all speaking is writing, by which he means the assertion of one *pharmakon* against another: "The *eidos*, truth, law, the *epistēmē*, dialectics, philosophy—all these are other names for that *pharmakon* that must be opposed to the *pharmakon* of the Sophists and to the bewitching fear of death." The *pharmakon* itself has no essence or *eidos* and so its assertion against another *pharmakon* ultimately finds no ground (124–26).

25. Theuth's *Book of the Dead* contained spells that were believed to reanimate the *Ba* (loosely, the soul) of a human being after death (see chapter 5, note 13).

26. De Vries (1969, 252n *ad loc*); Hackforth (1952, *ad loc.*); Yunis (2011, 230n *ad loc*).

27. Cf. Pl. *Ion* 530b–c.

28. Pl. *Ion* 533d–e, 535e–536d.

29. Klein (1965, 11).

30. Nehamas and Woodruff (1995, xxxv–xxxvii). Opposing opinions are listed in chapter 5, note 26.

31. Scholars have noted that Alcidamas anticipated Plato's criticism of writing on this very point, but the above considerations indicate that Plato went much further and in fact envisioned a "living *logos*" beyond oral and extemporaneous discourse (cf. Alcid. *Soph.* 27–28).

32. See the discussion of technique in chapter 4.

33. Plato deliberately contrasts the vision of the beings with the flowers in the gardens of Adonis with his usage of the verb "behold" (*theōrein*) in the *Phaedrus*, only four times in total, twice in reference to the former (247c1, d4) and twice in reference to the latter (276b4, d5).

34. The "gardens of Adonis" were pots and boxes used to force plants so they might quickly flourish, and would be discarded after use in festivals (de Vries 1969, 253n.276d3;, Yunis 2011, 233n.276d2–3). These festive boxed plants are likely named on the basis of the myth, reported by later mythographers, that Adonis was born out of a smyrna tree (from which myrrh flows) and then hidden in a chest and given to Persephone. Once the box was opened, Persephone delighted in the infant's beauty and refused to part with him (Apollod. 3.183–85; Hyginus, *Fabulae*, 58). Persephone's experience clearly parallels Socrates's portrayal, in his palinode, of the ecstatic experience of *erōs* (251e3–252b3).

35. Xen. *Smp.* 2.24–26; Pl. *Smp.* 176c, 214a.

36. For example, Pl. *Phd.* 84b-c, *R.* 509b, *Smp.* 175a–b, 220c–d, 221e.

37. A notable example being the conclusion of Plato's *Symposium*, when all others are drunk or utterly exhausted (223b–d).

38. Pl. *Smp.* 221d–222a; see also *Ep.* 2.314c. On the continuity between Platonic myths and Socratic irony, see Friedländer (1958, 1.137ff).

39. Pl. *Lg.* 637b ff., Xen. *Mem.* 2.24–26. It is possible that the present passage in the *Phaedrus* also serves to mock Isocrates's valetudinarian advice to Demonicus with respect to symposia—assuming that Isocrates was speaking his opinion and was not in this case adapting his words to his audience (*To Demonicus* [Isoc. 1], 32; cf. McAdon 2004, 27).

40. Benardete (1991) writes that "the peculiarity of Plato's art consists in his showing the nature of philosophy in general while showing the impossibility of deducing from its nature the nature of a philosophic argument in particular" (2).

41. This problem is taken up in the *Parmenides* (137c–d, 138e).

42. The use of myth is related to the use of semblance in *antilogic*—these imprecise images are very suggestive to souls that do not demand utter precision. They allow agreement or deception in the same way long rhetorical speeches and unexplored opinions do.

43. Burger (1980, 4).

44. Cf. Pl. *Ep.* 7.341c–d.

45. Compare how Socrates "is led" by Phaedrus's "shining head" and enthusiasm while reading Lysias's speech (234d4).

46. This is anticipated in the last sentence of Lysias's speech: "But if you miss [or: long for, *pothein*] something with respect to love, believing [*hēgoumenos*] it has been left out, ask" (234c6). Also note how Lysias, perhaps inadvertently, links *hēgoumenos* with the desire for secure and unending friendship and pleasure (232b).

47. This also lends new significance to Socrates's question: "Do you not believe that Eros is a son of Aphrodite and a god?" (242d9). In other words, is not the mere fact that you come to believe something to be true proof of some leading power that exists beyond mere words? Phaedrus could hardly think that persuasion or learning exist if it was true that *erōs* and that which is outside of speech were nothing but madness.

48. Note the antithetical construction *men* . . . *de* at 277d9 (*men*), the ignoble writing, and 277e5 (*de*), the noble writing.

49. The priests who attended the Pythia at Delphi delivered oracles to the supplicant written in hexameter verse. The Sibyl's oracles were also written in hexameter (Parke 1988, 6).

50. Inspiration by Lysias's speech is mentioned at 234d, by Socrates's first speech at 241e, 265a, and by Socrates' palinode at 257c, 263d, 265a.

51. For example, Pl. *Grg.* 449b–d, 457c–458c, 471e–472c; *Ion* 541e–542a; *Phd.* 90d–91c; *Prt.* 328d–329b, 334d–338e; *R.* 344d–e.

52. Pl. *Smp.* 176b.

53. Socrates describes how this befell a number of his young associates, particularly Aristeides, who told Socrates that "I never learnt anything from you, as you yourself know, but I advanced, whenever I was with you," but "now that entire state has flown out" (*Thg.* 128c–130e). In the *Symposium*, the experiences of Apollodorus, Aristodemus, and Alcibiades are even more radical, where Apollodorus finds nothing worthwhile when separated from

Socrates, Aristodemus is only able to imitate Socrates's physical appearance, and Alcibiades sees divine images in the older man yet flees from him in shame (172e–173b, 221d–222a).

54. *Contra* Derrida (1981, 117), who writes that: the use of *logos* is an "act of both domination and decision."
55. See also Pl. *Ep.* 7.340c.
56. Pl. *Mx.* 247a–c.
57. Pl. *Ep.* 7.340c.
58. Friedländer (1958) writes that "irony guards the Platonic secret" (1.153).
59. Mackenzie (1982, 70–72).
60. "It is in these such cases [of contradiction] that the soul, summoning reasoning [*logismos*] and the intellect, attempts to see whether each of the things reported to it is one or two" (Pl. *R.* 523c–e).
61. Klein (1965) argues that the *Phaedrus* does not in fact provide a particularly robust account of good writing; in elenchic fashion, Socrates is primarily concerned with understanding what is bad speaking and writing. Klein asks whether "the answer to the question as to what constitutes good and proper writing has been deliberately and playfully withheld?" (16). Werner's (2007b) characterization of the art of rhetoric as a "regulative ideal" should be resisted, because it is too easily construed as an imaginative ideal, a constructed fiction, that obscures the real force of Plato's "ideas" or "forms," which are not merely normative principles, but ontological principles necessary to explain the existence of the phenomena we perceive (297–98). The perfected art of rhetoric explains how it is that we persuade and are persuaded, which depends upon a natural desire for truth that is obscured in cases of imperfect rhetoric.
62. In his letters, Plato states the value of this kind of repetition for careful study (*Ep.* 2.314a, 6.323c–d). Plato also notes in the *Theaetetus* that some students of Socrates had already begun memorizing and writing down his conversations for study (142d–143a).
63. Plato thus goes beyond Alcidamas's criticism that writing is unable to adapt to the momentary needs of action and extemporaneous speech (Alcid. *Soph.* 9–10).
64. In the *Sixth Letter*, Plato suggests that the static nature of writing is useful, especially if it counteracts natural habits (*Ep.* 6.323c–d).
65. White (1993, 256), *contra* Derrida (1981, 115).
66. Consider again Zeno's dialectical refutation of the hypothesis that the many are one—that is, the hypothesis contrary to his beloved Parmenides's (Pl. *Prm.* 127b, 128a–e). The latter's poetic declaration requires argumentative support, of which a refutation of the contrary is the strongest.
67. While Plato has addressed the defects of writing through the dialogue form, it does not follow that this is the only manner of noble writing. The writer must know what it is he writes on, be able to defend his writing when called on to do so by refuting what is explicitly said, and show that the writing itself is wretched. It is fathomable that a treatise may also perform these functions.
68. Plato's depiction of Socrates's life is frequently understood as an unproblematic celebration, even though Socrates's life is itself characterized as being constituted by the problem he posed for himself (229e4–230a6). See, for example, Nicholson (2001, 86–87), Capra (2014, 139–48).
69. Plato omits the politic concern of self-preservation for careful writing that he expresses in the *Seventh Letter* (*Ep.* 7.341e).
70. For example, Pl. *Phd.* 60c–61c. See Strauss (2001, 245–46).
71. Since "reminding" is the only use of writing explicitly mentioned by Plato, this must be what al-Fārābī (1962) means by his opaque suggestion that the *Phaedrus* shows "what it is that writing achieves and the extent to which conversation fails in this respect" (2.6.28).
72. Jaeger (1944, 2.74).
73. Strauss (2001, 246–47).
74. Strauss (2001, 246).
75. Pl. *Phd.* 89b–c.
76. For example, Pl. *Ep.* 2.311b–c.
77. For example, Pl. *Ap.* 34e–35b, *R.* 336c.
78. Lebeck (1972, 267), emphasis in original. See also Santas (1982, 108).

79. D. H. *Demosthenes*, 3.

80. Al-Fārābī (1962, 2.10.36). This is ultimately the inspiration for Strauss's approach to "the problem of Socrates"—that is, the historical Socrates versus the Platonic Socrates—and is therefore a significant influence on his approach to the question of why Plato wrote and Socrates did not (Strauss, 2001 246–47).

81. For example, Pl. *Smp.* 216a.

82. Pl. *Smp.* 215a–b.

83. See Pl. *Phd.* 61b. Zuckert (2009) emphasizes that Socrates "distances himself from his own speeches," in keeping with his professed ignorance and attendant need to approach the nature of things "indirectly" through dialogue between opinions, semblances, and the appeal to desires (303–4, 323, 332).

84. Diogenes Laertius recounts the story that Plato had written the *Lysis* while Socrates was still alive, which upon reading the latter exclaimed, "By Heracles, this young man utters so many falsehoods about me!" (D. L. 3.35).

85. Pl. *Ep.* 7.324e.

86. Capra (2014, 139–42) discusses the literal monumentalizing of Socrates as a statue in Plato's Academy, which if true gives even greater significance to Phaedrus's similar promises (235d4–e1, 236a7–b4) and Socrates's thematic collection of "statues" and "monuments" under the form of "reminders" of true being (249c4–8, 251a4–7, 252d5–e1), which includes words written and spoken. Plato's warning against monumentalizing these reminders as if they were the beings themselves would extend to the figure of Socrates. So puzzling to himself and his followers, Socrates's *logos* can only be reproduced by keeping that puzzle alive through examination and refutation.

87. Friedländer (1958, 1.144).

88. Rosen (1990, 188, 202–3). This seems a more promising explanation for Socrates's (and Plato's) interest in Phaedrus than "the ordinariness of Phaedrus' character" (Irani 2017, 160). Although Phaedrus's ordinariness may serve as a useful model of "the many" and therefore the general audience of the *Phaedrus*, who are all themselves naturally capable of reasoning, it does not explain why Plato chose him specifically for this function rather than another of Socrates's many associates.

89. In the *Seventh Letter*, Plato writes, echoing Thamos: "If it appeared possible for [these things] to be written or spoken sufficiently for the many, what nobler thing could I have done in my life than this, to write what would be of great benefit for humanity and bring the nature [of these things] into light for all? But if I undertook the endeavor of expressing this to human beings it would not be good for them, except for some few who are able to discover the truth for themselves through little instruction, and the others would be filled with an incorrect highmindedness that is in no way harmonious, and still others [would be filled] with a lofty and empty expectation, as if they had learned great things" (341d–342a).

90. Ferrari (1987, 4).

91. Although Isocrates wrote speeches in forensic, deliberative, and epideictic styles, he never delivered them in person, and instead circulated the speeches as pamphlets (in his own words, he "kept quiet" all his life [Isoc. *Letters* 6.2]). He claimed, at the end of his life, that he was driven to a primarily literary career on account of a weak voice and fear of public speaking (Isoc. *Panathenaicus* [Isoc. 12] 9–10; cf. Alcid. *Soph.* 15). Still, his rhetoric was entirely literary, given that he founded and taught in his own school of rhetoric (D. H. *Isocrates* 1; [Ps.–Plu.] *Lives of Ten Orators*, 4).

92. Plato may allude to Isocrates in the *Euthydemus*, as someone who "lies on the border between philosopher and politician" and "believes himself to be amongst the wisest of all human beings," having an interest in denigrating philosophers although unable to win in private arguments (304d–306c).

93. By all accounts, Plato would have written and published the *Phaedrus* well into Isocrates's career, since Plato wrote from 400 at the earliest to his death in 347, and the older Isocrates from 390–c. 342 (the plausible date of the *Panathenaicus*). Plato therefore would have been familiar with those of Isocrates's works that are most relevant here, including *Against the Sophists*, *Areopagiticus*, *Encomium of Helen*, *Panegyricus*, and possibly the late *Antidosis*.

94. Isoc. *Against the Sophists* (Isoc. 13), 1, 3, 7.
95. Clay (1979, 348).
96. Isoc. *Panegyricus* (Isoc. 4), 3–4. Isocrates reaffirms this at the end of his life (Isoc. 12.11).
97. Isoc. 12.26–8, *Antidosis* (Isoc. 15), 261–66.
98. Irani (2017, 15).
99. Irani (2017, 14). Specific examples include Isocrates's aristocratic appeal to the excellence of character for the sake of political unity and his conservative praise of an older age in which the greatest offices were allotted according to virtue (*Areopagiticus* [Isoc. 7], 23, 37), as well as his concern for the welfare of Athens, which inspires his pan-Hellenism (Isoc. 4, esp. 1–20, 120–32).
100. Scholars point to one passage in particular as evidence of Isocrates's contempt for Plato's school, although it is oblique: "There are some who think themselves great, once having made a strange and absurd hypothesis, who are able to speak on these things tolerably. . . [some] maintaining that courage and wisdom and justice are the same, that we have none of them by nature, but that there is one [kind of] knowledge concerning them all" (Isoc. 10.1). Isocrates never, however, mentions Plato by name, even when ridiculing the speculations of the sophists in the *Antidosis* (Isoc. 15.266–69). His argument that philosophy is for the sake of benefiting human beings in speech and action, using but not dwelling in speculative exercises, is not discordant with the *Phaedrus*'s emphasis on the return to the earthly things and the city (*pace* McAdon 2004, 30–35).
101. Brown and Coulter (1971, 408). Brown and Coulter's argument, that Plato did not consider Isocrates to be philosophical because he indulged in "amphiboly" and did not use "true definitions," is, however, untenable (407–14). The whole discussion of rhetoric in the *Phaedrus*, oral and written, shows that a definition is only true so far as it leads the audience to what is true, rather than being a plain statement of the facts or sufficient in itself for knowledge. They overlook Plato's own use of amphiboly for philosophic ends, and so misconstrue Plato's rhetoric as depending on the explicit presentation of "true theory," free of deception, which is curiously unrhetorical and indeed un-Platonic.
102. Isoc. 10.2, 7–8, 12–17, 21; 13.7–8, 17; 15.271.
103. Isoc. 10.7–8. Also consider the *Panathenaicus*, published after Plato's death, in which Isocrates discusses using a written speech not as a frank disclosure of his opinion, but as a test for his friends who were accustomed to agreeing with him, in order to see whether they noticed its true intent and use of double meanings. That is, he produced a writing to provoke refutation and hide the truth in order to speak to a variety of audiences (Isoc. 12.234–65).
104. Isoc. 10.7–8, 21. But cf. Isoc. 15.271: "It is in the nature of human beings to take hold of knowledge [*epistēmē*], which by holding we would see whatever must be done or said."
105. Brown and Coulter (1971) rightly compare Isocrates to the ethos of Socrates's first speech on the basis of Isocrates's defense of *doxa* over *epistēmē* (409–10). See also Irani (2017, 17), who argues that the love of honor is at odds with philosophy and may reduce philosophy to "a game of domination."
106. Isocrates explicitly seeks the immortality of heroes and legislators: "not the immortality enjoyed by the gods, but that which implants in future generations a memorial of those who distinguished themselves through some noble deeds" (Isoc. 12.260).
107. Perhaps not so surprisingly as Clay (1979) claims, although he points out how the *Phaedrus* is rich with allusion to Pan from the very outset.
108. Pl. *Tht.* 143a–144b, *Smp.* 221d–e, *Ep.* 2.314c; Xen. *Smp.* 4.19, 5.4–8.

# Bibliography

Adams, John C. 1996. "The Rhetorical Significance of the Conversion of the Lover's Soul in Plato's 'Phaedrus.'" *Rhetoric Society Quarterly* 26.3: 7–16.
Al-Fārābī. 1962. *Alfarabi's Philosophy of Plato and Aristotle*. Translated by Muhsin Madhi. Ithaca, NY: Cornell University Press.
Barney, Rachel. 2006. "The Sophistic Movement." In *A Companion to Ancient Philosophy*, edited by M. L. Gill and P. Pellegrin, 77–97. Oxford: Blackwell.
Beercroft, Alexander J. 2006. "'This is not a true story': Stesichorus's Palinode and the Revenge of the Epichoric." *Transactions of the American Philological Association* 136.1: 47–70.
Benardete, Seth. 1991. *The Rhetoric of Morality and Philosophy*. Chicago: University of Chicago Press.
Bentley, Russell. 2005. "On Plato's *Phaedrus*: Politics beyond the City Walls." *Polis* 22.2: 230–48.
Bett, Richard. 2000. "Immortality and the Nature of the Soul in the *Phaedrus*." In *Plato*, edited by Gail Fine, 907–31. Oxford: Oxford University Press.
Brisson, Luc. 1998. *Plato the Myth Maker*. Translated by Gerrard Naddaf. Chicago: University of Chicago Press.
Brown, Malcolm, and Coulter, James. 1971. "The Middle Speech of Plato's *Phaedrus*." *Journal of the History of Philosophy* 9.4: 405–23.
Buccioni, Eva. 2007. "Keeping It Secret: Reconsidering Lysias' Speech in Plato's 'Phaedrus.'" *Phoenix* 61.1: 15–38.
Budge, E. A. Wallis. 1955. *The Book of the Dead*. New York: Bell Publishing Company.
Burger, Ronna. 1980. *Plato's Phaedrus: A Defense of a Philosophic Art of Writing*. Tuscaloosa: University of Alabama Press.
Burnet, John. 1901. *Platonis Opera*, 2nd ed. Oxford: Oxford University Press.
Burnyeat, Myles F. 2012. "The Passion of Reason in Plato's *Phaedrus*." In *Explorations in Ancient and Modern Philosophy*. Vol. 2, 238–58. Oxford: Oxford University Press.
Campbell, David A., ed. and trans. 1991. *Greek Lyric, Volume III: Stesichorus, Ibycus, Simonides, and Others*. Cambridge, MA: Harvard University Press.
———. 1988. *Greek Lyric, Volume II: Anacreon, Anacreontea, Choral Lyric from Olympus to Alcman*. Cambridge, MA: Harvard University Press.
———. 1982. *Greek Lyric, Volume I: Sappho and Alcaeus*. Cambridge, MA: Harvard University Press.
Capra, Andrea. 2014. *Plato's Four Muses: The* Phaedrus *and the Poetics of Philosophy*. Cambridge, MA: Harvard University Press.

Clay, Diskin. 2007. "Plato Philomythos." In *The Cambridge Companion to Greek Mythology*, edited by Roger D. Woodard, 210–36. Cambridge: Cambridge University Press.

———. 1979. "Socrates' Prayer to Pan." In *Arktouros: Hellenic Studies Presented to Bernard M. W. Knox on the Occasion of his 65th Birthday*, edited by Glen W. Bowersock, Walter Burkert, and Michael C. J. Putnam, 345–53. Berlin: Walter de Gruyter & Co.

Collard, Christopher, and Cropp, Martin, eds. and trans. 2009. *Euripides VIII, Fragments*. Cambridge, MA: Harvard University Press.

Cook, Albert. 1985. "Dialectic, Irony, and Myth in Plato's *Phaedrus*." *The American Journal of Philology* 106.4: 427–41.

Cooper, John M. 2009. *Knowledge, Nature, and the Good: Essays on Ancient Philosophy*. Princeton, NJ: Princeton University Press.

Curran, Jane V. 1986. "The Rhetorical Technique of Plato's 'Phaedrus.'" *Philosophy & Rhetoric* 19.1: 66–72.

Davies, John K. 1971. *Athenian Propertied Families 600–300 BC*. Oxford: Oxford University Press.

De Vries, G. J. 1988. "Self-Knowledge in Plato's Phaedrus by Ch. J. Griswold." *Mnemoysne* 41.1–2: 161–64.

———. 1969. *A Commentary on the Phaedrus of Plato*. Amsterdam: Adolf M. Hakkert.

Derrida, Jacques. 1981. "Plato's Pharmacy." In *Dissemination*, translated by Barbara Johnson, 61–172. Chicago: University of Chicago Press.

Diels, Hermann. 1952. *Die Fragmente der Vorsokratiker*, 6th ed. Revised by Walther Kranz. Berlin: Weidmann.

Dorter, Kenneth. 1971. "Imagery and Philosophy in Plato's *Phaedrus*." *Journal of the History of Philosophy* 9.3: 279–88.

Dover, Kenneth James. 2016. *Greek Homosexuality*, 3rd ed. Cambridge, MA: Harvard University Press.

———. 1968. *Lysias and the Corpus Lysiacum*. Berkeley: University of California Press.

Farrell, Anne Mary. 1999. *Plato's Use of Eleusinian Mystery Motifs*. Unpublished PhD dissertation. Austin: The University of Texas at Austin.

Ferrari, Giovanni. 1988. "*Self-Knowledge in Plato's Phaedrus* by Charles L. Griswold, Jr." *The Philosophical Review* 97.3: 408–11.

———. 1987. *Listening to the Cicadas: A Study of Plato's Phaedrus*. Cambridge: Cambridge University Press.

Ficino, Marsilio. 1985. *Commentary on Plato's Symposium on Love*. Edited and translated by Sears Jayne. Dallas, TX: Spring Publications, Inc.

———. 1981. *Marsilio Ficino and the Phaedran Charioteer*. Edited and translated by Michael J. B. Allen. Berkeley and Los Angeles: University of California Press.

Friedländer, Paul. 1958. *Plato*. 3 vols. Translated by Hans Meyerhoff. New York: Pantheon Books Inc.

Furley, William D. 1996. *Andokides and the Herms, A Study of Crisis in Fifth-Century Athenian Religion*. Bulletin of the Institute of Classical Studies Supplement 65. London: Institute of Classical studies, University of London.

Gadamer, Hans-Georg. 1991. *Plato's Dialectical Ethics: Phenomenological Interpretations Regarding the Philebus*. Translated by Robert M. Wallace. New Haven, CT: Yale University Press.

———. 1989. *Truth and Method*, 2nd ed. Translated by Donald G. Marshall and Joel Weinsheimer. London: Continuum Publishing Group.

Giannopoulou, Zina. 2010. "Enacting the Other, Being Oneself: The Drama of Rhetoric and Philosophy in Plato's *Phaedrus*." *Classical Philology* 105.2: 146–61.

Griswold, Charles L. 2002. "Comments on Khan." In *New Perspectives on Plato, Modern and Ancient*, edited by Julia Annas and Christopher Rowe, 93–127. Cambridge, MA: Harvard University Press.

———. 1986. *Self-knowledge in Plato's Phaedrus*, 2nd ed. Pittsburgh: Pennsylvania State University Press.

Guthrie, William K. C. 1975. *A History of Greek Philosophy, Volume IV: Plato—The Man and His Dialogues: Earlier Period*. Cambridge: Cambridge University Press.

Hackforth, Reginald. 1952. *Plato's Phaedrus: Translated with Introduction and Commentary.* Translated by Reginald Hackforth. Cambridge: Cambridge University Press.
Hayase, Atsushi. 2016. "Dialectic in the *Phaedrus.*" *Phronesis* 61: 111–41.
Heath, Malcolm. 1989. "The Unity of Plato's *Phaedrus.*" *Oxford Studies in Ancient Philosophy* 7: 151–73.
Heidegger, Martin. 1997. *Plato's Sophist.* Translated by Richard Rojcewicz and André Schuwer. Bloomington and Indianapolis: Indiana University Press.
———. 1991. "Plato's *Phaedrus*: Beauty and Truth in Felicitous Discordance." In *Nietzsche, Volumes I–II,* 188–99. Translated by D. F. Krell. New York: HarperCollins.
Hermeias. 1971. *Hermiae Alexandrini in Platonis Phaedrum Scholia,* edited by P. Couvreur. New York: G. Olms.
Hobbes, Thomas. 1994. *Leviathan.* Edited by Edwin Curley. Indianapolis, IN: Hackett Publishing Company, Inc.
Howland, Jacob. 1991. "The Problem of Platonic Chronology." *Phoenix* 45.3: 189–214.
Hyland, Drew A. 2008. *Plato and the Question of Beauty.* Bloomington: Indiana University Press.
Irani, Tushar. 2017. *Plato on the Value of Philosophy: The Art of Argument in the* Gorgias *and* Phaedrus. Cambridge: Cambridge University Press.
Jaeger, Werner. 1944. *Paideia: The Ideals of Greek Culture.* 3 vols. Translated by Gilbert Highet. Oxford: Oxford University Press.
Jowett, Benjamin. 1892. *Phaedrus.* Oxford: Oxford University Press.
Kastely, James L. 2002. "Respecting the Rupture: Not Solving the Problem of Unity in Plato's 'Phaedrus.'" *Philosophy & Rhetoric* 35.2: 138–52.
Kelley Jr., William G. 1973. "Rhetoric as Seduction." *Philosophy & Rhetoric* 6.2: 69–80.
Kennedy, George A. 1980. *Classical Rhetoric and Its Christian and Secular Tradition from Ancient to Modern Times.* Chapel Hill: The University of North Carolina Press.
———. 1963. *The Art of Persuasion in Greece.* Princeton, NJ: Princeton University Press.
Kerényi, Karl. 1967. *Eleusis: Archetypal Image of Mother and Daughter.* Translated by Ralph Manheim. New York: Bollingen Foundation.
Kerferd, G. B. 1981. *The Sophistic Movement.* Cambridge: Cambridge University Press.
Klein, Jacob. 1965. *A Commentary on Plato's Meno.* Chicago: The University of Chicago Press.
Koritansky, John C. 1987. "Socratic Rhetoric and Socratic Wisdom in Plato's *Phaedrus.*" *Interpretation: A Journal of Political Philosophy* 15.1: 29–53.
Lebeck, Anne. 1972. "The Central Myth of Plato's *Phaedrus.*" *Greek, Roman and Byzantine Studies* 13.3: 267–90.
Lewis, David M., ed. 1981. *Inscriptiones Graecae.* 3rd ed. Berlin: de Gruyter.
Liddell, H. G., and Scott, R. 1996. *A Greek-English Lexicon.* Supplement by H. S. Jones. Oxford: Oxford University Press.
Linck, Matthew S. 2003. "Unmastering Speech: Irony in Plato's *Phaedrus.*" *Philosophy & Rhetoric* 36: 264–76.
Lincoln, Bruce. 1997. "Competing Discourses: Rethinking the Prehistory of *Mythos* and *Logos.*" *Arethusa* 30: 341–67.
Linforth, Ivan M. 1946a. "Telestic Madness in Plato, Phaedrus 244de." *University of California Publications in Classical Philology* 13.6: 163–72.
———. 1946b. *The Corybantic Rites in Plato.* Berkley: University of California Press.
Lloyd-Jones, Hugh. 1996. *Sophocles: Fragments.* Cambridge, MA: Harvard University Press.
MacDowell, Douglas M. 1978. *The Law in Classical Athens.* London: Thames and Hudson Ltd.
———, ed. and trans. 1962. *Andocides IV: On the Mysteries.* Oxford: Clarendon Press.
Mackenzie, Mary Margaret. 1982. "Paradox in Plato's 'Phaedrus.'" *Proceedings of the Cambridge Philological Society* 28: 64–76.
Mansfeld, Jaap. 1980. "Plato and the Method of Hippocrates." *Greek, Roman, and Byzantine Studies* 21.4: 341–62.
McAdon, Brad. 2004. "Plato's Denunciation of Rhetoric in the *Phaedrus.*" *Rhetoric Review* 23.1: 21–39.

McCumber, John. 1982. "Discourse and Psyche in Plato's *Phaedrus*." *Apeiron* 16: 27–39.
Moore, Christopher. 2015. *Socrates and Self-Knowledge*. Cambridge: Cambridge University Press.
———. 2014. "Arguing for the Immortality of the Soul in the Palinode of the *Phaedrus*." *Philosophy and Rhetoric* 47.2: 179–208.
———. 2013. "Deception and Knowledge in the *Phaedrus*." *Ancient Philosophy* 33: 97–110.
———. 2012. "The Myth of Theuth in Plato's *Phaedrus*." In *Plato and Myth: Studies on the Use and Status of Platonic Myths*, edited by Catherine Collobert, Pierre Destrée, and Francisco J. Gonzalez, 279–304. Leiden: Brill.
Morgan, Kathryn A. 2000. *Myth and Philosophy from the Presocratics to Plato*. Cambridge: Cambridge University Press.
———. 1994. "Socrates and Gorgias at Delphi and Olympia: *PHAEDRUS* 235d6-236b4." *The Classical Quarterly* 44.2: 375–86.
Mueller, Gustav. 1957. "Unity of the *Phaedrus*." *Classical Bulletin* 33: 50–53.
Murray, James S. 1994. "Interpreting Plato on Sophistic Claims and the Provenance of the 'Socratic Method.'" *Phoenix* 48.2: 115–34.
———. 1988. "Disputation, Deception, and Rhetoric." *Philosophy & Rhetoric* 21.4: 279–89.
Mylonas, George E. 1961. *Eleusis and the Eleusinian Mysteries*. Princeton, NJ: Princeton University Press.
Nails, Debra. 2002. *The People of Plato: A Prosopography of Plato and Other Socratics*. Indianapolis, IN: Hackett Publishing Company.
Nehamas, Alexander. 1999. "The *Phaedrus*." In *Virtues on Authenticity: Essays on Plato and Socrates*. Princeton, NJ: Princeton University Press. 329–58.
———. 1990. "Eristic, Antilogic, Sophistic, Dialectic: Plato's Demarcation of Philosophy from Sophistry." *History of Philosophy Quarterly* 7.1: 3–16.
Nehamas, Alexander, and Woodruff, Paul. 1995. *Phaedrus: Translated, with Introduction and Notes*. Indianapolis, IN: Hackett Publishing Company.
Newell, Waller R. 2000. *Ruling Passion: The Erotics of Statecraft in Platonic Political Philosophy*. Lanham, MD: Rowman & Littlefield.
Nichols, James H. Jr. 1998. *Phaedrus; Translated with Introduction, Notes, and an Interpretive Essay*. Ithaca, NY: Cornell University Press.
Nicholson, Graeme. 1999. *Plato's Phaedrus: The Philosophy of Love*. West Lafayette, IN: Purdue University Press.
Nussbaum, Martha C. 1986. *The Fragility of Goodness: Luck and Ethics in Greek Tragedy and Philosophy*. Cambridge: Cambridge University Press.
Ober, Josiah. 1989. *Mass and Elite in Democratic Athens*. Princeton, NJ: Princeton University Press.
O'Sullivan, Neil. 1992. *Alcidamas, Aristophanes and the Beginnings of Greek Stylistic Theory*. Stuttgart: Franz Steiner.
Parke, H. W. 1988. *Sibyls and Sibylline Prophecy in Classical Antiquity*. Edited by B. C. McGing. London: Routledge.
———. 1967. *The Oracles of Zeus: Dodona, Olympia, Ammon*. Oxford: Blackwell.
———. 1956. *The Delphic Oracle*. 2 vols. Oxford: Blackwell.
Pickard-Cambridge, A. W. 1927. *Dithyramb, Tragedy and Comedy*. Oxford: Oxford University Press.
Pieper, Josef. 1964. *Enthusiasm and Divine Madness; On the Platonic Dialogue Phaedrus*. Translated by Richard Winston and Clara Winston. New York: Harcourt.
Planinc, Zdravko. 2001. "Homeric Imagery in Plato's *Phaedrus*." In *Politics, Philosophy, Writing*, edited by Zdravko Planinc, 122–59. Columbia: University of Missouri Press.
Podlecki, Anthony J. 1998. *Perikles and His Circle*. London: Routledge.
Ramus, Petrus. 2010. *Arguments in Rhetoric against Quintilian: Translation and Text of Peter Ramus's Rhetoricae Distinctiones in Quntilianum*, edited by James Murphy, and translated by Carole Newlands. Carbondale: Southern Illinois University Press.
Rhodes, James M. 2003. *Eros, Wisdom, and Silence: Plato's Erotic Dialogues*. Columbia: University of Missouri Press.

Rinella, Michael A. 2010. *Pharmakon: Plato, Drug Culture, and Identity in Ancient Athens*. Lanham, MD: Lexington Books.
Robinson, Richard. 1953. *Plato's Earlier Dialectic*. Oxford: Oxford University Press.
Rosen, Stanley. 1990. "The Golden Apple." *Arion* 1.1: 187–207.
———. 1988. "Socrates as Concealed Lover." In *The Quarrel between Philosophy and Poetry*. New York. 91–101.
———. 1969. "The Non-lover in Plato's *Phaedrus*." *Man and World* 2.3: 423–37.
Rowe, Christopher J. 1989. "The Unity of the *Phaedrus*: A Reply to Heath." *Oxford Studies in Ancient Philosophy* 7: 175–88.
———. 1986. *Plato: Phaedrus, with Translation and Commentary*. Wiltshire: Aris and Phillips Ltd.
Rutherford, R. B. 1995. *The Art of Plato: Ten Essays in Platonic Interpretation*. Cambridge, MA: Harvard University Press.
———. 1988. "Plato and Lit. Crit." *Phronesis* 33.2: 216–24.
Sallis, John. 1996. *Being and Logos: Reading the Platonic Dialogues*, 3rd ed. Bloomington: Indiana University Press.
Santas, Gerasimos. 1982. "Passionate Love in the *Phaedrus*." *Ancient Philosophy* 2.2: 105–14.
Schleiermacher, Friedrich Daniel Ernst. 1936. *Schleiermacher's Introductions to the Dialogues*, edited and translated by William Dobson. Cambridge: Cambridge University Press.
Schofield, Malcolm. 1980. *An Essay on Anaxagoras*. Cambridge: Cambridge University Press.
Scott, Dominic. 2011. "Philosophy and Madness in the *Phaedrus*." *Oxford Studies in Ancient Philosophy* 41: 169–200.
Seeskin, Kenneth. 1987. *Dialogue and Discovery: A Study in Socratic Method*. New York: SUNY Press.
Sheffield, Frisbee C. C. 2011. "Beyond Eros: Friendship in the *Phaedrus*." *Proceedings of the Aristotelian Society* 111: 251–73.
Shorey, Paul. 1933. "On the Erotikos of Lysias in Plato's Phaedrus." *Classical Philology* 28.2: 131–32.
Sinaiko, Herman L. 1965. *Love, Knowledge, and Discourse in Plato*. Chicago: University of Chicago Press.
Skemp, J. B. 1967. *The Theory of Motion in Plato's Later Dialogues*. Amsterdam: Adolf M. Hakkert.
Slaveva-Griffin, Svetla. 2003. "Of Gods, Philosophers, and Charioteers: Content and Form in Parmenides' Proem and Plato's *Phaedrus*." *Transactions of the American Philological Association* 133: 227–53.
Sommerstein, Alan H., ed. and trans. 2009. *Aeschylus III, Fragments*. Cambridge, MA: Harvard University Press.
Strauss, Leo. 2001. *On Plato's* Symposium. Chicago: University of Chicago Press.
Taylor, Charles. 2016. *The Language Animal: The Full Shape of the Human Linguistic Capacity*. Cambridge, MA: Harvard University Press.
Thompson, W. H. 1973. *The Phaedrus of Plato, with English Notes and Dissertations*. New York: Arno Press Inc.
Vlastos, Gregory. 1991. *Socrates, Ironist and Moral Philosopher*. Ithaca, NY: Cornell University Press.
———. 1981. "The Individual as an Object of Love in Plato." In *Platonic Studies*, 3–34. Princeton, NJ: Princeton University Press.
Voegelin, Eric. 2001. *Order and History*. 5 vols. *The Collected Works of Eric Voegelin*. Vols. 14–18. Edited by Ellis Sandoz. Columbia: University of Missouri Press.
Weaver, Richard. 1953. "The *Phaedrus* and the Nature of Rhetoric." In *The Ethics of Rhetoric*, 3–26. South Bend, IN: Regnery/Gateway, Inc.
Wedin, Michael V. 1987. "Collection and Division in the 'Phaedrus' and 'Statesman.'" *Revue de Philosophie Ancienne* 5.2: 207–33.
Werner, Daniel S. 2012. *Myth and Philosophy in Plato's Phaedrus*. Cambridge: Cambridge University Press.
———. 2010. "Rhetoric and Philosophy in Plato's 'Phaedrus.'" *Greece & Rome* 57.1: 21–46.

———. 2007a. "Plato's *Phaedrus* and the Problem of Unity." *Oxford Studies in Ancient Philosophy* 32: 91–137.
———. 2007b. "Plato's Epistemology in the 'Phaedrus.'" *Skepsis* 18: 279–303.
White, David A. 1993. *Rhetoric and Reality in Plato's Phaedrus*. New York: State University of New York Press.
Wilamowitz-Moellendorff, Ulrich von. 1917. *Platon*. 2 vols. Berlin: Weidmannsche Buchhandlung.
Woodford, Susan. 1994. "Palamedes Seeks Revenge." *The Journal of Hellenic Studies* 114: 164–69.
Yunis, Harvey. 2011. *Plato: Phaedrus*. Cambridge: Cambridge University Press.
———. 2009. "Dialectic and the Purpose of Rhetoric in Plato's *Phaedrus*." *Proceedings of the Boston Area Colloquium in Ancient Philosophy* 24: 229–59.
———. 2005a. "Eros in Plato's *Phaedrus* and the Shape of Greek Rhetoric." *Arion* 13.1: 101–25.
———. 2005b. *Taming Democracy: Models of Political Rhetoric in Classical Athens*. Ithaca, NY: Cornell University Press.
Zaslavsky, Robert. 1981. "A Hitherto Unremarked Pun in the *Phaedrus*." *Apeiron* 15.2: 115–16.
Zuckert, Catherine. 2009. *Plato's Philosophers: The Coherence of the Dialogues*. Chicago: The University of Chicago Press.

# Index

Acumenus, 3, 7, 10, 14, 124–125
action; deed, xii, xvi–xvii, xviii–xix, 1–2, 10, 23, 32–33, 39, 40, 42, 51–52, 54, 56, 60, 71, 89–91, 101–103, 132, 137–138, 143, 146–147, 180, 191, 205n47, 209n63, 229n106. *See also* dramatic action
Adams, John C. 198n39
Adonis, 166, 174, 226n33–226n34
Adrasteia, 63, 115, 169
Aeschylus, 198n1, 200n21, 208n30, 216n21, 216n29, 216n33, 217n50
Agra, 4, 11, 15, 16
Aischines, 203n10
Alcibiades, 4, 183–184, 217n55, 226n53
Alcidamas, 218n62, 224n15, 225n31, 227n63, 228n91
Al-Fārābī, 183–184, 227n71, 228n80
Ammōn. *See* Thamos
Anacreon, 30–31, 204n34
Anaxagoras, 129, 202n51, 212n102, 220n97–220n101, 220n103
Andocides, 4, 199n5, 199n9, 199n12, 199n13
*antilogic*, 107–114, 115–119, 121–124, 132, 144, 149, 152, 158, 176, 178, 198n45, 216n35, 216n38, 217n49, 217n59, 226n42. *See also* dialectic; persuasion
Aphrodite, 46, 117, 226n47
Apollo, 6, 79, 117

Apollodorus, 199n10, 201n39, 201n41, 202n49, 202n56, 202n58, 204n31, 209n63, 223n1, 226n34, 226n53
*aporia See* perplexity
appearance, 9, 11–12, 16–17, 22, 25, 30, 31–32, 37, 43, 65, 70–73, 75, 80, 84, 102, 107, 109, 120, 142, 159, 161, 163, 172, 177–178, 181–182, 189, 191–193, 213n127
*archē*; principle, 52–58, 67, 74, 80, 113–114, 118, 209n49–209n50, 209n53; ruler (*archōn; archikos*), 58–59, 64. *See also* soul
Areopagus, 12, 97, 213n115
Ares, 12, 77, 84, 134, 212n114–213n116
Aristophanes, 5, 199n14, 200n17, 200n19, 202n50, 215n2, 220n96
Aristotle, 197n27, 201n41, 203n1, 204n30, 204n36, 205n39, 206n1, 206n57–206n58, 208n36, 210n67, 214n131–214n132, 214n137, 216n30, 217n39, 222n138, 223n150–223n151
art (*technē*), vii–viii, 18, 49, 51, 52, 76, 89–92, 95, 98, 103–110, 112, 115–118, 120–141, 144, 145–152, 155–158, 160, 162–163, 165–166, 168–169, 170–171, 174, 179, 183–184, 188, 192–193, 195n6, 201n35, 205n44, 207n26, 208n34, 212n102, 215n5, 216n28, 219n77, 219n89–219n90, 220n95, 220n107, 222n125, 222n137,

238  *Index*

223n148–223n150, 225n17, 226n40, 227n61–227n62. *See also* dialectic; medicine; poetry; prophecy; rhetoric; technique
Asclepius, 131, 200n31
Athena, 121, 202n58
Athens. *passim*: customs of, 11, 19, 71; institutions of, 71, 97, 144, 203n2, 205n38–205n39, 213n115. *See also* Eleusis; opinion, common

Bacchus. *See* Dionysus
Bacchic; Bacchants, 29–30, 51, 64, 79, 204n31, 205n51
background, xii, 4, 10, 101–103, 108, 114, 121, 153, 160, 180, 188–189, 193, 197n31, 217n42, 217n59
Barney, Rachel, 199n3
beauty; beautiful; noble (*kalos*), 2–3, 18, 35–36, 37, 47, 49, 54, 58–59, 64–65, 66, 68–77, 80–81, 84–86, 89–92, 95, 98–102, 99, 103, 107–108, 111, 117–118, 125, 128, 137, 138, 144, 146–147, 149–151, 152–153, 155, 157–158, 166–168, 171, 173–177, 178, 183–184, 185–190, 191–193, 206n58, 208n33, 210n74, 211n81, 212n94, 219n81, 224n13, 227n67, 228n89; itself; true, 69, 74, 76–77, 80–81, 83–87, 102, 108, 113, 117, 120, 151, 158, 178, 189–190, 192, 212n99–212n100, 215n1–215n2
becoming. *See* generation
Beercroft, Alexander J., 202n46, 207n12–207n13, 216n26
being (*ousia*; *to on; ta onta*), 34–35, 40, 41, 52–53, 55–57, 62, 65, 101–102, 108, 111, 120, 121, 132–136, 145, 148, 149, 151, 176, 206n58, 209n50, 210n70, 212n107, 216n37, 217n49, 217n59; itself; true, 60–61, 62–77, 79–81, 83, 85–88, 90, 97, 100–102, 106, 107, 108–109, 111, 113–114, 116, 120–122, 124, 132–133, 136, 139–140, 143, 145, 148, 155–156, 159, 162–165, 169–172, 175, 177–180, 188–190, 193, 207n22, 210n65, 210n68–210n69, 210n73, 211n81, 211n85, 211n87, 212n107, 212n109, 213n124, 214n131, 214n136, 215n14, 218n69, 218n75, 219n90, 223n5, 226n33, 228n86. *See also* becoming
Benardete, Seth, 74, 196n11, 198n48, 203n2, 203n7, 209n49, 209n58, 210n66, 212n103, 212n106, 212n110, 212n112, 213n121, 214n129, 221n121, 226n40
Bentley, Russell, 214n135, 214n137
Bett, Richard, 208n39, 208n45
body, 3, 5, 7, 14, 23, 35–36, 37, 39, 41, 46, 48–49, 51, 53–60, 63–65, 67–69, 71, 73–76, 79–80, 82, 87–88, 91, 95, 97, 98–101, 114, 124–126, 130–134, 139, 143, 153, 157, 163, 167, 169, 189, 208n37, 208n41, 210n72, 212n102, 214n131–214n132, 215n6, 218n61, 219n86, 220n103, 223n145
Boreas, 11, 14, 15, 46, 47, 199n14, 209n63
Brisson, Luc, 202n47–202n48
Brown, Malcolm, 206n61, 229n101, 229n105
Buccioni, Eva, 203n11
Budge, E. A., 224n6, 224n13
Burger, Ronna, 196n10, 196n11, 198n37, 198n48, 203n6–203n7, 204n20, 208n39, 209n49, 214n129, 215n15, 218n60, 221n122, 222n129, 226n43
Burnet, John, 209n52, 220n101
Burnyeat, Myles F., 43, 206n2, 208n35, 209n64, 211n78, 212n94, 212n106, 213n119, 218n72

Capra, Andrea, 197n35, 198n50, 212n99–212n100, 213n122, 215n14, 227n68, 228n86
Cephalus, 5
chance; luck, 8, 23, 27–28, 35–36, 63, 91, 147, 157. *See also* probability
Charmides, 183–184
cicada, 16, 98–102, 141, 148, 183, 185, 208n33, 215n17
Cicero, 217n53
Clay, Diskin, 202n47–202n48, 202n53, 206n7, 218n65, 229n95, 229n107
de Condillac, Étienne Bonnot, 197n21
Cook, Albert, 211n93
Cooper, John M., 196n15

Coulter, James, 206n61, 229n101, 229n105
courage; manliness, 60, 116, 143, 229n100; cowardice, 84, 143
craft. *See* art
Curran, Jane V., 219n76
custom. *See nomos*

*daimon*; *daimonion*; demon, 29–30, 30–31, 45, 51, 83, 156, 206n7, 215n15
Davies, John K., 199n4, 200n23
death, 14–15, 19, 60, 77, 87, 100–101, 114–115, 119, 125, 132–133, 162–163, 181–183, 200n22, 215n15, 218n61, 228n93, 229n103. *See also* immortal; mortal
definition, 26, 33–37, 39–42, 48, 72, 85, 92, 106, 110–114, 118–123, 126–127, 132–133, 140, 148, 165, 169–171, 187–188, 217n56, 219n81, 219n90, 229n101
Delphi, 6, 31, 49–50, 78–79, 202n61, 204n36–204n37, 207n27, 211n88, 225n22, 226n49
Delphic inscription, 6, 13, 79, 173–174, 204n37
Demeter, 3–4, 75, 199n9, 199n14, 209n63
democracy; democratic, 27–28, 204n14, 204n23, 214n139
demonic. *See daimon*
*dēmos* (people), 8, 24, 25, 26, 27–28, 31–32, 64, 96, 151–152, 182, 184, 204n15
Demosthenes, 200n19, 201n41, 204n25, 216n30
Derrida, Jacques, 224n12, 225n17, 225n24, 227n54, 227n65
desire. *passim*: *epithumia* and *himeros* , 48–49, 207n22; *See also erōs*
dialectic, xv–xvi, 47, 96, 106–107, 118–124, 126–128, 130–136, 139–142, 145–151, 156–158, 161, 163–164, 168–170, 173–176, 179, 183, 185–186, 192–194, 207n19, 219n76–219n77, 219n79, 219n89, 222n124–222n125, 222n138, 222n141, 223n150, 223n152, 224n10, 227n66; and *antilogic* , 118–119, 132, 149, 158, 198n45, 217n49; as method, xv, 118, 120,
127–128, 131–132, 148, 218n75, 219n90, 222n124; dialectician, 120–121, 135, 139–140, 150–151, 179, 222n141
dialogue form, xv–xix, 1, 155, 180, 183–185, 227n67; and opinion, xv–xvii. *See also* dialectic; dramatic action; opinion; writing
Diogenes Laertius, 109, 216n30, 216n34, 217n51, 217n53, 228n84
Dionysius Halicarnassus, 183–184, 203n3–203n5, 228n79, 228n91
Dionysus, 117, 201n34, 204n31–204n32, 206n54, 218n65
divine; divinity, 14, 29–30, 33, 36, 37, 45–46, 47–52, 54, 57–59, 61, 63–64, 67, 72–74, 76, 79, 83–84, 86, 88, 99–101, 116–117, 119, 131, 132–133, 145–147, 148, 151, 156, 158, 167–169, 172, 176, 179–180, 184, 187, 189, 205n38, 207n26, 208n34, 209n63, 211n83, 211n85, 214n130, 214n133, 215n17, 223n5, 226n53; *See also daimon*; god
Dodona, 49, 51, 161, 202n61, 225n22
Dorter, Kenneth, 206n54
Dover, Kenneth James, 199n8, 200n16, 203n2–203n6, 203n10
*doxa*. *See* opinion
dramatic action, xii, xvii, 1–2, 32, 34, 42, 44, 82, 95, 146, 148–149, 180, 198n48. *See also* dialogue form
drug (*pharmakon*), 11–12, 14–15, 18–19, 125–126, 130, 157–159, 207n19, 207n21, 225n17

education, 24, 39–40, 79, 130, 137, 144–146, 151–152, 156–157, 167, 169, 173, 211n80, 215n7. *See also* teaching
Eleusis, mysteries of, 3, 4, 15, 18, 33, 50, 71, 74–75, 168, 186, 199n9, 199n10, 199n11, 199n14, 200n15–200n16, 211n91
Empedocles, 212n104, 212n108, 212n113
enthusiasm; inspiration, xi–xii, xiii–xiv, 9, 16–19, 30–33, 36–37, 40, 43–45, 47–48, 50–51, 67–69, 71–76, 78–80, 82, 85–86, 90, 113, 147–148, 157–158, 174, 184, 188–189, 208n33–208n34,

212n106, 213n118–213n119, 226n45, 226n50, 227n61. *See also erōs*; madness; shame
Epicrates, 5–7, 15, 28, 167, 205n38
*eikos*. *See* probability
Eros (god), 45–46, 47–48, 51–52, 76, 89, 99, 117, 200n16, 208n33, 215n10, 226n47
*erōs*. *passim*: as desire for perfection or unity, xii, 62, 66, 70–72, 75–77, 92, 101, 130, 145, 148, 151, 153, 178, 183–184, 189–190, 192–193; as experience, vii, 46, 47–48, 69–70, 72, 73–75, 85–87, 92, 117, 150, 178, 183, 199n14, 226n34; for oneself, 41, 75–78, 86, 96–97, 145, 178, 212n113; as ground of *logos*, xii–xiii, xv, 29, 36, 40, 68–72, 118–122, 150, 180, 183, 191–192, 218n72; kinds of, viii, 28, 39, 46, 47–48, 49, 51, 73, 75–77, 87, 111, 119, 125, 129, 131, 132–133, 185, 187–188, 215n1; and madness or mania, xi, 3, 8–9, 18, 23–24, 31–33, 33, 35, 38–39, 43, 45, 48, 51–52, 68–71, 73, 86, 116–117, 119, 129, 132–133, 148, 168, 187, 189, 211n85, 218n72, 226n47; in tension with the city or community, 37, 38, 40, 68–69, 75–77, 83, 87, 187–189; true, 79–80, 87, 117, 119, 205n49, 206n58, 208n33. *See also* lover
*erōs* and *logos*, viii–ix, xii, xiii–xv, 2, 11, 28, 29, 44, 52, 66–67, 68, 79–80, 116, 122, 148, 191, 213n124, 226n47
Eryximachus, 3, 4, 124–125, 166
eternal; eternity, 44, 55–56, 61, 76, 92, 97, 115, 148, 153, 155–156, 162, 166, 172, 182–184, 209n55, 210n67, 211n86–211n87, 215n2. *See also* immortality
ethic; ethical, ix, 2, 4, 25, 28, 39, 42, 52, 59, 63–65, 70, 77–80, 87–89, 91–92, 95, 96, 118, 125–126, 128, 143, 145–147, 148, 151–153, 155, 166, 168–169, 176–179, 181, 186–189, 191–193, 225n19, 229n99; *See also erōs* and *logos*; philosophy; rhetoric
Euripides, 125–126, 199n10, 200n21, 204n31, 206n54, 207n17, 217n50, 217n53, 218n64
Euthydemus, 222n141
Evenus, 123, 177–178

falsehood; falsity, 12–13, 19, 39, 47–48, 62–63, 99, 101, 103, 107–109, 111, 149, 151–152, 155–157, 170–171, 174–175, 198n44, 206n57–206n58, 228n84. *See also* truth
family, 37, 39, 50, 87
Farrell, Anne Mary, 199n14
Ferrari, Giovanni, 16–17, 101, 108, 113, 185–186, 195n4, 196n10, 196n13, 197n31, 198n51, 202n60, 203n13, 203n64, 206n61, 206n68, 208n39, 214n129, 215n17, 216n19, 217n57–217n58, 218n75–219n76, 221n112, 228n90
Ficino, Marsilio, 17, 54, 208n32, 208n39, 208n46–209n47, 209n49, 209n56, 212n105
fitting (*kairos*), 125, 138–141, 149–151, 163, 166, 168, 171, 174, 179–180, 188, 189, 191–194
forgetfulness. *See* memory
form (*eidos*; *idea*), 12, 34, 35–36, 43, 46, 48, 51–52, 57–61, 65–67, 71–73, 74, 79–80, 92, 102, 108–110, 118–121, 127, 131–138, 140, 143, 145, 148–149, 156–157, 159, 169–170, 176, 179–180, 193, 205n44, 205n49, 205n51, 209n62, 210n73, 211n81, 212n106, 213n124, 213n125, 217n49, 218n69, 225n24, 227n61; and content, 28, 30, 32, 36, 40, 41, 44, 110, 113, 127, 205n43; Plato's theory of, xvii, 43–44, 57, 213n124
fortune. *See* chance
free; freedom, 8, 22–29, 33, 35, 38, 48, 56, 63, 82, 98–99, 101, 183, 187, 225n23
Friedländer, Paul, 44, 197n29, 197n32, 198n44, 198n48, 202n55, 206n3, 206n63, 211n85, 212n112, 214n128, 216n34, 226n38, 227n58, 228n87
friend; friendship, 24, 37, 39, 86–89, 143, 151, 189–190, 205n38–205n39, 214n131–214n132, 214n137, 215n10, 226n46
Furley, William D., 199n11

# Index

Gadamer, Hans-Georg, 219n77, 222n140
generation; genesis, 53–56, 57, 60–61, 144, 164–166, 184, 189, 210n72, 223n5. *See also* being
genuine (*etumos*), 46–49, 101, 105, 110. *See also* truth
Giannopoulou, Zina, 204n19
god; gods, 14, 32, 45–46, 50, 52, 54, 57–63, 67–69, 73–80, 81, 84–87, 97, 100, 117, 120, 139, 146–148, 150, 155–158, 160–161, 166, 169, 172, 179, 189, 199n14, 207n10, 209n64, 210n67, 210n69, 210n72, 211n78, 213n115, 213n124, 213n126, 215n10, 223n5–224n6, 223n145, 226n47, 229n106. *See also* divine
good; goodness, xii, xv, 2–3, 5, 23, 24, 27–28, 35–37, 40–41, 46, 48–52, 55, 56–59, 60, 61–62, 64–65, 67, 70–72, 75–76, 77, 79–81, 88, 91–92, 98–99, 101–102, 104–105, 110–111, 116–119, 121, 125, 129–131, 138–140, 143, 145–147, 149, 151–152, 158, 165–168, 171–172, 177, 189–190, 193–194, 211n80, 212n94, 214n137, 215n6, 215n10, 215n15, 215n17, 220n103, 220n106–220n107, 221n122, 223n149; itself; form of the, 55, 60–61, 72–73, 87–89, 92, 102, 139–140, 156–157, 223n149
Gorgias, 103, 105, 106, 108–109, 123–124, 127, 140–141, 151–153, 183, 216n24, 216n33, 217n44, 217n46, 217n50, 217n52, 218n61, 221n116, 222n126
Griswold, Charles L., 133–134, 195n5, 196n10, 196n11, 196n13, 197n29, 198n38, 198n46, 198n48, 201n35, 203n7, 204n29, 206n58, 207n19, 208n39, 208n46, 209n57, 209n59, 209n61, 211n83, 214n129, 214n141, 214n144, 218n71, 218n75, 219n89, 221n116, 221n119, 221n122–221n123
Guthrie, William K. C., 220n97

Hackforth, Reginald, 54, 196n18, 204n26–204n27, 206n56, 206n59, 208n39, 208n45, 209n52, 210n75, 213n118, 220n103, 221n109, 221n115, 225n26

Hades, 5, 46, 59, 199n14, 200n22, 216n29
Hayase, Atsushi, 218n69
health, xi, 7, 10, 18, 46–47, 50, 64, 125, 130–132, 139
Heath, Malcolm, 196n11, 198n52
Heidegger, Martin, 26, 72, 196n9, 196n10, 204n17, 212n95–212n96, 217n42, 221n112–221n113
Helen of Troy, 46–47, 72, 207n17–207n19
Hera, 16, 79
Heraclitus, 202n48, 214n132
Hercules, 16, 199n14, 228n84
Hermeias of Alexandria, 196n11, 208n39, 221n109
Hermes, 112, 200n15, 216n29
Herodicus, 7, 14, 125
Herodotus (historian), 11, 156, 201n39, 201n40, 202n47–202n48, 204n31, 207n14, 207n18, 207n27, 218n64, 219n87, 223n1, 223n3–223n4, 224n6, 224n16, 225n22
Herodotus of Thebes, 6–7, 57
Hesiod, 18, 58–59, 100–101, 173, 198n1, 202n46, 202n49, 202n57, 202n58, 203n65, 204n31, 207n22, 210n67, 215n12, 215n16, 222n131
Hestia, 59, 210n70
Hippias, 159–160
Hippocrates; Hippocratics, 18, 73–74, 131–134, 170, 208n31, 212n100, 212n102, 212n104, 221n114, 221n118
Hobbes, Thomas, x–xi, xvi, 194, 197n21, 197n22, 197n23, 197n24, 197n25, 197n26, 197n27
Homer, 46–47, 58–59, 76, 100, 173, 177, 199n14, 202n46, 203n65, 205n45, 206n57–206n58, 209n63, 212n114, 214n133, 215n11, 216n21, 216n29, 216n32, 218n65, 219n78, 219n87, 225n23
honor, 6, 23, 25–26, 37, 48, 65, 77, 80–82, 88–89, 96, 100–101, 182, 184, 188, 213n125, 229n105
Howland, Jacob, 198n46
Hyland, Drew, 213n126

Ibycus, 45, 207n8–207n9, 209n63
*idea*. *See* form

## Index

ignorance, vii, xiv, 13, 18–19, 30–31, 37, 47, 50–51, 65, 67, 70, 78–79, 88, 90, 96, 100, 103–104, 106, 116, 120–121, 123, 130–131, 144, 146–153, 160–162, 171–173, 183, 192, 205n52, 222n141, 228n83. *See also* self-knowledge; Socrates

illness; sickness, 9, 19, 21, 23, 37, 46, 50, 52, 73, 116, 200n31. *See also erōs*; health; madness

image, 43, 51, 57–58, 70–72, 77–79, 81, 83, 86, 90–92, 104, 107, 117, 122–123, 142, 147, 159, 163, 164–165, 167–169, 184–186, 192–193, 208n33, 209n62, 210n72, 211n88, 213n121, 215n14, 217n59, 223n145, 226n42, 226n53; phantom, 47, 71–72, 87, 115, 165, 167, 176, 181–182, 189–190, 207n18. *See also* phantom; semblance

immortal; immortality, 14, 52–58, 67, 80, 96–98, 100, 106, 115, 149, 153, 168–169, 175–176, 177–178, 181–183, 184–185, 206n5, 208n46, 211n81, 212n107, 215n1–215n2, 229n106. *See* mortal

intellect (*nous*), xi, 45, 60, 65, 82–83, 91, 124, 129, 145, 165–166, 170, 181–182, 198n51, 210n72, 213n124–213n125, 227n60; intellection, 66, 119, 156–157. *See also* mind

Irani, Tushar, 196n13, 196n14, 197n32, 205n43, 206n62, 207n22, 218n67, 220n105, 221n114, 221n122, 222n137, 228n88, 229n98–229n99, 229n105

irony. *See* Socrates

Isocrates, 186–188, 207n14, 207n17, 213n125, 217n50, 226n39–226n40, 228n91–229n94, 229n96–229n97, 229n99–229n106

Jaeger, Werner, 196n15, 196n18, 197n29, 203n65, 221n112, 227n72

Jowett, Benjamin, 196n11

judgment, xiii–xiv, 10, 29, 33, 38, 41–42, 48, 56, 65–66, 68, 80, 82–84, 88, 105, 129, 131–132, 140, 143, 148, 158–161, 164, 167, 188, 213n127, 220n103, 225n17, 225n19–225n20, 225n23

justice, 38–39, 41, 65–66, 70, 77, 97, 102–103, 105, 110, 119, 127, 130, 141, 143, 151–153, 160, 166–168, 171–177, 184–185, 213n115, 216n21, 229n100; injustice; unjust, 9, 77, 104, 109, 143, 171–173; itself; true, 60, 102–103, 211n81, 225n19–225n20

Kastely, James L., 195n1, 203n2
Kelley Jr., William G., 198n39
Kennedy, George A., 196n15, 216n30
Kerényi, Karl, 199n9, 199n14, 211n91
Kerferd, G. B., 216n35, 216n38, 217n49
king, 64, 77, 156–158, 211n79, 216n21, 223n5
Klein, Jacob, 198n48, 214n130, 215n9, 222n138, 225n29, 227n61
knowledge, vii, 18, 34–35, 43–44, 45, 47, 49–50, 53, 55–56, 59–61, 65–67, 70, 77–78, 81, 86–87, 90, 96, 97, 102–108, 111–114, 118, 119–131, 133–143, 147–149, 151, 156–161, 162, 163–171, 173–174, 175–177, 179, 181–189, 192, 201n35, 201n43, 208n34, 211n90, 214n141, 216n22, 216n37, 217n54, 217n56, 218n69, 218n75–219n76, 220n106, 221n114, 223n148–223n150, 224n6, 225n17, 225n19, 229n100–229n101, 229n104–229n105; personal, 9, 96, 106, 118, 169, 192; itself; true, 60, 70, 90, 112–113, 128–129, 137, 141, 148, 163–165, 170–171, 173, 181–182, 188, 211n81, 223n5. *See also* ignorance; self-knowledge
Koritansky, John C., 210n74, 219n76, 222n129

law. *See nomos*
Lebeck, Anne, 183–184, 199n14, 209n63, 227n78
Lewis, David M., 199n5
likelihood. *See* probability
likeness. *See* semblance
Linck, Matthew S., 205n50, 214n129
Lincoln, Bruce, 1n46 1n48
Linforth, Ivan M., 201n34, 204n31
Locke, John, 197n21

*logos*; speech. *passim*: communal nature of, xiii, 1, 13, 44, 177–178, 188–190, 193; constitutive power of, ix, xiii, xv, 2, 10, 18, 29, 45–46, 50, 82, 92–93, 96, 139, 191, 193; hatred of (misology), 197n32, 218n67, 225n24; as language, xii, 66, 114, 172, 183–184, 222n138; as leading the soul (*psychagōgia*), xv, xvii, 44, 58, 66, 104–108, 110–111, 115–117, 120, 122, 127, 133–134, 136, 138–142, 146, 149–150, 165–166, 168–169, 170–172, 174–176, 180, 191–194, 216n29, 225n17, 226n47; limitations of, xviii, 60, 66–67, 92, 101–102, 117, 122, 123, 148, 155, 163, 168–169, 171–174, 176–178, 181–182, 218n67; *logismos. See* reason; as mark, xi–xii, xiv–xv, 110–111, 114, 115, 118, 122–123, 132–133, 135, 138, 156, 158–161, 164–165, 172–173, 189, 192, 197n28, 224n14; and reality, xi, 22, 26, 29, 32, 33, 40, 43–44, 66–68, 73, 80, 96, 101–102, 106, 112, 174, 180, 191–194, 195n3, 210n71, 218n65. *See also* dialectic; definition; memory; myth; probability; reason; rhetoric; technique; writing

lover. *passim*: noble, 47–49, 56; true, 39, 86–87, 130, 150, 176, 177–178, 205n49, 206n58, 214n129; *See also erōs*

Lysias, 2, 3, 5; career of, 5, 21, 89, 95, 96–98, 123–124; rhetorical style of, 22, 26, 28, 30, 61, 110–116, 127–129, 140, 144–145, 146, 152–153, 165, 169, 171–172, 173, 177–178, 185–187, 193–194, 203n6, 204n19, 204n20, 205n42; speeches of, 5, 21, 97–98, 199n4, 200n20, 200n23, 200n24, 200n25, 203n6, 215n4–215n5. *See also* nonlover

MacDowell, Douglas M., 199n9, 200n24, 203n2, 222n133
Mackenzie, Mary Margaret, 120, 198n45, 218n74–218n75, 219n77, 227n59
madness (*mania*), 31, 39, 48–52, 54, 56, 59–61, 68, 73, 83, 90–91, 100, 116–117, 119, 125, 132–133, 148, 157, 204n31, 207n26, 208n30, 211n81, 214n128, 218n69, 218n72, 226n47; of *erōs. See erōs*
manliness. *See* courage
Mansfeld, Jaap, 219n92, 221n110, 221n112
McAdon, Brad, 226n39–226n40, 229n100
McCumber, John, 198n51, 204n19, 205n46, 219n76
medicine, 3, 14, 18, 124–126, 128–129, 130–133, 138, 151, 157–158, 166, 199n7, 212n102, 216n24, 219n85. *See also* physician
Melissus, 223n143
memory, 8, 9, 23, 30–31, 67, 69–70, 78, 83, 85, 91, 97, 108, 153, 157–160, 175–176, 177–178, 181–182, 185, 186, 227n62; forgetfulness, 8, 32, 63, 66–67, 69–70, 73, 77–79, 84–85, 87, 92, 100, 157–159, 167; recollection, xv, 43–44, 45, 50, 66–74, 77, 80, 81, 85, 87, 91–92, 100–102, 109, 113, 119–120, 148, 158, 162, 167, 181, 185, 211n83, 212n106, 212n109, 213n118–213n119, 214n134, 219n81; reminder; memorial; monument,– xiii, 24, 30–31, 32–33, 67–68, 70–72, 76–79, 81, 85–86, 90, 92, 95, 97, 101, 111, 118–119, 133, 146–148, 151, 158–161, 162, 164–165, 167, 168–169, 172, 174, 176–177, 179–180, 181–183, 185–186, 191, 192, 211n88, 214n131–214n132, 215n14, 225n17, 227n71, 228n86
method, xv, 118, 120, 127–128, 131–136, 140, 170, 183–184, 218n75, 219n90, 221n114, 221n120
mind (*dianoia*), 37, 38, 39, 58, 60, 67, 87–88, 97, 99–100, 102, 104, 111, 119–121, 129, 137–138, 159, 177–180, 185, 187, 212n106, 218n72, 220n101, 220n103
moderation; sound-mindedness (*sōphrosunē*), 3, 7, 18, 21, 22–24, 26, 30–31, 32, 33–34, 35, 37–42, 46, 49–51, 70, 80, 83–85, 87–91, 116, 129, 145, 167–168, 189–190, 192, 198n51, 205n49, 207n26, 214n130; immoderation, 34, 38; itself; true, 60, 83, 189–190, 214n130, 214n139; self-

mastery, 80, 82, 214n128; *See also erōs*; madness
Moore, Christopher, 104, 195n5, 196n10, 196n13, 197n34, 201n44, 202n50, 208n37, 208n39, 209n48, 209n53–209n54, 214n128, 216n23, 216n37, 222n134, 224n14, 225n17
Morgan, Kathryn A., 202n47–202n48, 205n38
mortal; mortality, vii, 14, 50, 58, 61–68, 71–72, 76, 89, 91, 100–101, 120–121, 141, 146, 151, 166, 181–182, 189–190, 213n126, 216n29, 217n45
Morychus, 5, 7
Mueller, Gustav, 196n10
Murray, James S., 195n7, 216n35, 216n38
Muses, 33–34, 43, 51, 63–64, 100–101, 117, 148, 205n45, 207n22, 215n17, 219n81
music; musical, 34, 63–64, 100–101, 125–126, 130, 201n34, 203n9, 204n31, 210n74, 211n77, 215n18
Mylonas, George E., 199n9, 199n10, 199n14, 211n91
myth, xiv, 3, 10–15, 16–17, 19, 34, 43–44, 46, 47, 57–59, 65, 69, 70–71, 80, 87, 91–92, 99–102, 104, 117, 141, 147–148, 155–162, 167, 170–171, 172, 185–186, 191–192, 201n35, 201n43, 206n6, 208n33, 208n37, 209n63, 211n85, 213n125, 215n9, 215n14, 222n132, 223n5–224n6, 224n14, 226n34, 226n38, 226n42; and *logos*, 10, 12–15, 57, 57–58, 67, 92, 185–186, 201n38, 202n47–202n48, 211n85–211n86, 212n107, 213n125, 215n145; mythology, 67, 167–168, 184, 201n38, 202n47–202n48

Nails, Debra, 200n16, 200n19
nature; natural, vii–x, xii–xix, 1–3, 6, 9, 12–15, 17–19, 21–22, 26, 28, 29, 31, 33, 35–36, 39, 41, 46, 48, 52, 54–58, 62–65, 72–74, 82–84, 90–91, 92, 95–97, 100–102, 106, 108, 115–116, 118–120, 124, 127–137, 141–143, 144–145, 148–153, 155, 158–159, 162–174, 176–183, 186–189, 191–194, 209n50, 210n75, 211n83, 211n88,
220n96–220n98, 221n114, 222n132, 222n138, 224n9, 224n13, 225n17, 226n40, 227n61–227n62, 228n88–228n89; human, 46, 62–68, 71, 73, 77–79, 81, 100–102, 136, 141–142, 145, 147, 150, 152, 163, 165, 175, 190, 210n73, 210n75, 212n109, 222n137, 229n104
necessity; compulsion, xviii, 9, 11, 23, 26, 28, 30, 31–32, 33, 34, 37, 38–39, 40–42, 45, 49, 54, 56, 62–63, 65, 71, 75, 76, 78, 82, 84, 89, 97, 101–103, 105, 110, 112, 115, 119, 121, 125, 137, 140–142, 148–150, 157, 168–169, 177–178, 179–180, 187–188, 205n42, 210n73, 211n81, 216n28, 219n93, 221n114, 222n134; logographic, viii, xviii, 110, 113–115, 118, 122–123, 125–127, 139, 140, 164–166, 170, 180; *See also erōs*
Nehamas, Alexander, 196n13, 203n10, 216n35, 217n41, 219n76, 222n124, 222n141, 225n30
Nestor, 103, 106
Newell, Waller R., 206n64
Nichols Jr., James H., 196n16, 197n20–197n21, 198n47, 198n48, 217n53
Nicholson, Graeme, 195n1, 196n13, 196n18, 198n38, 200n17, 208n39, 208n41, 227n68
noble: beautiful or fine (*kalos*). *See* beauty: well-bred (*gennadas*), 47–49, 56, 187
*nomos*; custom; law, 10–14, 21, 24–25, 31, 32, 33, 40, 41, 63–64, 71, 75–76, 82–83, 96–98, 105–106, 116–117, 127, 130–131, 141–142, 153, 156, 168–169, 171–173, 177, 203n9–203n10, 204n37, 216n33, 225n19–225n20
nonlover: character of, 29, 39, 73, 83–84, 87–89, 99, 110, 119–120, 141, 172–173, 182–183, 191, 214n129; speech of, xi, 3, 7, 21–42, 46, 98–99, 110–118, 120–121, 170, 177–180, 190, 191, 226n45, 226n50. *See also* Lysias
Nonnus, 209n63
Nussbaum, Martha C., 200n15, 203n6, 204n27, 207n21, 213n118, 222n136

Ober, Josiah, 197n27
Odysseus, 100, 106, 109, 121, 219n78
Oreithuia, 11–12, 14, 18, 46, 47, 65, 199n14, 201n39, 213n115, 214n133
opinion (*doxa*). *passim*: common, x, xvii–xviii, 5, 14, 22, 23, 24, 26, 27, 33, 39, 40–42, 47–49, 73, 75–76, 81, 92, 102–103, 128, 144, 159–160, 173–175, 179–180, 184, 188–189, 222n141; and *erōs* or desire, xvi, 35, 40, 80–81, 147, 149, 172–173, 174–175, 191, 228n83; as limit for human mind, xi, 62–63, 108–109, 147, 209n55, 215n14; and *logos*, ix, x–xi, xii, xiii, xvi–xviii, xix, 10, 13–14, 19, 23, 33, 35–37, 37–39, 40, 41, 84, 90–92, 102–104, 107–111, 117, 122, 142–147, 149–153, 172–173, 174–175, 191, 205n49, 206n6, 208n28, 216n37–216n38, 217n45, 222n138, 222n141, 228n83. *See also* dialectic; knowledge; rhetoric

pain, xiii, 3, 50, 74–76, 85–87, 90–91, 98, 100–102, 107, 141, 146, 207n19, 208n33, 215n6–215n7
Palamedes, 106–107, 108–109, 153, 156, 216n33–216n34, 217n50
palinode, structure of, 46–47, 207n17, 207n19. *See also* dialectic; purification
Pan, 112, 148, 189, 206n7, 218n65, 229n107
Parke, H. W., 207n25, 211n91, 226n49
Parmenides, 55–56, 109, 202n48, 207n9, 209n55, 209n62–209n63, 211n87, 214n132, 217n45, 217n49, 218n73, 221n111, 223n143, 227n66
Pericles, 5, 126–127, 128–129, 220n94–220n98, 220n102–220n103
perplexity (*aporia*), 50, 52–54, 75–76, 86–87, 91–92, 107, 150, 152–153, 177–178, 206n60, 212n94, 214n136
Persephone, 4, 46, 199n14, 226n34
persuasion, vii, xvii, xix, 19, 51, 56, 66, 70, 79–80, 82, 84, 89–92, 95, 97, 102–109, 107–112, 115–118, 122–123, 126–127, 129–131, 133–145, 149–151, 170–171, 172, 174, 176–179, 180, 183, 186–187, 191, 193–194, 208n37, 209n64, 211n83, 216n21, 216n28, 220n106, 222n126, 222n132, 222n137, 223n148–223n149, 225n17, 226n47. *See also* rhetoric
Phaedrus: character of, 2, 3–4, 7, 9, 29, 32, 41, 57, 65, 71, 75, 87–88, 90–91, 98–99, 141, 167–168, 170, 180, 185–186, 190, 191, 213n125, 228n88; and conception of rhetoric, xiii, 2, 3, 18, 29–30, 32, 37, 90–91, 98–99, 102–104, 111, 122–125, 129, 141, 143, 144, 146, 148, 159–160, 164, 166, 174–175, 177, 179–180, 185–186, 190, 193–194, 199n7, 215n14; as lover of speech, xiii, 2, 4, 6, 8, 18–19, 31, 32, 37, 45, 90–91, 98–99, 101, 185–186, 190, 215n9, 215n14; as nonlover, 18–19, 29, 32–33, 41, 87–88; and philosophy, xv, 89, 98–99, 101–102, 105–106, 136, 146–147, 148–150, 153, 167–168, 174–175, 179–180, 185, 190
Pharmaceia, 11, 15
*pharmakon*. *See* drug
Philodamus, 207n16
philosopher, vii, 64, 67, 77–79, 106, 125–126, 151, 179, 181, 186, 210n74, 211n79, 228n92
philosophy, 39, 101, 159, 211n77, 212n102, 214n137, 214n139, 215n18, 217n41, 226n40, 229n105; and conversation or dialogue, xii, 44, 57, 80, 130, 138–139, 148–149, 152, 177–178, 210n74; and *erōs*, viii, xv, 36, 37, 65, 71, 86, 89–90, 102, 148–149, 168, 177–178, 182, 187–190, 193, 210n74; and ignorance, vii, 86, 90, 146–147, 179; and knowledge, vii, 179, 188; and rhetoric, distinguished from, ix–x, 105–106, 128, 137, 147, 179, 222n124, 222n137, 229n101; and rhetoric, perfection of, 90, 105, 133, 136, 151–152, 179, 186–188, 194, 221n108, 222n124; as way of life; ethical nature of, ix, xiv, xv, xviii, 43, 52, 65, 78–80, 87–88, 89, 91, 95–96, 100, 125, 148, 150, 152–153, 155–156, 174–175, 177–180, 181, 185–189, 192–193, 196n13, 197n34, 198n45, 215n6. *See also* self-knowledge

physician, 65, 73, 124–127, 131–133, 139, 212n102, 216n24. See also medicine
Pickard-Cambridge, A. W., 204n32
Pieper, Josef, 28, 49, 72–73, 197n32, 197n36, 198n48, 204n24, 204n27, 206n2, 207n23, 208n30, 212n94, 212n97, 214n143, 218n72
piety, 3–4, 46, 92, 156, 173–174, 207n10; impiety, 46, 220n98. See also Phaedrus
Pindar, 6–7, 173, 200n27, 200n28, 200n29, 200n30, 202n49, 202n58, 209n63, 219n87
plane tree. See setting
Planinc, Zdravko, 202n61
Plato, works of: *Apology*, 70, 200n22, 200n25, 200n26, 200n27, 202n48, 211n90, 213n123, 214n140, 215n15, 217n50, 217n53, 219n81, 220n99, 223n152, 225n19, 225n23, 227n77; *Charmides*, 201n37, 214n129; *Cratylus*, 202n59, 208n28, 210n70, 213n116, 216n29, 217n54, 218n61, 218n65; *Euthydemus*, 215n18, 216n38, 222n141, 228n92; *Euthyphro*, 207n10, 212n98; *Gorgias*, ix–xi, 40, 106, 128, 130–131, 196n17, 196n19, 197n26, 199n10, 200n22, 204n15, 204n28, 206n64, 206n66, 216n20, 216n24, 216n31, 219n88, 220n103–220n105, 220n107, 222n139, 223n149, 225n19–225n20, 226n51; *Hippias Major*, 216n27; *Hippias Minor*, 225n18; *Ion*, 201n34, 204n35, 208n34, 225n27–225n28, 226n51; *Laws*, 196n19, 204n31–204n32, 207n20, 208n36, 208n42–208n44, 212n101, 212n113, 215n3, 219n86, 222n128, 223n148–223n149, 224n6–224n7, 224n11, 225n20, 225n22, 226n39; *Letters*, 198n41, 207n15, 213n118, 217n56, 224n13, 226n38, 226n44, 227n55, 227n57, 227n62, 227n64, 227n69, 227n76, 228n85, 228n89, 229n108; *Menexenus*, 220n94, 227n56; *Meno*, 212n104, 216n20, 219n83, 219n88, 223n149; *Parmenides*, 108, 198n49, 207n9, 208n42, 209n50–209n51, 209n55, 209n62, 211n87, 212n101, 214n132, 216n36, 217n43, 217n45, 217n47–217n49, 217n53, 218n73, 221n111, 222n130, 226n41; *Phaedo*, 200n22, 202n51, 202n54, 204n18, 211n77, 211n92, 212n102, 215n12, 215n18, 218n67, 220n103, 224n6, 225n24, 226n36, 226n51, 227n70, 227n75, 228n83; *Philebus*, 215n6, 217n46, 219n88, 223n149, 224n6, 224n10; *Protagoras*, 199n6, 200n31, 201n43, 202n48, 204n22, 215n10, 220n94, 223n153, 225n18, 226n51; *Republic*, 47, 55, 80–81, 125, 156–157, 196n19, 198n42, 200n22, 200n23, 200n31, 203n12, 203n66, 204n23, 206n55, 207n18, 208n36, 208n44, 209n49, 211n76, 211n79, 211n89, 212n111, 213n117, 213n125, 214n139, 215n6, 216n22, 216n27, 216n33, 219n79–219n80, 219n85–219n86, 220n107, 221n111, 222n135, 223n147, 223n149, 224n7–224n9, 225n19–225n20, 226n36, 227n60, 227n77; *Statesman*, 151, 196n19, 201n38, 222n128, 223n148–223n149; *Sophist*, 198n49, 209n50, 214n132, 217n42, 217n59, 221n111, 221n117, 223n144; *Symposium*, 3, 14, 46, 76, 99, 125, 167, 199n6, 199n7, 199n8, 200n15–200n16, 201n44, 203n10, 205n52, 208n33, 211n89, 212n94, 212n97, 213n117, 214n136, 215n2, 215n8, 215n10, 215n13, 217n41, 217n55, 219n84–219n85, 220n94, 226n35–226n38, 226n51–226n53, 228n81–228n82, 229n108; *Theaetetus*, 200n25, 201n36, 201n43, 203n63, 205n48, 209n60, 214n132, 214n134, 217n53, 225n19, 227n62, 229n108; *Theages*, 220n94, 226n53; *Timaeus*, 208n42, 211n76, 212n101, 217n40, 222n126, 223n1, 224n6. See also writing
play, xi, xvii–xviii, 2, 6–14, 16–17, 18–19, 21–22, 24, 28–29, 31, 41, 43, 51, 57, 70, 73, 92, 100, 111, 117, 140, 155, 157, 165–168, 169, 172–173, 177, 179–180, 183–185, 189, 222n141

pleasure, 18, 35–36, 37–39, 42, 48–49, 52, 65, 73, 75–76, 82, 88, 91–92, 95, 98–102, 107, 118, 125, 141, 146, 149, 158, 167, 172, 185–186, 188–189, 191–192, 207n22, 208n33, 215n6, 226n46
Plotinus, 212n112
Plutarch, 220n98, 223n3; Pseudo-Plutarch, 204n16, 219n82, 228n91
Podlecki, Anthony J., 220n97
poet, 6, 45, 46, 48, 51, 63–65, 79, 96–98, 117, 125–127, 205n44, 208n33, 211n78, 216n22, 225n19; poetry, vii, viii, 1, 3, 5, 15, 34, 43, 51–52, 58–60, 89–90, 124–126, 128–129, 131, 138–139, 157, 167–168, 170, 173, 177, 184, 185–186, 195n4, 198n50, 206n57–206n58, 208n33, 215n1, 215n10, 227n66
Polemarchus, 6, 200n16
political, ix–x, xii–xiii, 4–5, 21, 32, 64, 89, 98, 104, 109, 151, 160, 171–172, 177, 181–182, 186, 187–188, 193, 197n27, 213n125, 215n2, 219n86, 220n95, 223n148–223n149, 227n69, 229n99; politician; statesman, 64, 95, 96–98, 126, 149, 151, 153, 160, 220n95, 220n103, 223n148–223n149, 225n19, 228n92
Polus, 123, 222n139
practice, ix–x, xv, 6, 43, 47, 61, 78–80, 90, 105, 110, 121, 122, 127–128, 131, 135–143, 148–150, 158, 166, 167–168, 177, 184–185, 186–187, 188–189, 196n14, 197n21, 203n9, 220n106–220n107. *See also* action; ethic
pray; prayer, vii, 1, 27, 50, 89, 92, 176–177, 189–190
probability (*to eikos*), 12–13, 14, 15, 16, 17, 23, 26–27, 28, 40–41, 44, 52, 57–58, 62, 81, 97, 104, 112–113, 131, 141–147, 149, 152, 155–157, 163–164, 168, 183, 205n42, 213n126, 216n37, 222n134
Prodicus, 3, 123–124, 138, 140–141, 174, 219n83
prophecy, 1, 45, 50–51, 90, 161–162, 164, 187, 207n25–207n27; prophet;
prophetess; seer, 45, 49–50, 63–64, 78, 207n27, 208n34, 211n78
Protagoras, 12, 123, 201n43, 202n48
*psychagōgia*. *See logos*
psychology, x, xiii, 33, 36, 39–40, 111, 119–120, 122, 124, 137, 142, 170, 172, 180, 192, 218n72, 221n122. *See also* rhetoric; soul
purification, 15, 33, 45–46, 47, 50–51, 56, 71, 151, 158, 176

Ramus, Petrus, 197n27
reason (*logismos*), viii, ix–xv, xvi–xvii, 36, 39, 58, 66–68, 70–72, 75, 81, 85, 87, 90–92, 124, 129–130, 136, 145, 156, 170, 175, 177–178, 191–194, 195n3, 209n64, 211n82, 212n106, 213n126, 214n134, 218n72, 219n81, 223n151, 227n60, 228n88. *See* logos
recollection. *See* memory
rhetoric. *passim*: in Athens, ix–x, 6, 7, 22, 130, 191, 197n27; and deception, x, xi, 8, 22, 28, 36, 39–40, 103–105, 107, 108, 111–112, 116, 137, 143, 149, 151, 170–171, 216n28, 229n101; and desire or *erōs* ,– xi, 22, 36–37, 43–44, 66–67, 87–88, 99, 102–103, 116–118, 122, 129–131, 144–145, 148–149, 151–152, 183–184, 191, 194, 228n83; and dialectic, 96, 118, 120–123, 126–128, 130–136, 139–142, 145, 152–153, 157, 168, 179, 183, 192–194, 219n89, 222n124, 223n150; as flattery, ix–xi, 37, 39–40, 89–91, 151–153; as instrumental, xiii, 3, 40, 128, 130, 138–139, 193–194, 219n93, 220n106, 224n13; ignoble, 39–40, 131, 179–180; and knowledge, xv, 33, 66, 96, 102–108, 112, 114, 118, 120, 122–128, 143, 149, 151–152, 166–167, 174, 177, 185, 220n106, 223n148–223n150; modern conception of, ix–x, 193, 197n20–197n21; noble, 96, 103, 128–143, 144–145, 146–149, 151–152, 155, 170–171, 185–187, 188, 193, 216n21, 220n106, 222n138; omnipotence of, xii; and philosophy. *See* philosophy; private, xiii–xiv, 28, 33, 96, 103, 106–112, 136–137,

151–152, 170–171, 192–193, 217n55, 223n148–223n149; and psychology, x, xv, xvii, xviii–xix, 33, 36, 39–40, 44, 52, 59, 66, 80, 82, 87–89, 96, 104–108, 110, 113, 120, 122, 124, 127–142, 145–147, 149, 151–152, 163, 168–171, 180, 183, 185–186, 192, 196n14, 206n6, 216n29, 221n120, 221n122, 222n132; problem of reason and rhetoric, ix–xv, 124; public, xiv, 21, 28, 96, 103, 106–107, 109–112, 126, 136–137, 151–152, 170–171, 181–182, 192–193, 217n53, 223n148–223n149; rhetoricians, 19, 39, 43, 110, 122–124, 126–127, 136–137, 140, 151–152; true, xv, 96, 121, 127–129, 135, 140, 145, 146, 148–149, 163, 192–193, 196n19, 220n97–220n98, 220n107–221n108. *See also* necessity; technique; writing
Rhodes, James M., 197n32, 204n14, 204n23, 220n97
Rinella, Michael A., 199n14, 207n21
Robinson, Richard, 218n75, 219n90
Rosen, Stanley, 204n21, 205n50, 214n129, 228n88
Rowe, Christopher J., 7, 195n2, 196n11, 196n16, 198n46, 198n52, 200n32, 201n33, 201n34, 201n42, 202n52, 203n2, 205n44, 207n11, 207n26, 209n52, 220n97, 220n101, 221n115
Rutherford, R. B., 196n11, 198n47, 198n48

Sallis, John, 197n29, 198n48, 204n37, 208n41, 221n121, 222n127
Santas, Gerasimos, 218n72, 227n78
Sappho, 30–31, 204n34, 212n99–212n100
Schleiermacher, Friedrich, 196n11, 196n15
Schofield, Malcom, 220n100
Scott, Dominic, 198n51, 218n63, 218n72, 219n76
searching (*zētēsis*), viii, 44, 50, 67, 75, 77–81, 86, 90, 92, 116, 121, 146–152, 160, 172, 175–177, 179–180, 181–183, 193, 219n81; *See also erōs*; ignorance; philosophy; self-knowledge
seed, xviii, 63–64, 75, 150, 165–166, 169, 175, 177–178, 184, 185–186, 193, 210n74

Seeskin, Kenneth, 219n81
self-knowledge, xiv, xv, 6, 8, 10–15, 16, 17, 19, 30–32, 39, 42, 45, 70, 74, 77–79, 86, 116, 128, 135, 147–148, 160, 183, 201n44, 202n50, 204n37, 211n90, 214n130. *See also* Delphi; ignorance; philosophy; searching; Socrates
semblance, xiii, xiv, 26, 57–58, 69–72, 81, 88–89, 91, 107–108, 112–114, 116–117, 121, 123, 139–140, 142, 144–145, 148–149, 213n124, 217n59, 228n83; *See also logos*; memory
setting; plane tree, xviii, 4, 10, 11, 15, 16–19, 32, 45, 49, 51, 54, 99–100, 101–102, 161, 180, 189, 200n15–200n16, 210n72, 213n115
shame, xvii, 7, 21, 25, 33, 45–48, 51, 52–53, 56, 73, 80–81, 82, 96–98, 143–144, 149, 155, 160, 165, 171–172, 188, 212n98, 216n30, 217n53, 226n53
Sheffield, Frisbee C. C., 214n129
Shorey, Paul, 203n6
Sibyl, 49–50
Sinaiko, Herman L., 205n50, 206n2, 218n71
Siren, 100, 205n45, 215n11
Skemp, J. B., 208n39
slavery, 18, 75–76, 98, 145–146
Socrates: erotic art of, 89–92, 96, 140, 147–152, 177, 183, 214n141; ignorance of, xiv, 30–31, 70, 90, 122, 137, 140, 147–148, 150–152, 182–183, 198n44, 211n90, 214n141, 221n108, 222n137, 228n83; inspiration of, xi, 17–18, 70; irony of, xi, xvii–xviii, 22, 42, 73–74, 92, 127–128, 137, 161, 167–168, 171, 183–184, 198n44, 207n26, 220n96, 222n137, 222n141, 226n38, 227n58; and love of speech, 4, 98–99, 190; rhetoric, use of, xvii, xix, 17, 43–44, 89–91, 96, 99, 104, 115, 117, 122–123, 137, 138–140, 147–153, 155–156, 163, 173–175, 177, 179, 183–185, 185–186, 192, 208n37, 209n53, 216n37–216n38, 217n53, 218n63, 219n81, 222n137, 227n61, 228n86–228n87
sophist; sophistry, 11–15, 16, 17, 62, 63–65, 96, 138, 159–160, 188, 196n13,

201n44, 217n41, 222n124, 229n100; sophistic movement, 2–3
Sophocles, 125–126, 200n21, 202n57, 217n50
*sōphrosunē*. *See* moderation
soul. *passim*: erotic, xii, 106, 113, 121–122, 124, 148–149, 151–152, 163, 166, 182–183, 187–188, 191; form of, 57–61, 80, 134–135, 137–138, 210n73; motion of, ix, 44, 52–63, 65–68, 71–72, 73–75, 80, 82–85, 88–89, 91, 113, 121, 142, 148–149, 163, 169–170, 172–173, 185, 187–188, 191–192, 208n41, 209n53, 212n107, 218n66, 223n5; order of, ix, 58, 62, 73, 78, 80, 85, 110, 118, 124, 136, 139–141, 158, 193–194; parts of, 35, 42, 44, 54, 58–59, 61–63, 68–69, 73–74, 80–88, 92, 97, 120, 124, 131–136, 147, 164, 182–183, 185–186, 205n49, 205n51, 208n38, 209n64, 210n71, 210n73, 212n109, 213n125, 213n127, 214n131–214n132, 214n136, 221n111, 221n120; ranks or types, 59, 63–65, 100–101, 124, 125, 134–135, 137–140, 141–142, 144–145, 150, 152, 162–163, 166–167, 170, 173, 175, 180, 183, 185–186, 207n26, 221n120; self-constitution of, 128, 139, 176, 191, 197n34. *See eros*; *logos*; persuasion; rhetoric
Sparta; Spartan, 4, 5–6, 105–106, 213n115, 216n27
spiritedness (*thumos*), 80–81, 182, 184, 188, 213n125
Stesichorus, 46–47, 72, 177, 207n15, 207n18
Strabo, 205n38, 224n6
Strauss, Leo, 182–183, 198n48, 227n70, 227n73–227n74, 228n80
substance. *See* being
symbol, 15, 16–18, 42, 99, 186, 224n6–224n7

Taylor, Charles, 197n21, 197n28, 199n2
teaching; instruction,. *See also* education; philosophy; sophist; teacher 3, 11–14, 18, 28, 41, 52, 62, 90, 97, 103–105, 118, 125–128, 130–131, 133–137, 161–162, 166–167, 170–171, 174–176, 177–178, 181, 184, 188, 195n6, 196n16, 213n124, 220n106, 222n126, 228n89
teacher, ix–x, 123, 126–127, 130, 135–138, 160, 174, 182, 204n16, 215n7, 219n83, 220n95. *See also* education; philosophy; sophist; teaching
*technē*. *See* art
technique, xiii, 3, 26, 28, 51, 110, 112, 115–116, 118–119, 122–129, 131, 138, 140–141, 145–146, 172, 177–178, 208n40, 217n53, 219n90, 222n124, 223n148–223n149, 224n13. *See also* art; rhetoric
Teisias, 26, 123–124, 140–147, 149, 152–153, 155, 160, 163, 168, 183, 186–187, 216n37, 219n89, 222n134
Thamos; Ammōn, 156–165, 167, 181, 223n3, 224n6, 225n17, 225n22, 228n89
Theuth, 156–160, 223n5–224n6, 224n9–224n10, 224n13, 225n25
Thompson, W. H. B02n11
thought; thinking, xiv, xvii–xviii, 18, 23, 31–32, 34, 36, 40, 43–44, 47, 49–50, 52–53, 58, 66, 70, 96, 110, 120–121, 132, 136, 146, 150, 156–157, 161, 163–164, 167, 172–173, 175–176, 177–178, 189, 192, 200n22, 205n49, 209n50, 211n83, 213n126, 225n23. *See also* mind
Thrasymachus, 121, 123–124, 127–129, 152–153, 183–184, 193–194, 220n107
Thucydides, 199n5, 200n15, 202n47–202n48, 220n94
truth, xi, xvii, 11–13, 15, 17, 19, 30–31, 31, 34, 41–42, 43, 44, 45, 47–49, 56, 60–61, 62–64, 67, 69–72, 79, 81, 84–88, 91–92, 95, 100–103, 105, 109–110, 112–113, 117–118, 122–123, 135, 141–147, 149, 151, 156–163, 165, 166–168, 169, 171–172, 174, 177–178, 180, 183, 188–190, 192–194, 197n32, 200n22, 201n43, 202n47–202n48, 211n85, 213n118–213n119, 217n41, 218n65, 218n67, 220n106, 222n134, 225n23, 227n61–227n62, 228n89, 229n103. *See also* falsehood
Typhon; Typhonic, 13, 17, 19, 81, 156, 202n49, 202n50, 213n115

tyranny; tyrant, 28, 63–65, 109, 124

unity, 54, 56–58, 66, 80, 92, 106–110, 112, 113–116, 118–120, 122–124, 137, 144, 151, 153, 156–157, 163, 170, 183–184, 192–193, 211n81, 229n99; of the *Phaedrus* , viii, xix, 21, 196n11; textual. *See* necessity, logographic
urbane, xiii, 2, 8, 22, 40, 43, 46, 47–49, 71, 81, 88, 102, 143, 160–161, 191–192

virtue; excellence (*aretē*), 37, 46, 87–88, 116, 128, 130–131, 138–139, 141, 143, 150, 151, 153, 167–168, 174–175, 188, 189–190, 215n2, 216n27, 219n86, 220n106, 223n150, 229n99
Vlastos, Gregory, 198n44, 214n131–214n132, 214n137
Voegelin, Eric, 200n22, 202n47–202n48, 205n39, 211n79, 212n107, 213n118
de Vries, G. J., 195n2, 195n4, 196n11, 201n35, 204n33, 208n39, 209n52, 210n74, 220n101, 221n109, 225n26, 226n34

war; battle, 37, 60, 64, 77, 103–104, 143
way of life. *See* ethic
wealth, x, 5–6, 8, 23, 27–28, 34, 65, 75, 156–157
Weaver, Richard, 195n4, 196n13, 197n32, 198n40, 206n65–206n67, 211n84, 214n129, 223n142
Wedin, Michael V., 218n69, 218n71
Werner, Daniel S., 44, 195n5, 195n7, 196n11, 198n38, 202n45, 206n4–206n6, 207n19, 209n64, 210n71, 211n86, 213n125, 214n144, 218n75–219n76, 219n91–219n92, 221n108, 222n129, 227n61
White, David A., 195n5, 198n51, 206n3, 207n24, 208n39, 218n65, 218n75, 221n112, 221n114, 227n65
Wilamowitz-Moellendorff, Ulrich von, 200n17, 213n118
wise; wisdom, vii–viii, 6, 12, 14, 31–32, 47, 59–60, 64, 71–72, 88, 100, 109, 121, 126, 147, 151, 157–161, 167, 179, 183, 185, 189, 206n5, 210n74, 211n90, 215n6, 217n53, 228n92, 229n100
Woodford, Susan, 216n33
Woodruff, Paul, 225n30
writing. *passim*: dead, 14–15, 162–164, 165; living, 162–166, 169, 172, 175–177, 179, 181–183, 184–185, 198n45, 225n31; noble, 155, 167, 170–171, 173–179, 181, 186, 188, 226n48, 227n67; ignoble, 155, 173–175, 224n15, 226n48; Platonic, xiv, xv–xix, 17, 28, 29, 97, 123, 140, 155, 160, 162, 165, 169, 173–185, 186–187, 191–193, 209n63, 214n136, 224n16, 225n21, 225n31, 227n58, 227n63–227n64, 227n67, 227n69, 228n80, 228n89; playful, xvii, xviii, 28, 155, 167–168, 169, 172–173, 176–177, 183–185. *See also* dialectic; dialogue form; dramatic action; *logos*; necessity; rhetoric

Xenophanes, 202n48
Xenophon, 200n26, 217n50, 217n53, 222n131, 226n35, 226n39, 229n108

Yunis, Harvey, 195n2, 195n7, 196n11, 200n15, 203n8, 208n39, 209n52, 211n82, 212n99, 213n118, 213n120, 218n68, 219n76, 219n93, 220n96–220n98, 220n101–220n102, 220n106, 221n109, 221n115, 222n124, 222n137, 223n146, 223n150, 225n26, 226n34

Zaslavsky, Robert, 203n62
Zeno, 107, 108–109, 123, 216n34, 217n45, 217n49, 217n53, 227n66
Zeus, 31–32, 59, 64, 77–79, 86, 91, 106, 130, 134, 139, 156, 161, 172, 205n38–205n39, 209n63, 214n133
Zuckert, Catherine, 197n33, 203n7, 214n141–214n142, 215n1, 228n83

# About the Author

**Tiago Lier** is a research administrator at the University of Calgary and has taught in the Department of Political Science. He specializes in ancient Greek political philosophy, with research interests in rhetoric, philosophy of language, and moral philosophy. He has previously published in *Phoenix*.

www.ingramcontent.com/pod-product-compliance
Lightning Source LLC
Chambersburg PA
CBHW050901300426
44111CB00010B/1330